This is the first comprehensive study of the position of Soviet industrial workers during the Khrushchev period. Donald Filtzer examines the main features of Khrushchev's labour policy, shop-floor relations between workers and managers, the position of women workers and their specific role in the Soviet economy.

Filtzer argues that the main concern of Khrushchev's labour policy was to remotivate an industrial population left demoralized by the Stalinist terror. This meant persuading workers to surrender their defensive shop-floor tactics of lax discipline and poor-quality work. Yet, as this 'de-Stalinization' had to be carried out without undermining the essential power and property relations on which the Stalinist system had been built, the author convincingly demonstrates that labour policy was thus limited to superficial gestures of liberalization and tinkering with incentive schemes. Rather than achieving any lasting effects, the Khrushchev period saw the consolidation of the long-term tendency towards economic stagnation that was to become associated with Leonid Brezhnev.

In his conclusions, Filtzer shows how the labour problems of the Khrushchev years were the same as those which confronted Mikhail Gorbachev and his ill-fated *perestroika*. Thus he argues that reform of the Soviet system is impossible within existing property relations. Current moves towards the market will bring with them new forms of instability which only the creation of a democratic, decentralized, but non-market socialism can overcome.

This book is a sequel to Filtzer's well-received earlier study *Soviet workers and Stalinist industrialization: the formation of modern Soviet production relations, 1928–1941*. In addition to students and specialists of Soviet history and economics, it will be relevant to readers with a more general interest in labour-process analysis.

SOVIET WORKERS AND DE-STALINIZATION

Soviet and East European Studies 87

Editorial Board

Soviet and East European Studies, under the auspices of Cambridge University Press and the British Association for Soviet, Slavonic and East European Studies (BASSEES), promotes the publication of works presenting substantial and original research on the economics, politics, sociology and modern history of the Soviet Union and Eastern Europe.

Soviet and East European Studies

Series list continues after index

SOVIET WORKERS AND DE-STALINIZATION

The consolidation of the modern system of Soviet production relations, 1953–1964

DONALD FILTZER

Senior Lecturer in European Studies,
Polytechnic of East London, and Honarary
Research Fellow, School of Slavonic and
East European Studies, University of London

CAMBRIDGE
UNIVERSITY PRESS

Published by the Press Syndicate of the University of Cambridge
The Pitt Building, Trumpington Street, Cambridge CB2 1RP
40 West 20th Street, New York, NY 10011–4211, USA
10 Stamford Road, Oakleigh, Victoria 3166, Australia

First published 1992

Printed and bound in Great Britain by   ˙ ͺ ˙
Woolnough Bookbinding, Irthlingborough, Northants

A catalogue record for this book is available from the British Library

Library of Congress cataloguing in publication data
Filtzer, Donald A.
Soviet workers and de-Stalinization: the consolidation of the modern
system of Soviet production relations, 1953–1964 / Donald Filtzer.
        p.   cm. – (Soviet and East European studies: 87)
ISBN 0 521 41899 2
1. Working class – Soviet Union – History – 20th century.
2. Industrial relations – Soviet Union – History – 20th century.
3. Soviet Union – Economic conditions – 1955–1965. I. Title.
II. Series.
HD8526. F54 1992
305.5′62′0947 – dc20   91–40201   CIP

ISBN 0 521 418992 hardback

CE

For Eleanor and Liam

Contents

Tables

Preface and acknowledgements

This book is a follow-up study to my earlier work, *Soviet Workers and Stalinist Industrialization* (London and Armonk, NY, 1986), which examined the position of the Soviet working class during the formative years of the Stalinist system and the origins of modern Soviet production relations. The underlying theoretical premises of the two works are the same, namely that the atomized position of the individual worker within society and at the workplace has limited the means available to workers for defending their position against management and the ruling elite. Essentially, workers are confined to individual responses, in particular the exercise of considerable control over the way in which they execute their labour power, and this, in my view, has become a fundamental source of crisis in the Soviet system. Indeed, the problem facing Gorbachev and the market reformers in today's USSR is precisely how to change the workers' relationship to the labour process, forcing them to cede greater power to management. This is a complex argument which I elaborate in considerable detail in chapter 5 and the conclusion.

From the point of view of the consolidation of the USSR's underlying system of production, the Khrushchev period plays a crucial role. Stalin's successors were all keenly aware that the continued domination of society by the secret police and rule by terror was incompatible with any attempts to extract the country from the economic impasse into which the Stalinist system had finally led it after World War II. The question facing the elite was how to motivate the population to put in greater effort at the workplace without actually ceding political power and its control over society. Where industrial workers were concerned, this meant persuading or coercing them to surrender the complex network of shop-floor practices developed through the course of the 1930s in defence of their individual positions. Much of de-Stalinization was, in fact, aimed precisely at this objective, as I detail in chapter 2. My argument is that the Khrushchev regime failed in this historical project. On the contrary, once the terror was removed the Soviet elite found that the crisis-ridden relationship between itself and the workforce created by Stalinist industrialization, but partially held in check by the dictatorial regime, was now free to manifest itself in 'pure' form. On this interpretation, the Khrushchev period formed a transitional phase between the Stalinist origins of the Soviet system and its modern manifestation, which revealed its full tendencies towards decline and ultimate disintegration under Brezhnev.

The Khrushchev reforms, therefore, revealed the precise limits to which the Stalinist system could be modified and reformed while still keeping intact its essential class relations and mode of appropriating the surplus product. It is no accident that Gorbachev, though clearly a far more astute politician than Khrushchev, soon found himself caught in the same vice and was forced very quickly to opt for a transition to the market and the inevitable restoration of capitalism which this must bring.

Although the basis of my analysis has not changed, this study differs from my earlier one in several respects. In particular, I have devoted more space to two questions: the specific role of women workers in the elite's attempts to regulate the economy (chapter 7), and the labour process itself (chapters 6 and 8). In terms of the latter, I have tried to locate the issue in the context of the larger debate over skills and de-skilling that has been going on in the West ever since Harry Braverman published his important book *Labor and Monopoly Capital* in 1974. Although its scope is therefore broader, I must still make the same caveat as before: this book does not pretend to present an overall political economy of the Soviet system, but must be taken as a partial and highly incomplete contribution towards that task. Fundamental questions of class relations, the reproduction of everyday life, and ideology are beyond the scope of this study, although they are crucial to any all-sided understanding of the totality of social relations of the USSR.

Many individuals and institutions made the completion of this book possible. R. W. Davies and Mary McAuley gave invaluable assistance in the initial stages of the research, directing me to sources, helping me to gain a solid grasp of the history of the Khrushchev period, and offering comments on draft project proposals. Robert Service gave considerable time, discussing his research on the early phases of de-Stalinization which helped me to place my own work in a larger political context.

The research was supported by a major project grant from the Leverhulme Trust. The British Council enabled me to spend three months in the Soviet Union, where I found a wealth of information, in particular local newspapers and dissertations, without which this book could not have been written. The Bundesinstitut für ostwissenschaftliche und internationale Studien in Cologne, West Germany, gave me a three-month Fellowship in the autumn of 1989 which allowed me to revise the manuscript.

The research was carried out at the Centre for Russian and East European Studies, University of Birmingham. Nick Lampert devoted much time and effort as director of our project, helping to revise grant proposals, and commenting on the manuscript. His observations and discussions of numerous research problems were always insightful. The drafts of the chapters on the Khrushchev wage reform and women workers were discussed at sessions of the Soviet Industrialization Project Seminar and the Women and Society Seminar respectively, and I am grateful for comments and suggestions offered on these occasions, in particular from John Barber, R. W. Davies, Judith Shapiro, and Chris Ward. John Dunstan, the Centre's Assistant Director, gave liberally of his time to manage our grant. Jackie Johnson, the librarian at the Centre for Russian and East European Studies, contributed much-needed assistance with sources. Betty Benenett, Sandra Cumberland, Tricia Carr, Nancy Moor, and Marea Arries were equally generous in providing technical support.

Several people read and commented on all or part of the draft manuscript, and provided numerous suggestions for revision: Michael Burawoy, Mark Harrison, Nick Lampert, Alastair McAuley, Judith Shapiro, and Elizabeth Waters.

Much of the material in chapter 4 appeared originally as 'The Soviet Wage Reform of 1956–1962', *Soviet Studies*, vol. 41, no. 1 (January 1989), pp. 88–110, and has been used with the kind permission of the editors of that journal.

Needless to say, none of the individuals and institutions cited here bears any responsibility for errors or shortcomings in the text or for its analysis and conclusions.

Terms and abbreviations

ASSR	Autonomous Soviet Socialist Republic (Avtonomnaya Sovetskaya Sotsialisticheskaya Respublika)
Gosbank	State Bank (Gosudarstvennyi Bank)
Gosplan	State Planning Commission
kolkhoz	collective farm (kollektivnoe khozyaistvo)
kolkhoznik	member of a collective farm
Komsomol	*see* VLKSM
KPSS	Communist Party of the Soviet Union (Kommunisticheskaya Partiya Sovetskogo Soyuza)
krai	territory
oblast'	region (roughly equivalent to a province)
orgnabor	organized recruitment
Procuracy	Office of the Public Prosecutor
Procurator	Public Prosecutor
raikom	District Committee of the Communist Party (raionnyi komitet)
raion	district (administrative subdivision within a city, *oblast'*, or other larger territorial unit)
RSFSR	Russian Soviet Federative Socialist Republic (Rossiiskaya Sovetskaya Federativnaya Sotsialisticheskaya Respublika)
samizdat	underground publication (literally, self-publishing)
sovkhoz	state (literally, Soviet) farm (sovetskoe khozyaistvo)
sovkhoznik	state farm worker
sovnarkhoz	literally, Council of the National Economy (Sovet Narodnogo Khozyaistva), more commonly known as Regional Economic Council
SSSR	Union of Soviet Socialist Republics (Soyuz Sovetskikh Sotsialisticheskikh Respublik)

TsK	Central Committee (Tsentral'nyi Komitet)
VLKSM	All-Union Leninist Communist League of Youth (Vsesoyuznyi Leninskii Kommunisticheskii Soyuz Molodezhi)
VTsSPS	All-Union Central Council of Trade Unions (Vsesoyuznyi Tsentral'nyi Sovet Professional'nykh Soyuzov)

Introduction: the contradictions of de-Stalinization

When Stalin died in March 1953, he left behind a country in a deep state of crisis. No sphere of the economy, politics, or society was immune. The economy, despite its rapid recovery from the ravages of World War II, was in considerable difficulty. The crisis was most glaring in agriculture, which was poorly mechanized and unable to provide the country with more than the most basic foodstuffs. Industry, though not in the same obvious state of decline as the countryside, continued to suffer from the structural weaknesses created by Stalinist industrialization: management was overcentralized and top-heavy; productivity and technology lagged badly behind those of the West; and production of consumer goods was woefully inadequate. In 1952, light industry produced just three pairs of socks or stockings for each member of the population, and barely more than one pair of shoes. Consumer durables such as refrigerators or television sets were virtually unobtainable.[1] But the pitiful economic realities were themselves symptomatic of a more profound political demoralization affecting the Soviet population. The terror and the network of labour camps on which the Stalinist system had so heavily depended had clearly outlived their usefulness. Not only was it clear that the population could no longer be expected to accept the strain under which the terror placed them, but the camps themselves were becoming increasingly difficult to control and manage, as evidenced by a growing number of rebellions.[2]

It did not require a profound understanding of the political economy of the Stalinist system to recognize the direct relation between the population's discontent and the economic impasse. People alienated from the political system and resentful of the terror and the mass of bureaucratic restrictions on their lives were unlikely to display a great deal of enthusiasm or effort at work. It followed from this that there would be no substantial improvement in economic

1

performance unless the post-Stalin leadership could solve the problem
of how to motivate the population. In this sense, de-Stalinization was a
clear economic necessity, directed precisely to the issue of how, in the
face of profound popular demoralization, the regime could coax the
population into making renewed efforts at the workplace. There were
other objectives, to be sure, in particular the larger crisis of legitimacy
which the terror had created, but the issue of the economy was a
paramount factor behind the political thaw.[3]

This basic truth was perceived, albeit with different degrees of
clarity, by all those involved in the struggle for succession: Lavrenti
Beria, Lazar Kaganovich, V. M. Molotov, K. E. Voroshilov, G. M.
Malenkov, and Nikita Khrushchev. Ironically, Khrushchev, whose
name was to become synonymous with the term 'de-Stalinization',
was perhaps the most cautious in this regard. Instead it was Beria, the
dreaded and ruthless head of the secret police, who initially emerged
as the most 'radical' of the de-Stalinizers: he advocated a substantial
reorganization of agriculture to ease the heavy burdens on the
peasantry, proposed relaxing the Soviet Union's hold on Eastern
Europe, in particular East Germany, and held out prospects for less
repressive control over the non-Russian nationalities within the
USSR.[4] Malenkov, who as chairperson of the Council of Ministers was
nominal head of state, also proposed major changes. In April, barely a
month after Stalin's death, he lowered retail food prices – an empty
gesture at a time of dire scarcity, but clearly designed to win popular
approval for the new leadership. He also championed a reorientation
of industrial production towards light industry.[5] These trends were
carried further after the so-called Beria Affair in June 1953 when, at
Khrushchev's urging, the Communist Party Presidium had Beria
arrested and summarily shot, on the grounds that he was preparing a
coup d'état.[6] At the Central Committee Plenum held in July 1953, just
after Beria's execution, the new industrial policy was reaffirmed, and
there were even criticisms, albeit of a veiled nature, of Stalin himself.[7]

The need for reform presented the new leadership with a fundamental problem. Economic revival would require substantial improvements in productivity, that is, the extraction of greater effort from the
population. If the terror was no longer a viable method of social
control (and, in fact, was now recognized as counter-productive), how
was this to be achieved? Merely tampering with the economy, or even
offering greater material incentives would not on their own be sufficient. It required liberalization of the overall political and intellectual
climate to restore some legitimacy to the regime in the eyes of its

population, and to make people believe that they had some stake in the system, no matter how illusory this was in reality. Only then would they be prepared to make the sacrifices the regime would require. Khrushchev probably understood this point far better than his rivals. But, like the others, he also realized that such a policy was fraught with dangers and had definite limits. There would have to be change, but not so great as to threaten the ruling group's hold on power. Moreover, the political leadership did not exist in a vacuum: even under Stalin, the leadership had exercised power on behalf of a ruling elite of top officials, economic managers, and the upper echelons of the policy-influencing intelligentsia. The class position of this group, as expropriators of the surplus product created by workers and peasants, would have to be preserved. The system had to be reformed, but without undermining the basic class relations from which the elite drew its privileges.[8]

This fundamental dilemma was to be observed in virtually all of Khrushchev's major reforms: the attempts at political liberalization, industrial reorganization, the Virgin Lands and other agricultural campaigns, and the shake-up of the Communist Party apparatus. Because of his flamboyant style, his often appalling judgement when it came to selecting advisers, and the impetuosity with which he often pursued his policies, it has always been tempting to see the failures of Khrushchev's reforms as being largely the result of his personal idiosyncrasies. Yet a careful look at the reforms reveals that the problem lay far deeper, in the nature of the Soviet system itself. In some cases, like the reorganization of the Communist Party, the bureaucratic apparatus which had to implement particular policies distorted them or simply ignored them because they perceived that the changes would threaten their jobs and privileges.[9] In others, such as the Virgin Lands campaign, Khrushchev was unable to overcome the opposition of powerful industrial and defence ministries, who blocked any reallocation of resources away from their bases of power.[10] In still others, the leadership itself, including Khrushchev, were keenly aware that to go too far with liberalization would call into question their own legitimacy, as Stalin's heirs, to rule the country.[11] The common thread linking all these policies and campaigns was that the reforms that *had* to be made could *not* be made without threatening the integrity of the Stalinist system itself.

This same contradiction impinged upon efforts to change the basic pattern of worker–manager relations within industry, in particular the workforce's relationship to the labour process as it emerged historically from Stalinist industrialization. No reform of industry could succeed without coming to grips with this major issue, for it went to the very heart of the elite's difficulties: its limited control over the extraction and disposal of society's surplus product.[12]

Stalinist industrialization had created a highly specific network of worker–manager relations on the shop floor, which derived from the political relationship between industrialization and the emerging Soviet elite's consolidation of power. As I have argued elsewhere,[13] the bureaucratic apparatus that had grown up during the New Economic Policy, which derived its privileges from the inequalities bred by the predominance of the market in a country plagued by economic back-wardness and scarcity, could secure its position only by eliminating threats to its domination from two potential sources of opposition. First there was the peasantry, which produced for the market and whose economic activity was therefore governed by the law of value. Without the eventual transformation of peasant farms into socially owned, collective agriculture (which has nothing to do with the barba-rism of Stalinist collectivization), the peasantry's long-term needs could be met only by a restoration of capitalism. Secondly, there was the industrial working class, which though depleted by World War I and the Civil War, and further demoralized by its progressive exclu-sion from decision-making within the industrial enterprise and society at large, still retained the long-term potential to reconstitute itself and assume power in its own name. This residual power was evidenced by the widespread discontent and spontaneous resistance actually mounted during the early years of forced industrialization. The elite could thus secure its own class position as expropriators of the surplus product only by subordinating both of these other classes. It abolished almost all vestiges of market relations and production based on the law of value, while systematically breaking up the old working class of the Revolutionary and NEP periods. Because its power relied exclusively on its control over the state apparatus, rather than through the auto-maticity that comes with the market and the ownership of capital, it could safeguard its dominance only by atomizing the population and making collective resistance impossible, a task it accomplished through the terror.

The significance of this political struggle for the nature of the labour process is described in more detail in chapter 5. What is important here is that the workers, denied the opportunity collectively to defend their interests through political parties, genuine trade unions, or even industrial action, appropriated control over the one area left open to them: the individual labour process. In this they were aided by the chaotic, unplanned nature of Stalinist industrialization, which made coordination within and between enterprises extremely haphazard, and by the chronic labour shortage created by the breakneck pace of industrial development. This partial control over the individual labour process manifested itself most visibly in the area of labour discipline. Absenteeism and insubordination, especially in the period up to 1933, were extremely high.[14] As the standard of living fell and the labour shortage grew increasingly severe, labour turnover shot up, so that in 1930 the average sojourn in a job was a mere eight months (four months in coal-mining).[15] Attempts by the regime to curb job-changing and truancy met with little success, because managers would not enforce discipline regulations, lest it make the labour shortage even worse.[16]

Overt violations of discipline were not, however, the most crucial way in which workers reasserted control over shop-floor life. More important was their relationship to production itself. Workers exercised considerable control over work speeds, taking advantage of the almost constant disruptions endemic to the Stalinist system: supply shortages, lack of tools, equipment breakdowns, and even long queues caused by the chronic disorganization of factory dining rooms. They similarly showed a general disregard for quality, which deteriorated sharply with industrialization and became a defining characteristic of Soviet production. Here, too, because of the labour shortage, management was almost powerless to compel workers to abandon such behaviour. When the regime attempted to force the issue through its annual rises in output quotas (norms) and cuts in wage rates, and through speed-up campaigns such as shock work and Stakhanovism, managers often had to respond by colluding to protect workers through keeping norms low or inflating earnings through fictitious or semi-fictitious bonus payments.[17] Given the nature of the Stalinist system, where managerial success depended on high plan fulfilment under conditions where the availability of both labour power and supplies was highly uncertain, such collusion became a normal part of factory life.[18]

Labour policy in the Khrushchev years faced the basic problem of how to deal with this legacy and how to compel or persuade workers to surrender the various defensive devices they had developed during the Stalin period. First, there was the need to tackle labour turnover, which, although it never reached the dizzying magnitude of the pre-war years, nevertheless rose following the liberalization of labour legislation in 1956 and confronted various regions and industries with serious difficulties. Secondly, there was the related issue of the labour shortage, which manifested itself in both the newly developing regions of Siberia and the Far East, and in such traditional industries as engineering. Thirdly, there was the informal network of localized wage agreements between management and workforce which blunted the use of wages as a prod to greater work effort. Finally, there was the question of the labour process itself, and the endeavour to break down the larger fabric of worker–management concessions which stemmed from workers' imperfect, but nonetheless considerable control over the way they organized and executed their work.

Although each of these issues is treated more or less thematically in the course of this book, they were closely interrelated. High turnover fed off the persistence of the labour shortage, which allowed workers freely to abandon jobs in the knowledge that they would always find a new one. The unwillingness of workers to put up with the dismal working and living conditions in the new Siberian settlements, or with the restrictions on their control over work speeds and on earnings which the Khrushchev wage reform imposed in engineering, virtually guaranteed that high turnover would undermine other policies aimed at easing the labour shortage in these areas. Similarly, the relatively high intensity of labour and low wages in industries and trades reliant on women workers meant that women outside the workforce had little incentive to leave the home for jobs in the factory. Efforts to extend political de-Stalinization to the workplace, and thus to raise the regime's moral and political legitimacy among the workforce, had equally contradictory consequences. The repressive Stalinist labour laws of the 1940s were repealed, and the trade unions were given greater rights to veto dismissals. While such measures no doubt did something to reduce simmering tensions between the population and the elite, their immediate consequence was to make labour mobility more difficult to control. This pattern was perhaps even more striking in the case of the wage reform. For by attacking the long-established mechanisms through which managers more or less guaranteed most workers their 'accepted' levels of earnings, the reform, far from providing countervailing inducements, merely set in motion a new wave of circumventions and arbitrary local distortions which subverted the attempt to reconstruct a viable system of incentives.

In the end, however, the central problem which the regime had to tackle was the nature of the Soviet labour process itself. And here, as we shall see, the elite had no coherent strategy. Rather, it tried to weaken workers' control by limiting their field of action in more peripheral spheres, such as labour mobility or incentives. Yet its problems in these areas derived from the essence of the labour process, and so these issues, too, remained unresolved. Through their partial control over the actual execution of work, workers contributed to the persistence and reproducibility of the most basic causes of industrial disruption: supply shortages, poor quality, incomplete batches of parts, huge variabilities in labour productivity and the use of work time, and the general breakdown of coordination between the different links in the chain of production to which these all led. These uncertainties in the industrial environment in turn tended to reproduce the individual worker's enhanced bargaining power. They vastly increased the demand for labour power, and so made the labour shortage more or less permanent, thereby weakening the impact of any disciplinary sanctions that either the regime or management might try to impose. Of equal importance, the various dislocations plaguing production were so great that management constantly relied on workers' cooperation to try to attenuate their impact, so as to keep plan fulfilment within reach. In return, management had to tolerate workers' retention of traditional work practices and to compensate irregularities in earnings that the unpredictability of production caused. The elite was thus faced with an unsolvable dilemma. It could not impose greater conformity on worker behaviour without first restoring predictability and cohesion to the cycle of production and distribution. Yet it could not rationalize the management and organization of production without re-establishing control over workers' individual actions.

The roots of the elite's difficulties lay in the genesis of the Stalinist system, in particular the need to atomize the workforce so as to ensure the elite's political domination. But this atomization relied on an extreme individualization of the work process, which then acted to deprive the plans of any coherence they might have contained.[19] The effects were partially mitigated by the terror and the use of a huge slave-labour sector to take up the slack left by inefficiencies in the 'free' areas of production. Once the terror was removed, the regime had no effective means of controlling workers' behaviour. It could not rely on the coercive power of the market, in particular unemployment. Nor could it offer workers the positive inducements to labour that genuine socialist democracy would provide. Both would have necessitated a total transformation of the property and power relations of the Stalinist system and would, in their different ways, have deprived the elite of any basis for its continued rule: the one by restoring capitalism, the other by allowing a politicized and self-conscious society collectively to determine policies, priorities, and the ways these would be achieved.

The result was that under Khrushchev the basic tendencies governing the industrial environment, which had been spawned by Stalinist industrialization but at the same time had been kept partially in check by the police state, *could now manifest themselves in pure form*. Far from witnessing any major changes in the nature of workforce–management relations, de-Stalinization saw their actual consolidation. The Khrushchev years thus constitute a transitional period, during which the modern system of Soviet production relations came to maturity. If under Stalin the essence of the system had manifested itself in distorted fashion, now under Khrushchev this essence became clearly expressed in its concrete phenomena.

This point is of more than just methodological or analytical interest. The experience of the Khrushchev years has considerable significance for events in the USSR under *perestroika*. For it calls into question the reformability of the Soviet system. The problem which confronted the Soviet elite when Gorbachev acceded to power in 1985 was identical to the one it faced in 1953. The economy, and hence the society which it underpinned, were in stasis. In Marx's terms, it was nearing the point where it had exhausted the possibilities contained in the existing social form of production. The problem facing the elite was how to transform the system, make it more efficient, and reintroduce some dynamic to it while still keeping its basic property relations – and hence the elite's privileges – intact. This necessarily involved a frontal attack on the content of the labour process, that is, on the way in which the surplus was extracted and appropriated. The extent and rate of surplus extraction had to be increased and the elite's disposition over it made more precise. In political terms, this meant attacking the working class and the entire fabric of social relations within the workplace. The elite proved unable to develop a coherent strategy for such an assault (see my discussion in the conclusion). To a certain extent, this was due to splits in its own ranks and to resistance, albeit limited, from the workers themselves. The main reason, however, is that such a strategy still did not provide an effective economic regulator for the system. The Stalinist system survived for 60 years as a hybrid system based on neither the anarchic and crisis-ridden spontaneity of the market, nor the self-conscious planning of democratic socialism. From a historical point of view, it was thus highly unstable. As the system neared the end of its developmental possibilities, it became increasingly evident, including to the elite itself, that history offered no viable 'third way' between these two poles. Thus the elite under Gorbachev was left with no choice but to opt for the market and the eventual restoration of capitalism, for then at least some sections of it might have been able to retain their positions of dominance and privilege by entering the new bourgeoisie.

This dilemma was already present in embryonic form in the Khrushchev years. The entire experience of de-Stalinization was one where the more far-sighted sections of the ruling hierarchy attempted to bend the system without breaking it. This process was doomed to failure, because the system's inherent instability meant that radical changes, whether in the planning system, political life, or the process of production, would always threaten to burst through the system's fragile integument and bring about its total collapse. Thus, perhaps ironically, inertial forces, and not the reformers, were better placed to guarantee the system's short-term survival. This explains Khrushchev's failure, the longevity of the Brezhnevite reaction, and the ultimate collapse of Gorbachev's original conception of *perestroika*.

The argument of the book is set out as follows. Part I examines the main features of labour policy during the Khrushchev period. It opens with a description of the work environment encountered by the individual worker on the shop floor, so as to establish the context of constraints within which both workers and managers had to operate. Chapter 2 analyses the restoration of the labour market and the political moves which accompanied it, in particular the liberalization of labour law and the so-called 'democratization' of the trade unions, and their relationship to labour turnover. Chapter 3 deals with the complex issue of the labour shortage: its reproduction, the campaigns to draw women and young people into production, especially in Siberia and other developing regions, and the particular crisis that hit the engineering industry in the aftermath of the wage reform. Chapter 4 examines the wage reform and its ultimate failure to create a viable system of incentives, through which the regime hoped to regain some control over workers' actions within the labour process.

Part II provides a detailed analysis of the Soviet labour process as it emerged and consolidated itself in the Khrushchev period. It begins with a theoretical discussion of its historical genesis (chapter 5), and goes on to look at three main issues: control over the surplus product (chapter 6); the special position of women workers and the role they play in the elite's attempts to bolster its compromised control over the surplus (chapter 7); and the issue of de-skilling as it relates to broader debates about control over the labour process in capitalist society (chapter 8). The conclusion summarizes the main findings about the Khrushchev period and relates them to the problems confronting the Soviet elite in the USSR under *perestroika*.

Part I

Labour policy under Khrushchev: issues and results

1 The worker and the work environment

The industrial structure created by Stalinist industrialization was quite specific to the Soviet Union as a social formation. The elite attempted to exercise control through the extreme centralization of decision-making, enforced through five-year, annual, and quarterly plans. Because of the bureaucratic, authoritarian nature of the system, this over centralization in fact gave rise to its virtual opposite, as individual managers and workers tried to cope the best they could with conditions that were often outside their control. Coordination and predictability, which must form the basis of planning, constantly eluded both planners and executors of the plan, as they struggled to cope with uncertainties and shortages, and in so doing reproduced these same disruptions elsewhere in the cycle of production and distribution.[1]

For reasons that will be elaborated in more detail in Part II, the enterprise confronted both workers and managers as an alien, 'objective' environment through which they had constantly to wend their way, circumventing official regulations and prescriptions and nominal plans in order to achieve the production indicators that would secure workers their earnings and managers their bonuses and upward mobility within the political system. First, there was the planning system itself, which was bureaucratically top-heavy and thus divorced from the vital information that planners required to construct workable plans and instructions. The system was fiercely competitive: ministries jockeyed with one another for preferential investment allocations; enterprises within ministries did the same. Because the centre had no effective means of controlling how plans were actually implemented, the plans were constantly distorted at enterprise level. What and how much was produced rarely conformed exactly to original production programmes, and at times could deviate from them considerably. This was in part due to the non-availability of the appropriate supplies, in part because such departures made it easier for management to meet targets, and partly because the initial specifications of the plans were frequently arbitrary, irrational, and hence unfulfillable in the form in which they were transmitted to the enterprise.

Secondly, there was the constant problem of supplies, which arrived irregularly, were often of the wrong specification or product-mix, and were generally of poor quality or even unusable. The supply situation gave rise to a peculiarly Soviet institution, storming, that is, slack work at the start of a production period (a month, quarter, or year), followed by a rush to fulfil the bulk of the production programme at the period's end, when supplies suddenly became available.[2]

Thirdly, Soviet industry was badly and unevenly mechanized. Production shops were more highly mechanized than auxiliary operations, which became a bottleneck in every enterprise and soaked up an inordinate percentage of the workforce. Another bottleneck was the shortage of spare parts and fastenings, which, as we shall show, was a direct consequence of the bureaucratic way in which plans were constructed and implemented.

All of these problems had been well documented and extensively discussed in the press and journals during Stalin's time, and these discussions continued under Khrushchev. In some cases, as with the planning apparatus, they became the object of a major institutional and organizational overhaul, which, however, merely produced new difficulties that were often worse than those they had been meant to solve. In others, such as the chronic undermechanization of auxiliary operations, the problems were so deeply rooted in the production cycle that no 'reform' could begin to address them. The degree of mechanization and the proportion of auxiliary workers were virtually the same at the end of Khrushchev's rule as at the beginning. Even today, when the size and technological base of Soviet industry are obviously far more developed than they were 25 years ago, the basic outlines of this problem have altered little.[3]

The legacy of Stalinist 'planning'

Despite the Soviet Union's rapid recovery from the devastation of World War II, by the time of Stalin's death the Soviet economy was in serious difficulties. The plight of agriculture and Khrushchev's attempts (which began even before Stalin died) to reform relations between the state and the countryside are well described in standard works.[4] Industry, however, also faced enormous problems. At the July 1953 Plenum of the Communist Party Central

Table 1.1. *Industrial production in major Soviet industries, 1950–1965*

	1950	1955	1960	1965
Iron and steel products (million tons)				
Pig iron	19.2	33.3	46.8	66.2
Steel	27.3	45.3	65.3	91.0
Rolled steel	18.0	30.6	43.7	61.7
Steel pipe	2.0	3.5	5.8	9.0
Engineering industry				
Turbines (total capacity, million kilowatt)	2.8	5.6	9.2	14.6
Metal-cutting machine tools (1,000 units)	70.6	117.0	156.0	186.0
Forge-press equipment (1,000 units)	7.7	17.1	29.9	34.6
Lorries (1,000 units)	294.4	328.1	362.0	379.6
Light vehicles (1,000 units)	64.6	107.8	138.8	201.2
Tractors (1,000 units)	117.0	163.0	239.0	355.0
Energy and fuel				
Electric power (million kilowatt-hours)	91.2	170.2	292.3	506.7
Oil (million tons)	37.9	70.8	147.9	242.9
Natural gas (billion cubic metres)	5.8	9.0	45.3	127.7
Coal (million tons)	261.1	389.9	509.6	577.7
Chemical industry				
Mineral fertilizers (million tons)	5.5	9.7	13.9	31.3
Synthetic fibres (1,000 tons)	24	110	211	407
Synthetic resins and plastics (1,000 tons)	67.1	160	312	803
Light industry				
Cotton cloth (million square metres)	2,745	4,227	4,838	5,499
Wool cloth (million square metres)	193	316	439	466
Linen (million square metres)	257	272	516	548
Silk cloth (million square metres)	106	415	675	801
Leather footwear (million pairs)	203	271	419	486

Source: *Narodnoe khozyaistvo SSSR za 60 let*, pp. 201, 205, 206, 208, 213, 216, 220, 222, 227, 229, 245, 249.

Committee – the first such meeting after Stalin's death – it was, according to R. J. Service's account, openly admitted that 'whole industries "[were] backward." Industrial output [was] insufficient either to supply the collective farms with much-needed machinery or to satisfy the material and cultural requisites of the urban population.'[5]

It was obvious to all the contenders for power that the industrial and planning apparatus they had inherited needed thorough reform.

However, nothing substantial was done until Khrushchev had consolidated his political position. Then, in 1957, he introduced a reorganization of industry along territorial lines (*sovnarkhozy*, or regional economic councils), designed to achieve a more rational use of resources and to eliminate the old bureaucratic red tape and competition between industrial ministries. In 1958 he also abandoned the by then traditional emphasis on the five-year plan and replaced it with an ambitious seven-year plan, due to run from 1958 to 1965. The results were decidedly mixed. As table 1.1 shows, despite a considerable rise in physical output in several branches of heavy industry, in most industries the rate of growth declined during the period 1960–5 compared with the previous five years.

As can be seen, light industry did especially badly. Despite the express intention of the seven-year plan to cut the shortage of consumer goods by having those industries grow faster than heavy industry, the results of the plan were precisely the reverse.[6] Like virtually every plan except the Third Five-Year Plan of 1938–41 (which actually called for higher growth rates in heavy industry), the planned growth in consumer-goods production never materialized. The disproportion between heavy and light industry only deepened. Yet this was merely the phenomenal expression of deeper problems within industry. Even in heavy industry disproportions and problems with coordination abounded. Shortages of supplies, poor quality, and waste of resources remained endemic. Despite the very real boost in output during the Khrushchev years, much of this growth was self-consuming. The output of iron and steel may have doubled, but a large share of it ended up as scraps and shavings, as iron and steel mills and foundries in engineering factories produced billets and semi-finished components that were too large and too heavy, which then had to be pared down to usable size by machinists. On paper this was growth, but in real terms a considerable amount of new steel production made no contribution whatsoever to the production of actual use values.

To a large degree, the various distortions which plagued the economy during the Khrushchev years could be attributed to the structure of the bureaucratic planning system through which the elite had to try to exercise control. Under the old ministerial system which prevailed until Khrushchev's *sovnarkhoz* reform of 1957, the different ministries had built themselves up into quasi-autonomous empires whose actions, once the slack of the post-war reconstruction had been taken up, had clearly become a brake on further industrial growth. Plans, for example, were arbitrarily changed, as ministries and their subdivisions (Chief Administrations, or *glavki*) frequently imposed 'urgent' orders on factories, requiring them to suspend work on their regular plans. Factories often invested substantial sums in these 'urgent' orders only to have them cancelled half-way through, leaving the factory to bear the costs.[7] The tractor-parts industry provides a good illustration. At the Kaganovich tractor-parts factory in Tambov, higher authorities decided in late 1955 to close the factory's piston shop and then, a few months later, decreed that in 1957 the factory was to double its output of pistons.[8] Similarly, *glavki* imposed plans that in no way corresponded to the needs of customers. The Stalingrad tractor-parts factory, for example, was consistently given plans to produce parts for which tractor factories had absolutely no need, resulting in the accumulation of ever-growing, useless stocks.[9] The bureaucratic top-heaviness of the separate ministries exacerbated supply problems, as factories spent thousands – and sometimes hundreds of thousands – of rubles flying in parts and materials from opposite ends of the USSR, rather than acquiring the same supplies locally.[10]

One of the more baroque ministerial practices was to assign factories supplies from enterprises which did not in fact exist. In one case a 'pusher' (a supply agent sent out to expedite orders) from the Rostov agricultural-machinery factory was sent to Makeevka to track down a consignment of metal, only to discover that the rolling mill which was to supply the order was still in crates and had not even been assembled. This was not an isolated incident: the Rostov factory was scheduled to receive rolled steel from a plant in Enakievo which had been closed for *planned* capital maintenance, and sheet steel from a mill at Zaporozhstal' which was not yet under construction.[11] In 1955 the Kuznetsk iron and steel combine had to pay out 5.5 million rubles in fines for the non-delivery of metal products – products which it could not have supplied because the shops supposed to manufacture them were not as yet built.[12] The same was true of the Voronezh heavy-mechanical-press factory, which was deemed a working enterprise with its own production programme, despite the fact that most essential shops, for example, its pig-iron and steel foundries, the press shop, the oxygen and acetylene stations, and even its main building, had still to be erected.[13] Perhaps the most serious rebuke levied against the ministries, however, was their inability or reluctance to oversee the development and installation of new technology, an issue I shall return to later in this chapter.

In 1957 Khrushchev abolished the ministries and replaced them with regional economic councils, or *sovnarkhozy* (literally, Councils of the National Economy).[14] These were designed to break down the ministerial empires and allow for the rational integration of plans, production, and supplies on a regional basis. The reform was a failure, primarily because it merely replaced ministerial bureaucracies with local ones.[15] As a result, many of the problems of the pre-reform period were merely carried over, sometimes in a new form. Factories continued to suffer from arbitrary plan changes.[16] More seriously, the localism of the *sovnarkhozy* and the industrial administrations under them led to breakdowns of coordination as bad as those before the reform. Enterprises in one *sovnarkhoz*, or even under separate administrations within one and the same *sovnarkhoz*, found it difficult, if not almost impossible to obtain supplies from enterprises in other *sovnarkhozy* or administrative subdivisions without masses of time-consuming paperwork and resultant hold-ups in production.[17] Towards the end of Khrushchev's rule, as the failures of the *sovnarkhozy* were becoming apparent and a number of planning functions were being recentralized in new, Moscow-based State Committees (ministries in all but name), bureaucratic nightmares with supplies grew even worse. Chemical-equipment factories, for example, found it difficult to obtain metal in time to meet order completion dates: sometimes the metal was issued only after equipment should already have been manufactured.[18]

Mention should also be made of the perennial problems with construction. The issue of unfinished and/or poor-quality construction is too vast to deal with extensively here. Virtually every issue of the construction newspaper *Stroitel'naya gazeta* [Construction Gazette] bulged with accounts of projects lying incomplete because ministries had not issued adequate funding,[19] because building-materials factories could not provide required supplies,[20] or because of the incentive of factory managers and planners alike to spread their resources too thin and indulge in a dispersal of building projects which they could not then complete.[21]

These, then, were some of the most glaring features of how bureaucratic administration of the economy impeded coordination and efficiency. But beneath these macro-economic difficulties lay a more fundamental problem of coordination *within* the industrial enterprise, the most important aspects of which we shall now examine.

Storming and supply problems

Storming is a peculiarly Soviet phenomenon, whereby a factory is forced to concentrate the bulk of its production at the end of a planning period, for example, the last seven to ten days of a month, the final weeks of a quarter, or the last quarter of a year, in a rush to fulfil its plans before the relevant target date. The causes may range from lack of supplies to a shortage of workers in initial stages of production, such as the machining of parts for assembly. The phenomenon is well described in standard works on the Soviet economy, especially for the Stalin period,[22] but it is worth outlining how it manifested itself during the years we are dealing with here, in order to provide a clearer picture of the shop-floor environment within which Soviet workers were operating.

Given the problems of coordinating production between the different shops of an enterprise, however, storming tended to affect some sections more than others. As such it was only a reflection of the bottlenecks inherent within the Soviet cycle of production. This was a particular problem in the engineering industry, where assembly shops were perpetually held up by the failure of foundries and machine shops to provide them with parts and components.

What this meant concretely is shown by the experience of a brigade in the high-voltage apparatus shop of the Uralelektroapparat factory in Sverdlovsk in 1962. The brigade never had job assignments issued before the start of the month, so that it never knew beforehand what it was supposed to be doing. When the brigade finally received its targets, it had no materials to work with. Supplies did not arrive until the last ten days of the month. Even then, work could not proceed, since some of the materials were defective and could not be used. Still other supplies never arrived at all. The end result was repeated storming and massive overtime.[23] The assembly shop of the Azov forge-press equipment factory 'habitually' turned out between 60 and 70 per cent of equipment during the last part of the month. In May 1958 it produced not a single machine during the first ten days, 3 machines during the second, and 32 during the third. During this time, many workers never left the factory, merely catching a bit of rest when and where they could. At the start of the month they were given multi-day 'smoke breaks' to compensate them for the statutory days off they had had to work.[24]

Often the mad rush meant that all available hands – be they workers, clerical employees, or even higher level management – had to be dragged into production. At the Leningrad electrical-equipment factory, at the end of the month they transferred literally the entire factory to assembly work, using offices as workshops and drafting into production bookkeepers, planners, carpenters, or anyone else they could lay their hands on.[25] Understandably, this chain of dependency between different shops led to recriminations, as assembly shops blamed machine shops for the shortage of parts, machine shops blamed foundries for failure to provide semi-finished components, and foundries blamed the poor state of their equipment or poor attendance by workers.[26]

The effects of storming on equipment, morale, and manager–worker relations were profound. Machinery was perpetually overtaxed. In the words of a drill operator at Leningrad's Russkii dizel' factory, 'Even if smoke is coming out of the machine you either have to ignore it or rectify the problem in a rough and ready way. But treating equipment like this takes its toll a day or two later.'[27] The situation was exacerbated by the fact that during storming, repair and maintenance workers were often shifted on to production jobs, which meant that they were unavailable to service equipment.[28]

At a deeper level, storming was one of the issues at the centre of shop-floor bargaining between workers and management. The irregularity of work schedules reinforced tendencies towards slack discipline. If workers knew that they might have little to do other than hang around the foreman's office, they were not especially inclined to adhere to strict work schedules. Storming, understandably, also affected the concessions that management had to make over wages. At the Tambov chemical-equipment factory, where some 80 per cent of output was completed at the end of each month, management had to haggle with workers to get them to put in the overtime needed to clear backlogs. Workers were alleged to demand an extra payment of 500 rubles per machine before they would cooperate. If management refused, the workers responded that the equipment would not be ready on time. According to *Trud*, this was often just bluff on the workers' part, but there were equally occasions when they forced management to give in.[29] In coal-mining, managers were accused of greasing workers' palms (*namazki*), not with money but with alcohol, which in turn prompted the indignation of miners' wives who had to live with the effects of their husbands' drinking.[30] The other side of storming was that it became a source of intense aggravation and frustration for workers and led to considerable conflicts over overtime work.[31] These two aspects of shop-floor bargaining – concessions and conflicts – were inseparable, for the need to persuade workers to accept storming was a major factor compelling managers to grant concessions over wages and work speeds and organization.

As our account of storming suggests, difficulties in acquiring supplies were one of the chief scourges of production. Here, too, the causes were varied. One problem was the disorganization and poor state of internal transport.[32] Another was the bureaucratic maze that enterprises had to negotiate in order to acquire what they needed. At one point during the construction of a new synthetic-rubber factory in Bashkiriya (earmarked as a major centre of the newly expanding chemical industry), the builders ran out of cement. Construction came to a total standstill for three days while a nearby cement factory waited for instructions from the local *sovnarkhoz* to provide the site with an interim shipment.[33] In Leningrad, bureaucratic regulations governing the delivery of metal meant that some factories actually found it easier to send trucks to Moscow to pick up metal than to try and extract it out of the local supply depot, such was the chaos in which the latter found itself.[34]

Equally disruptive was the way in which plan targets were set, usually in terms of gross-output criteria that offered a positive disincentive to suppliers to achieve the correct product-mix. Construction firms, for example, found that iron and steel and building-materials factories tended to concentrate on producing the most profitable items rather than those that were actually required.[35] It made little difference whether plans were specified by weight, units of output, or ruble value: factories found themselves under pressure and/or encouraged to circumvent them. The response of managers to their supply problems was often to circumvent the official lines of production and distribution and simply barter with each other. Factories with unneeded stocks of certain supplies – primarily metal – would engage in direct exchange with other enterprises holding unwanted stocks of items they required.[36]

Difficulties with supplies and storming were also generated by the internal organization of production within the enterprise. The constant shortages of castings experienced by engineering factories was in large part the result of the relatively backward technology used in foundries relative to the machine shops which machined them.[37] The undermechanization of internal transport and warehousing operations was similarly a source of bottlenecks. Thus the problem of supplies, and hence of storming, was dependent not only on externally given factors, but on the organization of production within the enterprise itself. As will be argued in later chapters, the specific features of this organization were rooted in the contradictory relations between the workforce and management and between the workforce and the elite.[38] For the moment, however, we should turn to the issue of the uneven mechanization of production and its implications for the structure of the workforce within the enterprise and for the composition of the working class itself.

The swollen auxiliary apparatus

The managerial practice in the Soviet Union of hoarding workers above planned levels has long been common knowledge. To a large extent it is necessitated by storming, as managers have to keep on hand a flexible contingent of workers to meet the rush at the end of the month or quarter. In coal-mining, where the poor organization of production traditionally meant that a large proportion of workers was unable to meet its output quotas (norms), managers retained above-plan establishments in order to ensure plan fulfilment.[39] Staffing levels were also a function of the age of plant and equipment, especially in the iron and steel industry, where the older Ukrainian furnaces and mills routinely employed far more workers than the more efficient units at Magnitogorsk.[40] As we shall see in chapter 3, the need to retain overlarge establishments[41] creates a perpetual labour shortage, which in turn provides workers with the leverage needed to retain their partial control over the labour process – thus reproducing the very micro- and macro-economic dislocations which require the hoarding of labour power and its consequent ongoing shortage. In this way, workers are constantly reproducing the conditions of their own relative scarcity and the concessions from management which flow from this.

Historically, this control has made it extremely difficult for the elite to free labour power through the modernization of existing enterprises. Prior to the *sovnarkhoz* reform, management itself resisted modernization because the inevitable teething problems of introducing new equipment, new production processes, or new product lines would, at least temporarily, lower plan fulfilment and/or raise costs, with a subsequent loss of bonuses, wages, and career standing.[42] Despite an almost complete overhaul of managerial bonus systems under Khrushchev, this financial disincentive to modernization was never eliminated.[43] The fault did not always lie with factory management, however: *sovnarkhozy* themselves were often slow to approve or implement modernization plans or to provide factories with promised equipment.[44] Thus one of the main problems the *sovnarkhozy* were supposed to do away with – the failure of the old ministries to implement technical modernization – continued to persist.[45]

More fundamentally, workers themselves have had a clear interest in resisting those innovations which would either push up norms or weaken their control over how they carried out their work.[46] The press in this period is full of accounts of individual workers or managers devising inventions or innovations which promised to yield substantial improvements in productivity and at the same time make the work regime easier, yet the improvements were never adopted – almost certainly because managers wanted to avoid pressures to raise norms or to redeploy workers who might have been made redundant.[47] Even where new equipment was introduced, it was often so badly designed or constructed that workers refused to use it because it led to worse production results than the machinery it replaced.[48]

These impediments to mechanization by and large affected production workers whose labour was already largely mechanized, but who had a great deal to lose from further technical improvements in terms of loss of control, higher norms, and disruption to established work practices. But undermechanization was also responsible for the persistence of a vast auxiliary sector, workers whose jobs involved a great deal of heavy, manual, low- or semi-skilled, and usually low-paid labour. The existence of this sector of the factory workforce and the elite's inability to reduce it meant not only the subjection of a large number of industrial workers to difficult and poorly renumerated work; it severely disrupted industrial production and created or exacerbated bottlenecks and problems of coordination.

Workers in auxiliary operations carried out a vast array of tasks which, although vital to production, did not actually involve these workers in production proper. Among the most common auxiliary jobs were internal transport, loading and unloading, warehousing, quality control, packing, cleaning factory premises, tool-setting and adjusting, and repair and maintenance. There were also ancillary workers who carried out menial jobs such as removing finished output from the workbench or bringing production workers their tools. Other trades, such as crane operators, although usually classed as auxiliary workers, were considered by some labour economists more properly to be production workers, and I shall treat them as such here. As can be seen from this list, most of these jobs were relatively low-skilled. The exceptions were tool-setters and adjusters, and repair and maintenance workers. These were skilled manual workers who (despite the relatively poor quality of their work, especially in the repair sector) generally claimed to derive considerable satisfaction from their labour.[49]

Since the beginning of Stalinist industrialization, there had always been a disparity between the mechanization of production and auxiliary jobs, a factor which led, among other results, to far higher norm fulfilment by auxiliary workers, whose work was less easy to control.[50] The other side of this uneven mechanization was the constantly rising proportion of auxiliary workers in the overall industrial workforce. The proportion of auxiliary workers rose from 38 per cent in 1948 to just over 40 per cent in 1954. By 1958 they were nearly half of all industrial workers, and remained at that level for the rest of the Khrushchev period.[51]

According to the Occupational Census of 1962, there were over 9 million auxiliary workers in Soviet industry out of a total of 20,176,000 industrial workers. Of these, some 3 million were engaged in tra
and loading–unloading jobs, over 2 million worked on repair and maintenance, and 650,000 were on quality control.[52] The Occupational Census of 1965, which covered approximately 90 per cent of Soviet industry, listed 9.15 million auxiliary workers, or 46 per cent of those surveyed. This implies that there were over 10 million auxiliary workers in Soviet industry as a whole. Of the 9.15 million auxiliary workers recorded in the Census, 3,214,000 (16 per cent of industrial workers) worked on repair and maintenance, tool-setting, or making tools for use by their own factory. A further 3,103,000 (15.3 per cent of workers) worked on warehousing, internal transport, loading, ancillary jobs, etc. Together, these two groups accounted for 69 per cent of all auxiliary workers.[53] In addition, we must take into account the huge army of cleaners working in industrial enterprises. We do not know how large this group was, but in 1965 there were 183,000 in engineering, food, and light industry alone, suggesting a total of just under twice that number in the whole of industry. These workers were almost all women, and the work was low-paid and arduous.[54] By way of international comparison, albeit a very rough and indirect one, in 1975 approximately 14 per cent of Soviet industrial workers worked on internal transport and warehousing, versus less than 9 per cent in the United States during the same period.[55]

We can obtain a clearer picture of just what these figures meant for the internal structure of industrial enterprises by examining the situation in different major industries. In engineering, according to the

1962 Occupational Census, 18 per cent of workers were employed in repair and maintenance and a further 17 per cent on warehousing, quality control, loading jobs, and transport. Thus these two categories together made up 35 per cent of all engineering workers.[56] By 1965 the relative size of these two groups had swollen still further to 37 per cent.[57] The nature of most of these jobs is revealing. Clearing away scraps was almost totally unmechanized. At virtually all engineering factories, shavings were collected in buckets, wheelbarrows, and hand carts. Materials and components were delivered to the workplace by hand, despite their considerable weight. Attempts to rationalize transport operations by reorganizing shop lay-outs, so as to shorten the distances that parts and materials had to travel, went almost totally ignored.[58]

In iron and steel, the gap between mechanization of production and auxiliary jobs was equally sharp. Nearly half of all workers in the industry were in auxiliary shops (411,000 out of 874,000 iron and steel workers in 1965[59]). Yet within production shops there was also a large minority on auxiliary jobs. According to the 1962 Occupational Census, 17 per cent of blast-furnace workers worked on loading and transport; a further 24 per cent worked on repair and maintenance, making 41 per cent of the total. In steel-smelting, such auxiliary operations as the preparation of ladles and ingot moulds, refractory jobs, and clearing of ingot-mould stools were poorly mechanized. In rolling mills, 11 per cent of workers were employed on sorting, marking, and clearing away metal, and a further 17 per cent on maintenance. In all, maintenance workers accounted for 28 per cent of all iron and steel workers. A further 25 per cent were in loading and transport jobs, so that these two professions on their own accounted for over half the industry's workers.[60]

In coal-mining, the regime attempted in 1956 to establish quotas on the numbers of auxiliary workers employed in each pit, but these were consistently violated.[61] In the cement industry, 27.7 per cent of all workers in 1959 were employed on repair and maintenance. Of these, nearly two-thirds – over 17 per cent of all workers in the industry – were fitters or electricians engaged directly on the repair of machinery and electrical equipment. The remainder were welders, foundrymen, machine-tool operators, refractory-lining repairers, and workers in various building trades. Nearly three-quarters of repair and maintenance workers carried out their work exclusively by hand.[62]

In the chemical industry, in 1962 a mere 40 per cent of workers were employed directly in processing chemical raw materials. The rest were engaged in various servicing or maintenance operations. More revealing is the fact that over half the industry's workers carried out manual labour without the use of any form of machinery or mechanical assistance. Such jobs included measuring out materials, loading raw materials into and removing finished output from chemical apparatus, internal transport, packing, and washing vessels and containers. Although the predominance of manual labour was inherent in the nature of chemical production, the extent of undermechanization was considered significantly to exceed what was necessary. Certain isolated chemical plants managed to mechanize many of the operations that continued to be done by hand elsewhere.[63]

The problem of spare parts

The problem of mechanization had one other dimension which profoundly affected the structure of the factory workforce: the chronic shortage of spare parts, metal fastenings (nuts, bolts, screws, etc.), and small tools. The shortage of these items and their non-standardization compelled factories in virtually every industry to manufacture them in their own workshops under labour-intensive and highly wasteful and costly conditions. The absence of spares was a major contribution to the hypertrophied auxiliary sector of factory establishments.

One of the interesting features of this problem is that its morphology altered hardly at all from the beginning to the end of the Khrushchev period. Engineering factories that made machines simply did not make the spare parts for them. In 1954, iron and steel plants, for example, received some 8,000 tons of spare parts from equipment manufacturers, but had to make 230,000 tons of parts themselves in their own workshops.[64] The *sovnarkhoz* reform made little difference to the nature or the scale of the problem. On the contrary, in Leningrad, at least, it made matters worse. Whereas before the reform engineering factories had been able to acquire cutting tools from specialist tool factories in other parts of the country, the localism of the *sovnarkhozy* now made this impossible. They were therefore forced to begin making the tools themselves in tool shops which were already overburdened by extraneous orders which factory management had dumped on to them.[65]

In engineering, it was estimated in 1959 that between 50 and 70 per cent of spare parts were manufactured in shop-repair stations, which did not have the appropriate equipment and could not, therefore, guarantee the quality of what they produced.[66] The oil-refining and chemical industries of Bashkiriya were provided with less than a fifth of the parts they required for new pumping and compressor equipment, prompting *Trud* to remark that it was easier to acquire a new compressor than a spare part for an old one.[67] This same picture was repeated in other industries: ore-mining, paper and cellulose, textiles, iron and steel, footwear, and construction.[68]

The shortage of spares led to lengthy stoppages, as shops had to wait for parts to be manufactured.[69] To make matters worse, if factories were unable to make the parts themselves, they would purchase machinery they did not need simply to cannibalize it.[70] In general, however, factories coped the best they could by making parts, tools, and fastenings in their own shops by primitive, handicraft methods (*kustarnichestvo*). Costs, understandably, were enormous. In 1955, 143 factories in Leningrad *oblast'* manufactured for their own needs some 3,200 tons of fastenings at 10 to 15 times the cost of their manufacture at a specialized factory. By 1963 local factories in Leningrad still had hundreds of small shops making their own fastenings at 7 to 10 times the cost of their centralized production at the Neva general metal goods factory, and requiring 10 times as many workers per ton of output.[71] In Moscow there were in 1957 some 40 enterprises producing fastenings in small batches on non-specialized machinery.[72] In Siberian heavy engineering, a shortage of specialized founding enterprises in the region forced factories to set up their own foundries, pattern shops, and scrap-crushing yards, each with a small capacity and using backward equipment. Output was costly and quality was poor. The same was true of tool manufacture and spare parts for equipment repairs.[73] On the whole, in 1962 there were some 3,000 enterprises in the USSR making their own pig-iron castings.[74]

The shortage of spare parts and fastenings was largely the result of the planning system, which discouraged engineering enterprises from devoting machinery and labour power to manufacturing relatively cheap items which would do little to help plan fulfilment. In consequence, each factory – as with repair and maintenance – had to duplicate its own miniature parts industry, including foundries and machine shops, which soaked up large numbers of workers. The poor quality and low productivity of their work created bottlenecks in production, and at the same time acted to swell the demand for labour power in the auxiliary sector. The consequences were to be quite profound, for in the early 1960s the regime was to look to auxiliary workers as a source of recruiting new machine-tool operators at a time when the shortage of these workers was causing serious disruption in engineering. The campaign, which is discussed in chapter 3, was far from successful, largely because auxiliary workers were unwilling to become machinists (whose pay was relatively low and whose work was relatively tightly controlled), but also because these shops had few workers to spare. This in turn was a direct consequence of the technical backwardness of these shops – itself a result of the elite's historical emphasis on gross production as the main indicator of plan fulfilment. Enterprises, therefore, concentrated investment in production shops, and neglected auxiliary operations. The fact that managers had a ready pool of cheap female labour to take on many of the more unpleasant manual jobs justified this calculus on the surface. As with almost every other aspect of the Soviet planning system, however, what was rational from the point of view of the individual factory director acted as an obstacle to development for the economy as a whole.

APPENDIX: SOCIAL COMPOSITION AND STANDARD OF LIVING OF THE INDUSTRIAL WORKFORCE

Social composition

The number of industrial workers grew during the Khrushchev period as shown in table 1.2. Of the 3,741,000 workers listed in light industry in 1965, 1,697,400 were in textiles, 1,436,000 in the garment industry, and 594,700 in leather and footwear (of which footwear alone employed 404,000). Moreover, workers in light industry – the overwhelming proportion of whom were women – tended to work in smaller enterprises. In 1960, over 40 per cent of textile workers (34.2 per cent in cotton textiles) worked in enterprises employing fewer than 3,000 workers. In the knitwear industry, over 45 per cent of workers worked in enterprises of fewer than 1,000 workers, while in the garment industry the corresponding figure was 79 per cent.[75]

By 1965 the engineering industry employed over one-third of all industrial workers and over twice as many workers as were employed in light industry (excluding the food industry). This, among other things, is a good indication of the low standard of living in these years, despite attempts to raise it from the abysmal level of the Stalin

Table 1.2. *Industrial workers by major industry, 1953–1965* (thousands)

	1953	1955	1958	1960	1962	1965
All industry	13,179	14,281	16,279	18,574	20,176	22,206
Chemicals (including rubber and asbestos production)	404	452	494	584	705	935
Iron and steel	706	742	812	886	947	1,037
Coal	793	897	1,071	1,031	996	1,016
Oil-extraction and refining	107	122	138	145	150	—
Engineering and metalworking	3,837	4,256	4,932	5,655	6,586	7,579
Building materials	720	830	1,072	1,310	1,383	1,392
Light industry	1,975	2,158	2,515	3,371	3,544	3,741
Food industry	1,398	1,478	1,662	1,743	1,884	2,099
Construction	2,521	2,814	3,921	4,554	4,502	4,892

Sources: 1953–8 – *Promyshlennost' SSSR*, pp. 84–5; 1960–5 – *Trud v SSSR* (1968), pp. 84–5, 121. *Trud v SSSR*, which gives no figures for 1953 or 1958, lists 15,522,000 workers in 1955. Over half of the discrepancy is accounted for by light industry, where it gives 2,833,000 workers, a full 31 per cent higher than the figure in *Promyshlennost' SSSR*. This is perhaps partly due to the inclusion of workers in manufacturing artels into the industrial sector in 1960. The disparities in other industries are slight – on the order of 2 or 3 per cent. This means, however, that our figures for 1953 and 1958 are probably also too low and overstate the growth in the number of workers from 1953–60.

period. Even in the Ukraine, one of the country's major iron and steel areas, engineering predominated, accounting for a third of all workers in Ukrainian industry.[76]

In terms of age composition, the USSR had, by 1963, more or less recovered from the distortions created by the country's terrible losses in World War II. The proportion of workers under the age of 19 in industry fell from 12.4 per cent in 1950 to 5.3 per cent in 1963, and in construction from 12.6 per cent to 6.7 per cent. The proportion of workers over the age of 25 correspondingly went up from 62.7 per cent to 74.2 per cent in industry, and from 57.9 per cent to 69.8 per cent in construction. This was reflected in an appreciable rise in the proportion of workers with a relatively long uninterrupted record of employment – a full 30 per cent of all industrial workers by 1963.[77]

The workforce in these years also became increasingly urbanized.

Table 1.3. *Women workers in major industries 1960–1967 (percentage of all workers)*

	1960	1967
All industry	44	46
Engineering and metalworking	39	40
Metallurgy and metalworking	16[a]	—
Including iron and steel	29[b]	—
Oil-extraction	38[b]	—
Coal-mining	19[a]	—
Chemicals	57[a]	—
Including rubber	62[a]	—
Building materials, glass, porcelain, and glazed pottery	54[a]	—
Including the cement industry	36	36
Woodworking	18[a]	—
Printing and publishing	70	—
Cellulose and paper	43	47
Including paper	62[a]	—
Textiles	72	73
Garment	85	84
Leather and hides	64	64
Footwear	66	67
Food	54	55
Including: Baking	69	70
Confectionery products	70	72
Construction	18	29[c]
Including: Plasterers	54[a]	—
House painters	54[a]	—

[a] 1959 data.
[b] 1961 data.
[c] 1965 data.
Sources: *Zhenshchiny i deti v SSSR*, pp. 72–3, 86; *Itogi vsesoyuznoi perepisi*, p. 167; *Rabochii klass SSSR*, p. 139 (A. V. Smirnov); Korobitsyna, dissertation, p. 38; Brova, dissertation, p. 103.

Although by 1964 only just over half the USSR's urban population lived in cities of 100,000 or more, these centres accounted for three-quarters of all workers and clerical employees (*sluzhashchie*) and four-fifths of all industrial production. This trend was supported by a continuing haemorrhage of people from the countryside, whose population in the years 1959 to 1961 alone fell by 1 million, despite a high natural growth rate.[78] In the main, however, new workers from the countryside tended to go into construction rather than urban industry, which now drew the bulk of its recruits from the towns themselves.[79]

Yet for all this, it is important to remember that in 1958–9 industrial workers still represented a small proportion of the 99.1 million people recorded in all forms of employment (industry, agricultural, trade, and services and professions) by the January 1959 census. In agriculture alone there were 33.9 million working people, or twice the number of industrial workers. In addition, there was a substantial non-working population of working age (men aged 16 to 59 and women aged 16 to 54), made up of those tending private plots, 'housewives', and students. These came to a further 27 million people, which exceeded the total of industrial and construction workers combined.[80]

As for the sexual composition of the workforce, in 1960 women made up 44 per cent of all industrial workers. By 1967 this had risen to 46 per cent, with the breakdown by major industries shown in table 1.3.

The table shows that certain industries – primarily textiles, the garment industry, and individual branches of the food industry – were almost exclusively dominated by female labour. Women also formed a majority of chemical workers (thanks largely to their predominance in the rubber industry), and a sizeable minority of workers in engineering, cement, and even iron and steel. Insofar as light industry was concerned, these were low-wage industries with extremely arduous working conditions. As I shall discuss in some detail in chapter 7, even within industries such as engineering, chemicals, and certain building trades (which in the West have been traditionally dominated by men, but which in the Soviet Union women have entered in substantial numbers), women were marginalized into monotonous, low-paid, and often strenuous jobs. This provided the regime with an important margin of flexibility in tolerating concessions to male workers over wages and control over work speeds and organization. It also makes a nonsense of Soviet attempts to cite the large-scale employment of women workers in these industries as evidence of female emancipation.

A note on the standard of living

Wages in the Khrushchev period increased slowly. Alastair McAuley has estimated that the average annual rise in real wages was about 3 per cent per year between 1950 and 1964, which was virtually identical to the annual rate of growth in money wages.[81] Moreover, wages grew considerably more slowly than productivity.[82] At the same time, many more Soviet citizens moved out of rock-bottom poverty, pegged at the notional sum of 30 (new) rubles a month. The main beneficiaries of these changes were not the families of industrial workers, whose per capita monthly income in 1951 was already 38 rubles,[83] but peasants on collective and state farms, lower-paid clerical employees, and pensioners, who benefited from a substantial rise in the minimum wage, increases in pensions, and the incorporation of some 3 million collective farmers into state farms, where they became state employees.[84] Nevertheless, workers' incomes also rose. The studies done of an admittedly small sample of 92 workers' families in Moscow, Gor'kii, and Ivanovo, found that the percentage of workers with a per capita income of less than 40 rubles a month fell from 50 per cent in 1951 to 16.3 per cent in 1959, while those with a per capita income of over 70 rubles a month rose from 11 to 21.7 per cent.[85] The standard of living undoubtedly improved in other ways, too, in this period, due partly to the vast improvement in housing provision, partly to an expansion of communal services, and partly to the increased supply of foodstuffs during the first half of the Khrushchev period.

Still, conditions remained harsh. The output of light industry failed to meet its planned targets, which had already been set below so-called 'consumption norms' established by major research institutes.[86] The bulk of workers' incomes continued to be spent on basics. According to the Moscow–Gor'kii–Ivanovo study, in 1959 workers still spent some 49 per cent of their income on food, 4.4 per cent on housing, and 22 per cent on clothing, linen, furniture, and household goods.[87] There was little room for such luxuries such as food from the kolkhoz market. Those with a per capita income of under 40 rubles a month purchased a bare 6 per cent of their food from this source; for families with a per capita income of between 40 and 70 rubles this rose to only 8 per cent. Only those whose per capita monthly income exceeded 70 rubles could afford to make liberal use of the market, obtaining over 15 per cent of their food there.[88]

Pressures were increased by the failure of food production to keep pace with the rapid and partially unforeseen growth in the urban population. These were exacerbated by renewed restrictions on private plots, on which the society depended for over two-thirds of its production of potatoes, over 40 per cent of its supply of vegetables, meat, and milk, and over 70 per cent of its eggs. In 1962 food prices were raised, which led to open disturbances, including the mass demonstrations in Novocherkassk, which were brutally suppressed. Harvest failures in 1963 and 1965 forced the regime to import grain and added to already severe problems with livestock.[89]

Services, too, remained inadequate in both quantity and quality. In Moscow *oblast'* in 1958, for example, there was one dry-cleaning establishment for every 484,000 inhabitants, one furniture-repair shop for every 393,000, and one tailor or seamstress to repair clothing for every 23,000.[90] Outside the major cities the situation was near-catastrophic. In 1959 only two-thirds of towns in Armenia had any laundries at all. In Latvia the figures were one in 14.[91] In Lipetsk, a medium-sized industrial town of around 200,000 inhabitants, there were virtually no laundries as late as 1964. Establishments existed, but they were so poorly equipped as to be practically unusable. There were no facilities for repairing furniture, clothing, or shoes. To visit the public baths required a two-hour wait, while a visit to a women's hairdresser meant a wait of three to four hours.[92] Small towns and settlements, which were usually centred around small and medium-sized industry, and thus discriminated against in terms of funding, found themselves almost totally neglected. In Leninskii settlement in Tula *oblast'* in 1962, the only leisure facilities were drinking, playing dominoes, or just hanging around the streets. There was a municipal club, but it showed only old films. The building-workers' club held dances, but almost no one came because people were unwilling to wade through the mud to get there. The clubs of other factories were either closed for 'repair' (a common Soviet euphemism) or advertised entertainment programmes but were in fact locked when people arrived. The author of this survey claimed that the situation in Leninskii settlement was typical of small towns throughout central Russia.[93]

One major problem was the poor state of public catering. In a country where food shortages are endemic, the Soviet Union has always placed great emphasis on its plans to expand its network of cafeterias as an alternative to preparing and eating meals at home. Ideally, public dining rooms would produce wholesome, appealing food more cheaply than the housewife (for Soviet men were never expected to enter the kitchen), and thereby ease some of the woman's domestic drudgery. The reality was otherwise. Although most workplaces had catering facilities, the fare was poor and relatively expensive, and fewer than half of workers used them.[94] Queues were long and took up considerable amounts of work time. At one Leningrad factory the wait for a meal was so long that workers found it quicker to go out to other factories to eat.[95] Equipment was poor, and dining rooms found themselves short of even basic items like knives and tableware. Here they were not helped by the poor quality of the products they received from their suppliers. Drinking glasses were so badly made, for instance, that public catering establishments throughout the USSR went through 7.5 million of them during the first 10 months of 1962.[96]

Public catering epitomizes all that was wrong with public services in the USSR not only during the Khrushchev years, but right up to the present. The failure to provide adequate child-care facilities, laundries, repair shops, or dining rooms proved enormously costly to the regime. It had the benefit – perhaps unintended – that a population which had to devote so much of its time to standing in queues, chasing after scarce goods, and otherwise seeing to its daily needs had little time even to contemplate organized oppositional activity, much less engage in it. On the other hand, the experience added further to the alienation of the workforce, and undermined other attempts to have workers identify ideologically with the ruling elite and to surrender the practices they had developed to defend themselves on the shop floor. In more concrete terms, as we shall see in the discussions of control over the labour process (chapter 6) and of the political economy of female labour (chapter 7), the costs were high. The amount of work time lost simply in waiting for meals was incalculable, while the general scarcity of services meant that a huge section of the working population – women – was putting nearly half as much time into housework as it did at the workplace. Here, too, the impact in reduced productivity and output cannot be estimated. This is not to say that the regime did not make progress in these areas. The number of child-care places expanded; so, too, did the network of public eating places and the number of meals they served. Both politicians and economists were well aware of the losses that backwardness in this area entailed. But the real issue was that whatever advances occurred, they were simply inadequate to the needs of the system. This was more than a question of quantitative growth. The planning system, and indeed power relations within the elite, acted almost automatically to perpetuate the hypertrophy of heavy industry at the expense of consumer goods and consumer welfare. This, in turn, played a major role in reproducing the inherent conflict between the workforce and the elite.

2   The reform of labour legislation and the re-emergence of the labour market

De-Stalinization, if it was to have its desired impact, had to extend to the workplace. Repression, even in the 1930s, had simply failed to prove itself a viable stimulus to work. In 1956, therefore, the regime set out on a different path to try to create a popular feeling of identification with the system and its leadership. The 1940 criminalization of job-changing and absenteeism was repealed, so that workers could switch jobs without fear of legal reprisals. There was also an extensive reform of the trade unions, designed to give them the appearance, if not the reality, of greater responsibility to their members. As part of this reform, new labour regulations made it far more difficult for managers to fire workers except for serious discipline violations. A coercive element was to be retained, but this was to be enforced in the main not through labour law, but through the incentive system, as implemented in the wage reform of 1956–62, which is discussed at length in chapter 4.

The reform of labour law meant significant changes in the state of the labour market. Workers were once more free to move about at will and had less to fear from the threat of dismissal. These changes, which had been essential from the point of view of the political liberalization of Soviet society, at the same time pushed the balance of power on the shop floor a little more in workers' favour, and in this sense helped to undermine the regime's economic strategy. This was most immediately reflected in increasing labour turnover, which, though quite modest in comparison with that of the 1930s, nonetheless caused serious bottlenecks in key industries and regions.

The impact of the legal reforms should not be overestimated, however. It was not the law itself that constrained managers in their relations with workers, but *the labour shortage*. What the law did was to make the relations between managers and workers more open and transparent, removing a major set of obstacles that workers and managers previously had to circumvent in order to maintain a functional *modus operandi* on the shop floor.

The repeal of the Stalinist labour laws

One obvious area requiring change was labour law, which with the abatement of the terror remained the most visible political legacy of the Stalinist past within the workplace. It was through labour law, in fact, that the true attitude of the Stalinist regime towards the working class – an attitude of fear and contempt – became most transparent, piercing the populist veneer of Stalin's pronouncements and official propaganda. So great was its distrust of the workers that from 1938 onwards the regime stopped publishing the Soviet Labour Code (KZoT). When the Code was finally reissued in 1952, it was for the use of court and procuracy officials only.[1]

From their very outset, the 1930s had seen a gradual escalation of restrictions on workers' freedom of movement, as the regime attempted to cope with the seemingly uncontrollable problems of absenteeism, insubordination, alcoholism, and labour turnover. In October 1930 it issued a six-month ban on the hiring of job-changers within state industry – a virtually meaningless sanction given the labour shortage and managers' desperate need for workers. This was followed in November 1932 by a decree calling for truants to be automatically fired from their jobs, evicted from factory-tied housing, and deprived of their ration cards. Although this Draconian law had some effect in cutting absenteeism, it, too, was ignored wherever managers felt that they could ill afford to let workers go, even those with poor discipline records.

As the economy improved and the labour situation stabilized in the mid-1930s, the regime shifted its attention to the problem of raising productivity on the shop floor (culminating in the Stakhanov movement of 1935–7), but in December 1938, as the pressures of rearmament and the reintroduction of conscription placed further strains on the supply of workers, the regime tightened up the old 1932 ban in truants: a decree of 28 December 1938 reaffirmed that absentees would be summarily dismissed and evicted (together with their families) from factory housing; moreover, subsequent procuratorial rulings extended the decree to any worker arriving just 20 minutes late, who would now be classed as truant. When, despite its harshness, this law had little effect, the regime, in June 1940, declared both truancy and job-changing criminal offences. Truancy was punishable by a period of

corrective labour of up to six months at the worker's original enterprise, with up to a 25 per cent loss of pay. Quitting one's job without
the authorization of factory management made the worker liable to
imprisonment for two to four months. In addition, according to the
decree of 28 December 1938, job-changers and those fired for truancy
were to lose most of their pension and disability benefit rights, a
provision which remained in force after the 1940 legislation had made
most of the 1938 decree redundant. Even then, however, managers
and the lower courts proved less than willing strictly to enforce the
new laws, until the regime began to imprison them as well. Finally, in
October 1940, as war approached, the regime introduced compulsory
labour service, initially for youth, but extended to the general population once the Soviet Union entered World War II in June 1941.[2]

The Draconian labour legislation of June 1940 remained in force in
the post-war period and was still on the books at the start of Khrushchev's rule. Even before its official repeal in April 1956, its enforcement
had become haphazard, no doubt because it was essentially unworkable. Criminal penalties for job-changing and truancy had been partially relaxed in 1951 and 1952, although, like the main body of labour
legislation, the decrees announcing these changes were never
published. From 1951, handbooks on Soviet labour law began
publishing the 1940 edict without listing its criminal sanctions, but
prosecutions still took place after that date.[3] Nevertheless, evidence
suggests that prosecutions were rare. In 1951, approximately 2 per cent
of workers in heavy engineering – and 6 per cent of those under the
age of 18 – left their jobs without permission. Moreover, a further 10
per cent left 'with the permission of the administration', which in
many cases was almost certainly granted in order to protect workers
from possible punishment.[4] By 1954, some 12 per cent of all industrial
workers and 25 per cent of those in construction quit their jobs of their
own accord, so that sanctions could not have been a very strong
deterrent.[5]

Other, more anecdotal evidence supports this conclusion. A letter to
Trud in early 1952 from a worker at the Petrovskii iron and steel works
in Dnepropetrovsk complained that neither management nor workers
paid the slightest regard to truants or time-wasters. *Trud* noted that the
trade union organization at the factory had not held a single meeting
on labour discipline in the whole of 1951.[6] In 1955 construction of the
Karaganda steel works was delayed because 1,500 workers had quit
their jobs over the course of that year, giving rise to a labour shortage.[7]
The Penza chemical equipment factory had similar problems holding

on to workers in the same year.[8] More substantial evidence is found in court judgments on labour cases from this period brought under the anti-truancy and anti-job-changing laws, which tacitly accepted that requests for discharge were legitimate grounds for separation and which made no mention of prosecutions for absenteeism.[9]

The Draconian laws of 1940 were officially repealed on 25 April 1956, by an edict of the Supreme Soviet which allowed workers to leave their jobs of their own accord and made absenteeism a mere disciplinary offence to be dealt with by local management.[10] This move was not a total liberalization, however. In the first place, like previous relaxations under Stalin, it was not published in the national press, but only in the specialized legal notices. As we shall see, this did not prevent workers from learning of its provisions. Secondly, it kept in force the restrictions on benefits for job-changers imposed by the Stalinist law of December 1938. These were partially relaxed in 1957, to exempt those injured on the job or who contracted an industrial disease,[11] but were not repealed *in toto* until 1960.[12]

If the old Stalinist restrictions on workers' behaviour had outlived their utility, what was the regime going to put in their place? The regime clearly saw an improvement in the standard of living and stronger material incentives as a large part of the answer. According to a joint letter from the Party Central Committee, the Council of Ministers, and the leadership of the trade unions (VTsSPS), circulated to all party and government officials soon after the Stalinist laws were repealed,

> A decisive role in the struggle for high labour discipline belongs to economic incentives, to the creation of good production and cultural and living conditions. The creation of a personal material interest by each worker in the results of his [*sic*] own labour is one of the most important principles of socialist management, a powerful lever for improving labour discipline.[13]

These sentiments became translated into concrete policy with the initiation in 1956 of a thoroughgoing reform of the wages and norm-setting structure, which attempted (albeit unsuccessfully) to create a stable system of incentives as a spur to greater effort and productivity.[14] The only other vehicle at its disposal were moral appeals, based (like the general political thrust of de-Stalinization) on the attempt to convince working people that they were now full and equal participants in the management of society. The regime now tacitly admitted that it could no longer use coercion as a means of controlling the day-to-day conduct of its workforce. The new Model Internal

Labour Regulations, issued in January 1957, reflected this fact. Above all, their effect was to give workers guaranteed protection from dismissal and security of employment, not seen since the late 1920s when Stalin had begun his pernicious erosion of the original, very liberal Bolshevik Labour Code.[15]

The new provisions stipulated that a worker could only be dismissed for 'systematic' violation of discipline regulations. Short of that, the only other penalties were reprimands of various degrees of severity, and the eventual transfer of the worker to lower-paid work for a period of no more than three months. Workers could still be fired for absenteeism or drunkenness, but only as a last resort.[16] Even here there was certain protection. A USSR Supreme Court ruling in September 1957 stipulated that, to warrant dismissal, not only did discipline violations have to be systematic, but management must have tried all other social and disciplinary measures without success.[17] Moreover, a worker could not be dismissed for a violation if another penalty for the same infraction was already in force.[18] It also became easier for workers to appeal against dismissal. In the 1920s and early 1930s joint trade union and management appeal bodies known as Rates Conflict Commissions (RKK) had exercised considerable independence in defending *individual* workers against unfair dismissal.[19] With the growing repressiveness of the Stalinist regime, the RKK gradually lost most of their powers and were generally discredited. In an effort to revive at least the appearance of a fair appeals procedure the RKK in 1957 were replaced by a Commission on Labour Disputes, made up of equal numbers from management and the trade unions, designed (at least in theory) to prod the trade unions into taking a stance more independent from management.[20] This was followed in 1958 by a 'reform' of the trade unions which, among other provisions, decreed that no worker could be fired unless the enterprise trade union committee sanctioned the dismissal. If the trade unions did approve, then the worker could by-pass the Labour Disputes Commission and appeal directly to the courts.[21]

Security of employment was bolstered by other regulations, some of which dated from as early as 1952 or 1953, but which now promised to have greater force in the new context of liberalization. Workers, for example, could legitimately refuse transfer to a new enterprise or locality, or to a different job within their existing enterprise if it involved carrying out duties other than those for which the worker was originally hired.[22] In the same vein, regulations governing the use of temporary workers were tightened up to prevent management from retaining workers on a string of successive temporary contracts. A worker could be hired on a temporary basis only once. If management re-engaged the worker or kept her or him on past the two-month limit on temporary jobs, the worker automatically became a permanent member of the enterprise establishment, with all the attendant protection against being discharged.[23] Later court rulings made it extremely easy for workers who had decided to leave, but who subsequently changed their mind, to withdraw their notice.[24]

The effect of these various laws and regulations was to give a legal foundation to the haphazard, and at times quasi-anarchic, security of employment created by the labour shortage. The latter had always made it difficult for managers to dismiss workers, even in the face of repeated absenteeism or indiscipline. This state of affairs was now regularized by the law. The result was further to reinforce workers' relative independence on the shop floor and their limited control over the labour process. Without the sanction of unemployment, except against the most recalcitrant individuals, management had little leverage to apply other than tacit bargaining over wages and work organization. This does not mean that managers could not at times gain the upper hand – that they did not impose forced overtime, attempt to cut wages, or even dismiss workers they considered trouble-makers or otherwise expendable. But these 'abuses' resulted from the same pressures to meet their plans under uncertain conditions as did the need to grant concessions. They were, in fact, different phenomenal expressions of the same essential relationship.

The liberalization of labour law should not be taken as a sign of a new beneficence on the part of the regime. Although the partial restrictions on job-changing were eased in 1960, this was followed by moves in a more repressive direction. In 1961, the regime imposed its infamous law against 'parasitism', which was later to be used as a blunt cudgel with which to repress dissidents thrown out of their jobs.[25] The regime also did not shrink from using violent repression to quell workers' unrest, most notably the strikes and demonstrations in Novocherkassk, which followed the price increase on foodstuffs in June 1962.[26] Towards the end of Khrushchev's reign there was also a concerted press campaign calling for the reimposition of stringent legal measures against job-changers (this is discussed at the end of the chapter). Whether or not this was the signal for a return to repressive legislation we do not know. Khrushchev fell in October 1964, and his successors, faced with a mounting crisis of labour recruitment, especially in the engineering industry, and general discontent with the

Khrushchev wage reform, effectively adopted a policy of buying peace on the shop floor – while continuing the brutal repression of any overtly political opposition.

Moral appeals and 'democratization'

Denied any means of collective organization and opposition, Soviet workers, at least until recently, have adopted essentially defensive, and generally individualized, responses towards both management and the regime. In the early 1930s this manifested itself in high rates of absenteeism, insubordination, drunkenness, and a general disregard for the quality of their labour. There is no question that these continued to be problems in the post-Stalin years, although their exact extent is difficult to gauge. This is especially true of absenteeism. One Soviet historian estimates that the average worker was truant a mere 0.9 days in 1958 and 0.7 days in 1963, a figure supported by at least one Western study of lost work time.[27] These figures would seem to be backed up by data from individual factories. Factories whose workforces we know numbered several thousand were reporting total annual days lost to absenteeism of only 1,000 to 2,000.[28] These figures, if accurate, would indicate that absenteeism was trifling compared to its rather stupendous levels of the early 1930s.[29] Yet there are reasons to believe that this is not the whole story. Occasional press reports indicate that at least some managers and lower courts were prone to turn a blind eye to absenteeism or general indiscipline,[30] although just how common this was is difficult to estimate. Perhaps more important was the fact that in 1960 and 1965 the average worker received an additional five days a year off work with the permission of the administration, plus 12 to 13 days in sickness.[31] Given the pressures which the labour shortage placed on managers to go easy in their application of discipline regulations, it is reasonable to assume that at least some of this was either an attempt to cover up absenteeism after the fact, or to place it under a more benign classification by readily granting workers' requests for time off.

Truancy was not the only discipline problem against which the regime campaigned. Drunkenness was a perpetual problem, as was slacking or taking a generally careless attitude towards the use of equipment or work time.[32] In all, the issue of discipline went right to the heart of the regime's attempts to mobilize or, if necessary, compel the workforce to surrender its partial control over its work and to raise productivity – and with it the size of the relative surplus product. One means of dealing with poor discipline was the reform of the incentives system, which will be discussed in chapter 4. The regime also attempted to revitalize the use of moral appeals, which had been so prevalent under Stalin, but which workers had grown to treat with considerable scepticism, indifference, and even hostility.

One such device was the Movement for Communist Labour. Individual workers, brigades, and factories were encouraged to compete for this honoured title by improving output, developing improvements in the organization of labour, or campaigning to raise discipline among their workmates. It was claimed, for instance, that brigades of Communist Labour showed lower labour turnover, fewer losses of work time within a shift, and less absenteeism, and for this reason were enlisted to help counter poor discipline by other workers, including dissuading potential quitters. They were also used to try and 'improve norm-setting', a euphemism for tightening up norms.[33] Yet, as with other forms of Socialist Competition, the Communist Labour movement was not all that it appeared. Competition between brigades was frequently bogus, as workers or brigades were awarded honours and even cash bonuses when they had not in fact met their pledged targets.[34] Participation rates were often low. The Krasnyi proletarii factory in Moscow, for example, in 1964 had not a single shock worker of Communist Labour out of a workforce of several thousand.[35] Where factories did officially list large numbers of workers involved in the movement, the competition agreements which workers signed were often ill-defined and devoid of concrete content.[36] Managers also abused the brigades by using them as trouble-shooters to cope with rush orders and disruptions to production. Other managers allegedly ignored the achievements of those who took the competition seriously – not surprisingly, in view of the resentment 'rate busters' could cause among rank-and-file workers. The petty vindictiveness of shop management against workers who criticized them also put brigades under pressure, and some broke up.[37] The result of these various practices was, in the words of one Soviet historian, that rank-and-file workers 'lost faith in the prospect of competition'.[38]

Such claims probably had some grain of truth to them. Unlike Stalin and Brezhnev, Khrushchev clearly recognized that no long-term improvements in productivity would be possible unless the working population began to identify its own needs and interests with those of the regime. It was, therefore, a fundamental task of de-Stalinization to foster the belief among workers that, with greater democratization, they would become active participants in the management of their own enterprises, and indeed of society at large. That this campaign found a deep resonance among many young members of the intelligentsia is demonstrated by the growing number of largely sympathetic discussions of Khrushchev appearing today in the Soviet press. It is also surprising how many older historians and social scientists – now that they are free to express their views openly – look back on the Khrushchev years with considerable nostalgia, as a period when the USSR was once again 'building socialism'. Unlike *glasnost'*, however, de-Stalinization was not aimed primarily at the intelligentsia, whom Khrushchev often distrusted and who could not, in the end, solve the problem of expanding industrial output. The moral appeals of the time were directed squarely at workers and peasants, even if actual policies, especially those of incentives, placed these sections of the population under considerable hardship.[39]

In line with this goal, trade unions and management alike came in for vigorous attack for ignoring workers' rights. Managers were accused of taking 'a scornful attitude towards trade union and public organizations', and of 'reducing their educational work to just issuing innumerable orders teeming with penalties'.[40] Letters from workers critical of the 'domineering' attitude of lower-level management and foremen appeared frequently in the press.[41] Another target was alleged corruption by managers in allocating housing.[42] Factory trade union officials, for their part, were accused of irregularities in the conduct of trade union meetings and elections and, more importantly, of not exercising adequate control over managerial decisions to penalize workers or to impose new norms without consulting the trade unions (as was statutorily required).[43]

Another complaint was the failure of local trade unions to protect workers from unfair dismissal. While it was certainly true that some managers were more than willing to fire workers arbitrarily and in violation of established procedures, and that the trade unions frequently colluded in such practices,[44] the reality was that relatively few workers were victimized in this fashion. In Perm *oblast'*, for the first nine months of 1957 the *oblast'* procurator appealed against a total of 973 managerial orders on the grounds of improper application of the labour regulations, and at least half of these involved penalties other than dismissal.[45] In 1962 a mere 1,000 reinstatement cases came before the Leningrad courts, although this could have been influenced by the lower success rate of Leningrad plaintiffs.[46] Even allowing for the fact that only a small proportion of dismissed workers bothered to take their cases to court,[47] for the mass of workers the threat of being fired was unlikely to have been a burning issue.

Far more significant from the workers' point of view were complaints against managers for failure to provide proper working conditions. Chief among the issues was labour safety. Most safety violations were attributed to the dereliction of duty of individual managers,[48] but it was the planning system itself that was primarily to blame – either because it put pressure on managers to sacrifice safety to the drive for plan fulfilment and the need to meet targets, or because of the underproduction of the necessary safety equipment. In order to save on building costs, for example, designers cut corners on lighting and ventilation systems.[49] Other problems with ventilation arose because factories could not acquire needed equipment from suppliers or because the capacity of the machinery they received was too weak to cope with the job.[50] Similarly, throughout industry there was a chronic shortage of protective gear (goggles, gauntlets, etc.), with the demand for many items being met by only 35 per cent, mainly because neither the State Planning Commission (*Gosplan*) nor the *sovnarkhozy* saw fit to incorporate their production into the industrial plan.[51] Thus a closer look at the various press campaigns over the issue of labour safety reveals an inherent contradiction: a campaign designed to demonstrate the regime's defence of workers' interests against negligent managers led inevitably back to the nature of the system itself.

The same was true about the issue of forced overtime. Technically, the use of overtime had always been tightly controlled, although the regulations were violated with increasing frequency during the 1930s. Under no circumstances was overtime to be used to compensate for stoppages or to meet a factory's production plan. If overtime was applied, it had to be approved by the factory trade union committee, with three exceptions: urgent loading jobs; when a worker did not show up at the beginning of a shift and no one was available to replace her or him; and spontaneous disasters. In all cases, overtime was to be paid at a higher rate of pay, with a further supplement if the overtime was worked at night.[52]

Complaints about forced overtime were rampant. It may seem strange to those in the West, where workers often require overtime in order to supplement an inadequate wage, that this should have been a bone of contention in Soviet factories – especially since the absolute number of hours worked was often small (in the most serious cases reported, around 30 hours a month). But Soviet workers have always considered overtime an infringement of basic working conditions, an attitude which exists even today.[53] One reason is that overtime was not regular, but a consequence of storming. It was, therefore, concentrated into a relatively small time-span and subjected the workers to considerable stress. And because most of the overtime was illegal, management – often with the collusion of the trade unions – frequently refused to adhere to established overtime rates, so that the overtime would not show up on the ledgers of the factory's wages department.[54]

Managers were not averse, of course, to using overtime to compensate for their own organizational failures, as demonstrated by the experience at a number of Leningrad factories. At one, overtime was imposed to make up for time lost because workers on the evening shift had to leave work early to catch the last bus home. At another, new and allegedly 'labour-saving' equipment broke down so frequently and was so unproductive that the women running it could fulfil their plan only by storming. At a third, managers had a positive financial incentive to impose overtime, since the bonuses they earned from plan overfulfilment far exceeded fines they had to pay for violating labour legislation.[55] On the whole, however, overtime arose primarily from the pressures the system imposed on managers to fulfil their plans under difficult conditions. Some problems might well have been rectified by better organization of the workplace or production methods, but the effort to impose these may have entailed too many difficulties to make it worth while, or even possible. New equipment may have led to plan increases; more rational deployment of workers may have challenged the latter's control over work speeds and organization at a time when managers needed workers' cooperation to cope with everyday or unforeseen disruptions (non-arrival of supplies, equipment breakdowns, etc). The press accounts themselves make this amply clear.[56] There was thus an ongoing process of bargaining on the shop floor between managers and workers, each of whom confronted the need to pursue their particular goals and needs in a highly unpredictable environment. Overtime was a concession that management had to be able to extract if the larger fabric of manager–worker relations – which depended on the enterprise achieving at least apparent plan fulfilment – were to be preserved. It was thus a partial negation of workers' limited control over the labour process and at the same time a precondition for their ability to maintain it.

The aim of these campaigns against abuses of labour legislation was not so much their rectification as a desire on the part of the regime to give workers a feeling that the regime was 'for them', that after the years of alienation from the political process workers now had an ally in the regime, and together they would build socialism within everybody's lifetime. It is noteworthy that one major difference between discussions of problems of labour discipline in the Stalin and Khrushchev periods is that under Stalin, despite the demagogic populism surrounding the purges or Stakhanovism, the regime distrusted the working class and saw it as a potential enemy. Attacks on 'self-seeking minorities' of workers – workers who were 'selfish', who violated good discipline, who were lazy – were common in the 1930s: except these were not 'minorities', since the behaviour under attack (changing jobs to seek better conditions elsewhere, absenteeism, slacking, or pressing for lower norms in order to carve out an area of control insulated from the pressures imposed by the regime or factory management) was that of vast numbers of workers, if not the majority. Under Khrushchev such attacks virtually disappeared. The public admission of an adversarial relationship between the regime and its workforce had no place in a policy of de-Stalinization designed to improve popular morale as a precondition to inducing people to exert themselves more at the workplace. Press exposures of poor safety conditions and illegal overtime were far from uncommon in the Stalin period as well. Here the aim was more pragmatic: given the very real and potentially explosive grievances that the population had against the regime, the unnecessary antagonism of workers was to be avoided. What changed under Khrushchev was the political context in which these exposures were made. Nowhere was this clearer than in discussions of labour turnover.

Labour turnover in the Khrushchev period

When discussing labour turnover, Soviet commentators usually distinguish between the global number of workers leaving an enterprise and those leaving 'at their own desire or dismissed for violations of labour discipline'. For this they have another term, *tekuchest'*, or 'fluidity', which in English is also generally rendered as 'turnover'. The difference between the two concepts can be substantial, because turnover in the second, narrow sense excludes those leaving for officially sanctioned reasons: military service, retirement, poor health, death, transfer to another enterprise or locality, or maternity leave.[57] The Soviets have always considered *tekuchest'* as a problem of labour discipline, although the harshness with which they have dealt with it has varied over the years, as witnessed by the Stalinist labour laws and their repeal under Khrushchev. There was even a brief period in the 1930s when the regime more or less admitted that job-changing was, in most cases, a rational response by workers to bad working or living conditions.[58] Under Khrushchev this became the pre-vailing wisdom, and towards the end of his rule labour economists and sociologists (sociology was just beginning to emerge as an accepted 'social science') undertook numerous surveys, of variable quality, of the reasons why different groups of workers left their jobs. The change was not entirely due to de-Stalinization. While turnover continued to be a major problem for industry, especially in the newly developing regions of Siberia and the Far East and in the engineering industry, its levels, as we shall see, came nowhere near the astronomical figures of the 1930s. Turnover was serious; it caused innumerable difficulties within key regions and industries, but it was not a cause for panic.

According to Kaplan, turnover (*tekuchest'*) in 1956 was 'less than' one-quarter the rate in 1932.[61] This would put it at 33.8 per cent, meaning that, on average, one-third of Soviet workers changed their jobs of their own accord (or were fired for discipline violations) in that year. This was a sharp rise over the 12 per cent turnover rate of just two years earlier, and can be attributed to the immediate impact of the lifting of restrictions on job-changing. What is interesting, however, is that after the initial rush of people from their old factories to seek new jobs, turnover declined markedly, so that by 1960 it was only half its level of 1956 (or around 17 per cent), and it remained very close to this figure during the rest of the Khrushchev period.[62]

The pattern of turnover varied considerably from region to region. In the older industrial centres, such as Leningrad, Ivanovo, and Sverd-lovsk, turnover hovered near, or even below the national average.[63] In contrast, turnover in Siberia and the eastern parts of the USSR was extremely high, reflecting the enormous difficulties the regime had in developing these areas and creating a stable, indigenous workforce. If average turnover in the RSFSR hovered around 19 per cent in 1961 and 1962, it was a full 50 per cent higher in Eastern industrial centres (table 2.1).

While turnover in Siberia and the Far East in 1961 and 1962 was already far higher than the national average, there was a further jump in 1963, where the first-quarter figures were equivalent to a yearly average of over 40 per cent. As we shall see in chapter 3, enterprises and construction projects had enormous difficulties holding on to workers, many of whom were young recruits on temporary contracts,

Table 2.1. *Labour turnover, Eastern RSFSR, 1962 (workers leaving at their own desire as a percentage of all workers)*

	1961	1962	1st quarter 1963
Khabarovsk	27.1	26.8	11.7
Kuzbass	24.7	24.6	10.4
Krasnoyarsk *krai*	28.3	29.4	14.6
North-east region	25.4	27.2	12.8
Komi ASSR	24.8	25.7	11.7
Irkutsk *oblast'*	34.1	—	—
Kemerovo *oblast'*	23.9	23.5	20.9 (all of 1963)

Sources: Senyavskii, p. 178; T. P. Malakhova, pp. 136–7.

and failed dismally in their efforts to induce these people to stay on permanently. The result was a considerable out-migration and net population loss from Siberia in these years. What this meant in concrete terms can be gauged by the following examples. The construction firm for the Kazakhstan copper-mining industry (Kazmedstroi) in 1957 hired 5,653 workers but lost 5,205. Mining construction in Karaganda (Karagandashakhstroi) during the first quarter of 1958 lost 6,078 people, or 83 per cent of those it had hired. Perhaps more significant was the experience, of the housing-construction firm, Promzhilstroi, which was responsible for building the new housing that would, in theory, staunch turnover: in one quarter (sources do not specify the year) the firm hired 812 workers but lost 1,679, or twice the number it took on.[62] Under these circumstances it was nearly impossible to create the conditions that might have allowed the evolution of a stable workforce – a problem which was never solved throughout the Khrushchev years.

Turnover also varied considerably from industry to industry. In chemicals, for example, it was relatively low, being 13.9 per cent of the average workforce in 1961 and 14.3 per cent in 1962. Yet the outflow of workers still exceeded the number of new workers being trained, putting pressure on enterprises to take on above-plan numbers of trainees.[63] Moreover, turnover fluctuated considerably from factory to factory and from shop to shop within enterprises, making the worst-hit sections bottlenecks which could hold up the work of those whose workforce was fairly stable. In the Kuzbass, turnover was highest in auxiliary shops, affecting turners, fitters, train marshallers and couplers, and railway-roadbed repair workers, and in some cases reached as high as 50 per cent of the workers in these shops. The main cause was wages: fitters and turners could earn 15 to 20 per cent more in engineering than in chemicals in the same locality.[64]

In coal-mining, where, together with construction, turnover has always been highest, turnover in some major coal trusts and pits reached 50, 60, or 100 per cent (the equivalent of renewing the entire workforce in a single year). Whether or not this was typical of the entire industry it is difficult to tell. On the whole, turnover was greatest not among the youngest workers, but among miners aged 25 to 30, who represented 40 per cent of all leavers. The prime causes cited by workers were poor housing and a fall in earnings as a consequence of the wage reform.[65] Similarly in construction, turnover in some trusts could reach what for this period were astronomical proportions. In one trust of the Krivoi Rog Basin construction combine, turnover in 1960 was 66 per cent.[66] In general, the problem in construction was not low wages but poor working conditions. In Leningrad, for example, building workers were the second highest paid group in the *sovnarkhoz*, after workers in iron and steel and non-ferrous metallurgy, yet over 60 per cent of building workers who changed jobs also left the industry.[67]

In terms of occupation and age, roughly half of leavers worked with machines, including a large share of skilled workers. Thus in engineering turnover was greatest among machine-tool operators; in coalmining it was largest among stope workers (except for combine and coal-cutting machine operators); in construction among carpenters, plasterers, and concrete-layers. As for age, turnover was highest among younger workers under the age of 25, who represented half of all leavers.[68] This is not surprising, since younger workers are freer to move and are likely to be most anxious to improve their pay and promotion prospects. Nevertheless, this implies that a large share of those giving up their jobs were older workers with considerable experience, whose departure entailed the greatest economic loss for the enterprise.

The economic impact of labour turnover

Although turnover in the period after 1956 never even remotely approached the levels of the 1930s, its disruptive effect was still severe. Job-changing caused considerable economic damage in the form of days lost between jobs and reduced productivity of workers in the last weeks of an old job and the first weeks of a new one. In general, a worker quitting her or his job would take three or more weeks before starting another, although this varied from a low of two weeks in Moscow *oblast'* to a high of one month or more in the Urals.[69] However, surveys of both Leningrad and Chelyabinsk showed that the longest breaks in employment were among women, many of whom had to give up work in the summer months to look after children.[70]

These were not the only economic costs, however. Retraining workers who, when leaving their jobs, also changed occupations[71] was estimated to cost between 150 and 500 rubles, depending on their skill.[72] Moreover, when changing jobs workers only regained their previous level of productivity in from three to four weeks if they remained in the same trade, or within four to six weeks if they switched to a new one.[73] The converse was also true: when workers left it was necessary to replace them; many of these new workers were inexperienced and had to be trained, during which time they often had difficulties handling their machinery.[74]

Still, it is necessary to place these economic costs in perspective, both historically and in relation to other forms of lost work time. Lost production from labour turnover was far less than in the 1930s, not just for the obvious reason that turnover was itself lower, but because it no longer brought with it the problem of training an almost entirely new workforce which took years to acquire the skills, experience, and cultural habits required by modern industry. Secondly, the economic costs of turnover were far below those due to sick leave, maternity leave, and other officially sanctioned absences, which averaged about 27 days a year for each industrial worker. The number of person-years lost from these causes was 10 times the number due to labour turnover. Days lost due to stoppages and lost work time *within production* were even greater.[75] Even if we allow for the lost efficiency associated with moving from one job to another, the costs were still well below those due to other causes. However, this is not the real issue. The impact of turnover was highly differentiated, affecting some areas of the country and some industries severely, others much less so. In those regions or industries where it was high, as in Siberia or Leningrad engineering, its disruptive effect was considerable and it constituted a major economic problem.

The three main reasons behind decisions to change jobs were, not surprisingly, discontent over housing, working conditions, and wages. Nationally, some 16 per cent of job-leavers quit because of housing.[76] The figures were highest in those branches of industry with the most

rapidly expanding workforce, namely engineering, electrical technology, iron and steel, building materials, and chemicals.[77] The Stalin
years had seen a drastic neglect of housing construction, which
Khrushchev tried to rectify through a campaign of rapid building
using prefabricated components and materials. In coal-mining and
construction the failure to provide workers with adequate housing
was a traditional problem, caused largely by the pressures which the
planning system placed on managers to concentrate on capital construction at the expense of house-building.[78] Large numbers of young
workers still lived in dormitories, where conditions were notoriously
bad. Many had no heat and hot water. Overcrowding was such that
workers sometimes had to sleep two to a bed. Facilities such as
kitchens and laundry rooms were inadequate. Cultural and recreational diversions were sadly lacking, and residents complained of
boredom.[79]

Under Khrushchev, the annual rate of housing construction was
nearly doubled. During the Fifth Five-Year Plan (1951–5) some 6
million new flats were built, providing 240 million square metres of
living space. In the five years from 1956 to 1960, a further 11.2 million
flats were put up, covering 474 million square metres, while the period
1961–5 saw the construction of another 11.5 million flats with 490
million square metres. In all, some 108 million Soviet citizens (not
families) in both town and country were allocated flats between 1956
and 1965; of these, 84 million moved into quarters that had been newly
constructed.[80] Despite this considerable expansion of the housing
stock, housing was still a major problem, as the turnover figures show.
Shortages and housing queues in large towns remained long, but were
not as bad as in outlying areas. As late as 1965, large chemical plants in
the Kuzbass were still unable to provide living quarters for between a
quarter and a third of their workers. The situation at enterprises
undergoing rapid expansion was, understandably, worse.[81]

Housing, both old and new, suffered from a lack of basic amenities.
A survey of 156 women workers at major factories in Sverdlovsk,
carried out between 1959 and 1961, found that 122 of the women lived
in communal flats, of which only nine had all basic utilities and
services. Forty-seven had central heating, plumbing and sewerage; 24
had plumbing and sewerage, but no central heating; and a staggering
42 – or one quarter of the entire survey – had no amenities whatsoever.[82] A similar survey carried out in Moscow, Gor'kii, and Ivanovo
in 1959 found that of the 103 workers' families questioned, barely half
had a bath, gas, and a telephone.[83] These problems were reproduced

in newly constructed housing. New flats for Leningrad's Barrikada factory, which were touted at the time as the cheapest to build in the city, were filthy: although the local housing office had accepted the flats as completed and ready for habitation, new occupants moved in to find dirt, building wastes, spots on the walls, and the like, which they had to clean up and rectify themselves.[84] In 1963 the All-Union Central Council of Trade Unions (VTsSPS) issued a statement attacking the appalling state of housing construction in Chelyabinsk. Blocks of flats were left unfinished, with a great deal of defective work requiring rectification.[85] In Okhta, a workers' settlement near Leningrad, housing was erected without the completion of essential public services, including child-care facilities or adequate landscaping. Residents had to walk around in the mud.[86] In Kuibyshev, construction trusts were earning huge profits by claiming completion of – and payment for – jobs which were not in fact finished. Windows were left without handles, plumbing and sewerage was not properly installed, and doors had no locks.[87]

Another factor influencing labour turnover was actual working conditions. Workers doing unmechanized and manual labour or working on internal factory transport were well over one-third of all job-leavers.[88] This does not mean that the nature of their work was the sole cause of their leaving. Manual labour, except in such highly skilled jobs as fitters, electricians, or tool-setters, was also associated with low pay and poor prospects for advancement. Nevertheless, factories like the Red Star (Sarkana Zvaigzne) moped factory in Latvia, could point to a direct connection between their high rates of turnover (27 per cent in 1962) and poor working conditions. Poor lay-out of machinery forced workers to spend a lot of time in uncomfortable positions; others had to put up with bad lighting, no changing rooms, and no showers or even washbasins.[89] The absence of these same basic facilities allegedly contributed to high turnover at a number of factories in Sverdlovsk *oblast'*.[90] Monotony, too, was a factor, especially in factories with large-scale assembly-line production.[91] Dissatisfaction with poor working conditions was especially high among women. Over a fifth of women leavers in Leningrad cited this as their reason for going.[92] Although this was smaller than the proportion who quit because of poor housing and services, it is worth noting that the Leningrad textile industry was one of the few able to guarantee child-care places to all those who needed them. This led at least one commentator to insist that turnover in textiles was due overwhelmingly to the grim working conditions which prevailed in that industry.[93]

The other major cause of labour turnover, of course, was wages. The issue was not simply low wages, but the opportunity to improve one's position by going to another factory. As I shall note in chapter 3 when discussing turnover among machine-tool operators in engineering, the issue of control over the labour process was also important, and workers often accepted lower-paid jobs in exchange for less regimentation of their work regime. Understandably, wages became more important the lower they were. The Leningrad survey found, for example, that for those on the very bottom of the pay ladder a change of job could mean a considerable increase in earnings. Some 95 per cent of leavers earning 40 (new) rubles a month or less at their old job improved their position, a full 63 per cent of these by between 20 and 60 rubles. For those on 40 to 60 rubles a month, 70 per cent moved to new jobs offering more money. The ability to make such radical gains declined sharply, however, as the pay at a worker's old job went up.[94]

The lack of uniformity between enterprises in the wages they paid continued to influence turnover, as it had in the 1930s. Fitters and turners in the Kuzbass chemical industry could earn far more not only by working in engineering,[95] but by changing shops within their own enterprise. This applied especially to young workers in auxiliary shops, whose starting wage upon leaving training school was a mere 40 to 50 rubles a month, and who had to wait at least five years before they could expect to move into the higher-skill grades – something they simply were not prepared to do.[96]

High turnover was also a direct consequence of the higher norms imposed by the wage reform of 1956–62. Although the new norm-setting regulations were frequently circumvented to protect the earnings of essential groups of workers, difficulties in meeting norms were a direct cause of turnover in ore-mining and even in some engineering factories, especially among younger, less experienced workers who were new to their trade.[97]

There was one group of workers for whom the causes of turnover did not fit neatly into the conventional categories of wages, working conditions, and housing. Women workers, in keeping with their highly specific role in the political economy of Soviet industry, tended to change jobs for reasons which grew precisely out of their dual position as wage earners and domestic labourers. In Leningrad, dissatisfaction with living and social conditions, in particular the inadequacy of child-care provision, was the greatest single cause of turnover among women workers. Over a third of all women who quit their jobs cited this as their reason. Not surprisingly, it therefore accounted for a

large share of turnover (over a third) in industries with a high proportion of women workers (chemicals, textiles, garments, and leather and
footwear).[98] These were not, however, the only industries affected.
The Vozhd' proletariata textile combine in Egor'evsk (Moscow *oblast'*)
lost 470 skilled women because it could not offer child-care places for
their children.[99] Women construction workers in Perm were quitting
firms with poor child-care facilities to look for jobs where child care
was better.[100] So, too, did women in iron and steel and engineering
factories in the Urals, where they represented just under 10 per cent of
women leavers.[101] This may have been a lower proportion than among
women leavers in Leningrad, but it was hardly insignificant. As we
shall see in chapter 3, however, the shortage of child-care places was
far more important in keeping women out of the workforce altogether
than in prompting those already in work to quit.

The campaign against turnover, 1963–1964

The problems caused by high turnover, especially in industries
and enterprises (such as engineering) where it was causing serious
disruptions to production, placed the regime in a quandary. The entire
project of de-Stalinization, with its renewed emphasis on 'socialist
legality', demanded that it attempt to regulate the newly re-emergent
labour market without recourse to repression. Yet the pressures to try
and stop the haemorrhage of workers were mounting and seemed to
demand some form of action. *Trud* openly acknowledged the dilemma
when, in late 1962, it admitted that the relaxation of restrictions on
receipt of benefits by job-changers had helped to increase turnover,
but then cautioned that 'those leaders who fight for a return to the
methods of naked bureaucracy, which limit the shift of workers from
one enterprise to another, are profoundly mistaken. In our time such
methods are unacceptable.'[102] One solution was to try to persuade
quitters to change their minds. The Movement for Communist Labour,
as noted earlier, had this as one of its main objectives. Some factories
established a procedure whereby they would authorize requests to
leave only after they had had a chance to discuss it with the worker
concerned and possibly deal with her or his grievances. At least one
factory claimed some limited success for the scheme.[103]

Despite periodic articles in the press deriding job-changers for their
individualism and lack of loyalty to the collective, most discussion of
turnover treated it as essentially a rational response to legitimate
grievances. This atmosphere changed in 1963 when the national and

local press began a full-scale assault on alleged 'flitters' and habitual absentees. Articles complained that managers were taking no action against drunkenness and truancy. Others expressed indignation that truants and job-changers were entitled to the same rights to annual leave, rest-home passes, and housing allocation as disciplined workers. Some accused young trainees of coming to a factory simply to obtain a skill and wage grade assignment before moving on.[104] There were still occasional dissenters from the prevailing mood who continued to challenge the idea that job-changers were after the 'long ruble' rather than trying to rid themselves of poor working and living conditions, and who attacked the growing momentum behind a return to punitive measures.[105] But these became very much minority views. The campaign was not, after all, simply an exercise in propaganda. It was designed to pave the way for precisely the 'administrative' measures against which the minority had warned. The spirit of the new official line was summed up in the words of a milling-machine operator from the Kirov engineering works in Leningrad:

> If some[one] doesn't yield to admonishments, if he pays no attention to anything – neither a friendly word, the advice of comrades, nor warnings – but loafs about, leads a parasitic life, and robs society, then to stand on ceremony with such a person means harming society. In this case it is necessary to use force. A relentless struggle against flitters, who bounce from factory to factory in the search for easier earnings, with truants and parasites who fling hours of work time to the wind – this is what we need.[106]

Throughout 1963, the press printed letters from workers and managers together with reports from factory meetings – all of which were surely highly orchestrated – putting forward various schemes and proposals for dealing with job-changers and truants. In January, articles and letters appeared in *Leningradskaya pravda* demanding that discipline infractions be entered in workers' labour books – an interesting foretaste of the campaign to introduce the 'labour passport' launched in 1964.[107] Some went further and suggested that workers wanting to quit a factory should require permission from the factory 'collective' before they could go.[108] A group of works in Bashkiriya demanded that, in enterprises where management was reluctant to punish truants, the collective be empowered to dismiss them.[109] One construction worker wanted a regulation whereby building workers who quit their jobs would have to surrender housing received in connection with their work – at least until the critical housing shortage among building workers had been resolved.[110] Other proposals included depriving truants of rest-home passes or housing allocations, cutting their annual leave by the number of days they were truant, or transferring them to lower-paid work (already provided for by existing labour legislation).[111] Some commentators suggested that job-changers should have their pensions cut, a view which one otherwise hard-line labour economist opposed on the grounds that it would be ineffective: most quitters were young and were not worried about their pensions.[112] Finally, there were calls to allow managers to oblige trainees to stay on at the factory which trained them for a period of 18 months to two years.[113]

The drive for stricter discipline culminated, in early 1964, in a campaign to introduce a labour passport. The campaign was launched via a letter from a group of workers at the Donetsk iron and steel works, who complained that the existing system of labour books did not allow managers – or society – to differentiate conscientious workers from 'flitters' or 'parasites'. The existing labour book was not an adequate record, since a worker could conveniently lose it, and it cost only 5 kopeks to replace. Equally important, there were numerous occasions where documents had to be presented outside of the immediate work situation, and the ordinary passport contained no details of the holder's work record.[114] Over the following months, the Donetsk workers' call was taken up all over the country, as local papers produced the ritualistic letters of approval from workers in their areas.[115] Dissent from the proposal was rare.[116] Yet the campaign withered on the vine, as no legislation was issued to back it up. Whether such legislation would have been forthcoming if Khrushchev had remained in power we do not know. The issue became a dead letter under his successors, who preferred to solve the labour crisis through less confrontational means.

Conclusion

In the eight short years between the repeal of the last vestiges of Stalinist labour law in 1956 and Khrushchev's fall in 1964, the Soviet labour market underwent profound change. The supply of labour became fully dependent on the behaviour of individual workers for the first time since the end of the 1930s. It would be a mistake, however, to seek close parallels between the two periods. Labour turnover in the 1930s was a truly massive phenomenon which mirrored the chaos inherent in Stalinist industrialization as a whole. It was an extreme response by workers to an equally extreme situation, as they gave up their jobs to seek other jobs that might offer better pay, less dismal housing, or better rations. It was an elemental response by a workforce traumatized by collectivization and the crushing of organized resistance from peasants and workers alike. Turnover in the Khrushchev period never even remotely reached these levels, although the factors which provoked it remained very similar to those of two and three decades before: bad housing, inadequate services, dangerous or unpleasant working conditions, and pressure on wages.

Despite its more modest magnitude, the re-emergence of large-scale labour mobility fundamentally stamped the entire fabric of relations between workers and management and between workers and the political authorities. On the one hand, the reform of labour legislation and the ability of workers to leave their jobs whenever they wished meant that the labour market once again became a 'seller's market'. Workers could not be dismissed against their will, yet they could come and go virtually as they pleased. These legal guarantees would have meant nothing without the persistence of the labour shortage, but given the labour shortage they provided workers with the confidence that their position within the enterprise was protected – so long as they remained isolated individuals and made no attempt to articulate or press collective demands.

Efforts to create a greater popular ideological identification with the regime also had contradictory results. The more ephemeral campaigns, such as the Movement for Communist Labour, did little to alter workers' attitudes towards their jobs to any substantial degree. The more concrete gestures towards 'democratization' embodied in the trade union reform helped to increase the worker's boldness when it came to quitting her or his job or protesting against unfair dismissal, but without a compensatory willingness on the worker's part to make any sacrifices on behalf of the regime's political goals. This was inevitable, since the democratization on offer was only a sham. Workers still had no real freedom to form their own trade unions or political parties. They thus remained without genuine collective organizations to defend their interests inside the factories or to press their demands in the larger political arena.

The legal changes and the 'democratization' campaigns thus did nothing to help the elite assert greater control over the process of surplus extraction. For a workforce not subject to effective disciplinary sanctions, in particular the threat of unemployment and starvation, proved difficult to control, all the more so as this control had to be exercised over millions of isolated, atomized individuals, each relating to the labour process in her or his own idiosyncratic way. Effective political activity could be eliminated, but only at the expense of alienating the worker *and at the same time* providing the worker with the conditions necessary to express that alienation directly in the production process.

3 The labour shortage

Introduction: the emergence of the labour shortage

Since the 1930s the Soviet economy has been beset by a virtually permanent shortage of labour. The morphology of the labour shortage has, however, altered radically over the years, and so, too, has the pattern of its reproduction. Initially, the labour shortage was the direct consequence of the unplanned process of primitive accumulation inherent in the five-year plans. The hypertrophic pace of new construction and industrial expansion created an unanticipated demand for labour power which the countryside simply could not meet. The matter was compounded by the tragedy of collectivization. Consistent with earlier stages of capitalist primitive accumulation, industrialization and collectivization saw millions of peasants forced off the land to become the new proletariat in the towns and on new construction sites. But the very methods of collectivization and the counter-reaction they provoked among the peasantry, who slaughtered livestock, ran down grain reserves, and generally adopted a hostile, sullen attitude towards the regime, spelled the death of any hopes that collectivization would lead to a capitalist-style modernization of agriculture. The numbers of peasants who could be let go from the land became limited by the demands of agriculture itself. Indeed, the regime imposed the internal passport in 1932 precisely to stanch the haemorrhage of peasants fleeing the land for higher wages on building projects or as unskilled workers in the factories.[1]

Once created, however, the labour shortage became a central factor determining shop-floor relations. The scarcity of labour power, and the consequent elimination of unemployment as a sanction, meant that managers were almost powerless to enforce rigid discipline. On the contrary, they openly disregarded increasingly severe disciplinary legislation because they simply could not afford to dismiss workers, no matter how troublesome their behaviour. This also went some way towards redressing the workers' loss of collective power within the enterprise: a worker who worked slowly, left the workbench for a stroll or a chat, or who abused equipment and turned out a high proportion of defective products, was still better than no worker at all. The labour shortage thus helped provide workers with the leverage needed to exert limited control over their individual labour process.

In this way, the labour shortage assumed a specific cycle of reproduction. The limited control which the labour shortage allowed workers to exercise over the execution of their labour became a prime source of the myriad of dysfunctions and disruptions plaguing production and distribution. The breakdown of coordination, manifested most strikingly in storming, in turn created pressures on managers to hoard labour: first, because the inefficiencies of Soviet production caused it to consume more labour per unit of output, and secondly, because the irregularities of production schedules meant that managers had to retain a permanent surplus of hands to help meet targets during rush periods. All this took place within a planning environment which offered managers a positive financial incentive to expand their labour force.[2] The end result was that structural paradox so well documented in Western studies of the Soviet economy: the hoarding of labour by individual enterprises and the perpetual shortage of labour power within the economy as a whole.

In the Khrushchev years two different types of labour shortage emerged simultaneously. In Siberia and the Far East, regions which the regime had earmarked as areas of rapid new development, there was a perpetual ingress and egress of workers, reminiscent of the European parts of the Soviet Union during the early five-year plans. New recruits came in from other regions of the country to work on construction projects or to take up work in factories, while other workers – native workers looking for better conditions in less remote localities, recruits unwilling for the same reasons to renew, or in many cases even to complete, their labour contracts – were rushing to leave. The result was a net population loss which seriously jeopardized the regime's plans for Siberia's economic development.

In the older industrial centres, what we might call the structural labour shortage made itself felt. It became most serious in the engineering industry in the wake of the wage reform of 1956–62, as workers, especially machine-tool operators, struggled to escape from the downward pressure on earnings and to *retain control over the labour process*, but it was, in fact, a general crisis, affecting industry as a whole.

Although the rapid increase in industrial employment in the immediate post-war years partly disguised the economy's natural tendency to overconsume labour, by 1951 partial shortages had already begun to emerge. There were absolute shortages of workers in northern and eastern regions, and in such labour-intensive industries as coal-mining and construction, but more established industries were able to take advantage of their ability to offer skilled and better-paid jobs to attract young, first-time entrants to the labour force and to hoard workers above planned establishments.[3] By 1957–8 this situation had been almost totally transformed, as a generalized labour shortage began to affect all major cities.

According to Senyavskii, this was due to the restrictions placed on migration into Moscow, Leningrad, and other industrial centres, in an attempt to curb their 'gigantically growing' populations.[4] The limits on migrants were in turn made necessary by the weak infrastructure of the large towns: work opportunities existed, but shortages of food, housing, and communal services made a further influx of people insupportable. This, however, was not the only cause of the labour shortage. The numbers of workers and clerical employees continued to grow at a rate sharply in excess of the natural growth of the working-age population, a trend made worse by the low productivity of agriculture and the *relatively* limited recruitment that could come from this sector.[5] Other factors were also at work: the lack of facilities needed to allow large numbers of non-working women to enter the labour force, failures in the recruitment and training network, and the wage reform of 1956–62.

The net effect of all these influences was a serious shortage of workers in both the older industrial centres and newly developing industries and regions. If Siberia and the engineering industry were the most dramatic examples, other industries were equally involved. New chemical plants starting up in the Mid-Urals could not find enough workers for construction, installation, or operation. Some factories were operating with from one-half to one-third their planned establishments.[6] In 1966 – nearly two years after Khrushchev's fall – Leningrad textile factories still could not fill all the places in their factory training schools.[7] In the coal industry of the Kuzbass, a shortage of semi-skilled workers compelled managers to put skilled workers on to less skilled jobs.[8]

In response to this growing crisis, the Khrushchev regime launched a number of campaigns designed to increase the supply of labour power to the regions and industries affected. It launched a major drive to attract non-working women into production, overhauled the recruitment and training systems, and initiated a 'Social Call-up' to draft tens of thousands of young workers into Siberia and the Far East. Engineering factories were encouraged to transfer auxiliary workers to production jobs, increase their hiring of demobilized service personnel, and improve the efficiency of equipment use so as to get by with fewer hands. Yet not one of these campaigns achieved its objectives. Low wages and lack of child-care facilities made industrial work an unattractive option for millions of women. Volunteers for Siberia found living and working conditions so difficult that they returned home at the first opportunity. In engineering, the job of the machine-tool operator had been rendered so unpopular by the wage reform that few workers from other trades could be persuaded to take it up. At the end of Khrushchev's reign in 1964 the labour shortage still showed no signs of abatement.

I. THE CRISIS OF RECRUITMENT

The non-working population

It is perhaps surprising to discover that in a society in which, we have come to assume, virtually all those of working age hold down some form of employment, there was, during the Khrushchev years, a large pool of potential workers who stayed outside the workforce. According to the 1959 census, there were in the USSR 119,821,618 people of working age, defined as men between the ages of 16 and 59, and women between 16 and 54. Of these, 92,695,658 were employed. This meant that just over 27 million people of working age were not working. This included slightly more than 5 million – including 4,800,000 women – engaged more or less full-time on the private plot; 3,300,000 students; and another 12,860,000 non-student dependants, of whom 11,465,000 were women. Over half of these women (6,752,000) had children under the age of 14.[9] There was thus a total of around 17 million people, 90 per cent of whom were women, who were potential entrants to the labour force. Taken together, they represented 15 per cent of the total population of working age.

Not surprisingly, labour economists focused their attention throughout this period on the problem of how to draw these women into social production. In reality, the number actually available for work was smaller than the census figures suggest, since, as Sonin points out, many of those engaged in tending the private plot were women looking after children, who would not have been able to work in any case.[10] On the other hand, there were millions of pensioners who were able to work, and could have been drawn into social production. Indeed, in 1959 there were already 5.9 million pensioners working in the national economy.[11] Thus, the potential number of new workers was large, and the regime did not succeed in drawing them fully into production until well into the 1970s.[12]

The severity of what we may call the 'crisis of the able-bodied' (*trudosposobnye*) varied from region to region. In Siberia at the start of 1961, between 21 and 33 per cent of the working-age population (depending on locality) were looking after either the home or the private plot, and 90 per cent of these were women.[13] In Eastern Kazakhstan this group accounted for between 33 and 38 per cent of the potentially employable.[14] The reasons women gave for not working reflected the general lack of services and provisions which, as we have seen, were also a prime cause of female turnover (see chapter 2). The crisis of child-care provision was especially acute. In both Siberia in early 1962 and Leningrad in 1966, half of all women who sought child-care places could not find them.[15] In the Kuzbass, 60 per cent of non-working women cited the absence of child care as their reason for not working.[16] For the whole of the USSR, as late as 1967 there were pre-school places for only 23 per cent of children in that age group.[17] Even allowing that many parents had no wish to make use of these facilities, the shortage was still chronic.

Another factor allegedly inhibiting female employment was the occupational structure of many regions. In Siberia, for example, most non-working women lived in localities dominated by iron and steel, coal-mining, and other branches of heavy industry. In Kemerovo *oblast'*, light industry in 1962 accounted for only 1 per cent of production and only 7 per cent of workers and clerical employees – as against 65 per cent employed in coal-mining, iron and steel, chemicals, and building materials. As a result, women were a much smaller proportion of workers and clerical staff in Kemerovo (36 per cent) than in the USSR as a whole (49 per cent). This figure would have been even lower but for the relatively large number of women who took up heavy manual jobs in construction and roadworks.[18] The same picture prevailed in Eastern Kazakhstan, where new investment was concentrated on expanding that region's non-ferrous metallurgy industry.[19] Sagimbaeva claimed that high turnover in new settlements in

Kazakhstan was in large part explained by the fact that, when women were unable to find work due to the local specialization of production, their husbands also had to quit their jobs and move.[20]

This problem was not confined simply to Siberia and the Eastern USSR. The Urals – where in 1959 1,385,000 women of working age remained outside social production – was also characterized by a predominance of heavy industry, which left women few openings except in low-skilled manual jobs, where they were an exceptionally large share of the workforce. The problem was especially acute in medium-sized and small towns, which accounted for a large proportion of the region's population but offered practically no work opportunities in light industry. Moreover, when planning new industrial towns planners took little account of the need to provide employment possibilities for women.[21]

The difficulties of drawing women into production were compounded by the fact that for many families it was simply unprofitable for the woman to work. In small Siberian towns, women tending the private plot earned on average over 1,100 rubles a year. These people, argued Sonin, could not be enticed to work through the provision of better communal services, but only by offering them more lucrative financial incentives.[22] His argument was amply supported by Sakharova's findings in the Ukraine. In relatively high wage areas – that is, in regions dominated by heavy industry, where employment opportunities for women were limited in any case – the husband's wage was sufficient not simply to allow women to stay at home, but actually to make their entry into the labour force uneconomical.[23]

What is interesting about these arguments, in particular the complaint about the unbalanced occupational structure of regions like Siberia and the Urals, is the assumption, even among women economists and commentators, that *the appropriate sphere of female employment was light industry*. The proffered solution – to build more light-industrial enterprises in areas dominated by heavy industry – would, if carried out, merely have perpetuated the ghettoization of women workers into low-paid jobs with a high intensity of labour, in other words, into jobs characterized by a high rate of exploitation. Nowhere do we find in these discussions arguments about the need to reorganize and reform working conditions in heavy industry so that women could participate equally alongside men in jobs that were highly skilled, well-paid, and carried out in conditions safe for everybody, men and women alike.

The campaign to ease the labour shortage by bringing women into production did not produce substantial results while Khrushchev was in power. Only in the late 1960s and early 1970s was this reserve of new workers soaked up, as the service sector was expanded and as women were brought into industries such as automobiles to take up unpopular jobs which men would not do. The Khrushchev campaign contrasts oddly with the drive during *perestroika* to push women back into the home – a drive motivated partly by the desire to boost the birth rate, and partly by a need to find a means of introducing unemployment in a way that is politically acceptable to men.[24] During the Khrushchev period for many women the regime simply could not offer sufficient inducement for them to take up employment in the state sector. Either the job opportunities were not there or the incentives to prompt women to leave the home were too meagre. Wages were too low, and communal services were too undeveloped to allow those women who wanted to work to do so. Thus one avenue out of the labour shortage was momentarily closed. Stalin's policy of depressing the standard of living, starving light industry, and under-funding public services and welfare now became a major source of contradiction within the economy. The economy – and industry in particular – needed workers, but millions of potential recruits either would not or could not come forward to fill the gap because the conditions that might have allowed them to do so were inadequate. This was not a product of the poverty the Bolsheviks had inherited from Russian capitalism. It arose rather from deliberate decisions about industrial development made by the elite in the interests of consolidating its power within Soviet society.

The regime's failure to attract these millions of women into social employment was the obverse of the position of women within production, where they constituted a reserve army of the low-paid, doing primarily unattractive and heavy jobs. As under capitalism, the worker in the Soviet Union finds little scope for the all-rounded development of the human personality through socialized labour which Marx foresaw under socialism. Even within this general truism, however, there was a vast gulf between the existential position of men and women workers. What few opportunities existed within Soviet industry for interesting, creative labour were overwhelmingly the province of men. Under these conditions, the *confinement* of women to the home was not as unattractive an alternative as it might have seemed, especially since participation in socialized production did nothing to ease their domestic burden.

The labour shortage in Siberia and the Far East

The industrial development of Siberia and the Far East was a major part of Khrushchev's plans for industrial expansion. The logic behind this seemed, on the surface at least, irrefutable. The Asiatic part of the Russian Federation (that is, east of the Urals) and Kazakhstan together accounted for nearly 70 per cent of the country's territory, but only 16 per cent of its population. The area was rich in raw materials and natural resources, but the industrial infrastructure was weak. Insofar as these resources were exploited, it meant transporting them over vast distances to the older industrial centres of the western USSR, which was expensive and inefficient. Economic rationality therefore dictated that new industries should be brought to the raw materials, rather than the other way around. Such a policy, if successful, would have had the added benefits of creating a more even distribution of population and wealth across the territory of the USSR, thus easing the pressures on the large conurbations of Moscow and Leningrad.

In the eyes of labour economists, the main obstacle to this strategy was the lack of adequate 'labour resources', that is, labour power. The issue was seen not so much as an absolute shortage of available workers, as an inability to draw people into production. Like the USSR as a whole, Siberia had a large working-age population that did not participate in production. In nine towns of Novosibirsk *oblast'* in 1965, there were over 33,000 people who did nothing but tend private plots. Yet industrial enterprises in these towns were unable to recruit even a few dozen workers needed to meet their planned establishments.[25] As noted above, most of the non-working population were women. A study of Krasnoyarsk *krai* and Novosibirsk *oblast'* carried out between 1960 and 1963, found that two-thirds of non-working women between the ages of 16 and 35 were looking after young children. Moreover, well over half of non-working women in large towns had a trade, and so could have been ready entrants into the workforce had conditions permitted.[26]

By the same token, Siberian agriculture was not a promising source of recruitment, since it was already highly labour-intensive and suffered its own labour shortage.[27] There was movement from the countryside to the towns, but this was inadequate to cover the out-migration of urban residents to other parts of the Soviet Union. In general, Siberia experienced a net outflow of population, despite considerable recruitment of new workers on mostly temporary contracts from European USSR. During the whole of the Seven-Year Plan

(1959–65), 360,000 more people left Siberia than came in. This long-term trend continued well after Khrushchev fell: between 1961 and 1973 over 1 million people left Siberia, including more than 800,000 of working age.[28] This virtually nullified the influx of recruits, who had totalled nearly 1.5 million people between 1956 and 1960.[29] Siberia became a kind of revolving door, with population movements reminiscent of the 1930s, although on a smaller scale. People left the village for the towns, because the latter offered better amenities and a higher standard of living. At the same time, urban residents were becoming keenly aware of the relative backwardness of Siberia's towns and migrated to other parts of the USSR.[30] So serious did the situation become that the regime imposed a ban on new construction in its major European cities (including Moscow, Leningrad, Sverdlovsk, Kiev, Kharkov, and Gor'kii), at least partially in an attempt to create a surplus of labour power available to go to the newly developing regions.[31]

Of the workers who came into Siberia, the greatest share – 46 per cent in 1960 – went into construction. Another 17 per cent became mine workers; 17 per cent took up jobs as drivers and machine operators; and only 10 per cent entered skilled manual trades as fitters or electricians.[32] Such recruitment patterns clearly reflected the priorities of building new enterprises, but at the same time contained within them the seeds of the high turnover which lay behind the regime's inability to develop a stable workforce. In 1960, turnover in Siberia was 50 per cent above the RSFSR average,[33] but this fails to reflect the chaos that turnover caused to the industries and localities affected. A survey of migrants into three urban settlements in Krasnoyarsk *krai* during 1956–60 found that by the end of three years over half had left; between one-quarter and one-third went in their first year alone.[34] In 1959, enterprises in Omsk took on 21,000 workers but lost 22,500. Construction, timber, and woodworking were the industries most badly hit. In Tyumen' *oblast'* the timber and woodworking industries lost the equivalent of 80 per cent of their workers in 1959 and 1960. In construction Krasnoyarsk *krai* took on 42,000 building workers during 1959–60, and lost 31,000. Construction organizations in the Kuzbass hired 146,000 workers in this same period, but lost 151,000, a trend which continued in both industry and construction in the *sovnarkhoz*, at least through 1962.[35] The picture was the same in Irkutsk *sovnarkhoz*, which in 1961 hired 70,000 workers but discharged 69,000. The building-materials industry in Siberia reflected the same trend: during the fourth quarter of 1962 its enterprises hired 40,588 workers but lost

49,150. The situation eventually deteriorated to the point where, as in the 1930s, enterprises began inflating recruitment requests in order to cover anticipated losses from labour turnover.[36] This pattern was reflected in the fact that in 1960 newly hired workers made up between a third and a half of the total workforce in Siberia's different *oblasti* and regions, a picture which began to change only in the 1980s.[37]

As might be expected in a region characterized by a harsh climate and weak infrastructure, conditions rather than wages were the primary cause of outward migration. A 1960 study of turnover in Krasnoyarsk found that the overwhelming share of workers who quit their jobs because of dissatisfaction over pay actually remained in the same town, whereas those who left due to housing and living conditions moved elsewhere.[38] Indeed, wages were not the main problem, since up to 1960 workers in Siberia received an extra allowance (known as a 'zonal coefficient') to compensate for the hardships and higher prices of foodstuffs in the region. This, as one group of labour economists acknowledged, was often sufficient to entice young workers to come to Siberia, but was totally inadequate when it came to convincing them to stay.[39] However, in 1960 the regime, for reasons that are not clear, reduced, and in some areas totally abolished, the zonal coefficients, so that even this lever for attracting workers was removed. The effects were immediate: by 1961 real wages in Siberia had fallen to only 92 per cent of those in the European USSR.[40]

Even with adequate wages, the problem was that workers had little to spend them on. Food supplies in Siberia (but not, surprisingly, in the Far East) were even worse than in the centre of the country. Moreover, the situation appears to have deteriorated over time. In 1958 per capita sales turnover in state and cooperative retail trade in Western Siberia was 84 per cent of that in the European USSR, and in Eastern Siberia 97 per cent. By 1961 these figures had fallen to 66 and 76 per cent respectively, with the worst shortages being in agricultural produce and mass consumer goods. The poor state of public catering meant that there was no compensation for the general lack of foodstuffs, leaving families with little alternative but to have a wife or grandmother tend a private plot.[41] This, of course, only acted to exacerbate the labour shortage, thus retarding the region's potential development and postponing even further the day when its economic backwardness might be alleviated.

Housing suffered from the same problems. As elsewhere in the USSR, plans for industrial expansion did not incorporate provisions for new housing to accommodate the increased workforce. Karaganda *sovnarkhoz*, for example, planned to recruit 62,000 new workers in 1959, but expanded its dormitory space by a mere 16,000 beds. Even allowing for the fact that some workers already living in dormitories would be leaving, this in no way compensated for the planned shortage of living space.[42] The planning authorities in general made no attempt to give Siberia priority status for housing construction: the Seven-Year Plan called for the urban housing stock in Siberia to grow at virtually the same rate as that in the rest of the USSR. Thus the gap in housing provision – and it was this disparity which was important in determining turnover and outward migration – was not going to close.[43]

Other services and amenities lagged equally far behind. The number of doctors, hospital beds, and rest-home and sanitoria places per head of population in Siberia was far below the levels in the European USSR. Residents of Siberia were far less likely to have running water, sewerage, central heating, or gas. To make matters worse, investment in these amenities was actually planned to be lower in Siberia and Kazakhstan during the Seven-Year Plan than in the European RSFSR.[44] We have already noted the inadequacy of child-care provision in Siberia. The effect of the shortage was drastic, as many young girls, who came to Siberia originally to work, got married and had children, and then had to drop out of the workforce because they could not find child care. Other young couples when faced with these problems – compounded by the general lack of communal services such as laundries and canteens – simply decided to return home.[45]

The instability of the Siberian workforce and the labour turnover through which it manifested itself was, therefore, qualitatively different from that which affected workers in the European parts of the USSR. It was rather reminiscent of the quite extraordinary population movements of the First Five-Year Plan, when workers in some industries were changing jobs on average two, three, or even four times a year, as they wandered about looking for anywhere which offered slightly better conditions than where they had just been. The scale on which this occurred in Siberia and the Far East in the late 1950s and early 1960s was obviously much smaller, but the nature of the phenomenon was the same. To some extent, this was to be expected in a newly developing region where the infrastructure was poor. Indeed, recruits anticipated that conditions would be harsh, especially in construction. The problem, however, as many labour economists pointed out, was to move away from a situation where industry and construction depended on migrants, to one where the region could rely on its own stable, indigenous workforce. The failure to do this then became an obstacle to the region's development. Like the USSR as a whole in the 1930s, development did take place. Industrial output in Siberia during the Seven-Year Plan rose by 80 per cent, against only a 20 per cent rise in the size of the workforce. For all the disruptions which turnover caused, new enterprises eventually were finished and went into operation. In some industries, such as chemicals, non-ferrous metallurgy, electric power, and building materials, the expansion was quite dramatic, as output increased two- and threefold.[46] This says nothing, however, about the quality of growth, which differed not at all from the problems besetting industrial production all over the USSR. In terms of the labour market, the growth that occurred in no way resolved Siberia's inherent labour problems. Far from becoming a new industrial centre, offering a counter-pole of attraction to the overburdened resources of Moscow and Leningrad, the outflow of people from Siberia proceeded apace until the early 1980s.

The failures of the recruitment and training networks

Over the course of the 1950s and 1960s, the methods by which factories recruited and trained workers underwent fundamental change. Recruitment – both organized and spontaneous – became increasingly urbanized and less reliant on migrants from the countryside.[47] Enterprises also became dependent on new sources of recruits, especially demobilized military personnel.[48] At the other extreme, older institutions, such as the system of organized recruitment, or *orgnabor*, which had led such a chequered existence in the Stalin years, virtually disappeared as a major source of hiring. Similarly, the old system of Labour Reserve Schools, established by Stalin in 1940 as an instrument for compulsory labour for young people, was replaced by vocational training schools or technical colleges (PTU), which were deemed more able to meet the economy's need for better-educated and better-trained workers.

Recruitment in this period followed a steady trajectory towards spontaneity, as mirrored by the declining importance of *orgnabor*. In the 1930s *orgnabor* had provided the economy with an average of 2.87 million workers a year,[49] although the high turnover of recruits greatly undermined the effectiveness of the system.[50] The number of recruits fell sharply in the post-war years, from an annual average of 700,000–800,000 during the period 1946–54, to 500,000 in 1958, and just 249,000 in 1962. By the 1950s *orgnabor* was recruiting mainly for construction, coal-mining, and certain other labour-intensive industries, although even here it was unable to cope with their demands for new workers. It was barely able to provide recruits for construction and a small number of industrial enterprises in Siberia and the Far East.[51]

The system had always been riddled by inefficiencies. Ministries, then later the *sovnarkhozy*, and enterprises all inflated recruitment requirements. Enterprises wished to protect themselves against the effects of high turnover, while ministries and *sovnarkhozy* had little real knowledge of the real labour needs of enterprises.[52] The cumbersomeness of the system made it difficult for construction projects to obtain workers with the correct skills. In many cases, only a tiny minority of workers had experience in the building trades, so that building sites constantly had to employ them on jobs other than those for which they had been trained. This, in turn led to disputes, since it was in violation of existing labour legislation, which guaranteed workers the right to work only in their appropriate specialism. The workers' grievances were understandable, since many of them were in highly skilled, but non-construction, trades and could be employed only on unskilled, manual labour. The economic costs of this practice were high. If workers agreed to stay on they had to be retrained, which took time and was costly. Others, however, were not so flexible and simply quit.[53] Turnover was aggravated by the bad conditions workers found when they arrived. At one minerals trust in Irkutsk *sovnarkhoz* as late as 1962, workers were housed in ramshackle barracks without baths or even drinking water (for the latter, workers had to travel two to three miles). In another construction trust the dormitories had no toilets, and the food was so bad that workers had to travel two hours to the nearest town to get breakfast. The barracks were also located some 20 miles from the actual building site, and to get there the workers had to cram themselves into overcrowded buses for what must have been a long and unpleasant journey.[54] The cost of conditions such as these was not simply high turnover. Workers returning from Siberia undoubtedly told of their experiences, and this must have made it increasingly difficult to attract new recruits. Indeed, in 1962 the Ukraine was able to meet less than half its recruitment plan of 'several thousand' workers for the Northern timber industry.[55]

A similar fate befell the so-called Social Call-Up, an appeal issued by the government to persuade young people to volunteer for work in newly developing regions. Initially introduced in 1954 to recruit agricultural workers for the Virgin Lands campaign,[56] it was extended in 1956 to sign up volunteers for industry and construction.[57] Following an initial enlistment of 200,000 people in 1956, the Komsomol was able to recruit nearly 600,000 in 1958, about half of whom went to construction sites in Siberia, the northern USSR, and the Donbass, and slightly less than this (250,000) to projects in their own *oblasti*. Over the next four years, annual recruitment declined, but still provided a total of 800,000 workers.[58] Not surprisingly, the new recruits encountered the same conditions as their colleagues hired through *orgnabor*. Housing was bad, and there were no recreational facilities. Enterprises offered little by way of training, and there were cases of intimidation of young workers by local managers. Turnover among volunteers was, therefore, high. In one section of a Krasnoyarsk construction trust, more than half the Komsomol members quit because of managerial abuse; sometimes whole brigades gave notice *en masse*. The construction of the nickel combine in Pechenga (Murmansk *oblast'*) lost nearly half of its Social Call-Up volunteers during 1956 and early 1957, while the construction of the Urals aluminium works lost around one-quarter.[59]

As enterprises came to rely increasingly on their own ability to recruit and hire, the training system – both trade schools and factories' own training programmes – acquired greater significance. The failures of this system, therefore, placed a further obstacle in the way of attempts to solve the labour shortage. In October 1940 the regime had imposed labour conscription for youths aged 14–17, who were assigned places on training courses in industrial and transport trade schools.[60] This system, known as the Labour Reserve System, was made voluntary in March 1955, although the schools were to continue in operation under a Chief Administration (*glavk*) of Labour Reserves.[61]

The inadequacies of the Labour Reserve System were discussed openly in the press. Enterprises were reluctant to take on graduates from the schools, partly because they did not want the added burden of providing them with housing, but primarily because the young workers often did not possess the skills enterprises needed and were almost all poorly trained. Students were taught on outdated and worn-out equipment, usually by instructors who themselves did not have adequate training. Practical work made up only a small proportion of study time (less than a quarter of total instruction), during which it was impossible to acquire a decent level of expertise. Nevertheless, the schools awarded their graduates nominally high skill grades, because this allowed instructors to claim extra bonuses. Once the trainees arrived at the factories, however, the latter found that they had either to retrain the workers from scratch or to regrade them downwards.[62] Prior to the *sovnarkhoz* reform, these problems were compounded by the fact that the numbers of students to be trained in each trade were decided centrally by ministries, and it was only a matter of chance if these corresponded to the skills which enterprises actually required. Coal mines – which were already training five times as many workers on their own pit courses as the mining training schools were turning out – often refused to take these workers on; of those they accepted, about half had to be retrained.[63] Similar complaints were levied against the schools in construction: instruction was poor, and the period of training (10 months) was too brief to allow students to acquire the necessary trades and levels of skill. Training was minimal – in one training school in Dnepropetrovsk, students spent six months without a single hour of work on-site. As a result, the schools became unpopular and found it difficult to attract entrants.[64] However, the alternative of on-site training was hardly more successful. New workers were trained in brigades, where instruction was haphazard and varied enormously in quality. Frequently they were used simply as navvies or unskilled labourers, and failed to acquire a skilled trade. These failings were not always intentional, but often arose as a natural by-product of stoppages and disruptions due to lack of supplies.[65]

Despite occasional attempts to justify the Labour Reserve System,[66] it continued to decline in importance. In 1959 it was replaced by the system of vocational education (literally, Professional-Technical Education, or PTO), which in fact had been initiated as an adjunct of the Labour Reserve System in 1954.[67] Although in many areas the new technical colleges (PTU) represented an important modernization of the Soviet Union's vocational-training network, the vast majority of young workers (90 per cent) now received training directly on the job, through individual instruction in work teams (brigades), or via various short courses.[68]

This system, too, had crucial drawbacks. As part of the Khrushchev education reforms, enterprises were supposed to be tied to a technical college (PTU). Enterprises would provide students with work experience and training, and the colleges would filter graduates to these factories as new workers. Yet by 1965 some 65 per cent of large-scale enterprises had no ties to a PTU, while newly built enterprises were being put into operation without a PTU being created to service them.[69] Those enterprises that were tied to a PTU found that relations were often caught up in bureaucratic in-fighting between *sovnarkhozy* and local officials in charge of technical college administration, who insisted on training workers for jobs for which local enterprises had no openings.[70]

Training provision within enterprises was also inadequate. Factories did not have suitable premises, while instruction prepared workers for only a narrow range of skills with little account taken of the demands that might be posed by eventual modernization.[71] This was especially true in engineering, and did nothing to help that industry cope with its labour shortage. Workers at Leningrad's Kotlyakov factory, for example, complained that their 'training' consisted of standing around watching experienced machine-tool operators at their jobs. Shop superintendents maintained that they could not afford to entrust equipment to inexperienced workers, yet without machine time there was no hope of their acquiring a skill.[72] Training in the chemical industry shared many of the same drawbacks. The failure to build technical colleges to feed new chemical plants left the latter with a serious shortage of skilled workers, which in turn led to delays in starting up operations and to excessive equipment stoppages. Factories ran their own courses, but these were of short duration and poorly designed.[73]

Finally, training faced one other obstacle, already inherent in the education reform, but which spilled over to affect young workers once they entered the factory. A central feature of Khrushchev's reform of the secondary school curriculum had been the restoration of 'polytechnical' education. In fact, polytechnical instruction in any meaningful sense of the word was never established. Children did not receive exposure to a variety of skills and trades, nor did they learn about enterprise management or planning procedures, as had been the professed ideal in the 1920s. The emphasis was really on vocational training in the most narrow sense. Under the terms of the reform, an extra year was added to secondary education, and pupils were to spend about one-third of their time in the last three years acquiring a particular trade. Farms or industrial enterprises were to provide a large part of the training. The reform foundered, among other reasons, because enterprise managers resented having to bother with schoolchildren, who in most cases probably just got underfoot and added to the already chaotic conditions in the factory, and because skilled workers refused to take time away from production to teach them, as this cut into work time and jeopardized earnings.[74]

Such attitudes were directed not simply to visiting school students, however. There is considerable evidence that the reception given by older workers to their younger workmates was, in many factories, indifferent at best, and hostile at worst. The main reason was money. Some feared that time taken to train newcomers would not be compensated. In engineering factories, where the wage reform and constant disruptions to production combined to put pressure on wages, established workers also worried that there would not be enough work to go around if younger workers were taken on. In other factories older workers were able to monopolize the most lucrative jobs, which they protected by forming brigades of Communist Labour, made up only of their most skilled and productive comrades and from which younger or less able workers were excluded.[75] The press continuously maintained that this type of behaviour was indicative of only a minority of skilled workers, and that most continued to treat trainees fairly and to deem it a matter of pride to take them on for training.[76] There is no way to verify which was most prevalent. At the very least we can say that the behaviour of a significant share of older workers contributed to the host of problems young workers encountered when starting their first job. Neglect, poor training, and use as dogsbodies were not just confined to new recruits on construction sites in Siberia, but carried over into established industries like engineering – where, ironically, the labour shortage was perhaps most disruptive and new workers were desperately needed. It was these very disruptions, however, that, by putting pressure on earnings, no doubt reinforced any paternalistic, craft chauvinism that may have existed. In a society where the working class's internal cohesion had been undermined by three decades of political repression and atomization, and reinforced by a near-extreme individualization of work organization and remuneration, solidarity and generosity were likely to be the first casualties when earnings or a worker's general welfare were threatened. This had the benefit for the elite of keeping the workforce politically neutralized, but at the cost of reduced coordination and control over production, which was the inevitable consequence of the individualization of work.

II. THE LABOUR SHORTAGE IN THE ENGINEERING INDUSTRY

The labour shortage, as we have already indicated, had a very different morphology in the older industrial centres of the USSR. Whereas in Siberia, workers – or prospective workers – were leaving their jobs or refusing to enter the workforce because of the primitive conditions, the low standard of living, and the difficulties of working in a relatively undeveloped region, in cities like Moscow, Sverdlovsk, and Leningrad the problem was compounded by the unwillingness of workers who were available and looking for work to take up certain jobs, most notably those of machine-tool operators in engineering. While other industries and occupations were also affected,[77] it was in engineering that the labour shortage was most serious and posed the most severe threat to the economy. The shortage affected mainly machine-tool operators, because the wage reform of 1956–62 had regraded masses of these workers into the lowest skill and wage grades at the same time as their jobs were made subject to tighter norms. As earnings suffered, workers simply abandoned their jobs, either to find comparable employment in the same occupation at factories offering better pay, or to take up new trades altogether. Wages, however, were not the only factor. There has always been in Soviet industry a trade-off between wages and control over the work process. Many workers have been willing to tolerate earning only an average wage if this allowed them to preserve some form of control over work speeds and organization. As we shall see, a significant minority of machine-tool operators were willing to take lower-paying jobs which gave them greater scope for individual control. Conversely, if workers were to become machinists or to stay in that trade, their earnings had to be higher than the terms of the wage reform generally allowed. The regime recognized this very late in the day, when it changed bonus regulations for machinists in 1964, but it was only under Brezhnev and Kosygin that the wage reform was eventually dismantled and the crisis of machinists resolved. In the mean time, the high turnover and shortage of machine-tool operators set in motion a vicious cycle of delays and disruptions within factories which had knock-on effects throughout the economy. Without enough oper-ators to machine parts, fitters in assembly shops were constantly behind schedule in meeting their targets. Storming became a way of life in engineering, and factories awaiting overdue deliveries of equip-ment had their own plans disrupted. These problems were compoun-ded by the backwardness of most foundry shops, which increased the pressure on machine shops even further.

The shortage of machine-tool operators affected virtually the whole of the engineering industry. In 1964, engineering factories in the 15 largest *oblasti* and territories of the RSFSR had a shortage of 600,000 workers. Moscow alone had a shortage of 100,000, only one-fifth of which could be met by a campaign then under way to persuade some 20,000 auxiliary workers to become machine-tool operators.[78] Only in

Leningrad, however, was the full extent of the crisis well documented. This is partly because of the thorough and comprehensive study of labour turnover carried out by Leningrad sociologists in the early 1960s; but it is mainly because the local newspaper, *Leningradskaya pravda*, was, unlike the national and other local papers, willing – for reasons that I have not been able to discover – to print graphic and extremely detailed reports of how the labour shortage was affecting Leningrad industry. The problem was no less serious in other towns, but their newspapers simply did not report it with the same frequency or candour as *Leningradskaya pravda*.[79]

However, even these infrequent accounts give a very good indication of how the labour shortage deformed the cycle of production in those enterprises which were affected by it. The Kommunist mining-equipment factory in the Krivoi Rog, for example, was unable to fulfil its orders because of a shortage of turners. One shop, which used to have 20 turners on each shift was, in late 1962, working with only seven or eight.[80] In the Urals there was a sharp rise in turnover (not just at engineering factories) between 1960 and 1962, which led to many enterprises being unable to employ their full planned establishment. Moreover, the rise was most marked amongst more experienced workers, whose share of leavers rose from 48 to 59 per cent.[81] Even in 1960 the Turbomotor factory in Sverdlovsk had lost twice as many machine-tool operators as it hired, whereas in all other trades it was at least able to replace those who had quit.[82] The Uralmash and Uralkhimmash factories – two of the largest engineering enterprises in the Urals – also reported that a shortage of machinists was leading to bottlenecks.[83]

In Moscow, press reports of a labour shortage did not begin to appear until late 1962, although it is obvious that the problem had been affecting production for some time. The first detailed account, for example, pointed to the extremely poor utilization of equipment which the shortage of machinists was causing in major engineering enterprises.[84] The picture painted was the standard one: machine shops were short of turners and other machine-tool operators, while workers in assembly shops were left idle waiting for the big rush at the end of the month. As elsewhere, the shortage of turners was made worse by the poor work of foundry shops, which, because of their relatively primitive technology, often could not provide those machine-tool operators on hand with a full day's work.[85] In general, turnover among machine-tool operators was alleged to be three to four times that prevailing in Moscow industry as a whole.[86] This prompted

Moskovskaya pravda to single out those enterprises which, by putting in some effort at improving working or housing conditions, had been able to recruit the workers they needed and improve their use of equipment.[87] The fact was, however, that these enterprises were merely attracting machinists and other workers who had left other factories. As we shall see when discussing the labour shortage in Leningrad, the trade of a machine-tool operator was an unpopular one. The overall shortage could not be solved merely by redistributing the operators between the general mass of equally desperate enterprises, and indeed it remained severe in Moscow right up to the end of the Khrushchev period.[88]

The labour crisis in Leningrad engineering

The Leningrad press began extensive reporting of the impact of the labour shortage in March 1961, with an article on the Vpered engineering works. The emphasis at the time was on the factory's inability to compensate for the shortage of workers by making use of potential 'reserves' for raising output: tighter discipline, more efficient work schedules, and better mechanization.[89] This was followed at the end of March by the publication of an 'appeal' from five major engineering works calling on factories to make better use of metal cutting and forge-press equipment, and on Komsomol members and other young people to take up the trade of machine-tool operator.[90]

The extent of the labour shortage can be gauged by the fact that the machine shops of 32 Leningrad engineering enterprises did not have enough workers to run a second shift.[91] The problem was not that factories were short of workers. They simply could not hire enough machinists. The Elektrik factory reported that it was short of 50 machine-tool operators.[92] The Machine factory was so short of machinists that it could not run all of the equipment in its machine shops even on its first shift, much less on the second, which was able to meet its targets only by having foremen work the machine tools in the evenings. Yet the factory had 57 *former* machinists working as assemblers, quality controllers, packers, and drivers, *none of whom could be persuaded to go back to their old jobs.*[93] The story was the same at the Excavator factory: in the first machine shop, 28 out of 86 machine tools had no one to run them; in the second machine shop the figure was 18 out of 50. The factory was supposed to move 70 of its own workers from other trades to machinists' jobs, but had managed to switch only seven. In the meantime, six other machine-tool operators had quit, leaving the factory with a net gain of only one.[94] A letter from a foreman at the Leningrad tool factory explained how they were short of turners, because young turners wanted to leave the trade and take up jobs in machine assembly, where the work was cleaner, easier, and much better paid. Of the young trainees on work practice from secondary school, none wanted to be turners – all wanted to work in assembly.[95] The Admiralty ship-building factory in late 1963 ran an advertisement for machine-tool operators to work in its machine shops, but had virtually no takers.[96] In all these reports the shortage of machinists was tied to a self-reproducing cycle of production difficulties and disruptions. Machine shops were not providing assembly shops with complete batches of parts. As parts came in at the end of the month, assembly shops could meet their targets only by storming. The Excavator factory even had to draft in extra fitters from other towns.

The reluctance of workers to take up jobs as machinists was based on quite legitimate grievances, which in turn were perpetuated by the labour shortage, making it almost impossible for enterprises to break out of a vicious circle. The printing and publishing machinery factory, for example, lost 745 workers in 1961, including 293 machinists. Unlike other factories, it actually managed to recruit nearly 100 more new machine-tool operators than had quit, but it was still short of skilled workers. By mid-1962, the factory had lost approximately one-third of its machine-tool operators, primarily due to the constant overtime these workers had to put in, in a vain attempt to keep assembly shops supplied with parts. Older workers began leaving, some to take up easier, although probably lower-paid work, in workshops of scientific research institutes. Their replacements were invariably younger workers with insufficient experience, but the factory had trouble holding on to them as well. Those who were doing part-time courses at technical colleges or higher education found it impossible to keep up their studies while working so much overtime. Other young workers complained of rudeness and ill-treatment by foremen and shop superintendents,[97] which may at least in part have resulted from the pressures the latter felt themselves under to meet their plans when they were short-staffed. At the Reduktor factory the high turnover of machinists was blamed on a similar combination of factors. Conditions in shops were appalling. Workers arrived to find workplaces filthy from the previous shift, with shavings and bits of parts everywhere. General hygiene and safety were poor. Work was also badly organized. Workers had to hunt down tools and wait around for job assignments, because no one had prepared them the night before.

Young machine-tool operators were also leaving because they were not receiving any training to upgrade their skills – a matter of vital importance given the low wage and skill grades into which most machinists were classified as a result of the wage reform.[98] The picture in the reduction-gear shop of the Kotlyakov factory was almost identical. So serious was the shortage of machinists that at times this particular shop had as many as 30 machine tools standing idle. Most workers who left complained of low pay, low skill grades, and dirty working conditions.[99]

Thanks to a massive study of 10,500 job leavers in Leningrad carried out in this period, we are able to supplement these press reports and construct a more systematic picture of the factors behind, and the impact of, the shortage of machine-tool operators. To begin with, the overwhelming proportion – over 60 per cent – of engineering workers who quit their jobs nevertheless stayed in engineering. This still left a substantial share of new openings that were filled by people fleeing jobs in industries where pay and conditions were even worse, primarily building materials, light industry, and the food industry.[100]

Perhaps not surprisingly, the study found that nearly half of machine-tool operators who changed enterprise when giving up their jobs[101] also abandoned the trade. This compares with only 27 per cent of fitters, three-quarters of whom stayed in the same occupation. Although in 1964 there were approximately the same number of fitters and machine-tool operators in Leningrad industry, the latter had twice the level of labour turnover. What is most interesting is the fact that, despite press accounts implying a flood of machine-tool operators into assembly jobs, among those interviewed in the survey, only 6.6 per cent found new jobs as fitters, as against 7.5 per cent who became auxiliary workers, 13.5 per cent who took up 'other' (unspecified) industrial trades, and 7.4 per cent who left industry completely (for example, to work in machine shops of research institutes). What this means is that a substantial share of machine-tool operators were willing to take up lower-paying jobs as auxiliary workers simply to get out of this line of work. This was most pronounced among young machine-tool operators under the age of 18: while 26 per cent expressed a desire to become fitters or electrical fitters, 31 per cent said they were willing to move to less skilled jobs as auxiliary workers.[102] What is common to virtually all the jobs that machinists sought as alternatives is that *they offered greater control over the labour process.* Pay was less important than the opportunity to ease the strain of work, which in machine-tool operation was more closely controlled by the nature of the technology used than in assembly or auxiliary jobs. The latter may at times have been unpleasant or even badly paid, but, precisely because they were poorly mechanized and largely manual, they still gave workers more control over the pace and intensity of their labour.[103] This is indirectly confirmed by the fact that fitters had only the third best wage in Leningrad industry, after workers in metallurgy and construction, yet it was the most stable occupation.[104] Few fitters were going to take up jobs in iron and steel or the building trades, with their incomparably worse conditions, just for a few extra rubles a month.

These survey data show that the problem of recruiting and training machinists was more complicated than it was portrayed by the press and many labour economists, who attributed it to wages alone. There was clearly a trade-off here: machinists were willing to take jobs with lower pay if this eased the intensity of their labour. But this does not mean that they would not have stayed at their jobs if their wages had been substantially increased. The experience of the Brezhnev years, when wage ceilings were greatly relaxed and the shortage of machine operators was solved, suggests that this was, in fact, the case.

Attempts to ease the labour shortage

As the intractability of the labour shortage became increasingly evident with each passing year, factories, local economic authorities, and the regime in Moscow launched a number of campaigns and measures designed to reverse the trend. One of the most prominent was to urge factories to re-employ and retain auxiliary workers as machine-tool operators. This was bound to be a difficult undertaking, not just because of the resistance of many auxiliary workers to the idea of becoming machinists, but because of the undermechanization of auxiliary operations, which made them highly labour-intensive. The availability of such workers was, therefore, limited.[105] By the same token, the few factories that had succeeded in mechanizing their auxiliary shops had managed to cut this portion of their workforce considerably, thus showing the potential benefits that could be reaped.[106]

On the whole, however, the results of the campaign were meagre. In Sverdlovsk *sovnarkhoz*, moves to mechanize the manufacture of sinter machines at Uralmash freed only 11 workers. At the Bogoslovskii aluminium factory, mechanization of electrolysis operations released a mere 28.[107] A plan to retrain 900 auxiliary workers in Moscow's

Kuibyshev district by November 1963 had found only 500 workers with just three months to go.[108] A similar campaign at Moscow's Kompressor factory netted only 23 new machinists – although the press touted this as a great success.[109] Reports from Leningrad were if anything even less sanguine, as factories reported mere handfuls of auxiliary workers shifting to machinists' jobs.[110] Overall, engineering factories in Leningrad succeeded in cutting their auxiliary workforce by a mere 1.4 per cent over the course of 1961–2.[111] Like Moscow, even if all plans had been successful, this would have provided only a fifth of the number of new machine-tool operators needed to allow Leningrad's engineering factories to work on two shifts.[112]

In the face of the labour shortage, engineering enterprises began to rely heavily on demobilized soldiers for new recruits. Here, too, the results were less than heartening. The Admiralty ship-building factory lost 40 per cent of the demobilized soldiers it had taken on as machine-tool operators over the course of 1962.[113] The printing and publishing machinery factory fared slightly better: of the 350 ex-soldiers it hired in 1963, it lost only a quarter.[114]

The real problem behind all the efforts to attract new recruits, however, was that auxiliary workers, young trainees, or ex-service personnel might come to the factories, but, even if they stayed on the job themselves, other machine-tool operators were leaving, thus negating any successes of the recruitment campaigns. Leningrad's Voskov factory managed to shift 283 auxiliary workers to machine tools during 1963 – which must have been quite a success, relative to the small numbers being reported elsewhere – but during this same period 409 machine-tool operators quit.[115] The printing and publishing machinery factory complained that even when it trained auxiliary workers as machinists they would see help-wanted notices at other factories and leave to take up new jobs – as auxiliary workers![116]

The press and most labour economists argued that the main obstacle to the recruitment of machine-tool operators was wages, and unless the regime was prepared to redress this problem efforts to attract more workers to the trade were simply doomed.[117] Although, as we have seen, this issue was more complex, and workers had a clear idea of a trade-off between remuneration and control, clearly a change in wages policy was going to be central to any attempt to solve the shortage. The problem had been built into the provisions of the wage reform, which narrowed the scope for norm overfulfilment and reduced overfulfilment payments. In theory, these were to be compensated by new bonus payments for plan fulfilment and quality, although the bonus systems proved for the most part a failure.[118] In engineering, however, machine-tool operators found themselves the victims of a tight regrading procedure, which left them in lower skill and wage grades (*razryady*) than workers in other industries. In 1962, nearly a quarter of engineering workers were in the first skill grade, over half in grades one and two, and over three-quarters in the first three grades. By 1965, improvement in this situation had been negligible. Forty-eight per cent of workers in engineering and metalworking were still trapped in the first two skill grades, and 73 per cent in the first three. This pattern was repeated in every branch of engineering, and was observed nowhere else in Soviet industry, where workers were concentrated in the middle grades.[119]

At the same time, the relatively high degree of mechanization of their jobs made them subject to more rigorous norms (so-called 'technically based' norms), so that norm fulfilment for machinists was well below that of fitters or workers in auxiliary trades (whose earnings may still have been less due to lower basic rates). The combined effect of tighter norms and regrading was intense pressure on earnings. In 1964, 42 per cent of Leningrad machine-tool operators were earning less than 80 rubles a month, a full 20 rubles a month less than the average wage in engineering; 14 per cent earned less than 60 rubles, making them the only production trade in heavy industry with so many low-paid workers. Only industries dominated by women workers, such as textiles, garments, and footwear, had more workers concentrated in low-paying jobs.[120]

To try to overcome the difficulties created by the wages system, managers were often forced to ignore a grading structure which in practice was simply unworkable. Experienced workers were paid not by their own wage and skill grade, but according to the work they actually did. Although this helped compensate workers for their potential loss of earnings, it also made them dependent on shop management actually giving them higher-paid work.[121] It also gave rise to anomalies which then led to further resentments among workers. Workers in different skill grades would have to carry out exactly the same work. Those in lower grades resented what they saw as unfair differentials, while those in higher grades refused to be paid below their grade. This actually prompted one unnamed factory in Leningrad's Moscow district to allow workers to elect their own brigade councils, which then decided each worker's skill grade, as well as penalties for shoddy work or discipline violations.[122] It is doubtful that management would have ceded such a large share of its traditional prerogatives had shop-floor discontent not forced it do to so.[123] The important point, however, is that the spontaneous action of managers to try to stem the exit of skilled workers served actually to promote turnover by undermining the uniformity of pay between factories.[124]

Turnover was not the only problem caused by discontent over wages. With potential earnings already limited, workers, especially machine-tool operators, refused to work with so-called 'technically based' norms; these were designed to reflect the full technological capacities of equipment, rather than be calculated (as most norms were) on the basis of the existing organization of work, including average time lost on stoppages. According to bonus regulations originally laid down by the wage reform, workers working with technically based norms were granted, by way of an incentive, a paltry payment of 1.5 to 2 per cent of their monthly piece-earnings for each percentage by which they overfulfilled such norms.[125] The problem was that these norms were so much more rigorous than those ordinarily in use, and overall fulfilment was so low, that the financial incentive to accept them was almost non-existent.[126] They thus became an impediment to plans to rationalize or reorganize production. Managers, for their part, were reluctant to apply them because they would only exacerbate turnover. On the contrary, holding norms down and allowing artificially high fulfilment was often the only way to raise earnings in engineering to a level high enough to dissuade workers from quitting.[127]

In 1964 the State Labour and Wages Committee liberalized the bonus rules, but only by way of an experiment tried out at 90 engineering enterprises throughout the country. Production workers and tool-makers in engineering who accepted technically based norms would receive a bonus equal to 10 per cent of their piece-earnings merely for fulfilling such norms, plus an additional 1 to 2 per cent for each percentage of overfulfilment, up to a maximum of 25 per cent of piece-earnings. In certain sections of engineering, for example, the manufacture of high-precision machinery and tools, workers were to receive bonuses only for quality indicators, providing that they also fulfilled their norms.[128] Despite the limited application of the new regulations, some enterprises which applied it, such as the Moscow Small-Capacity Automobile Factory (Moskvich) claimed that it raised earnings and therefore helped cut turnover.[129] Such caution notwithstanding, the experiment showed that the regime had finally decided that some relaxation of the wage reform in engineering was essential.

Yet the form of this relaxation was revealing. The regime clearly did not want to surrender what it felt it had gained in terms of controlling machinists' wages and imposing tighter norms. It would not beat a retreat and relax either the use of technical norms or strict regrading, but would merely give workers a financial incentive to accept them. As we shall see in chapter 4, managers often intervened at shop-floor level and solved the problem in their own way – by refusing to apply technically based norms.

The campaign to improve equipment utilization

One method by which the regime attempted to come to grips with the labour shortage in engineering was to impel enterprises to improve their utilization of equipment. If factories could not recruit enough machinists to run the machinery, then it was hoped that they could, through various improvements in work organization, cope with the task using the workers they had.

Equipment utilization was measured by a so-called 'shift index' (*koefitsient smennosti*), which was calculated by dividing the total number of machine-shifts worked by the total number of machines. Thus a factory with 100 machine tools working without interruption over three shifts would have a shift index of 300 machine-shifts/100 machines = 3.0, a perfect score. Conversely, if this same factory worked only one shift, its shift index would be 1.0, which was relatively low. Obviously, no enterprise could afford to keep all of its machine-tool stock constantly in production, as some had to be kept in reserve to cover breakdowns or other unforeseen contingencies. But equipment utilization in engineering was notoriously low, hovering in many of Leningrad's major engineering firms at around 1.5 – which meant that these factories could not even operate their equipment productively over two full shifts. Other cities reported similarly poor results. In early 1963 the majority of Moscow engineering factories had a shift index of 1.3–1.4.[130] In Sverdlovsk many of the Urals's leading engineering works had an index as low as 1.2, which meant that they were barely in operation for more than one shift; others operated at a figure between 1.5 and 1.6.[131] Factories in Ivanovo were also working within this same range.[132]

Initially, the campaign to raise equipment utilization was seen as an end in itself, rather than as a device for dealing with the labour shortage. In Moscow the drive to raise the shift index contained not a hint that a labour shortage even existed.[133] In Leningrad, as we have

noted, the two were linked, but only insofar as the recruitment of more
machine-tool operators would permit enterprises to make better use of
machinery. Indeed, it was soon recognized that bringing idle equipment into operation or running machinery longer would actually
increase the demand for machinists,[134] which explains the intensity of
the drive to recruit auxiliary workers to these jobs. When the latter
campaign, as well as the increased recruitment of demobilized service
personnel, failed to have the desired impact, the emphasis shifted to
finding ways to run more equipment with *existing* personnel. Indeed,
certain Leningrad factories reported improved shift indices by getting
machine-tool operators to tend more than one piece of equipment,
amalgamating inefficient shops, or reorganizing transport and some
stages of production.[135]

For all these reports of success, the campaign still came up against
serious difficulties. To begin with, figures for equipment use were
often overstated, in part because official *sovnarkhoz* criteria for calculat-
ing the shift index were easy to manipulate. The latter allowed enterprises to exclude from their calculations all equipment in auxiliary
shops plus machines that had no workers attached to them (one of the
problems the campaign was intended to solve in the first place). Using
this formula, the Kotylakov factory was able to calculate its shift index
based on just over half its stock of equipment, and the Admiralty
ship-building factory on less than one-third.[136] Another issue was
whether machinery that was in operation was being used *productively*.
Many factories improved their formal utilization, but only by increasing their amount of defective production, which other workers had to
spend countless hours rectifying.[137] In such cases, 'improved' use of
equipment was in no way matched by an increased output of actual
use values. Materials, equipment, and workers' labour time were
simply squandered to no purpose. They may have all gone into the
statistics as contributing to 'production', or 'plan fulfilment', but
society did not benefit from these expenditures.

Improving equipment utilization in many cases merely created
bottlenecks in interrelated areas of production. Even leaving out of
account the increased demand for machine-tool operators, raising
machine time placed additional demands on supplies of castings,
parts, and semi-finished components coming from foundries and other
auxiliary shops which, because of their undermechanization, were
barely coping with existing requirements even when working flat out
on three shifts. These same disproportions existed within machine
shops: some machine tools were working at less than half their

capacity because they depended on the output of other, less productive pieces of equipment. By the same token, increasing the productivity of some machines could at best have only a limited effect, and at
worst prove pointless, unless the productivity of others with which it
was interconnected in the production process could be raised propor-
tionately.[138]

To a large extent, poor equipment-use was due to the vast amount of
old or uninstalled equipment which factories hoarded. One section of
the Ekonomaizer factory in Leningrad was littered with turning lathes
unsuitable for that shop's production.[139] Approximately one-third of
all metal-cutting machine tools in Leningrad industry (that is, not just
engineering) were in auxiliary shops where, by the nature of the work
there, they were used only sporadically. This was especially a problem
in repair shops, which, because of their inefficient organization and
decentralization, had to keep on hand the entire range of equipment
they might need to make replacement parts, no matter how rarely
such parts were required.[140] But factories also simply accumulated
stocks of equipment as a matter of course, keeping on old equipment
even when purchasing new. From the point of view of enterprise
directors, such behaviour was perfectly rational. New equipment often
arrived 'incomplete' – that is, with essential parts missing – and could
not be used. Managers also retained old equipment as a hedge against
storming or unanticipated plan changes. Factories might also be
ordered by the planning authorities to buy equipment which they
could not use. The build-up of stocks was exacerbated by extremely
long delays in getting new equipment into service: time spent in the
store-room, assembly, and operational development could take from
two to three years. In the mean time still more modern equipment was
developed which enterprises wanted to acquire, yet they could hardly
write off 'old' equipment that had never been put into operation.[141] As
of 1 January 1964 there were in Leningrad over 1,800 machine tools,
685 units of forge-press equipment, and 267 units of foundry equipment still awaiting installation, some of it for as long as five years.[142] A
census of uninstalled and surplus equipment carried out in Ivanovo
oblast' in 1963 found 14,986 uninstalled machine tools and other pieces
of machinery, a full third of which was lying out in the open air
because there was nowhere to store it.[143]

The amount of aged equipment was quite staggering. Leningrad's
printing and publishing machinery factory had 40 metal-cutting
machines between 20 and 40 years old.[144] At the Kotlyakov factory,
nearly a quarter of equipment was older than 20 years, and 15 per cent

over 40.[145] Workers at the electrical-appliance factory in the city of Pushkin, near Leningrad, refused to work on certain pieces of equipment because they were so decrepit that it was impossible to make anything on them.[146] In Moscow, as of 1 August 1962, 46 per cent of all metal-cutting equipment at Dinamo was over 20 years old. At ZIL, 37 per cent was more than 20 years old and another 27 per cent was over 10.[147]

The accumulation of outdated or otherwise idle equipment had a profound effect on the technological profile of the engineering industry, for it meant the retention of a large stock of outmoded universal cutting tools alongside more modern specialized equipment (carousel lathes, boring machines, and so on) which tended to be underutilized. This imbalance was further heightened by the fact that universal cutting tools continued to make up a large share of *newly acquired* machinery. Commenting on this phenomenon, one economist claimed that doing away with this old equipment would actually improve production capacity, by making way for the introduction and use of newer, more productive machinery which would then be better utilized.[148]

A major cause of this accumulation of aged and outmoded machinery lay in the problem of unfinished construction, since equipment ordered for new shops would arrive while the shops were still not built. Managers made matters worse by ordering new machinery before they had actually acquired the funds to construct new shops or sections. And, of course, problems of unfinished construction were aggravated by the common practice of dispersing investment funds over too many projects, so that none of them could be completed until managers could wrench more money out of the central authorities.[149] Beneath these practices lay still more profound causes, tied to the difficulties of modernizing existing plant and equipment in the Soviet economy. Despite policies designed to direct new equipment purchases to the re-equipping of existing shops and the replacement of obsolete machinery, managerial practice went in precisely the opposite direction. Although in the Ukraine, for example, the growth of capital investment during the period 1959–64 vastly exceeded the construction of new factories, managers merely used this equipment to stock new shops, rather than retire outmoded machines.[150] This meant, however, that old machinery had constantly to be overhauled in order to be kept in service, placing greater strain on the repair and maintenance sector, as well as raising production costs.[151] But this tendency was not the result of managerial arbitrariness. On the one hand, it was a logical response to the pressures of the planning system, which militated against the introduction of new technology, and at the same time encouraged managers to start as many new investment and construction projects as they could win approval for.[152] On the other hand, it arose equally from workers' limited control over the labour process. New equipment would necessarily have brought with it the need for redeployments and redundancies. At best managers would have had to find displaced workers alternative employment. At worst it would have provoked open hostility on the part of workers whose jobs might be threatened. Managers were simply unwilling to face the problems on the shop floor that lay-offs would have caused. This, then, proved a major structural obstacle to attempts to solve the shortage of machine-tool operators by reducing industry's demand for these workers.

By 1964 the campaign to improve equipment utilization had achieved almost nothing. In fact, the shift index in Leningrad was actually deteriorating.[153] Nationally, the average shift index in engineering stood at 1.4. A survey of 42 engineering plants revealed that barely half of metal-cutting machine tools were fully utilized even during the first shift and 17 per cent of them did no work at all. On third shifts, as we might expect, only a quarter of machine tools were in full-time use, while 65 per cent lay completely idle. The figures were even worse for forge-press equipment.[154] Perhaps most astonishing of all, Soviet engineering was never to improve on this performance, even when the shortage of machine-tool operators ceased to be critical. For all of Leningrad industry (not simply engineering), the shift index in 1986 was 1.2, rising to a mere 1.38 in 1987.[155] Admittedly, this figure may have been lowered by poor utilization in certain areas of industry less efficient than engineering, but these will be more than balanced by industries like textiles and iron and steel, where equipment is used continuously over two and three shifts. Only now is there renewed discussion in the Soviet press about the need to adopt multi-shift work schedules. This suggests that the obstacles to more effective utilization of machinery were not simply conjunctural, but have been structurally rooted in the system of production and planning. The symptoms are the continued backwardness of Soviet equipment, including the limited use of machine tools with programmed controls – machines which became standard in the Western engineering industry a long time ago. In large part this is due to the resistance of workers to this type of machinery (a resistance which was manifested even in the Khrushchev period), because it further reduces operators' control over the work process.[156]

Conclusion

The labour shortage in the Khrushchev period, although a generalized problem affecting industry as a whole, had a number of different components. In Siberia and the Far East it stemmed initially from the underpopulation of the region, which the regime hoped to solve through the in-migration of labour recruits from the western USSR, who would hopefully stay as permanent workers in the enterprises then under construction. In the older industrial conurbations, the shortages were more structurally rooted in the economy's tendency to overconsume labour power. In engineering this was exacerbated by the effects of the wage reform, which prompted many machine-tool operators to abandon their jobs – and often their trade – to seek better pay and working conditions elsewhere in industry.

Our review of the different policies designed to improve the supply of labour power shows that each of them failed, not because they were particularly ill-designed, but for structural reasons endemic to the Soviet system. There was a huge reserve of non-working women who could have entered industry both in Siberia and in the country's older industrial regions, but the regime failed to persuade them to do so. In many areas the predominance of heavy industry limited the employment opportunities for women, a problem that might have been attenuated had the regime found a way to improve general working conditions. As we shall see in chapter 7, however, this was a more complex issue than it would appear. Most heavy manual auxiliary jobs were already done by women, but they might have taken up certain production trades had working conditions been improved. At the same time, job discrimination, which kept women's wages at about two-thirds those of men and effectively barred them from the more skilled manual trades, such as mechanics and tool-setters, meant that potential earnings were too low to attract many non-working women into industrial work. For this reason, an expansion of employment possibilities in light industry might not have been the panacea that was claimed, since non-working women could see the relatively poor pay and high intensity such jobs offered.

Shortages might also have been eased if the recruitment and training system had been more efficient. Both were dogged by deep-seated weaknesses. In Siberia and the Far East, the social infrastructure was so poorly developed that recruits simply refused to stay, often leaving before the expiration of their initial contracts. In older industrialized centres, factories sharply reduced their reliance on both organized recruitment and the vocational-training network because these proved too unreliable and unable to supply workers with the training, trade, and skill profiles demanded. This left hiring and training to the spontaneous activity of enterprises themselves, which had their own internal difficulties. The reform of vocational education, which was supposed to provide enterprises with training schools to feed them new workers, failed to achieve this objective. Only a minority of factories were tied to such schools, and the recruits did not always possess the trades and skills enterprises needed. Inside the factories, older workers sometimes resented the need to train newcomers. They showed even more resentment to school students sent for vocational instruction as part of Khrushchev's education reform: the students got underfoot and their instruction time ate into workers' output and earnings.

In terms of the labour shortage in engineering in the 1960s, this was a crisis of the regime's own making. While engineering would no doubt have suffered the same general shortage of labour that affected other sectors of the economy, its particular severity was caused by the unwillingness of workers to enter a trade where wages were more tightly circumscribed and control over the labour process was more limited. The regime was thus held hostage to the unplanned actions of its population, which simply did not behave as the elite had wished or predicted, but persisted as individuals in pursuing their own needs and interests through whatever channels they found available. This meant leaving jobs they did not want and seeking better conditions wherever they could find them – irrespective of the disruption this caused to factory production programmes and central plans. As with recruits to Siberia, by defending their own individual position in this way, workers helped to perpetuate the poor working conditions and earnings which had provoked their spontaneous actions in the first place.

4   The wage reform

If, as I have argued so far, the central task of de-Stalinization was to improve economic efficiency and raise productivity, the true centre-piece of this strategy was the wage reform. The reform was first introduced into coal-mining and some engineering enterprises in 1956, covered all major branches of industry by 1960, and the rest of the economy by 1962. The reform sought to re-establish what the regime considered to be a systematic relationship between the price paid for labour power and the amount of labour performed, a relationship which had broken down during the 1930s under the pressures of industrialization and had deteriorated even further in the last years of Stalin's reign. While the reform achieved some of its more nominal objectives, such as reducing levels of norm overfulfilment and the weight of norm-overfulfilment payments in piece workers' earnings, it did not succeed in turning Soviet wages into a coherent, predictable, and centrally controllable system of incentives.

This is not to deny that the reform also had other goals. For example, it sought to ease the plight of the very low-paid, although, as we shall see, the actual narrowing of differentials among wage labourers was at best modest.[1] Similarly, the regime attempted to use wages policy to influence the allocation of labour between industries and regions. Here, too, the results were questionable. In Siberia and the Far East the application of so-called extra 'zonal' payments singularly failed to stem population-loss and high labour turnover in these regions.[2] In engineering the wage reform actually contributed to a serious shortage of machinists. Even had these aspects of the wage reform been more successful, however, the creation of an effective incentive system remained, in my view, the reform's major goal, and it is in these terms that it must be judged.

I shall not give a detailed account of the mechanics of the wage reform or of the more technical issues involved in its implementation.

This has been comprehensively treated by Leonard Kirsch in his excellent book on Soviet wages.[3] Rather, after outlining the major features of the Stalinist wages system, the reform, and its general results, I shall look in more detail at the different problems the reform encountered in individual industries. This is all the more important in that Kirsch based much of his analysis on his observations of the engineering industry. While this is perhaps justified by the fact that engineering in this period accounted for just under one-third of industrial workers,[4] the pattern of difficulties varied considerably from one branch of production to another.

The Soviet wages system prior to the reform

Stalinist wages policy had always been essentially coercive in character. The vast majority of workers were placed on piece-rates, with remuneration tied to output quotas, or norms. The norm was set so that if a worker fulfilled her or his quota by 100 per cent she or he would earn the basic wage (*stavka*). Overfulfilment obviously meant higher earnings; the system of progressive piece-rates, favoured for a time in the 1930s and again after World War II, allowed the rate paid for each unit to rise as overfulfilment increased, thus allowing the boost in earnings to accelerate. Underfulfilment, on the other hand, meant that a worker earned less than the basic wage, which under Soviet conditions entailed real material hardship. The theory behind Stalinist policy was that the basic wage should be kept relatively low, so that workers would exert as much effort as possible to overfulfil their norms. To maintain the pressure, especially as workers mastered the old norms, or as new technology and improved organization made fulfilment easier, norms were 'revised' – that is, raised – usually in the spring of each year, and job prices were cut. At times, as during the 1930s, the rises could be extremely steep.

This system never functioned as intended because managers were unwilling to allow workers' earnings to fall below a tolerable minimum. They thus resorted to a whole range of devices to protect workers from the worst effects of norm rises or downward pressure on wage rates. Norms were manipulated and kept deliberately low; workers were given opportunities to falsify their work results; managers awarded them specious, and sometimes totally illegal, bonus payments.[5]

In the post-war period these distortions had, if anything, grown worse. Basic wage rates had changed little from their pre-war level,[6]

forcing workers to rely more heavily on payments for norm overfulfilment. Although the earnings of piece workers had more than doubled
since the war, this was only because norms were being kept artificially
low, partly through the efforts of factory managers who refused to
permit earnings to drop below prevailing levels, and partly due to the
fact that during the war norms had been lowered to allow the influx of
new workers, including many inexperienced women and young
people, to cope with them. Thus by 1955 norms were so low that the
basic wage in engineering accounted for only about 50 per cent of
piece workers' earnings compared to 75–80 per cent before the war.[7]
The situation was the same in other industries (see table 4.1).

This, however, was not the end of the story. Workers on time-rates,
who obviously had no norms to overfulfil, saw the differential
between piece workers and themselves widen, prompting managers
to resort to other devices to protect their earnings. Various bonuses for
time workers, allegedly tied to their quantitative performance and the
quality of their work, were simply paid automatically, becoming, in the
words of one labour economist, merely 'a constant, monthly additional
payment to time workers' wages'.[8] Time workers were placed in
higher wage and skill grades (*razryady*), paid at the higher scales set for
piece workers, or put on so-called 'fictitious' piece-rates. In the latter
case they were paid piece-rates for jobs on which it was difficult to
establish verifiable norms and where the output or performance could
not be precisely measured, thus allowing the results easily to be
exaggerated.[9]

The outcome of these multifarious distortions was a patchwork of
wage scales, wage rates, and locally determined norms, which led in
turn to a truly vast number of wage anomalies. In the building-
materials industry – one of the first to introduce the wage reform –
many brick and glass factories were using wage rates introduced in
1939 or 1940. Moreover, as the industry had (prior to the *sovnarkhoz*
reform of 1957) been administratively split between the ministry of the
Building Materials Industry and various all-union construction ministries, workers in analogous trades found themselves earning different
amounts depending on which authority they worked under.[10] In iron
and steel bonuses for plan fulfilment, smelting high-grade steel, economizing on electricity consumption, and similar indicators routinely
came to 50 per cent of earnings – despite the widespread application of
progressive piece-rates. Moreover, factories applied a plethora of
different wage rates and wage scales so that workers carrying out
allegedly equivalent types of work received higher earnings at some

factories than at others. The arbitrariness of norm-setting also led to the creation of a hierarchy of 'profitable' versus 'unprofitable' jobs, with workers shying away from work on which it was difficult to overfulfil the norms – a factor which in turn gave rise to large amounts of unfinished production.[11]

A similar set of problems was encountered in engineering. Throughout the industry anomalies were common, as workers in analogous trades earned more in some shops than in others, and less skilled workers could earn more than skilled workers.[12] Moreover, the ease with which norms were fulfilled meant that workers showed a greater tolerance towards production difficulties which, in a more tightly regulated system, would have jeopardized their earnings and (or so it was alleged) prompted them to show greater effort in overcoming them. In practical terms this meant that norms could be vastly overfulfilled while factories failed to meet their production plans.[13]

Difficulties were compounded by the enormous bureaucracy that the norm-setting system created. With industrialization, the breakdown of the labour process had proceeded to such an extent that factories were operating with literally hundreds of thousands of norms, often specifying jobs worth just a few kopeks. One worker in the machine-assembly shop of the Novo-Kramatorsk engineering works was one month paid for 1,424 job orders, including 484 jobs worth from 3 to 50 kopeks. Total wages for these 1,424 jobs came to just 1,389 rubles. What is more, to work out his pay the factory had to write out and process some 2,885 documents containing 8,500 signatures, using up a total of 8 kilograms of paper and costing the factory 309 rubles – more than 22 per cent of the worker's actual wages.[14]

It should be said, however, that these various subterfuges were not able to protect earnings in every industry. Wages in textiles, traditionally low-paid since the First Five-Year-Plan, remained almost uniformly so despite the presence of considerable anomalies between trades and factories. The only groups of workers who achieved even modest rises in earnings in the post-war period were auxiliary workers,[15] many of whom were men (for example, skilled maintenance fitters).

If the regime was contemplating any reform of industry, it was clear, therefore, that the incentive system, which had remained unchanged virtually since the First Five-Year Plan and unworkable almost from that date, would have to be overhauled.

The basic provisions of the reform

All branches of large-scale industry and construction were scheduled to have completed a reform of their wages system by 1960. The remainder of the national economy was to implement the reform during 1961 and 1962. Initially, the reform affected six industries: engineering, iron and steel, non-ferrous metallurgy, coal-mining, chemicals, and building materials. Of these, coal-mining was the first to apply the reform on a large scale. The Ukrainian coal-fields introduced shorter hours (see below) and new payment regulations during 1956, so that by 1 January 1957 some 99 per cent of Donbass pits were working under the new system. The remainder of the coal industry introduced the reform only in 1958.[16] In 1956, 14 Moscow engineering enterprises introduced the wage reform on an experimental basis, but the results were so unsatisfactory that a year later three plants – the First State Ball-Bearing Factory, the Kalibr instrument factory, and the Vladimir Il'ich engineering works – implemented a revised reform for a further trial.[17] The rest of the engineering industry began implementing the reform in 1959.[18] Likewise, five major iron and steel works (Magnitogorsk, the Kirov works in Makeevka, Azovstal', Zaporozhstal', and Dneprospetsstal') began preparing a wage reform in 1956, with the rest of the industry introducing the reform during 1957 and 1958.[19] In the chemical industry the reform was equally staggered, with factories in Moscow, Perm, Stalingrad, Omsk, and Tula ordered to introduce the reform during late 1957, and remaining enterprises to follow suit before September 1959.[20] The building-materials industry introduced the reform between 1958 and 1960, depending on the branch of production.[21]

The wage reform, the detailed provisions of which differed in each industry, had a number of objectives:

1. *Basic wages were to be raised*, so that they represented a higher share of earnings. In this way it was hoped that, with workers less dependent on norm-overfulfilment payments, there would be less pressure to distort norm-setting. In engineering and iron and steel, for example, the target was to have the basic wage make up 70 to 75 per cent of the earnings of piece workers and 75 to 80 per cent of those of time workers.[22] In chemicals the target was somewhat lower: 70 per cent for piece workers and 75 per cent for those on time rates[23] (eventually to become the vast majority). To this end the basic wage in basic chemicals, for example, was raised by 70 to 83 per cent for piece workers and 67 to 85 per cent for time workers.[24]

2. *Norms were to be raised* to limit their overfulfilment. This was to be achieved not just through large norm rises, but by pushing enterprises to adopt so-called technically based norms, which (at least in theory) would accurately reflect the full production potential of equipment and improved methods of labour organization.

On the whole, norm rises were steep. In engineering, norms were to be raised by 65 per cent. In chemicals, where norm fulfilment before the reform was considerably lower, rises were to average 30 per cent, although the first factories to adopt the reform raised norms well above this figure. In coal-mining, norms were raised indirectly by shortening the working day to six hours and keeping total shift norms unchanged – thus, it was claimed, leading to a *de facto* rise of some 33 per cent. Moreover, about one-third of workers working in mines deemed to have norms that were too low had their nominal norms raised even further, by between 6 and 18 per cent, depending on the basin.[25] As all of these were average targets, workers in some enterprises suffered norm rises far in excess of these figures.[26]

3. *The number of wage scales and wage rates within each scale were to be sharply reduced and simplified*, with the aim of eliminating the patch-work of scales and skill grades, which could vary from factory to factory within a single industry. In chemicals, after some initial experimentation with an eight-skill-grade scale, most workers were put on a uniform scale with seven grades. Building materials (except for cement) and engineering were each to have a single scale with six skill grades.[27] Moreover, wage rates within the scales were to be rationalized. Whereas before the reform each enterprise might operate with dozens of different wage rates in the bottom skill grade, in most industries there were now to be only a handful of separate rates, depending on whether a worker was on piece- or time-rates and worked in normal or 'hot' and dangerous conditions.[28]

In coal-mining this rationalization took on a rather different form, as most workers began working in integrated brigades and were paid on various forms of collective piece-rates. In line with this, the number of different occupations was cut initially by 80 per cent, and for production workers (that is, excluding auxiliary jobs like roofing or delivering timber) eventually down to just two basic trades, stope workers and preparatory workers (*prokhodchiki*), each paid a basic wage of 75 rubles per shift. The logic behind this was that in integrated brigades all workers were now called on to carry out different jobs interchangeably, and so should earn a uniform basic rate.[29]

4. *Progressive piece-rates were to be eliminated*, except for certain limited areas of the iron and steel industry. Piece workers were to be put either on straight piece-rates or on piece-rates supplemented by various bonuses.

5. With the de-emphasis on norm-overfulfilment payments and the attempt to control the arbitrary and often capricious award of bonuses to time workers, *new bonus regulations were introduced to reward workers for meeting various production and quality indicators*. In coal-mining, workers were to receive a simple bonus for fulfilling or overfulfilling their production plan.[30] In engineering, piece workers on assembly lines and conveyors were to receive a bonus of 10 per cent for fulfilling the monthly plan plus 2 per cent for each per cent of overfulfilment – up to a maximum of 20 per cent of their piece earnings. In addition, as an inducement to prompt piece workers to work with so-called technically based norms, those who did so were to receive a bonus of 1 to 2 per cent of their basic wage for each percentage by which they overfulfilled them. Time workers were to receive bonuses for the quality of their work and for carrying out job assignments on time.[31]

Piece workers in the chemical industry were to be allowed to earn bonuses of up to 20 per cent of their basic wage for fulfilling monthly plan targets plus additional bonuses for meeting various quality indicators (economizing on materials, increasing output of top-grade products, adhering strictly to operating procedures). Later regulations governing both piece and time workers (most workers in basic chemicals were on time-rates; most workers in the rubber industry were on piece-work) stipulated that quality bonuses could not exceed 15 to 20 per cent of the basic wage and that *they were not to be paid if workers did not meet their production plan* – a provision which, as we shall see, was open to considerable abuse.[32]

Similar quality bonuses were encouraged in the iron and steel industry, but they were rarely applied.[33]

6. *Various groups of piece workers* whose jobs were now deemed incompatible with piece work (those carrying out maintenance and repair of equipment, for example), *were to be shifted on to time-wages.*

At the same time, there were two further provisions which directly affected the reform. First, the working day was cut to seven hours for industries previously on an eight-hour day, and to six hours for those, such as coal-mining, where a large proportion of workers had been on a seven-hour day. Certain workers in industries involving continuous processes, such as iron and steel, were excluded from this provision, but they were to be compensated with extra days off.

The second major change was in the procedure for carrying out norm revisions. From 1957 norms were no longer to be revised through annual campaigns. Rather, responsibility for revising norms was devolved on to local enterprises, and in larger factories on to individual shops, to be implemented as circumstances demanded. The purpose was not merely to reduce the amount of bureaucracy in norm-setting, but to encourage management more quickly and accurately to reflect technological improvements in norm increases.[34] At the same time, however, the trade union reform gave the unions a greater role in approving norm rises, which were not to be implemented without prior consultation with factory trade union committees – a responsibility the latter did not always exercise with much vigour.

General results of the reform

A survey of the formal aspects of the reform shows that it achieved many of its more general objectives, although it did not succeed in its most important aim, namely to develop a consistent and viable system of incentives.

The reform's most visible success was in the regulation of piece work. The number of piece workers in Soviet industry declined, so that by 1 August 1962, 60.5 per cent of industrial workers were on piece-rates and 39.5 per cent on time-wages. Of those on piece-rates, just under half were on straight piece-rates and just over half on some form of bonus system, whereby their piece-earnings were augmented by one or more of the bonus payments described above. Progressive piece-rates were almost totally eliminated, accounting for less than 0.5 per cent of all piece workers.[35]

The share of the basic wage in workers' earnings also rose to about 73 per cent in 1961, being slightly lower (71 per cent) for piece workers and somewhat higher (76 per cent) for time workers. The proportion of piece workers' earnings that derived from payments for norm overfulfilment correspondingly fell to about 13.5 per cent, although the percentage in engineering (nearly 20 per cent) was higher than that in industries like chemicals (just over 11 per cent) where overfulfilment possibilities were limited by the nature of production.[36]

Not surprisingly, the reform also drastically reduced levels of norm overfulfilment among piece workers, as table 4.1 shows. The greater difficulty workers now had in achieving large overfulfilment figures was reflected in a significant number of workers not meeting their norms, together with a decline in those overfulfilling by substantial amounts. In October 1962, some 11.4 per cent of industrial workers

Table 4.1. *Average norm fulfilment in selected industries*

Industry	Pre-reform	October 1963
All industry	169	120
Engineering and metalworking	209	133
Coal-mining	123	106
Iron and steel	137	115
Non-ferrous metallurgy	142	115
Building materials	144	113
Oil-extraction	134	127
Chemicals	158	120
Woodworking	170	120
Textiles	146	111
Garment industry	155	113
Meat and dairy	157	107[a]
Baking	134	111[a]
Printing and publishing	184	112[a]

[a] Figures obtained by special survey conducted after introduction of the wage reform. The date is unspecified, but probably 1958 for printing and publishing; possibly as late as 1960 for the baking and meat and dairy industries.
Source: Batkaev and Markov, p. 198.

fulfilled their norms by 100 per cent or less, ranging from the fairly modest figures of 5.1 per cent in iron and steel and 6.9 per cent in engineering, to 31.4 per cent in coal-mining and 20 per cent in oil-extraction.[37] These latter two industries were also the two most highly paid, and in fact their low norm fulfilment was blamed directly on the prevailing bonus system, which allowed workers to earn full bonuses for plan fulfilment while still underfulfilling their norms (as is noted below).

Finally, in stark contrast to the pre-reform period, the wage reform allowed the regime to keep wages within planned limits. In fact, average wages for workers and clerical employees in the entire state sector (not just industry) during the Seven-Year Plan (1959–65) actually rose more slowly than the plan had predicted, showing a seven-year rise of 22.9 per cent, as against a planned growth of 26 per cent.[38] Nove, however, has pointed out that much of this control over wage-spending was due to the incorporation of 3 million *kolkhozniki* into state farms. Although this meant a rise in their personal standards of living, as state farm workers their earnings were 23 per cent lower than the national average, and 27 per cent below the average for industrial workers.[39] Nevertheless, according to Soviet figures at least, workers in industry were definitely affected by this squeeze. During the Seven-Year Plan, their wages rose on average by just 19 per cent, well below the average for the economy as a whole.[40]

More important from the regime's point of view, wage rises during the wage reform lagged well behind rises in productivity. Data for the RSFSR indicate that between 1959 and 1962 wages rose a mere 7 per cent compared to a rise in productivity of nearly 20 per cent. This pattern was fairly uniform among all major industries. At some enterprises the gap was quite striking: at Magnitogorsk, between 1959 and 1963 productivity per employed person (not just workers) rose 27.5 per cent, while workers' wages rose a mere 1.4 per cent. At the Vladimir Il'ich engineering works in Moscow, during the period 1959–62, productivity rose by 50 per cent while wages went up by only 1.7 per cent.[41] One might think that this was a welcome result from the regime's (but not the workers') point of view, but the gap was so large, argued Manevich, that wages now had to be raised.

All of this might, on the surface, seem like impressive achievements. In particular, it would appear that the reform had allowed the regime to regain a substantial degree of control over events on the shop floor and to break the process of managerial collusion with workers over earnings that had undermined Stalinist wages policy since the start of industrialization. This conclusion, however, would be premature.

First, these global results were in large part the product of the sexual division of labour within the Soviet economy which allowed far more success in controlling the earnings of women workers than it did those of men. Overall, women in industry earned less than 70 per cent of the average male wage. They were marginalized into the lowest-paid industries and trades. In light industry, basic wages were low and additional earnings were restricted by the fact that the prevailing technology gave women far less control over the labour process, and hence reduced scope for extracting looser norms as a concession from management. Within heavy industry, women worked either on assembly-line production, where they faced the same difficulties as women in light industry, or in auxiliary jobs doing primarily heavy manual labour. Here they may have exercised more control over the pace and quality of their work, but pay was still low. The importance of this reserve army of low-paid women cannot be underestimated. It gave both local management and the regime as a whole the leeway to tolerate violations of wage and norm-setting regulations designed to protect the earnings of workers – usually male – in favoured industries and trades.[42]

Secondly, the aim of the reform was not simply to control overall wages expenditure, but to develop an effective system of incentives which would act to control the behaviour of *each individual worker*. This, as we shall see, the reform failed to do. As a result, the global averages were an almost accidental balance of countless deviations from official regulations, with many workers able to prompt managers to protect their earnings, while others were not. In both cases the wages system could not provide an adequate incentive to convince or compel workers to surrender defensive shop-floor practices or to accept a rise in the rate of exploitation. In engineering, as we have already seen, the reform may have succeeded in keeping overall earnings within desired limits, but only at the expense of arousing so much discontent among machine-tool operators that they quit their jobs and seriously disrupted the work of that industry. Where workers, especially women, were not in a position to exercise this kind of influence, they effectively subsidized the concessions which had to be made to those workers whose cooperation was deemed by management to be more vital to production.

In short, the wage reform failed to make the process of producing and appropriating the surplus product predictable and controllable. Resolving some of the more glaring idiosyncrasies of the Stalinist wages system, it merely created new difficulties for workers which managers in many, if not most, cases felt obliged to rectify. Managers and workers readily circumvented those aspects of the reform that threatened established earnings, so that while average earnings may have stayed within planned limits and total earnings lagged behind growth in productivity, *for the individual worker* the application of the reform took on a random character and thus lost its main force as a coherent system of incentives.

The failures of the reform

1. Wage Anomalies

One of the major problems the regime had sought to redress with the wage reform was the patchwork of anomalies which undermined planned differentials. While it managed to attenuate or eliminate some disparities, it tended to encourage others, as managers had to protect the earnings of individual groups of workers (those whose skills were in short supply or whose cooperation was vital to production) who had suffered from one or another aspect of the new policy. To a large extent this reflected the contradictory nature of the reform, which sought to reduce inequalities by raising the wages of the lowest-paid workers while limiting the earnings of those at the top. At the same time, however, the reform carried over the Stalinist period's campaign against so-called 'egalitarianism'. The two aims were simply incompatible with one another. Moreover, by putting pressure on the earnings of numerous groups of workers, the reform reinforced 'egalitarianism' by forcing managers to protect earnings irrespective of the amount of effort workers put in or of the quality of the work they performed.

Although both the minimum-wage law of 1956 and the increase in basic wages tended to pull up the wages of the low-paid, the reform did nothing to redress the disadvantage suffered by workers in low-priority industries, primarily light industry and consumer goods, where the workforce was almost exclusively women. In 1965 the best-paid workers were those in the fuel industry (coal-mining and oil), non-ferrous metals, iron and steel, and chemicals, in that order.[43] Engineering ranked only in the middle of the table (slightly lower than the national average), while the food industry and light industry were at the bottom, as table 4.2 shows. The average monthly wage in coal-mining was thus nearly 2.5 times that in light industry.[44] In fact, such differentials have always been part of Soviet wages policy, partly to ensure the attraction of skilled workers into heavy industry, and partly as a reflection of the regime's appalling discrimination against female workers.

If the wage reform was never intended to do away with disparities between high- and low-paid industries, it *was* supposed to do away with anomalies *within* each sector. This it failed to do.

In coal-mining, for example, at least up to the late 1950s each basin had its own, highly divergent norms for identical jobs. The problem was rooted in the fact that unified norms had last been issued in 1933, since which time each basin had introduced its own successive local alterations. Although new handbooks for norms on mechanized operations were issued in 1954–6, *these were not obligatory*, allowing coal managers to alter them on the pretext of adjusting for local geological conditions, 'organizational-technical' difficulties, and the like. In reality, the norms were manoeuvred whenever managers deemed it necessary to protect workers' earnings.[45] The reform equally gave rise to, or reinforced, disparities between different trades. Under the old system the basic wage of extraction workers was some 40 to 50 per cent higher than that for maintenance workers. To prevent such a wide gap in actual earnings, maintenance workers were given low norms.

Table 4.2. *Average monthly wage of industrial workers by industry, 1965* (rubles)

All industry	101.3
Coal-mining	191.4
Iron and steel	124.2
Forestry	111.1
Cellulose and paper	102.0
Chemicals	101.9
Engineering and metalworking	100.8
Electric energy and heating	100.7
Building materials	99.2
Food industry	84.7
Light industry	77.7
Including: Footwear	80.8
Textiles	80.6
Garment industry	72.2
Construction	106.5

Source: Trud v SSSR (Moscow, 1968), pp. 141–5.

However, when the reform gave both extraction and maintenance workers the same basic wage, many pits either allowed the latter to keep their old, artificially depressed norms or imposed only nominal norm rises.[46] At the other extreme, the reform had set the basic wage of certain auxiliary occupations so low that the mines simply did not apply them. They either raised them by awarding these workers extra payments (*doplaty*), or by diverting on to this work other workers whose basic wages were higher.[47] Disparities also arose between different sections of one and the same mine, due to divergent levels of plan fulfilment (and hence plan-fulfilment bonuses).[48]

In engineering, as we have seen, the reform caused a distinct deterioration in the relative – and in many cases absolute – position of machine-tool operators. The nature of their work meant that they were more easily subjected to tighter norms than mechanics or other workers with a large degree of manual labour in their work (for example, those in small-batch or single-item production, or repair and maintenance personnel). At the same time, they suffered far worse than workers in other industries during the regrading into new skill grades that was part of the reform. The result was high turnover, especially among machinists, and serious disruption to the work of engineering enterprises.[49]

To try to deal with this situation, managers in engineering had to engage in numerous circumventions of official regulations. In order to attract young workers as trainees, factories allowed them a special, higher basic wage during their first three months on the job. Many enterprises went further and gave them relatively easy production targets, so that the combination of piece-earnings and the higher basic wage allowed them to earn more than experienced workers. It was even alleged that young workers 'developed a taste for such generous extra payments', and would quit their jobs in order to be taken on as 'trainees' somewhere else.[50] Because norms on some items were more rigorous than others (giving rise to a division between 'profitable' versus 'unprofitable' jobs – with workers shunning the latter), managers had to be careful to parcel out work assignments in such a way as to guarantee all workers an equal earnings potential.[51] In general, it was common practice in engineering simply to keep norms low, so that workers could use overfulfilment payments to compensate for low skill grades or the use of nominally technically based norms.[52] In some cases, managers even allowed workers to decide their own skill grades through brigade councils.[53]

Despite these difficulties, piece workers as a group – including machine operators – were nonetheless privileged relative to those on time-rates. Kirsch has maintained that although the reform failed to eliminate the large gap between piece- and time-earnings, it nonetheless made it less severe.[54] We can question whether this was of any practical import. The discrepancy between actual earnings of piece and time workers was almost everywhere greater than the prescribed differences in their basic wages, which was only to be on the order of 10 to 15 per cent. In engineering, the average earnings of piece workers at the end of Khrushchev's rule were a full 33 per cent higher than those of time workers. Among workers in the middle and upper skill grades, the gap was 60 per cent. A comparable pattern was true in iron and steel. In some enterprises – not simply in engineering – piece workers could be earning twice as much as time workers in the same skill grade.[55] A similar gap emerged between production and auxiliary workers, a fact at least partially accounted for by the shift of many auxiliary workers from piece- to time-rates as part of the reform. The result was that managers had to intervene to protect the earnings of those workers who were falling behind. In the chemical and building-materials industries, time workers were paid at piece workers' rates. In iron and steel and non-ferrous metallurgy, they were paid for doing 'hot' or dangerous work when they were actually working under normal conditions.[56] In Leningrad engineering, time workers were compensated by putting them into higher wage and skill grades, which allowed their earnings more or less to keep pace with those of piece workers.[57] In general, the manipulation of skill grades was an important vehicle for adjusting earnings of workers in shortage trades when other methods, for example, paying additional or illicit bonuses, were not available.[58]

The retention of local control over norm-setting, together with the greater power of some enterprises as opposed to others to win higher wage funds added a further random element to differentials. In some industries and enterprises the use of outdated norm handbooks, combined with deliberate violation of regulations when assigning workers a basic wage, meant that many workers could wind up earning more than those with greater skills.[59] Because norm-setting materials differed so widely even among factories within the same industry, norms on allegedly identical jobs could vary by a whole order of magnitude. A study of the engineering industry found norms on one and the same metal-cutting operation to be two and half times higher at some factories than at others. In the building-materials industry the discrepancies could be as much as sixfold. The reason was that each factory set its norms using totally disparate and non-equivalent criteria.[60] In another experiment, norm-setters at six different instrument factories were told to calculate rates for a particular job, for which they were all given the same drawings and specifications. Yet the norms varied from a low of 7 minutes to a high of 143, because each norm-setter had used a different handbook: some were quite recent, but others had been issued some 12 years before and were hopelessly out of date.[61]

In engineering many factories were able to win larger wage-fund plans than others, allowing them to retain established earnings levels by putting workers in higher skill grades or applying low norms. Factories with less financial clout and, as a result, tighter wage plans, found themselves with insufficient room to introduce effective bonus systems. Such discrepancies were even built into *sovnarkhoz* wage plans by the *sovnarkhozy* themselves.[62] Those factories with the easiest production plans also found themselves with the greatest flexibility when it came to increasing their workers' earnings. The other side of this, of course, was that industries and enterprises whose plans were tightest had the greatest difficulties guaranteeing their workers bonuses. In construction the wage fund was based on gross output, and not on the actual labour content of jobs. This meant that workers found it unprofitable to take jobs on building sites during the initial stages of construction, which were the most labour-intensive (and recorded the lowest 'gross output'), and indeed labour turnover in construction was highest precisely in this phase of the work. Similarly disadvantaged were workers in factories trying to introduce new product lines or new technology, or building workers on projects outside major cities – all of whom tended to earn lower bonuses than workers in major factories for the same expenditure of labour time. In coal-mining the gap in earnings between workers who fulfilled their monthly plan and those who did not could be as much as 100 per cent, although the differences in their respective performances or labour expended could be very small.[63]

It was almost inevitable that these various anomalies – some due to the wage reform itself, others to managerial distortion of it – would affect labour mobility by making some enterprises more attractive than others. Although it was certainly true that wages were not always the prime motive in job-changing, it was nevertheless the case that in some areas workers could greatly improve their position by switching jobs. The institutionalization of such disparities was, therefore, a device by which managers confronted with a labour shortage could hire or hold on to workers, or win their cooperation when dealing with internal difficulties. High-priority industries or enterprises which were in a position to win larger wage funds were better placed to make these kinds of concessions. But once such a system was set in motion it acquired its own internal dynamic, as other factories attempted to follow suit, even if they were not so financially powerful. This kind of 'stock-jobbing', although never reaching the heights it acquired during the 1930s, nevertheless gave the wages system its apparently patch-work and haphazard appearance, an appearance that was exacerbated by the structural rigidities of the system and the reform's own internal inconsistencies.

2. Violations of wages and norm-setting regulations

The wage reform, at least in its early stages, led to a fall in earnings for considerable groups of workers, usually those who, under the old system, had had their earnings propped up by low norms or other devices which had now been eliminated. At the Kalibr instrument factory in Moscow, for example, the experimental wage reform reduced the wages of transporters and electric-trolley operators by about 10 per cent.[64] The earnings of sharpeners in the tool shop of the Dmitrov milling-machine factory suffered an even sharper drop.[65] A similar fate befell auxiliary workers in the non-ferrous metallurgy plants of Sverdlovsk *sovnarkhoz* and quarry workers at the Minsk reinforced-concrete products factory.[66] In addition, we have already noted the pressure that machine operators were under due to regrading, as well as the fact that for industry as a whole wages failed to keep pace with productivity.

These trends, which resulted from the implementation of the reform itself, were in places exacerbated by managers who used the reform as a pretext to slash wages. Building-site managers in Gor'kii were setting maximum bonuses below the levels stipulated by bonus regulations.[67] In the chemical industry, bonus regulations made it clear that managers could hold back bonuses only for failure to meet specified quality indicators. Despite this, workers found themselves losing their bonuses for a host of real or alleged infractions that had nothing to do with product quality (for example, discipline violations or ignoring safety procedures), or even without any explanation at all.[68] Similar violations of bonus rules were reported in iron and steel, non-ferrous metals, and woodworking.[69] Wages were cut in other ways as well. The manager of an asphalt and concrete factory in the Donbass received eight months' corrective labour for imposing forced overtime on his workers without so much as offering them time off in compensation.[70] In other cases managers 'implemented' the wage reform by imposing norm rises that even the regime considered unjustifiably high, by pushing as many workers as they could into low skill grades, or by delaying paying workers their wages.[71]

Abuses such as these cannot simply be attributed to the capriciousness of individual managers. The pressures which, as we shall presently describe, forced managers to manipulate wages and norms in order to preserve the earnings of individual groups of workers could, in other enterprises, operating under different conditions and constraints, push management in the other direction. If, for example, an enterprise or its *sovnarkhoz* failed to obtain a generous wage fund or to make the new investments needed to meet plans for productivity improvements, then economies would have to be made by cutting rates, trimming bonuses, or resorting to unpaid overtime.[72] Sometimes management found itself in the position of having to jeopardize the earnings of one set of workers in order to protect a group it considered more important.[73] The bureaucratic nature of the system also deprived workers of money they had legitimately earned.[74]

In the main, however, the reform confronted managers with a need to maintain or even push up earnings, both directly through wage and bonus payments, and indirectly through low norms. Despite overall adherence to the wages plan and the slow rise in wages relative to productivity, *within* these global figures managers had considerable room for manoeuvre. The need to retain this kind of flexibility was vital in a work environment where managers had only limited control over workers' behaviour and required their cooperation at key junctures in the production cycle.[75]

We have already noted how managers raised the wages of various groups of auxiliary and time workers by paying them the basic wage for piece workers or for workers with unpleasant or dangerous conditions. There were, however, many other devices which managers could use. In engineering, assemblers (as opposed to machine-tool operators) were compensated for the lower skill grades imposed by the wage reform, by being put on jobs rated – and paid – at a higher grade.[76] The stress which the reform placed on bonus systems also made these an easy loophole. In coal-mining, the tying of bonuses to fulfilment or overfulfilment of production plans, as opposed to norms, meant that workers could underfulfil their norms and still retain high earnings via their plan-fulfilment bonuses. This was more than just a hypothetical possibility: throughout the coal industry, pit managers met production targets not by improving individual output, but simply by taking on additional workers. In this way, norms became separated from the key determinant of additional earnings and lost much of their coercive force.[77] This was especially important in an industry where traditionally large numbers of workers underfulfilled their norms, since it allowed them to protect their earnings even when production difficulties (or lack of effort) made high norm fulfilment impossible.

In other industries, managers routinely paid bonuses for indicators other than those stipulated in the bonus regulations. This is well illustrated by the experience of the chemical industry, which is worth describing in detail because it covers virtually all of the abuses reported in other industries.

1   Quality bonuses, which were to be paid only if workers achieved better results than stipulated in the plan, were awarded simply for meeting planned levels.
2   Regulations also stated that production workers were to receive quality bonuses only if they simultaneously fulfilled their production plan – yet this, too, was ignored at major factories.
3   The Leningrad pharmaceutical factory also paid many of its piece workers bonuses for fulfilling and overfulfilling their norms,

despite the fact that this practice was expressly forbidden throughout the chemical industry (except for certain workers in synthetic fibres).

4   Workers were paid bonuses in excess of the maximum allowed (15 to 20 per cent of the basic wage).

5   Auxiliary workers were to receive quality bonuses only if the shift, section, shop, or equipment they served met its plan, but were not to receive plan-fulfilment bonuses *per se*, on the grounds that their work did not directly influence the magnitude of production. Nevertheless, such workers as store-room attendants, cleaners, and loaders were paid bonuses for plan fulfilment.

6   Bonuses for economizing on materials were paid irrespective of the size of the economies achieved, so that workers at one particular plant actually received higher economy bonuses one year than they had the year before, when savings had been three times as large.

7   Workers were paid bonuses for such vague criteria as working 'well' or 'excellently', without any definition of what constituted 'good' or 'excellent' work.[78]

Payments for work not performed (*pripiski*), or for stoppages or defective work in excess of permitted levels had been common devices for increasing workers' earnings in the 1930s and post-war periods, and they remained so after the wage reform. They were most common in coal-mining and construction where, due to the nature of work under Soviet conditions, stoppages (against which workers' earnings had to be protected) were a frequent occurrence, and falsification of work results was not difficult. Stoppages – for which workers were to receive reduced pay, even if the interruption was not their fault – were routinely paid in construction at the full rate, as work properly carried out. Similarly, building workers were paid for redoing or rectifying poorly done work (which should have been unpaid), as well as for work they had not actually performed.[79] In coal-mining, some managers rewarded workers who agreed to help clear out backlogs or who overfulfilled their production targets not with money, but with alcohol – to the great consternation of the regime.[80] Other methods, in addition to *pripiski*, were found to raise wages in the coal industry, especially those of younger or less skilled workers. Miners in lower-skill grades would be included in the integrated brigades of skilled workers, and thus be paid at the higher prevailing rate. New, untrained workers, who according to regulations were to be paid at a lower rate during their training period, were instead paid the full wage reserved for skilled and more experienced workers.[81] This particular abuse of wage regulations must certainly have been in response to high turnover among young, low-paid miners.[82] However, such payments were made in other industries too. At the Second State Ball Bearing Factory in Moscow workers were granted special payments to compensate for production time lost carting boxes of parts over to the workbench.[83]

For piece workers, earnings could also be controlled through the use of low norms. Although the magnitude by which norms could be manipulated clearly shrank in the wake of the norm rises and falling norm fulfilment imposed by the wage reform, this still played an important role in protecting the earnings of individual groups of workers.

During the early years of the wage reform in coal-mining, workers on direct piece-rates at a number of mines were able substantially to boost their earnings because their norms were being kept down, sometimes at levels below those prevailing before the war – a move which managers in some coal-fields again justified as necessary to cut turnover.[84] In iron and steel, engineering, and the cement industry, managers used low norms to compensate workers for heavy or dangerous work when stipulated wage rates failed to create an adequate differential.[85] Low norms were also employed to compensate workers for lost earnings. Factories producing reinforced concrete products in Sverdlovsk *sovnarkhoz* found that wage rates and bonuses specified by the reform were too low to allow workers to retain their customary earnings, and so made up for this by deferring the application of technically based norms.[86] In some cases, norm-setters deliberately set norms low enough to make sure that workers retained their customary earnings.[87] At one iron and steel works in Sverdlovsk, shop management carefully regulated the recording of norm fulfilment: if actual fulfilment was too low, they bumped it up to protect earnings; if management considered fulfilment to be too high, they understated it, on the grounds that consistently elevated fulfilment figures might prompt norm-setters to raise the norms. Job sheets recording norm fulfilment were actually filled out before the end of a shift.[88]

In general, the new procedures providing for decentralized norm-setting allowed many managers simply to fail to revise norms at regular intervals or in line with technical improvements.[89] Managers at a number of engineering factories merely raised norms in proportion to the rise in the basic wage,[90] thus creating the appearance of applying the wage reform without putting any pressure on earnings. Other enterprises used outdated norm-setting handbooks.[91] Another device was for managers to accumulate minor technical improvements which, on their own, were too small to warrant norm rises, but which, when accumulated over time, made norm fulfilment far easier.[92] Managers also made use of regulations allowing them to introduce lower, temporary norms on new products or processes. These were permitted for a period of up to three months while the enterprise and its workers overcame teething difficulties. At the end of this time, managers either failed to raise the norms or set them at levels below what was actually being achieved.[93]

Yet such ruses were not always necessary. Managers, whether it be at highest or lowest level, in many cases simply refused to raise their norms. In doing so they had on occasion the cooperation of the trade unions, whose refusal to sanction norm rises could either have been genuine or simply a pretext behind which managers could justify their own inaction.[94] On the whole, norm revisions were a time-consuming, cumbersome exercise,[95] and those enterprises or shops which could meet their production plans without introducing technical improvements or raising norms opted to do so.[96]

The end result was that enterprises could claim to be carrying out the letter of the wage reform by having a high percentage of 'technically based' norms, while the norms themselves were relatively easy to fulfil. In April 1963 engineering factories in Estonia could report from half to three-quarters of their norms as 'technically based', while at least a third (and often more) of their workers were fulfilling their norms by 150 per cent or more.[97] Throughout engineering generally, norm fulfilment soon began creeping up after an initial fall at the start of the reform, with many factories achieving *average* fulfilment of 140 to 150 per cent.[98] Even individual enterprises in the iron and steel and building materials industries were able to go against the general trend of lower norm fulfilment by failing to revise norms in line with technical advances.[99]

To try to counter this general trend, the regime in 1962 launched a campaign to persuade workers to police their own norms.[100] Eventually this became crystallized in the formation of so-called Public Norm-Setting Bureaux. In theory, the aim of these Bureaux was to enlist the views of both activists and rank-and-file workers on which norms had become outdated and how production could best be organized to allow them to be raised. We can be sure that, although they may have enlisted the enthusiasm of some sections of the workforce, they were by and large well-orchestrated affairs, engineered by party, trade

union, and management officials. Their justification was that they
were a more democratic form of raising norms, in contrast to managers
who abused norm-setting regulations and set norms without consulting the trade unions.[101] Despite the alleged success of the Bureaux,
press accounts make it clear that their achievements were modest, at
best. The entire Upper Volga *sovnarkhoz* recorded a mere 281 Bureaux
by the end of 1964.[102] Considering that each factory was to have
several Bureaux, this indicates that the number of enterprises claiming
them was relatively limited. Even then, their existence was often only
on paper. At the turbine-motor factory in Sverdlovsk there were 19
Bureaux involving just 246 people, which is an indication of how little
rank-and-file workers were willing to participate in them. By the
factory's admission, the Bureaux did little of practical importance.[103]
This was built into the norm-setting procedures. There were simply
too many norms for the permanent members of the Bureaux to keep
track of.[104] The Bureaux also clearly did not always know what they
were doing, and were accused of setting rates too high for less skilled
workers to cope with.[105] The main value of the Bureaux, however, was
very likely not as a vehicle for regulating wages directly – it would
have been unrealistic to expect them to be able to manage a task which
norm-setters found overwhelming – but as another form of 'mobilization'. In this they were consistent with other campaigns during
de-Stalinization designed to co-opt rank-and-file workers and to foster
the illusion that they were now co-managers of the economy and
society along with the ruling elite. In this case, however, the regime
was probably overambitious. Workers were unlikely to participate
willingly in attempts to increase the intensity of labour and put
pressure on their own earnings when they had such a clear interest in
keeping norms as low and as manageable as possible.

3. Dysfunctional bonus systems

One of the central strategies behind the wage reform was to
give greater weight to bonus payments for plan fulfilment and quality
indicators, so as to relieve pressures on managers to circumvent wage
regulations. In practice, the bonus rules themselves were easily
abused. As Kirsch has noted, workers came to see the bonuses as a
stable component of wages, guaranteeing their earnings.[106] We have
already seen how managers manipulated bonuses by paying them for
a far wider array of criteria than those specified by the regulations. Yet
at the same time, and partially undermining the use of bonuses to

ensure earnings, the bonuses actually paid for specific criteria the regime wished to encourage – namely, quality, economizing on the consumption of materials, and adherence to technical procedures – were too small to offer adequate incentives.

Here their effectiveness was further undermined by the need for managers to regulate earnings in order to avoid disputes. One construction trust in Tula *oblast'* vastly expanded the list of workers eligible to receive bonuses because management feared discontent if it awarded them only to the 'best' workers. The result was that no one received a bonus large enough for it to serve as any kind of incentive.[107] In some cases, a clear conflict arose between workers and managers, whose bonuses were both paid out of the same wages fund. In construction, new regulations governing payments for on-schedule completion of building projects provoked workers' complaints that the lion's share of the bonuses were being gobbled up by top management, leaving only a pittance for the workers themselves.[108]

In 1961, bonuses amounted to a mere 6 per cent of piece-earnings.[109] In engineering, the introduction of more rigid, technically based norms (at least where such norms were actually imposed) tended to nullify the impact of bonuses awarded to workers who overfulfilled them. In theory these bonuses could rise to a maximum of 25 per cent of piece-earnings, but in practice they amounted to no more than 2 to 4 per cent, a level so low that regulations governing them had to be revised in 1964.[110] At many enterprises, bonus funds for both quantitative and quality indicators either did not exist or were trivially small, in some cases (as in chemicals) because *sovnarkhozy* did not grant these enterprises enough funds to pay bonuses at the levels set down in official regulations.[111]

Low bonuses for meeting various quality indicators were a particular problem in precisely those industries where they were deemed most important. In the chemical industry, where adherence to technical procedures was essential to achieving high-quality output, managers consistently ignored them. In the aniline dye and rubber and asbestos branches of the industry, for example, materials made up some 75 to 80 per cent of production costs, yet bonuses for economizing on their consumption were not widely applied.[112] In iron and steel, managers had the right to pay bonuses for quality indicators *instead of* plan fulfilment in sections where quality was deemed especially important; but regulations set these bonuses at only half of what workers received for meeting or exceeding the plan, and so managers did not use them.[113]

Individual enterprises in a number of industries tried to deal with these limitations by tying bonuses for plan fulfilment to the simultaneous reduction of defective or poor-grade output. Among the enterprises where such schemes were tried were two Urals engineering works, the Tambov automobile and tractor parts factory, the Serp i molot and Elektrostal' iron and steel works, the Gigant and Sebryakovskii cement factories, and the textile enterprises of Kalinin *sovnarkhoz*. Virtually all these enterprises claimed that the change led to lower defective output. Given its punitive nature, however, and the fact that the one enterprise which revealed its effect on earnings (Elektrostal') admitted that a large proportion of workers lost money as a result, we can be sceptical as to how widespread this system became.[114]

Conclusion

The essential feature of the wage reform's implementation was the acceptance by management that earnings must not fall below 'established' levels – that is, those levels which had prevailed before the reform or had come to be expected as normal over the ensuing years. Officially the reform itself stipulated this condition insofar as the average wage within each industry was concerned, but the regime openly conceded that individual groups of workers whose earnings were deemed to have been 'artificially' high would see their wages fall. Even if this had not been official policy, the fact was that the inherited wages system was a patchwork of locally established norm-setting practices, differentials, and devices for compensating individual groups of workers for difficulties imposed by the punitive nature of official wages policy or by the production chaos of Soviet industry. These local practices had led to a dizzying array of local anomalies and disparities between workers which effaced officially prescribed differentials based on skill, favoured trades (piece versus time workers, production versus auxiliary workers), and working conditions (so-called 'hot', heavy, or dangerous jobs versus those performed in normal conditions). Under these circumstances, to regularize the wages system and re-establish coherent incentives necessarily implied that some groups of workers who had benefited under the old system – or, as in the case of workers in less favoured industries or trades, at least were protected by it – would suffer, either absolutely or relative to other groups.

As neither the workforce nor management were willing to accept this situation, implementation, while achieving some of the regime's objectives and doing away with some of the more bizarre distortions of the pre-reform period, merely recreated others. Insofar as the regime was able to use the reform to contain the growth of average earnings, this came at considerable cost, and helped to undermine attempts to develop an effective system of incentives. Attempts to de-emphasize the role of payments for norm overfulfilment – which had forced managers to hold norms down – and replace these with bonuses for fulfilling or overfulfilling the plan, for economizing on the consumption of materials, and for achieving better quality merely led management to manipulate payments for these criteria instead. Efforts to do away with some of the worst excesses of the piece-rate system, by shifting on to time-rates workers whose jobs depended on precision rather than gross output or speed, ended up cutting earnings of many former piece workers, who then had to be compensated through various devices (fictitious piece-rates, overgenerous bonuses, regrading into higher skill grades, and so on). It is also worth bearing in mind that by raising the share of the basic wage in overall earnings – which was supposed to eliminate the need for workers and managers to circumvent wages policies – the regime merely restored them to the level prevailing in the 1930s, when such circumvention was just as widespread as after the war. Where workers were unable to protect themselves adequately from the effects of the reform, as in engineering, their resulting dissatisfaction caused severe difficulties within production which were eased only when Khrushchev's successors relaxed controls over earnings. Looking at the reform as a whole, we can see that, as under Stalin, each set of restrictions and regulations prompted attempts by workers (and managers eager to retain these workers' cooperation) to find new ways around the system. There were, of course, more vulnerable groups of workers – primarily women – less able to defend themselves in this way, and it was probably largely at their expense that both management and the regime were able to tolerate violations of the regulations by others.

If the wage reform failed in its main objective – to create a stable and predictable system of incentives – its causes lie not simply in the wages system itself, but in the wider problems of Soviet production and the pattern of manager–worker relations and concessions that are an essential part of it. The question of whether or not a worker met her or his norms or whatever other criteria the regime may have wished to impose depended on a host of variables over which the workers themselves often had no control: the irregular availability of supplies, their uncertain quality, the uneven mechanization of the different stages of production, and the often irrational division of labour within the Soviet factory. These various problems, singly or in concert with others, led to substantial losses of work time (in the order of 15 to 25 per cent), which in turn jeopardized workers' abilities to meet norms and plan targets. Similarly, the quality of materials and equipment could make the fulfilment of different quality indicators a purely random occurrence. In construction, illegal extra payments (*pripiski*) were regularly paid out to compensate workers for disruptions to production, and it is in fact their prevalence which made it so difficult to extend bonus systems and contract payments into that industry.[115]

Industry's almost permanent dependence on storming equally threw up a number of issues which by necessity could be resolved only outside officially prescribed wages regulations: forced overtime, how it was to be compensated, and even bribes or palm-greasing (*namazki*) which had to be paid to induce workers to agree to meet the plan on time.[116] The threat which storming posed to earnings should not be underestimated. In one shop of Leningrad's Krasnyi vyborzhets engineering works, disputes were reported to have broken out between brigades over which ones would be allowed to make use of late-arriving components.[117] It is not surprising that tempers should flare in such a situation, since the brigade which lost out would be forced to stand idle, with a subsequent loss of earnings – unless, that is, management should intervene with some other form of compensation. By the same token, the impact of uncertainties on earnings made both workers and managers reluctant to adopt even simple measures that might have improved coordination.[118]

If the reform could not digest the uncertainties and irregularities imposed on each enterprise from outside, it equally failed to help break down the considerable degree of control that workers exercised over the labour process and the work routine *within* production. In the 1930s the regime had tried – without success – to use shock work and Stakhanovism to coerce workers into ceding this one area of freedom. The wage reform attempted to achieve the same end through more pacific means, via what it thought would be a tightly structured system of sanctions and incentives. It, too, achieved little in this regard, because it was precisely this control that helped create the conditions which might have jeopardized earnings, thus requiring managerial intervention to maintain them at 'established' levels.

An analysis of the wage reform cannot, therefore, stand in isolation, but must be placed within the larger context of the Soviet labour process as a whole.

Part II

De-Stalinization and the Soviet labour process

5   The historical genesis of the Soviet labour process

In the introduction it was argued that one of the central contradictions facing the Soviet elite in the Khrushchev period was that, to effect any substantive rejuvenation of the economy, it had to restructure the labour process, yet it proved unable to develop any coherent strategy for accomplishing this task. Instead, as has been shown in Part I, the main areas of labour policy attempted to impose changes on worker behaviour indirectly, by enhancing the elite's control over labour mobility and the incentives system. By failing to come to grips with the problem of the labour process, however, its success in these other spheres remained extremely limited. What control it did gain, for example over general levels of wage-spending and the imposition of tighter norms for production workers in engineering, caused so much knock-on disruption in the rest of the economy that these policies had to be rescinded by Khrushchev's successors.

On this analysis it might seem that, had the elite mounted a head-on confrontation with both managers and workers over the question of control of the labour process, it might have been able to achieve the restructuring it required and to enhance its control over the surplus. Such a conclusion would, in my view, be wrong. From a strictly empirical standpoint, during the 1930s the Stalinist elite was constantly at war with the working class over the labour process. The mass campaigns of shock work, and even more so Stakhanovism, were designed precisely to resolve this issue, and yet they failed to bring about the changes that were intended. Workers and managers each found ways to get around the pressures these campaigns imposed. More basically, the actual nature of the Soviet labour process makes it impermeable to reform within the bounds of the property relations of the Soviet system. These of necessity introduce so many uncertainties into the production process that it both enables and requires the individual worker to exercise substantial control over her or his labour. Such control becomes inseparable from the essence of the system itself, so that it cannot be broken short of undermining the overall fabric of production relations.

In this chapter I shall analyse the historical determinants of the Soviet labour process and define its underlying contradictions. This forms the theoretical basis of the rest of the discussion in Part II, which is devoted to an analysis of the morphology and dynamics of the labour process as it emerged in the Khrushchev period. I shall concentrate on three themes. Chapter 6 analyses the problem of surplus extraction, dealing with two central issues: control over the use of work time, and the problem of waste, that is, the tendency within the Soviet system for growth to be self-negating through physical losses, the need to rectify defective or deformed products, and the over-consumption of labour power and means of production in the course of production. Chapter 7 examines the special position of women workers in the Soviet economy, and argues that in female-dominated trades and industries the elite had greater control over surplus extraction, which gave it some leeway to tolerate its relative loss of control among what it deemed to be more strategic sections of the workforce (primarily skilled, male workers in heavy industry). Finally, chapter 8 takes up the problem of de-skilling in Soviet industry, and relates this to the broader international debates over de-skilling and decision-making within the labour process under capitalism.

Theoretical analysis of the Soviet labour process

My theoretical starting point is that the Soviet Union is a 'class' society, whose reproduction is based on exploitation. There is a ruling stratum, an elite, based in the bureaucracy, but not coterminous with it (since the bureaucracy is far larger than the ruling group), which extracts a surplus product from a workforce. I refrain from labelling these groups a ruling class and a working class because, in my view, the Soviet Union does not represent a stable mode of production, but rather a historically unstable social formation that is neither capitalist nor socialist, and as such has no effective regulator either of the economy or of the reproduction of its social structure.[1] The system evolved in this form precisely because the emerging bureaucratic elite was unable to consolidate its position as a ruling group through market relations. Thus the spontaneous, although crisis-ridden regulation of the economy through the law of value was eliminated as a historical possibility. Socialism, by which I mean the democratic, collective control of society over its development, was also excluded, since this would have meant the liquidation of the elite in favour of working-class power.[2] Rather, the Soviet elite has attempted to regulate the economy through the nominal process of planning, but here, too, the results have been unstable and highly contradictory, in the last instance because of the absence of democracy in the society.

Without society's collective determination of priorities, assessment of resources, and decision-making on how policies are to be fulfilled, planning cannot succeed. Indeed, as I have argued extensively in an earlier work,[3] it is impossible to call such a system planning in any meaningful sense of the word. Planning must be based on calculation, which in turn presupposes accurate knowledge. The results of the plan must conform more or less closely to the designs and intentions of the planners, who, in turn, must have a reasonable knowledge of how the economy works, what its resources are, and *the ability and willingness of the implementers to carry out the plans*. This cannot happen if, as in the Soviet case, the implementers falsify the information they transmit to the planners by hiding capacities or reporting fictitious results. More basically, it cannot happen if the conditions of production are so unstable that the results deviate substantially from what was intended because supplies are irregular; parts, tools, and materials fail to meet required specifications; or there are widespread defects in finished output. The problem is not just the scale on which such disruptions occur, but the fact that their extent and location are essentially unpredictable, and therefore cannot be anticipated and compensated for when drawing up the plan. Under these circumstances, accurate calculation becomes impossible. In the end the epistemological basis to planning can be assured only if the planners and the implementers are the same people, that is, if the society is socialist and democratic, for only then is the incentive to distort instructions or falsify results reduced to a marginal factor.

The emergence and evolution of the Stalinist system must be viewed historically, as the unstable outcome of the class conflicts which took place in the Soviet Union during the decade following the October Revolution. The Bolsheviks had emerged victorious from the Civil War, but the cost of their victory had been high. Already a poor, overwhelmingly peasant country before the outbreak of World War I, that war and the attempted counter-revolution which followed it, left the Soviet state in a precarious economic and political position. Its industrial plant and equipment had been badly run down, and the already small working class underwent a partial disintegration, as large numbers of workers responded to the dire conditions in the towns by returning to the countryside. Internationally, the failure of the German revolutions in 1919 and 1923 had left the Bolsheviks isolated. This isolation was reproduced inside the country, as the Bolsheviks, uncertain about the security of their political position, banned the Left Mensheviks and Left Socialist Revolutionaries after the Civil War. The resulting political monopoly of power in a poor country, forced to seek a non-capitalist path of development using its own meagre resources, had disastrous results. The adoption of the New Economic Policy in 1921 had been a matter of political and economic necessity, because without the restoration of a market it was impossible to re-establish viable trade relations between the town and country. But the market, especially in the context of a one-party state, meant that from the very beginning a privileged bureaucratic stratum arose whose members became conscious of their own individual and group interests, which were tied to their functions as administrators of the state and managers of the economy.

It was this group that Stalin represented in his ascendancy to power. The economy confronted a serious crisis at the end of the 1920s, as the peasants began withholding grain from the market at a time when resources were needed for the regime's belated plans for industrial expansion. The young bureaucratic elite had to resolve this crisis in a way that would still preserve its power and privileges. This meant that further concessions to the peasantry and the extension of market relations were excluded. Equally, there was no question of ceding power to the working class – a prerequisite of a socialist solution to the problem – even if the working class, already demoralized by NEP and the systematic political bureaucratization of the society, had been prepared to challenge the elite for power. The elite, therefore, could consolidate its position only by attempting to create a system that was neither capitalist nor socialist, but which was organized around the elite's bureaucratic and political administration of the society. What the elite had not anticipated was the violence of the peasantry's reaction to collectivation and, to a lesser extent, of the working class's resistance to the pressures of forced industrialization, both of which it had to suppress by force.

The elite's attempts to run the economy through planning, therefore, never evolved past the stage of bureaucratic administration and organization. Real plans were impossible, because the elite, which was itself only taking shape as a coherent social stratum, was in a state of effective class conflict with the rest of society. The only method by which it could consolidate its rule was the use of brutal force and the political atomisation of all potential opposition. This meant not just the atomization of workers and peasants, but of all prospective opponents, including those within the elite itself. No one, except perhaps Stalin's innermost circle, could function or organize themselves collectively. People could operate only as atomized individuals. This does not mean that at the workplace workers did not exercise some forms of collective solidarity with one another in their bargaining relationships with management, or that managers did not press their interests as a group when seeking resources or defending their economic position through their various ministries. It does mean that, at a political level, collective action and even collective discussion and deliberation of problems was impossible. Under Stalin the penalties for miscalculation in this area were long-term imprisonment or death. Even after Stalin, open dissent still landed one in a labour camp. What this meant, however, is that, without the spontaneous regulation of the market, or the collective regulation of the economy through democratic planning, the elite could establish and maintain the underlying economic relationships of exploitation and surplus extraction only through its political control of the state. However, this political control proved incapable of establishing a system of production which could automatically reproduce itself without the maintenance of the political superstructure. There is a definable pattern of the reproduction of social and production relations within Soviet society, to be sure, but the system they reproduce is so unstable that without the elite's ongoing political domination the economic relations would begin to unwind – as evidenced by the current moves towards market reforms.[4]

The result of this system is that economic and political life in the Soviet Union became characterized by an extreme individualism, for it was only as individuals, or (as is the case on the shop floor) as relatively small groups of individuals, that people could function. Other avenues of response were closed off. This is the essential feature governing relations between planners, industrial managers, and workers. Each was compelled to articulate and pursue her or his personal interest within the bounds set by the bureaucratic system. This, in turn, created an economy driven and reproduced by a large degree of spontaneity and anarchy, within a superficially 'planned' integument. No other result was possible, because of the social antagonisms that exist between the elite and those whom it attempts to govern. Similarly deep antagonisms exist under capitalism, as well, but there the market acts as a disciplining agent, against both capitalists and workers. A firm can go bankrupt or be taken over; workers can be thrown out of their jobs. But in the absence of a market in the Soviet Union, the elite had no means to compel the implementers of its plans and instructions to carry them out. Even the terror of the 1930s was unsustainable over a long period, and did extreme damage to the economy. More to the point, the terror had only limited effect on actual workers, even after the war. It could atomize the society and keep it politically quiescent, but it could not control people's behaviour at the workplace.

From the very beginnings of the five-year plans, people – managers and workers alike – constantly bent and deformed the plans to meet their own needs and requirements. The plans themselves incorporated and reflected the outcome of intense political competition between ministries, each anxious to bolster its economic importance through the acquisition of greater resources (generally at the expense of other sectors of the economy).[5] The distortions which resulted then presented themselves as an objective circumstance, defining the environment within which planners, ministry officials, managers, and workers all had to operate and survive. This gave rise to very definite social relations within production. It is only through these relations that planners, managers, and workers could attempt to pursue their individual interests, and their actions and counter-actions then became the mechanism through which those relationships were reproduced.

This has long been illustrated concretely through the positions of the planning bureaucracy and industrial managers. As a group, managers formed part of the ruling elite, and their privileged position was absolutely tied to the perpetuation of the existing social structure. Yet, as individuals, they were compelled constantly to take actions which circumvented or subverted the instructions of the central authorities, in order to ensure both their own advancement and the practical fulfilment of their plans. One part of the elite was therefore in perpetual conflict with another. The central planning agencies compiled and issued instructions (already distorted by bureaucratic competition). Managers, on the other hand, sought to keep their plans low and relatively easy to fulfil, all while creating the appearance that they were working at near full capacity (lest too much success led to plans being raised). They consistently understated capacities and applied for greater resources of investment and labour power. Thus the information which the planners used to calculate their plans was always falsified. But the falsification had other, deeper roots. In a situation of constant shortage and scarcity – a phenomenon whose historical genesis also lies in the nature of Stalinist industrialization – managers had consistently to deviate from supply and output plans. They by-passed official supply channels and entered into informal bargaining arrangements with other managers. They altered their product-mix, partly so that it would conform to the supplies they actually had on hand, and partly so that they could concentrate production on those items that would make their fulfilment figures look most impressive. For that was the only way to get ahead in the system: achieve good plan results and win promotion. The end consequence, however, was that the planners never actually knew what was being produced or where any given set of products was in the circulation network. The plans became a fiction because what was actually produced and put into circulation had only an approximate resemblance in both quantity and quality to what had been planned for.

What I attempted to do in my study of the 1930s, and here, is to take this analysis to a more basic level, and locate the roots of this system in the relations between the elite and the workforce and between the workforce and management within production. For managers do not operate in isolation, or simply in terms of their relationship with other sections of the elite. The most essential relationship in the society was and remains that between the elite as expropriator of the surplus product and the workforce which creates that product. The elite's relationship with the workforce was essentially unstable, reflecting the inherent instability of the Soviet system of production. At a general level, the elite–workforce relationship was reproduced in a fashion similar to that between capitalists and workers under capitalism. The elite controlled the means of production, while the worker controlled only her or his labour power. The latter was put at the disposal of the elite through a transaction that was partly one of buyer and seller and partly based on direct coercion. The worker applied labour to the means of production and the elite appropriated the surplus product, using the necessary product to replace worn-out means of production and to pay wages to the workers, so that the latter could acquire means of subsistence and renew their ability to provide labour power in the future. At the end of the production period, the worker had once again to 'sell' her or his labour power to the elite, because she or he had no other means of survival; for its part, the elite had to re-engage the worker who alone could produce the surplus product on which the elite survived. At a deeper level, however, unlike the capitalist, the elite had no direct relationship with the workforce, and had no means of establishing one. Its relationship was primarily mediated through the shop-floor relations between workers and management, with a corresponding loss of control over the labour process and work discipline, and ultimately over its ability to expropriate and dispose of the surplus product. In this sense, regime labour policy, even in the 1930s, was always dependent on management's willingness or ability to enforce it. Management for its part found (far more than industrial managers do under capitalism) that it had constantly to adapt its demands and behaviour to the particular work practices that workers had built up and defended on the shop floor.

Here the historically specific nature of the Soviet workforce is crucial. The elite was able to consolidate its position by atomizing real and potential opposition. Where the working class was concerned, this meant breaking down its collective traditions and suppressing all forms of collective protest. Strikes and mass protests, which were common right up to 1934, were put down and organizers arrested. More important, the working class's ability to organize itself collectively, even within a single workplace, was severely undermined by a combination of factors. Political demoralization, already fostered by the growing bureaucratism of the Bolshevik Party in the 1920s, deepened. Factory meetings were rigged, and workers soon lost any hope that they could voice their criticisms of official policy, much less force any changes. The trade unions gave up any semblance of defending even basic working conditions, and became conduits of government policy to increase production. At the same time, the standard of living was falling precipitously due to the catastrophe of collectivization. The struggle for individual or family survival soon began to take precedence over concern with collective discussion and action. This latter process was in turn buttressed by the shock-work system and the extensive individualization of the labour process. Work quotas were constantly raised and wage rates lowered, making it hard for workers to eke out even a basic existence unless they overfulfilled their norms. The production records of shock workers were used as a basis of general norm rises, and rank-and-file workers were in many cases compelled to try to keep up with the shock workers just to sustain their earnings. At the same time, the privileges granted to shock workers, and the upward mobility such workers could enjoy, further divided the ranks of the workforce and undermined its internal cohesion. Within production, the stress on individual record-breaking was combined with a fractionation of the division of labour, with most workers being paid on piece-rates and put to work on relatively minute, repetitive tasks. This, too, had an enervating effect on solidarity. A further factor was the huge changes in the social composition of the workforce. Millions of peasants were brought into production who had little experience of industrial life. Had they found there a strong culture of working-class organization, no doubt they would soon have integrated into those traditions, but what they found instead was an experienced workforce already in the process of atomization, who were increasingly replacing collective defences of their needs and interests with individualistic actions like absenteeism, insubordination, frequent job-changing, and drunkenness. The influx of peasants strongly bolstered this process, although it must be kept in mind that the new workers, when they adopted individual responses, were behaving perfectly rationally given the limited range of options available.[6]

In this environment, workers soon found that the only room for manoeuvre open to them was to attempt to exercise control over the immediate work situation. This meant not simply high absenteeism or labour turnover, but more importantly the reappropriation of partial control over the labour process itself. Workers were aided in this by the very methods of Stalinist industrialization which, on the one hand, created a severe labour shortage (which meant that managers were soon deprived of effective sanctions against recalcitrant workers), and, on the other hand, undermined and violated basic coordination between sectors of the economy. Scarcity, irregular supplies, frequent plan changes, poor-quality materials and components became the standard conditions in which enterprises had to work. In such an environment, once the pressures of the first breakneck years of industrialization had subsided, workers found it both necessary and relatively easy to exercise control over work speeds, the intensity of their labour, and the quality of their work. The regime's policy of individualizing the work process as a means of *politically* controlling the working class strengthened this tendency. The pressure on each worker, each shop, and each enterprise to concentrate on individual output records further wore away the foundations of economic coordination. Too many of one item would be produced alongside too few of another, with no regard for integration. Similarly, quantitative records took precedence over quality, so that masses of goods might be produced which either could not be used or which demanded the considerable additional expenditure of labour time and materials remaking or adapting them to a usable form. Production became inordinately wasteful.

If this was the historical genesis of the system, once in place it confronted each individual worker and manager as an externally given, objective world within which they had to learn to function. Since neither managers nor workers could collectively exercise any effective control over the system, they had to respond as individuals. This does not mean that they operated as isolated, autonomous units. Rather, managers (both at higher echelons and on the shop floor) and workers entered into quite specific relations with each other, but these relations were structured by the seemingly alien and out-of-control work environment and by the narrow range of responses open to each. For managers, the fundamental drive was quite transparent: how to maximize the gap between perceived capacities and perform-ance results. What was important was the difference between the two magnitudes, and not absolute plan fulfilment in and of itself. For too low a plan and too high a level of overfulfilment would lead only to a higher plan in the next period which might not be realized. The problem was how to achieve these results under such highly unstable conditions. In a world where most things are out of control, people attempt to regain control by influencing what factors they can. For Soviet managers this meant – and still means – trying above all to establish stability wherever possible – trying to retard the introduction of new technology, because output will fall during settling-in periods and eventually plans will be raised; within the gross plan, ignoring the planned product-mix and concentrating on those items easiest to produce or which show the best indicators (heavy parts if the plan is in tons; large numbers of easy-to-manufacture items if the plan is by number of pieces); by-passing established supply channels if neces-sary, in order to guarantee supplies; and perhaps ultimately most important of all, working out a *modus operandi* with the workforce, to reduce the destabilizing effects of externally given problems and of the workers' own behaviour.

From the workers' point of view, the problem was twofold: first, how to cope with the internal chaos of the workshop (lack of supplies and tools, poor-quality materials and components), and secondly, how to ease the strains imposed by the central authorities and/or manage-ment. Sometimes the two aims were in conflict with each other: if the production programme fell too far behind, it meant overtime and storming (the break-neck attempt to clear out backlogs at the end of the month, quarter, or year), which were unpopular but unavoidable. At other times they were mutually compatible or self-reinforcing. Where possible the worker tried to slow down the pace of work, largely by controlling aspects of work organization which, in a smoothly running system, would have been the prerogative of management but, in the Soviet system, only the worker could affect. This was easiest in manual jobs, where the worker could simply work more slowly. But even for workers on assembly lines or machine production, the myriad of interruptions – waiting for supplies or a crane, having to leave the workbench to hunt down tools or parts in the store-room, or taking advantage of the long queues in the dining room to extend the dinner break – all allowed workers to shorten the effective working day and place definite limits on the elite's ability to extract a surplus.

Because of the continuing labour shortage, it was difficult for managers to break this system. Rather, they had to adapt to it. In the main they had no choice but to cede to workers considerable control over the work process, because they needed their cooperation not to make matters worse, to help rectify various disruptions to the work routine, or to agree to overtime and storming. If earnings suffered, either because of external circumstances or because workers simply had not produced enough to make their customary wage, managers were generally willing to allow various fiddles so that pay packets did not suffer. If discipline was lax but the worker or workers involved were too important to dismiss, management would turn a blind eye. Thus there evolved a sophisticated system of shop-floor bargaining between workforce and management over areas of control.

The features of this bargaining reflected the specifically Soviet conditions in which it took place. First, these were not collective arrangements worked out formally or informally between management as a group and collectives of workers. They were essentially individual concessions made to individual workers and extracted from individual shop or section managers, which might or might not be tolerated by higher factory officials. In this sense they were arbitrary. Some sections of workers were better placed to extract concessions than others. Generally – although by no means exclusively – these were male production workers in the more essential trades and industries and workers in skilled auxiliary trades, such as tool-setters, electricians, and mechanics. A major exception were auxiliary workers in less skilled, non-mechanized jobs, whose work was essentially uncontrollable, even though in other terms (low pay and poor working conditions) they were not a favoured group.

Secondly, and more importantly, the social relations of production, which grew out of the interactive responses of managers and workers to the externally given work environment, acted spontaneously to reproduce that environment, and with it these production relations. When managers changed the product-mix to make it easier to meet production targets, or because the materials they had received did not allow adherence to the original plan; or when plans were not met because workers took excessive breaks away from their machinery or too often came late to work, this then became an objective circumstance for other factories, which found that supplies were late or of the wrong specifications. Similarly, when steel workers ignored operating procedures and produced defective metal; or engineering workers manufactured defective machines that broke down frequently or were dispatched with vital parts missing, this, too, became an objective circumstance for those factories receiving the steel or the equipment. For the managers and workers in these enterprises, these all became part of *their* objective work environment, which called forth from them the same responses as in other factories: delayed production, violations of product-mix, and defective output, all based on similar patterns of concessions between workers and management. In this way the spontaneous actions of each individual became generalized and reproduced throughout the system in a self-perpetuating cycle. Attempts by the elite to intervene and break down this pattern of relations have had the effect only of reinforcing them. In the Stalin period, the regime resorted to progressively repressive labour legislation, culminating in the actual criminalization of job-changing and truancy. The effect of these interventions was simply to exacerbate instability on the shop floor, driving managers to collude with workers to find ways of circumventing them. The same was true of wages policy, which was used under both Stalin and Khrushchev as a disciplining force, to try to force a restructuring of worker–manager relations within the factories. Here, too, the discontent and destabilizing effect of what were essentially coercive incentive systems pushed managers to by-pass official wage regulations, thus bolstering the pattern of shop-floor bargaining which the regime was trying to break. On the contrary, it is precisely because of their reproducible character that the production relations that have evolved within Soviet industry have proved so resistant to outside political pressure.

6   Limits on the extraction of the surplus

The primary problem which the Soviet elite faces in its attempts to administer the economy is its limited control over the production, appropriation, and disposition of both the absolute and relative surplus product.[1] This manifests itself in a number of ways. First, the actual size and location of the surplus in pure physical form is to a large extent simply unknown. Enterprises falsify output figures or understate capacities. Part of output is literally lost in transit or warehousing. It is quite impossible to dispose of a product whose physical dimensions and whereabouts cannot be determined. Secondly, control is also undermined by the circumvention of planning directives and instructions by enterprise managers and their workers. Orders to produce a specified quantity of a particular good are frequently distorted, or even supplanted at enterprise level. The good in question is produced in the wrong amount or to the wrong specifications, or the enterprise manufactures something else altogether – either because this allows it more easily to fulfil its plan or because external circumstances (for example, the absence of the right kinds of supplies) leave it no other choice. Here, too, the centre simply has no idea of the fate of investment decisions or product orders, thus undermining attempts at coordination. Thirdly, disposition over the surplus product is constrained by the fact that the size of the actual surplus lies far below what the economy could potentially produce (or what the planners expect it to produce, which is not the same thing), essentially because of lost output.

The main sources of lost production lie within the labour process itself, where we find a close and often complex interconnection between losses directly attributable to the worker's own behaviour and those imposed on the worker by external circumstances. Superficially, when the worker goes off for a smoke or to chat with workmates this appears substantially different from the work time lost because the worker has to leave off production to track down missing parts or tools, is delayed starting work because job assignments or drawings have not arrived, or because she or he has to take extra time to trim down oversized or overweight metal components into a usable form. But hunting down tools and parts, however exasperating workers may find it, also provides an important break in the work routine which alleviates strain and monotony. So, too, do long queues in factory canteens or illicit breaks for a stroll or conversations, many of which can be concealed behind the ordinary disruptions imposed by the internal disorder of the Soviet factory. At another level the survival of a huge, undermechanized auxiliary sector gives the workers in these sections considerable scope to regulate the way they apply their labour, since by making their performance more unpredictable and spasmodic, it causes further uncertainties to other workers who depend on them.

These limits to the size of the surplus product all arise from the fact that the worker is not able (or compelled) to expend her or his labour power on the production of use values. In the worst case she or he is left idle for a substantial part of the working day – one or two hours, or even an entire shift. However, even when the worker is 'on the job', she or he is constantly being diverted from her or his main tasks due to the need to deal with all manner of disruptions to the work regime.

Another major source of limits on the surplus is losses through waste, a subject we shall deal with more fully in the second part of this chapter. By waste we refer to the tendency within the Soviet economy to consume means of production and labour power without a commensurate production of finished output. For example, a great deal of Soviet industrial production is defective. Means of production and labour power have been expended on its production, but the goods in question have either to be scrapped or remanufactured. In both cases, means of production have been applied to no useful purpose. The effect on production can actually be worse than if the fixed and circulating capital (including labour power) had simply lain idle, since the raw materials will have been squandered (perhaps irretrievably) and fixed capital depreciated. Alternatively, defective output will not be scrapped, but will be accepted by the consumer because there is no alternative. Where these products are to serve as means of production, they enter into the next phase of production as defective means of production used in the manufacture of other products which will then turn out defective as well. In this way the production of defective output takes on a reproducible character. Its implications for the economy are profound. Machinery made from second-grade or defective metal cannot function as intended. It will break down or wear out prematurely, and the goods manufactured on it will themselves suffer in quality. To compensate for low-grade inputs, factories have to increase their consumption of these inputs. For example, if steel is too brittle or of insufficient strength, factories have to compensate by using more metal. This raises the demand for steel production beyond the level dictated by the given state of technique. But this, in turn, requires the building of more steel mills, whose construction and equipping puts greater pressure on supplies of cement, coal, steel, etc., whose own productive base (quarries, coal mines, and engineering factories) must then be expanded, raising further the demand for all of these diverse means of production. In this way the whole productive apparatus becomes hypertrophied.

Similar losses occur when fuel and materials (coal or pig-iron, for example) are overconsumed. Here, too, a portion of the means of production and labour power used to extract and produce these materials will have been expended to no purpose, while demand for these products rises relative to real technological need, again exacerbating the hypertrophic production of means of production. There are, however, other dimensions to the problem. When products are of poor quality (but not scrapped), or of the wrong size and specifications, they require a considerable amount of additional labour to rectify the defects or adapt them to serve as means of production in subsequent stages of production. Steel ingots regularly arrive in machine shops several times the weight of the parts to be machined from them. A large percentage of the metal – sometimes the overwhelming proportion – ends up as scraps and shavings. The waste here occurs in three forms: (1) workers have to spend a lot of time trimming the metal down to a workable size, which time is, therefore, lost to production; (2) machinery and cutting tools undergo unnecessary depreciation, thus raising the demand for new machinery and necessitating the retention of an oversized repair and maintenance sector; and (3) the metal scraps have to be recycled through the process of smelting and rolling, that is, turned into metal a second time. In reality, many of the new billets or ingots made from these scraps will also be of poor quality and oversized, so that much of this metal will once more end up as scrap, to be recycled yet again through the process of steel production. The cycle by which this form of waste is reproduced is virtually never-ending, and the losses which it inflicts on the economy are probably far more serious than those caused by outright defective production.

The issues of waste and loss of work time are closely interconnected. The generation and reproduction of waste diverts countless quantities of labour power from production. The relative control over the labour process which the Soviet system of necessity allows the worker is reflected not just in lost time, but in a general indifference towards the quality of the products the worker produces, an indifference reinforced and encouraged by the system of bureaucratic planning and the stresses this places on managers to disregard quality, product specifications, and correct product-mix in favour of gross output. What further links these two phenomena is that their roots lie in the specific relations of production which prevail within the Soviet enterprise, most notably in the reproduction of the labour shortage, which provides workers with the 'bargaining power' needed to extract concessions from management on the shop floor. The same features of these production relations which cause such severe losses of work time also generate the pressures leading to waste. The worker relates to the labour process as an alienated, atomized producer, who strives to reduce the intensity of labour and who, because of the labour shortage and the relative security of employment that it brings, is under relatively little pressure to ensure that what is produced is of suitable quality. On the contrary, the product which emerges from these production relations is a deformed or defective product, a product which deviates from the demands of productive or individual consumption, but which is appropriated as a use value anyway, causing further deformities throughout the production cycle.

Already in the 1930s, limits on surplus extraction arising from within the labour process were clearly discernable. Workers routinely reappropriated large parts of the working day wandering the shops looking for tools or parts, queuing at factory dining rooms, or simply stealing extra rest time to chat with workmates. Indeed, one of the primary motivations behind the Stakhanov campaign of 1935–7 was, in my view, to break workers' emerging partial control over the labour process through speed-up and the imposition of more streamlined methods of work organization. By 1937 Stakhanovism was a spent force in the factories, although it retained a nominal existence until Stalin's death, and there was little to impede the incipient patterns of worker–manager bargaining from developing into a mature system of shop-floor relations.[2] The same was true of waste, which appeared as a specific feature of the Soviet system from the very start of industrialization and was analysed as such by economists.[3] Thus, by the 1950s these two phenomena were integral features of the Soviet system of production. Yet it was precisely these two most central issues that labour policy under Khrushchev failed to address, not because there was no recognition of the problem – on the contrary, as we shall see, they were described in great detail in the press and academic literature – but because the regime had no means of attacking what had by then become established and accepted work practices. De-Stalinization, because it had no direct answer to the question of how to enable the elite to regain control over job execution, witnessed the evolution of the modern Soviet labour process into its mature, contemporary form. Thus by studying the problem of control in its concrete detail as it emerged in this period we are, in fact, looking at the problem as it has persisted for over three decades. At the same time, such a study helps make clear the depth of the structural impediments that confronted Gorbachev and his efforts at *perestroika*.

I. THE USE OF WORK TIME

The morphology of lost work time

Soviet discussions of work time in the Khrushchev period routinely cite workers losing on average about 15 per cent of each shift. These figures are similar to those calculated by McAuley and Helgeson, who estimated that the average industrial worker lost just over 14 per cent of shift time in 1960 and just over 13 per cent in 1965. In other words, the average Soviet worker lost the equivalent of 33 days of the working year in 1960 and 30.3 days in 1965 without ever leaving the factory. This is merely the time spent idle within the working day. It takes no account of time lost from production due to labour turnover, sickness, maternity leave, officially approved absences, and truancy. These taken together gave the average industrial worker an additional 27 days off work over and above paid and public holidays in 1960, and 26.3 days in 1965, all but a tiny fraction of it legally sanctioned (truancy averaged less than one day a year per worker in both these years).[4]

Shop-floor surveys revealed considerable variation in the use of work time both between and within factories.[5] Far more important was the structure of losses. A March 1961 survey of over 100,000 workers in Chelyabinsk revealed that 26 per cent of workers registered losses of 30 minutes a day; 21 per cent lost an hour; and over a third lost more than 90 minutes. Only 20 per cent suffered losses of less than 15 minutes. It is quite striking that of the 100,000 observations recorded in the study, not a single worker reported spending an entire shift without losing some work time.[6] A 1960 study of 1,000 workers in iron and steel, engineering, and textiles found a roughly similar distribution. Among turners on the first shift at the ZIL automobile plant in Moscow, for example, over a third of losses lasted from one to three hours; only a half were of less than an hour.[7]

A more detailed picture of the different forms and causes of lost work time emerges from specific studies of the engineering industry and coal-mining. A survey of 670 machine-tool operators, carried out in either 1958 or 1959, at factories in Yaroslavl', Moscow, Minsk, and Novorosiisk found that they spent only 60–70 per cent of time in production tending their equipment. The rest was taken up in transporting, setting up, and removing parts from their equipment, carrying out necessary measurements, cleaning up the workplace, and other minor manual operations.[8] A similar survey in Kiev found that machinists there spent even less time – two to three hours per shift – on actual machining; the rest went on various auxiliary operations which they carried out themselves.[9]

Coal-mining was an altogether different kind of industry which had traditionally been plagued by uneven mechanization and poor organization of production. Stoppages and lost work time had, therefore, always been high. Although the shift to a shorter work day and the reorganization of workers into integrated brigades allegedly led to substantial improvements in work organization and use of shift time, losses nevertheless remained high – in the order of 25–30 per cent.[10] Illustrative of the complex of problems affecting coal-mining was the Kuznetsk basin (Kuzbass), where an extensive study of work time was carried out in late 1959 and early 1960. Losses in the Kuzbass were actually somewhat lower than in the older Donbass region, averaging around 22 per cent. This was still high, and a full half of all stopes suffered stoppages in the course of each day.

The structure of losses differed according to the methods used by each pit to extract coal. There were in this period three basic techniques: (1) relatively new coal-cutting combines allowed for the almost total mechanization of cutting, hewing, and loading jobs; (2) mines also used coal-cutting machines, where only the cutting itself was mechanized and all other operations (loading, hauling, etc.) continued to be done by hand; (3) coal was also blasted out. Although blasting was not itself mechanized, it more or less did away with such labour-intensive operations as hewing and loading. Each of these methods had their own attendant difficulties. Mines using coal-cutting combines found that the combines were out of action over 50 per cent of a normal shift, in large part because of the faulty design of the combines then in use. Every time combines were to be shifted to a different part of the seam, for instance, they had to be dismantled. They were also prone to frequent breakdowns. Despite their almost extraordinary amount of down time, the combines were still more productive than alternative blasting methods, where stoppages were only half as great, but the large number of non-productive jobs associated with this technique reduced overall productivity.[11]

A major problem affecting all these methods was the frequent breakdown of conveyors and underground transport. An even greater difficulty was uneven mechanization. Such jobs as loading rock and coal, carting timber to the coal face, and roofing and maintenance were all highly labour-intensive. Moreover, because roofing, hewing, and loading, were each mechanized to different degrees, and yet had to be done in a particular sequence, *mechanized operations were not significantly quicker then those that were unmechanized.* Quite simply, unmechanized jobs became a bottleneck throttling the potential gains in productivity associated with mechanization.[12] It should be noted here that the Kuzbass was not exceptional in this regard. In the Donbass, workers operating coal combines lost 40 to 60 minutes out of each six-hour shift waiting for roofing jobs to be completed, at the same time as auxiliary workers – who made up more than half of all coal workers – themselves stood idle from 40 to 50 per cent of shift time.[13]

This, then, was the general picture in Soviet industry in terms of total time lost and its major causes. What this picture does not reveal, however, is the interrelationship between work time and the labour process. We must, therefore, concretize our analysis and examine the different moments of the phenomenon in more detail.

Workers' appropriation of work time

Even in the 1930s, labour economists had been quick to point out that poor discipline by workers while on the job was far more costly to the economy than either job-changing or absenteeism, both of which were notoriously high. The extent to which workers succeeded in appropriating large portions of the working day as their own was surprisingly well documented in the Stalin period. In part this was because the problem took on such major proportions, and became such a fundamental source of disruption to industrial life, that labour economists had to address it. They carried out countless studies of the work routine in different industries and factories (so-called 'photographs' of the working day), which revealed quite candidly the complex interaction between workers' wilful squandering of work time and the disorders caused by Stalinist methods of industrialization and 'planning'. In part, however, their preoccupation with this issue was also a result of the political attitudes of the regime which, as has already been argued, despite its populist rhetoric, saw itself as essentially at war with its own working class and recognized that its survival depended on the destruction of that class *as a class*.[14]

Labour economists in the Soviet Union never abandoned this tradition of observing and cataloguing the work routine, but under Khrushchev the focus of attention shifted. De-Stalinization brought with it a reluctance to attack workers openly, not just for blatant violations of labour discipline or for alleged 'self-seeking' when changing jobs, but also as those responsible for losses of work time. Whereas in the 1930s, journal and press articles routinely singled out individual workers for study and even attack or ridicule, such detailed analyses of the work routine were relatively infrequent in the Khrushchev years. Where they do appear, the worker is presented as the victim of circumstances created by negligent managers, and not as the culpable agent. This cannot, however, be the sole explanation for the change in emphasis. The incidence of overt and flagrant squandering of work time by workers almost certainly declined as the new workforce created under Stalin became acculturated to the new system of work relations and as the system of production relations evolved and matured. At the same time, the worker's partial control over the organization and disposal of work time became an accepted part of shop-floor life, so that the behaviour of the worker became merged into the general fabric of production as an integral part of the pattern of disruptions and dislocations affecting Soviet industry. This then became the norm, which defined the contours of the system of shop-floor relations within which both management and workers now accepted that they had to work. This was not a sudden process, but had been evolving since the 1930s.

The press reports that did appear make clear that flagrant violations of the work regime were still a problem at many factories. Young workers at Leningrad's printing- and publishing-machinery factory were constantly getting involved in group discussions about new films, clothes, or sports.[15] Workers at the Orenburg hydraulic-press factory were said routinely to leave off work to wander about and 'find out the factory news'.[16] In Moscow in 1964 the Stal'most factory installed monitors on its machine tools to record when workers left their machinery, and at least one worker had his pay docked for going off for too many smoke breaks.[17] Skilled manual workers, such as maintenance fitters and electricians, were especially able to take advantage of the high degree of control they had over their work to set their own work schedules, refuse certain jobs, or even to negotiate their own private 'contracts' with factories desperate for their services.[18]

The most common way in which workers could directly reduce working hours was simply by showing up late for work, leaving early, or extending their dinner break. Leaving work 15 or 20 minutes early, or starting up a quarter of an hour after clocking in were common.[19] Soviet workers in the Khrushchev period were supposed, for example, to work a half day on Saturdays. Yet a study of Saturday working at Leningrad's Kotlyakov engineering works found that in two of its shops not a single worker had begun work a full 20 minutes after the start of the shift. Some were in the store-room, others were gathering around the grindstone waiting to sharpen tools. At 12 noon – two hours before the official end of the shift – workers in another shop took down their tallies and sneaked out. In other shops workers began knocking off between 1 and 1.30 p.m.[20]

A 'raid' on the Neva ship-repair and ship-building factory in Leningrad during the summer of 1963 found that virtually all the workers in the ship-building shop started work 10–12 minutes late and went for dinner 10 minutes early. The shop was deserted 10–15 minutes before the end of the shift.[21] Similar 'raids' at other factories around the country found comparable violations of the work regime, although allegedly on a much smaller scale.[22] Workers may have had good reason for such actions, however. At Leningrad's Lentrublit rolled-pipe factory, workers on the second shift had to leave from 45 minutes to an hour before the end of the shift in order to catch the last bus home.[23] The fact that several press reports singled out textile factories for their lax attitudes towards work schedules suggests that foremen were willing to let the women go early in order to queue for groceries, collect children, or get started with household chores.[24]

In the immediate aftermath of the wage reform, the regime attempted to tighten up timekeeping procedures, since it had identified these as a major loophole through which workers could take time off undetected. The 'reform' was combined with an effort to reduce the huge army of timekeepers in industry, as a way of effecting general cuts in the auxiliary workforce. There is no question that the traditional system of recording workers' arrival and departure either at the factory gates or at shop entrances allowed workers considerable scope for coming late or leaving early. For one thing, the old system was incredibly cumbersome, and soaked up the labour not just of timekeepers, but of numerous support staff who had to set up clocks, boards, tallies, punch-in cards, and related timekeeping paraphernalia. Moreover, it did little to guarantee strict discipline. Workers could hang up the tallies of absent workmates. Factories on three shifts rarely bothered with timekeeping on the third shift, and sometimes not even on the second. Even where lateness was accurately recorded, timekeepers were completely unable to keep a check on workers' whereabouts and actions once a shift had started.[25]

In some cases the attempted cure was worse than the original disease. In August 1956, the Taganrog combine factory received instructions from its ministry to lay off 15 timekeepers and 'centralize' timekeeping at a smaller number of check-in points. The result was chaos. Timekeepers had a mere 2.5 seconds to process each worker, which included taking the factory passes off those starting a shift and rooting out and handing back the passes of those just leaving. The resultant queues were so long that many workers were made late for work, even when they showed up at the factory gates on time. Many left work 20 to 30 minutes before the end of a shift in order to queue up to clock out. Because the factory extended over such a large area (160 hectares), with some shops located 20 minutes' walk from the main gate, it was impossible to determine just how early a worker might have stopped work, which in turn led to huge arguments between workers and timekeepers. Moreover, the new system did nothing to rectify the old problem of how to verify a worker's presence at her or his workplace during the course of a shift.[26] It is interesting that when this 'experiment' was abandoned after just a few months, the factory did not return to the old method of registering attendance directly in the shops, but made timekeeping the responsibility of the despatchers who handed out work orders. A similar system was adopted at a number of enterprises in Moscow, where timekeeping was given over to foremen or related personnel, who kept a special register of 'deviations from normal working conditions and the normal length of the working day', in which the foreman noted all cases of absenteeism, lateness, extended dinner breaks, etc.[27] We do not know the fate of these two experiments, but what is significant about them is the fact that they made enforcement of a key element of labour discipline directly dependent on shop management – in this case foremen or work despatchers – and therefore subject to the pattern of shop-floor concessions and bargaining that takes place within Soviet industry. It is very likely that enforcement became highly selective, since foremen would have had to avoid conflicts with some groups of workers while being free to apply regulations more strictly to others. In other words, by granting foremen additional power, it localized workers' ability to extract concessions over the execution of that power directly on the shop floor, in a way that could not have happened when timekeeping – no matter how inefficient it was – was carried out impersonally at the factory gates. Rather than leading to a more systematic and rigid enforcement of discipline regulations, the new procedures may well have worked to workers' advantage.[28]

Insofar as long dinner breaks were concerned, workers were abetted by the perpetually dismal state of factory dining rooms. Canteens were undersized and underequipped, and simply could not cope with the demand. The inevitable result was long queues. The dining room servicing the construction site at the Elektrostal' iron and steel works could hold only 48 of the 200 workers who needed to use it. It took each person 90 minutes to get a meal.[29] Construction workers at the Novolipetsk iron and steel works in Lipetsk had to bring their own food with them. The site had a dining room, but it required a 20-minute walk each way, and the queue was over an hour long. As the author of the letter complaining of this situation noted, 'Who is going to allow two hours for dinner?'[30] It should hardly have been earth-shattering, then, to discover that engineering plants in Moscow, Kaluga, and Gor'kii were able to cut losses of work time in the dinner break by lengthening it from 20–30 minutes to 45 minutes or an hour.[31] The most graphic account of the problems which dining facilities caused to production was a *Trud* article about the state of public catering in Novosibirsk.

> There are still 15 minutes to go before the horn announcing the dinner break, but the workers have already begun to abandon the shop. Some of them guiltily and embarrassedly glance around before shutting down the machine, others, obviously used to this, do it quickly without any hesitation.
>
> Ten minutes before the start of the break no one is left in the shop. Then in the dining room a long line has been forming. Those who faithfully worked right up until the end wound up right at the back. They had to stand in line a long time and were late getting back to the shop. However, there are so many of these latenesses that at

Sibsel'mash, the instrument and machine-tool factories, the leather footwear combine, the No. 6 housebuilding combine, and other enterprises in the city they've grown used to them. Workers, technicians, engineers eat in three or four shifts, yet for all that people still do not manage normally to eat a bowl of soup, a helping of cutlet, and to drink a cup of tea.

... The people of Novosibirsk experience major difficulties even after the working day ends. There is a Komsomol youth dormitory on Vatutin Street. Thousands of workers live in a large, multi-storey building. There is a comfortable, bright room for every two to three people. Very good! Only there's no dining room. The young people leave for work at 8 in the morning, while the nearest dining room for four blocks opens also at 8 and closes early.

The situation was aggravated by the fact that what little new construction of catering facilities was undertaken was partially nullified by local Soviet decisions to take many existing dining rooms out of operation on the grounds that they were 'unprofitable'. 'In the mean time,' continued *Trud*, 'this unprofitability is perfectly explicable if one considers that in the buffets that were closed down the only things sold were chocolates and fossils being passed off as cakes.' The city had a local meat-packing combine which could have provided buffets and dining rooms with cheap *pirozhki* (a meat-filled dough similar to a small pastie), but these were also deemed unprofitable because their low price impeded canteens from fulfilling their turnover plans. However, the combine was in an obsolete building and could not have met the city's full demand in any case. And *Trud* concluded:

> And here, as a result, throughout the city 20,000 people are late for work following the dinner break. Meanwhile this figure is the minimum. Given the shortage in Novosibirsk of 20,000 places in dining rooms, snack bars, cafeterias, etc., the number of people late from their dinner break is in fact far greater than 20,000. It is long past time to decide which is better: to build several dozen new, modernly-equipped dining rooms and factory kitchens, or to put up with the sour mood of thousands of people and with tens of thousands of hours of lost work time.[32]

Factories were generally unwilling to invest in expanding canteen facilities or building new ones, since they preferred to concentrate resources on capital construction in production shops. This, and only this, they felt would aid plan fulfilment. The losses incurred in lost work time did not enter into the calculation. From the worker's point of view, this was a double-edged sword. The travails and aggravation involved in the simple process of acquiring a meal were considerable;

on the plus side, this was time away from the tedium and strain of work. What is more, the chaos and disorder in dining rooms gave workers an additional pretext for stretching meal breaks beyond the delays they genuinely encountered. As we shall see, this same duality applied to losses incurred because of the inherent disorganization of Soviet production.

Work time and the organization of production

Labour economists constantly pointed to the large increases in production that could be achieved if only work could be more rationally arranged. This is hardly surprising, since Soviet time and motion studies purported to show that workers lost far more time due to the so-called poor organization of production than they did from violations of labour discipline. Given the magnitude and persistence of these organizational failings, there is little reason to doubt this claim, although we can question the relative proportion of lost work time attributed to each category.

Workers' attitudes to the disruptions they encountered must have been ambiguous. As with the long queues in factory dining rooms, time away from the machine could provide a valuable and welcome respite from the strains of work. At Leningrad's Lenmashzavod, because tools were not delivered to the workbench, milling-machine operators had to leave work every 30 to 40 minutes to make a 10-minute trip to the store-room to fetch a new mill.[33] On the other hand, the disruptions themselves could make work harder, as workers had to ferry parts around the factory, fetch and carry heavy supplies, track down tools, etc.[34] Long stoppages could seriously eat into earnings, unless management was willing to find ways to compensate workers for the time they spent idle. Another factor, completely overlooked by Soviet commentators (and which is discussed in more detail in chapter 8), was that many of the problems workers faced acted to nullify the tendency to remove them from the decision-making process which was inherent in mechanization and automation, and required them to exercise a considerable amount of independence and initiative (for example, redesigning plans when the right parts were not available or blueprints were missing). The more such active intervention was required, the stronger workers' bargaining power was on the shop floor, since management required their cooperation to overcome bottlenecks and meet shop plans.

The impact of disruptions on worker's behaviour was well

illustrated by an account of the work routine at the Izhora works in Leningrad. Machine-tool operators routinely started work 10, 25, or even 40 minutes late, and began shutting down their machine tools from 25 to 40 minutes before the end of the shift. Many were already out of the gates 10 minutes before the final horn. Yet the author of this account blamed such losses not on the wilful actions of the workers, but on the poor state of internal organization (although workers were unlikely to have complained about this imposed reduction in work hours). At the beginning of a shift, workers had to wait around to receive work orders because foremen had not drawn them up the day before. If workers finished a particular job 30 or 40 minutes before the end of the shift, foremen had no other work for them to do, and so they stood idle.

These problems were not unique to the Izhora works, but were allegedly common to the majority of engineering enterprises.[35] At the Saratov machine-tool factory, for example, the shortage of tools meant that some workers spent 10 times as much time making the tools themselves as they did machining the articles for which they needed them. There were no ancillary workers on night shifts, so machinists had to interrupt work to fetch their own supplies. Some workers (allegedly a minority) then took advantage of these externally imposed delays to chat with friends.[36] The difficulties which this type of disorganization could cause workers should not be underestimated. Machine-tool operators at Leningrad's Elektrik factory saw their earnings drop because the factory simply could not provide them with enough work to do. They would finish a job and then hang around the foreman's office reading a newspaper. If the foreman found a job for them, this often meant they would have less work the following day. The situation was so bad that workers opted to use more backward, less productive machinery, just to reduce the time they spent idle. As a result, young workers became disgruntled and quit their jobs.[37]

The most striking thing about many of the sources of lost work time was their sheer irrationality. Some coal mines, for example, insisted on keeping tools on the surface rather than in each section underground, so they had constantly to be ferried from surface to pit and back again. Up to the late 1950s, miners used accumulator lamps, which burned out every two to three hours, and required a special worker to replace them. For some reason, this trade was eliminated without there being any improvement in lamp technology. Lamps still burned out before the end of a shift, but now the miner had to stop work to replace them himself.[38] Other mines appear to have found it impossible to organize rational work schedules. At one mine in the Stalinugol' trust, gas measurers stood around waiting for bore holes to be drilled prior to blasting, while in other sections blasters were idle because they were waiting for the gas measurers to show up.[39]

The most detailed taxonomy of production difficulties, however, was in engineering. The most common problem was the shortage of tools and parts, and the lost time involved in tracking them down could be staggering. At Leningrad's Vulkan factory, machinists complained that they regularly lost 40–50 minutes a day walking to storerooms and receiving and filling out work orders.[40] At the city's Znamya truda factory, one turner lost two whole shifts trying to find the drawings and tools to turn *one* part.[41] At other factories, workers could lose as much as a third of their time because workplaces were poorly prepared, shops had no equipment for sharpening cutting tools or lacked necessary drill bits, because simple items like nuts and bolts were not standardized and sometimes had to be specially machined (often by workers in other shops), or even, in the case of Leningrad's Vibrator factory, because one day the plant had no lights.[42] Because of the chaotic provision of supplies and parts, machinists lost further time doing their own carting, a job which in theory should have been done by ancillary workers.[43]

A striking testimony to the inherent disorganization which reigned in most Soviet factories was the fact that the most simple, commonsense improvements were treated as near earth-shattering innovations. A number of engineering factories were able to revolutionize their store-rooms by installing basic shelving and specially marked boxes. Parts and supplies could now be put in a specified place and clutter could be reduced. The Vorob'ev engineering works introduced the novel idea of scheduling workers responsible for preparing shifts, such as crane operators, store-room attendants, auxiliary workers, and foremen, to come in ahead of the main body of workers to allow the latter to begin work straight away.[44] Similar 'innovations' were introduced in optical-machine enterprises in Leningrad: workers were given work schedules and plans the day before, so that they could anticipate their need for tools and arrange their acquisition. Machine shops were given advance plans, so that they knew which parts to produce.[45]

The problem was that most factories had neither the incentive nor the ability to implement even such primitive alterations as these. Advance planning could be rendered totally worthless if supplies were not forthcoming or if plans had to be changed at the last moment.

More to the point was the fact that, as Sonin noted, enterprises had little incentive to improve the use of work time, since they were generally able to overfulfil their plans without altering existing work practices and their attendant losses.[46] He might also have added that any rationalization of the organization of labour would have involved increasing the intensity of labour, and would surely have met with resistance from workers. This would have been the case with the prior preparation of shifts, which would have effectively lengthened the working day by reducing the time production workers spent away from their machines. Any such reorganization would have entailed a direct attack on work practices developed by workers over a number of decades, and which were designed specifically to insulate them from the regime's periodic attempts to raise the rate of exploitation. Managers tolerated the persistence of these practices because, as Sonin said, they could still meet their plans if they were left intact. In fact, to challenge them would have jeopardized the cooperation of workers that managers needed in order to minimize the impact of disruptions, especially at a time of permanent labour shortages.

It would be difficult to overestimate the importance of poor internal planning, the breakdown of coordination, and shortages of supplies in determining losses of work time. The intrinsic disorganization of factory life also had other roots. Undermechanization, the poor state of internal transport, and the rigid division of labour within production, if anything, had a more profound impact, because they imposed structural limits on attempts to reform work organization and intensify the utilization of equipment and labour power.

Structural determinants of losses of work time

1. Undermechanization

While many of the difficulties catalogued above acted to increase workers' free time within the work day, others, as we have noted, did not. The storming cycle, for example, meant that workers had to 'pay back' idle time from the beginning of the month with overtime and considerable strain at the end. Clearly, many of the sources of lost work time aggravated storming, over and above difficulties with external supplies or conjunctural shortages of labour power, and did not, therefore, necessarily grant workers greater control over the pace of work. In the same vein, equipment stoppages and breakdowns – which were aggravated by storming – did not always lead to more rest, because of the extra work involved in rectifying the cause of the stoppage or shifting work to other machines.

What all of these disruptions to production had in common, however, was that they placed strict limits on the extraction of the surplus. This was particularly the case with undermechanization, which took up a great deal of worker's time because of the persistence of manual operations, and acted to negate the effects of mechanization elsewhere.

In coal-mining, for example, despite the increasing mechanization of extraction work, the persistence of manual labour in such jobs as roofing, hauling, and even hewing coal meant that *even by Soviet measurements* labour productivity in the Donbass grew by less than 2 per cent a year between 1950 and 1959. In the Stalinugol' trust, as late as 1959 less than a quarter of extraction workers were on fully mechanized jobs and over half worked strictly by hand. Even on long-walls worked by the new coal combines, which were designed to mechanize virtually all operations, nearly two-thirds of workers were employed on *manual* auxiliary jobs such as roofing and transporting conveyors. On long-walls employing coal-cutting machines (where loading of coal was still unmechanized), almost three-quarters of workers carried out manual labour. The end result was that the labour content of a ton of Donbass coal was actually higher in 1959 than it had been in 1940.[47]

A further problem was the large amount of manual labour *within* mechanized jobs. Machine-tool operators, for example, had to shift and mount on to their machine tools parts and semi-finished components which could weigh anywhere from several hundred to several thousand pounds. Because Soviet industry did not produce up-to-date hydraulic, pneumatic, or electrical devices for mounting, machinists might spend up to a quarter of their time on these types of operations.[48] Metal-cutting operations were themselves slowed by the snail's pace at which outdated equipment (cutting tools with manual feeds, for example) were retired from service. Not only were the machine tools themselves less productive, but they required the worker's constant attention, as opposed to automated equipment which would have allowed the worker to tend several machines simultaneously.[49] This uneven mechanization led to distinct problems with coordination. Managers concentrated investment in basic production operations (although even here it did not always lead to proper modernization) at the expense of auxiliary jobs. Thus, of the more than 520,000 workers in the engineering industry in 1959 employed on lifting, transport, and cleaning up, a mere 20 per cent worked with even the most primitive kinds of machinery or mechanical devices.[50] This posed just as much of a problem for assembly-line workers as it did for machine-tool operators. Workers on flow lines suffered innumerable little disruptions in the course of a work day – primarily interruptions in the delivery of components – which added up to considerable amounts of lost time. Essentially, workers on more mechanized operations were held up by auxiliary workers whose work was more labour-intensive and who had greater freedom to regulate the speed with which they worked.[51]

The uneven mechanization of production was exacerbated by resistance to innovation from both managers and workers, which was discussed briefly in chapter 1. At times this was a rational response to the faulty design and construction of new equipment, which worked so badly that workers found it easier to go back to using old machinery or work methods, even if this meant working by hand. Sometimes factories simply could not get the new equipment to work, no matter how much they modified it. In other cases, workers and specialists did not know how to operate it properly, even after making special trips to the original manufacturer in order to learn. In the end, shops just shunned their new purchases, leaving them to rust.[52] The result was that attempts to mechanize certain operations could actually end up costing more time and labour than when these jobs were done manually.[53]

At other times, however, this resistance was a product of overt managerial hostility, as at the Ul'yanovsk automobile factory, where management actually closed down the plant's Department of Mechanization and Automation.[54] Even without such open obstructionism, inventions could become tied up in endless bureaucracy and never see the light of day.[55]

Managers, as we have noted, had numerous reasons for caution in this area, as successful modernization could lead to plans and norms being raised, making it harder for managers themselves to meet success criteria, while at the same time provoking the hostility of workers who would then have had to fulfil higher targets. An excellent illustration of just how strong managerial recalcitrance in this area could be was the experience of the Leningrad machine-tool and automatic-machine factory, which, despite the more than adequate quality of its machines, could not find customer factories willing to take them, precisely because they would cut production time vastly, in some cases by as much as 80 per cent over capstan lathes then in use.[56] There were equally examples of factories or coal mines which acquired labour-saving equipment but did not use it.[57]

Workers' hostility to new technology was due not simply to the possibility that their norms would go up, though that was a prime concern, but to the loss of control that automated equipment would impose. It is probably this that explains the difficulties the regime had in introducing machine tools with programmed controls, since these would have further removed the worker from any independent command over the organization of work and the speed of its execution.[58]

2 Internal transport

In 1962, nearly one out of every six industrial workers was engaged in some form of loading or transport operation, most of which was unmechanized.[59] The factors behind this were several. As with auxiliary jobs in general, enterprises considered investment in the mechanization of transport and warehousing of secondary importance compared to investments in basic production. In addition, Soviet industry simply did not make much of the equipment needed to rationalize internal transport operations. Thus machines that were commonplace in every capitalist factory (fork-lift trucks, electric carts with lifting platforms, small stackers, light transporting machinery) were more or less non-existent in Soviet enterprises.[60] A survey of 186 engineering and metalworking factories, carried out in the early 1960s, found that 179 of them still collected metal shavings (which came to between a quarter and a third of the weight of metal castings and forgings used in machining) by hand, using buckets, wheelbarrows, and pans and brushes. Two-thirds used manual labour to deliver materials and components to the workbench and to move assemblies and parts from one machine tool to another. Only half used cranes to assist in these operations, and only 22 moved materials and components with mechanized carts and wagons.[61] Problems were exacerbated by the often irrational organization of transport work. Parts and components were shunted back and forth within and between shops and between shops and store-rooms, quite needlessly multiplying the volume of loading and haulage, which was already done inefficiently by hand.[62] Efforts to mechanize loading jobs were often undermined by suppliers, who provided goods in containers which, because of their size, weight, or the materials used, were unsuitable for mechanized handling.[63]

Transport jobs were afflicted by the same deficiencies as other areas of industrial life. Factories might have electric trolleys, but since they did not have lifting platforms, loading and unloading still had to be done by hand, negating much of the labour saved by the carts.[64] What mechanization there was was often so faulty that workers could not use it. At the Leningrad metal factory a shipment of new electric carts was rendered useless by the fact that the factory could not change the batteries on them. Workers abandoned the carts and carried on delivering parts and semi-finished components by hand.[65]

Pressure on internal transport came also from other sources. The adulteration of coal supplies with ash and slag meant that factories had to divert extra workers to cart away what were in effect deliveries of useless waste.[66] Delays in construction of new warehouses further retarded the mechanization of transport and storage. The Bogoslovskii aluminium factory in Sverdlovsk was supposed to be building brand-new mechanized warehouses, but the date of their completion was anybody's guess. The construction of one warehouse had begun in 1945, yet it was still unfinished 17 years later.[67]

The disorganization and poor technical state of internal transport was, therefore, a major factor in perpetuating the swollen auxiliary sector within Soviet industry. But it also cost production workers dearly in lost work time.[68] From the point of view of factory management, this was not without its compensatory benefits. A high proportion of these workers were women and low-paid. Managers may well have calculated that it was more economical to rely on large numbers of low-wage workers carrying out their work highly inefficiently than to divert resources from production to the mechanization of internal transport. So long as plans could be kept within achievable limits, the cost in disorganization and lost production could be tolerated. As in so many areas of factory life, what was rational for the individual enterprise director proved extremely costly to the economy as a whole and to the elite's ability to increase the surplus product.

3. The internal division of labour

Even if the regime had been able totally to eliminate all the causes of lost work time which we have discussed so far, there were certain groups of machine-operators who would have continued to suffer sizeable losses because of the fact that they could not set and adjust their own equipment, but had to depend on specially trained tool-setters to do it for them. This frequently left machinists facing long stoppages, while they waited for tool-setters to reset their machines. The largest group affected were machine-tool operators in engineering and other industries. Textile and assembly-line workers also did not do their own set-ups, but because this was not expected of them, the losses incurred waiting for tool-setters were seen as unavoidable. For one thing, these workers were largely women, who were viewed as intrinsically less skilled than many really were. For another, by maintaining control over the setting of textile equipment, and even more so of assembly lines, management could better control the speed and intensity of work. There was, therefore, no desire on the part of either managers or the political authorities to cede this prerogative to the workers.

Machine-tool operators were an altogether different matter, since the retention of tool-setting and tuning functions in the hands of a special trade did not allow management to increase the intensity of labour. While it served the function of divorcing the worker from decision-making and control over the labour process, the production lost while machinists waited for adjustments now seemed to outweigh these benefits.

Historically, the separation of machine-tool operators from tool-setting was a product of forced industrialization in the 1930s, when, according to Soviet labour economists, the influx of large numbers of new, unskilled workers into industry required a simplification of work tasks and the breaking up of what had been integrated production processes into innumerable, minute jobs, with each worker carrying out only one particular type of operation. Machine-tool operators lost all responsibility for technical servicing and maintenance of their equipment, the responsibility for which was now invested in highly skilled trades of tool-setters, electricians, maintenance fitters, and others.[69] This explanation, while certainly accurate, is not the whole story. Right through the NEP period, engineering workers had essentially been generalists, carrying out the entire range of production and auxiliary functions within the overall production process. This afforded these workers a considerable degree of control over the planning and execution of the labour process. The worker determined how a particular job was to be carried out and the sequence of production and auxiliary operations (machining, fetching tools, carrying finished output from the work bench), and set and maintained the equipment. Needless to say, this allowed workers to determine not just the organization of labour, but its speed and intensity. Such a division of labour came into open conflict with the methods of Stalinist industrialization, which invested all decision-making in the hands of factory management, and for whom the continued control by generalists–machinists over the labour process was an obstacle to the imposition of speed-up and raising the rate of exploitation. The issue, therefore, was not simply how to reorganize production to make it easier for unskilled recruits to master a trade and carry out assigned tasks, but how to ensure that all workers – both experienced and new – were removed from the decision-making process and control over job execution. This was a question not so much of economic efficiency as of *political control over the labour process*. The breaking down of the division of labour was part of a larger process of atomizing the workforce which proceeded along several fronts: the suppression of collective action, the rigid imposition of one-man management, the desperation imposed by the fall in the standard of living, and the impoverishment of the vocational curriculum in schools (where rote-learning and acquisition of a narrow range of skills replaced a polytechnical exposure to all aspects of production and enterprise planning).[70]

The results of these attempts to remove the worker from control over the labour process were contradictory. The atomization of the workforce allowed workers to reappropriate in another form much of the control over the labour process which they were in the process of losing. Workers may not have had direct or open responsibility for organizing their work, but the labour shortage and the intrinsic chaos of Soviet production allowed them a great deal of leeway to determine this organization surreptitiously. Moreover, the hyperspecialization of the division of labour carried within it the seeds of future problems which, by the 1950s, had become an obvious brake on productivity.

In flow production in engineering, the rigid division of labour between machine-tool operators and tool-setters meant that the former were allowed to carry out relatively simple, repetitive operations, such as transporting parts between stages of machining, or setting up, securing, and taking down parts from the machinery, while even the most basic adjustments to equipment, such as changing tools, usually had to be done by a tool-setter.[71] The amount of time lost waiting for tool-setting could be substantial. At the Ryazan' machine-tool factory it accounted for 18 per cent of all stoppages to machine-tool operators, and an even greater share for workers on production lines.[72] At the Lyubertsy agricultural-equipment factory, the frequent stops for adjustments and readjustments to automated lines took up between a quarter and a third of equipment work time.[73] The wait for tool-setters to come and make an adjustment could be three or even seven times as long as it took for the adjustment itself.[74] Moreover, this had a debilitating effect on the skill levels of machine-tool operators, many of whom had actually been trained in vocational school to do minor adjustments and set-ups, as well as major tool-setting. Once they took up work at an industrial enterprise, however, the vast majority of them had no opportunity to use these skills and eventually forgot them.[75]

The result was not just lost work time for production workers, but the inefficient use of the tool-setters themselves. The Kharkov tractor factory and Moskvich car factory (Moscow) had to keep on hand one tool-setter for every five to six machine-tool operators, all because the latter were not trained or permitted to do their own tool-setting.[76] In general in engineering, tool-setters were assigned five or six machine tools, in effect dividing up the sections of each shop into highly parochial mini-sections, each with its own tool-setter. Cooperation between sections was rare, and tool-setters would not assist other tool-setters who needed assistance. In part this must have been because of the need to draft them in as trouble-shooters to help clear out bottlenecks, which left them little time to help out elsewhere in the shop. It was estimated, for example, that tool-setters spent only half their time working on machine tools, 20 per cent of their time transporting parts or fetching cutting tools, a further 5 per cent of their time filling out work orders, while a full quarter of their work time was simply lost and unaccounted for. The other problem was the fact that tool-setters' earnings depended strictly on the production results of the machines which they serviced. They therefore had no financial interest in assisting other tool-setters, since they would not be paid for it. Nor would they adjust machinery even in their own subsection if it was nearing the end of a shift, because the next shift would end up using the equipment and being paid for its output.[77] Tool-setters also jealously protected their job delineation. They refused to rectify minor defects in machine tools, or electrical and hydraulic systems, forcing workers to wait for fitters, electricians, or hydraulic engineers.[78]

It is not surprising, therefore, that at least some factories attempted to change the basis on which tool-setters were paid and/or to streamline their internal division of labour to allow machine-tool operators to do their own tool-setting. As early as 1957 the Magnitogorsk general metal-goods and metallurgical factory adopted a so-called 'link' system, where tool-setters worked as machine-tool operators. When a machine tool needed setting its operator simply switched over and ran the equipment of the tool-setter, while the latter carried out the necessary adjustments.[79] More common were attempts to train machine-tool operators to do their own tool-setting. The evidence, however, suggests that such experiments were limited and enjoyed little success. For one thing, they appear to have been concentrated almost exclusively in the automobile and tractor industry.[80] With the exception of the First State Ball Bearing Factory in Moscow, and the Krasnaya Etna works in Gor'kii,[81] there is barely any mention of machinists being allowed to tune and set their own equipment at major machine-building or related engineering enterprises. Even within the automobile industry, the application of such experiments was limited. At the Gor'kii Automobile Factory it was applied only in individual shops, in part because existing wage and skill handbooks made it difficult to upgrade machine-tool operators who took on tool-setting functions, and in part because of drawbacks in the training system, which still turned out workers with very narrow specialisms.[82]

It is interesting that the issue of tool-setting provoked two dia-metrically opposite attitudes. On the one hand, many managers and labour economists accepted the existing situation as evidence that it was a waste to employ skilled machine-tool operators on production lines; others argued precisely the opposite, that the stoppages caused by such a narrow division of labour were an avoidable loss to pro-duction which required an expansion of machinists' job profiles.[83] In effect, the advocates of the latter position were calling for at least a partial return to the old generalist–machinist of NEP. They were reacting to the fact that the Stalinist division of labour was now choking production potential, at least in engineering. What they did not address was the fact that their proposals, if carried through, contained an important internal contradiction. They might have rationalized the use of work time by both machinists and tool-setters, but only at the expense of granting machine-tool operators greater control over their work process, precisely at a time when the regime was attempting to increase the intensity of their labour.[84]

The reproduction of lost work time

Throughout the Khrushchev period, various local or national campaigns were mounted to try to improve the use of work time. One of the more prominent was the revival of the multi-machine tending movement, which had warranted a great deal of publicity (with only limited results) before the USSR's entry into World War II. The idea

behind the scheme was quite straightforward: workers were encouraged to tend more than one, and in some cases several, pieces of
equipment, in exchange for higher pay. In theory, workers should be
able to do this without substantially raising the intensity of labour,
since in engineering, for example, there were large amounts of time in
the overseeing of equipment during which workers were performing
very little physical work and could be looking after additional
machinery. The attractiveness of the system was obvious, especially in
Leningrad, where it was applied as a method of easing the labour
shortage.[85]

Nevertheless, the multi-machine tending movement does not
appear to have enjoyed great popularity or success. For one thing,
workers were not always offered sufficient incentives to make it worth
the extra work involved. In principle, workers looking after two
machines were to have their job prices cut, but not fully in proportion
to the additional amount of equipment tended. Thus, if they operated
two machines, the job price would be reduced not to half of that for
working just one machine (which would have left earnings
unchanged) but, say, to 70 per cent. In this way, workers would be able
to boost their earnings without leading to an explosion of the wages
bill. The problem, however, was that different factories applied different incentive systems, many of which were bizarrely complex and/or
posed a risk of lower earnings if workers could not meet the norms for
multiple equipment set by management.[86] On the whole, participation
rates were low. At the Lenin engineering works in the Neva district of
Leningrad, less than 1 per cent of workers were multi-machine
tenders; in some sections there were none at all. In the first machine
shop of Leningrad's Karl Marx works, only 5 per cent of production
workers took part.[87] The potential for using this campaign to streamline production and the use of work time was, therefore, limited.

Other experiments were even less broadly based in their application. A construction trust in Krasnoyarsk reported a scheme whereby
brigades appointed 'worker–statisticians' from within their own ranks,
whose job it was to investigate the magnitude and causes of lost work
time. The campaign claimed a certain amount of success in reducing
hold-ups, but there is little evidence that this was more than just a local
aberration.[88] I have already mentioned such mundane improvements
as rationalizing work schedules or centralizing tool-sharpening, so
that workers could plan their work in advance and arrange to have all
the necessary implements and supplies at the time they were
needed.[89]

The main failing of all these diverse experiments and campaigns was that they merely addressed a few of the external manifestations of the roots of lost work time and not its essential causes. They were certainly incapable of ameliorating the labour shortage, which gave workers much of their bargaining strength in their dealings with management. In a larger context, they could not affect the complex pattern of relations between workers and management that had developed out of Stalinist industrialization in the 1930s and consolidated themselves in the post-war period, in particular during de-Stalinization.

This argument, that workers' appropriation of control over work time was a specific response to Stalinist industrialization, has come in for a certain amount of criticism by those who claim that it underestimates the importance of the cultural attitudes and forms of behaviour developed in pre-Stalinist times in determining workers' responses to Stalinist industrialization itself.[90] Without denying the significance of such legacies, the basis of our analysis has been that workers were essentially developing rational responses to structural and political constraints imposed by the Stalinist regime, not dissimilar to those exhibited by workers in developed capitalist societies when faced with strict controls on the labour market and the freedom of collective action.[91]

The experience of the post-Stalin period adds a further dimension to the argument. It might be feasible to assert that the work practices characteristic of Soviet industry in the 1930s were admixtures of carry-overs from the past and newly developed responses to the specific conditions of the time, but the relative importance of these cultural legacies receded as the system stabilized and matured. By the 1950s the Soviet workforce was a well-defined, fully developed social group, recruited primarily from among workers' families. Yet workers' limited control over the labour process – over work speeds, over job organization, and even over the relative surmountability or insurmountability of bottlenecks and disruptions – had clearly become an established feature of industrial life and part of the basic fabric of how production was carried out. Cultural background obviously plays an important role in shaping workers' attitudes and behaviour. It helps determine why people chose certain forms of action from among various alternatives as opposed to others. But structural factors are equally, if not more, important, for these set the limits to what is perceived as possible or reasonable at any given moment. If seemingly older, even pre-industrial attitudes and forms of behaviour were able to sustain themselves and become an essential part of the reproduction of material life, it is because they found a basis for their own reproduction in the specific conditions of economic and social activity – conditions which workers' actions helped to create and perpetuate.

Western studies from around the same period are useful, because they show that in those areas of capitalist industry where strong trade union organization allowed workers to insulate themselves from the workings of the labour market, they were able to exercise limited control over their labour process similar to that witnessed in the Soviet Union. The Devlin Report on work organization in the British Docks in the mid-1960s, for example, pointed out that one part of a gang might be working, while the rest were resting, smoking, taking a tea break, and so on.[92] Lupton was able to go further and specifically relate workers' appropriation of free time to management's failure to ensure disruption-free production.[93] As will be discussed at greater length in chapter 8, there are important differences between Soviet and Western factories, most notably the dependence of Western workers on strong shop-floor organization for their control over work practices, in contrast to Soviet workers, who derive their control precisely from their atomized position within the society and the enterprise.[94] What is significant about these examples, however, is that they show the actions of Soviet workers to be logical responses to their work situation and the social relations that prevail within it, independently of cultural traditions.

If the actions and behaviour of Soviet workers remained fairly stable over both the Stalin and Khrushchev periods, it was because de-Stalinization did remarkably little to alter the major features of Soviet shop-floor organization. Workers still found themselves confronting both the elite and enterprise management as atomized, politically powerless individuals. The bureaucratic planlessness (*besplannovost'*) of Soviet planning meant that control by the elite over production was imperfect because the plans themselves were subordinated to the needs of both managers and workers to protect their own interests (interests which in the case of managers were largely defined by the planning system itself). Information was constantly withheld or falsified, and implementation of central instructions was distorted or disregarded. Once set in motion, such a system reproduced itself as automatically as the production relations of capitalism. Central to this was the reproduction of the relationship between workforce and management. Bureaucratic planning and political repression had simultaneously allowed and compelled workers to appropriate considerable control over how they worked. Workers then became a central element in determining the form and reproduction of this planlessness.

The dislocations, shortages, or poor quality which confronted a given set of workers as externally caused, 'objective' circumstances were the result of the active disregard of work schedules, operating procedures, or quality standards by workers at earlier stages of production and distribution. In addition, the inefficiency and waste engendered by workers' actions led, among other things, to a tendency for the economy to overconsume labour power, thus sustaining and reproducing the labour shortage and undermining any possible attempts to break down workers' defensive practices through effective sanctions.

Like the labour shortage (from which it derives and which it subsequently re-engenders), losses of work time are not a transitory or conjuncturally specific phenomenon, but are *constantly reproduced* through the reproduction of workforce–management and workforce–elite relations. The various reforms of work organization which might have seemed so logical on paper came up against inbuilt resistance from both workers and managers who distrusted the potential changes they might have introduced in shop-floor relations. Workers, naturally, had an interest in obstructing any changes that might have reduced their control over the work process and led to an intensification of labour; management distrusted anything that might have led to plan increases, on the one hand, and jeopardized stable relations with the workforce, on the other.

The overconsumption of labour power derived not simply from the way in which workers used their work time. Its other major determinant was waste, the tendency for the system to consume inputs of means of production and labour power without their comparable translation into the production of use values. Here, too, the workforce was instrumental in the reproduction of waste, and with it the reproduction of its own partial control over the labour process.

II. THE REPRODUCTION OF WASTE

General forms of waste

1. Duplication of labour and the overconsumption of metal

From the beginnings of Stalinist industrialization in the 1930s, one of the most visible consequences of waste has been the need to duplicate work that has already been done, or to expend additional time adapting materials or equipment to prevailing conditions of production. The Khrushchev period was no exception. The most obvious example of this phenomenon was the need to rectify defective production. But the unnecessary expenditure of labour had other causes equally as important.

The problem of redoing work already performed was perhaps greatest in engineering, where the need to rectify or adjust poorly machined parts during assembly operations partially negated efforts to mechanize these jobs, leaving them just as labour-intensive and heavy as before.[95] Even before parts reached the assembly stage, however, machine-tool operators had themselves had to cope with the thankless task of working with semi-finished components and castings that were vastly oversized. The amount of metal wasted in this way was simply staggering. A large-scale survey of engineering enterprises in the early 1960s found that a third of castings and a quarter of forgings ended up as shavings,[96] although on some parts the waste could exceed 50 per cent or even two-thirds of original weights.[97] The Gor'kii car plant created enough metal scrap in one year to meet the demands of the neighbouring milling-machine factory for nine years.[98]

This massive overconsumption of metal had its roots in various aspects of the Stalinist planning system. For one thing, parts were not standardized, even on identical pieces of equipment. In the tractor industry, for example, three different factories all produced the same model of tractor using allegedly analogous parts, but their weights varied significantly.[99] More important was the built-in incentive of iron and steel factories to produce heavy ingots and billets in order to facilitate plan fulfilment. This calculus prevailed even within foundries and component shops in engineering, which boosted the weight of parts and components in order to meet shop plans, even though it proved extremely costly to machine shops in their own factory.[100]

The emphasis on planning by weight may at least partially explain the slowness with which Soviet factories adopted more efficient methods of parts manufacture, in particular the stamping of parts, instead of machining them out of forgings.[101] The quality of forgings and castings was also to blame, however: management at the Lenin works in Leningrad's Neva district cited the need to compensate for poor quality as one reason for increasing the weight of semi-finished components.[102] What was clearly the case was that oversized and heavy forgings, castings, and semi-finished components involved the considerable waste of materials and labour power. As *Leningradskaya pravda* commented on the situation at the Machine-tool and automatic-machine factory, people and equipment were working at full capacity, 'but just how great is the useful return on such work?'[103]

2. Incomplete production

One of the characteristic features of Soviet production is the manufacture and shipment of goods which, though nearly finished, cannot be used because some essential part or piece is missing. A factory might receive a machine that has no transformer or lacks something as trivial as a few bolts. Equally, it might be sent consignments of materials or parts which have the wrong specifications, for example, too much second-grade steel and not enough steel of high quality, or too many of one type of component and not enough of another. The Soviets even have a special term for this phenomenon, *nekomplektnost'*, or 'incompleteness' (literally, incomplete batching). The economic effects of incompleteness are that enterprises can nominally fulfil their plan by producing equipment or semi-finished products which, in the best case, cannot be put to the uses for which they were intended, and, in the worst case, cannot be used at all.

The origins of incomplete production date back to Stalinist industrialization of the 1930s and the extreme emphasis on gross plan fulfilment and individual production records. Shock workers might vastly overfulfil their targets on some items, while other workers in interconnected stages of production or assembly more or less just barely coped with their norms. The shock workers or Stakhanovites would build up mounds of components which could not be used because other workers could not, or would not, match their pace and produce comparable quantities of parts or components that were equally vital to assembly. At the other extreme, managers, by concentrating on producing those items which made plan fulfilment easiest, consistently violated the correct product-mix. Expensive machinery might wait months for final assembly because factories had not produced enough nuts or bolts, whose production was scorned because such cheap items – although vital – did nothing to help factories meet their overall targets.[104]

It is doubtful if incompleteness during the Khrushchev period attained the levels of the 1930s (indeed, as the system stabilized many of the more conjunctural causes, such as shock work, would have disappeared), but it nevertheless continued to cause serious bottlenecks. Factories still violated their product-mix in order to meet gross plan fulfilment.[105] One reason for the persistent shortage of building supplies was that building-materials factories concentrated on the most profitable or easy-to-produce items, at the expense of those which construction sites actually required.[106] Some sections of the brick industry went over to collective piece-rates precisely because brick-making was a highly integrated and interdependent process, and individual piece-rates encouraged workers in some stages of production to turn out excessive quantities of materials which, given the prevailing technology, workers in other stages could not use.[107]

Similar problems affected manufacturing industry. The Krasnyi kotel'shchik factory in Taganrog was the USSR's main supplier of boilers. Its store-yards were full of millions of rubles' worth of undispatched equipment which could not be finished because essential parts had not arrived from suppliers.[108] A number of Soviet factories which had purchased equipment from the Gor'kii milling-machine factory were unable to use it because essential fittings and accessories were missing. These, it turned out, had to be purchased separately by 'special order' – but the orders were never filled, and the machines could not be put into operation.[109]

3. Physical losses

It is striking how much of the social product was actually lost or spoiled due to internal disorganization or neglect by workers and management. It was common for equipment or parts to be left out in the open air to rust, either through negligence or because enterprises did not possess adequate premises in which to store it. Some of this machinery was new and was ruined before it ever reached the enterprises for which it was made.[110] At the Izhora works in Leningrad, forgings and other metal goods were abandoned in the snow, including one shipment of rolled steel shafts which should have been sent to an iron and steel plant four years earlier.[111]

Losses of raw materials were equally great. In most cases the problem was lack of premises. At the Turbomotor factory in Sverdlovsk, sand for the foundry was stored outdoors, where it absorbed too much moisture and ruined castings.[112] The construction of a new warehouse at the Leningrad metal supply depot was two years behind schedule – meanwhile, metal pipe sat outside being turned into 'second-grade raw materials'.[113] More ominous was the situation at the Sukhoi Log cement factory in Sverdlovsk *oblast'*, which for want of warehouse space kept asbestos outside and uncovered where it was trampled into the ground or mixed in with the snow.[114] Here the hazard posed to workers' health must have been far more serious than the lost materials.

Products would also be lost due to changes in factory plans and cancelled orders. Equipment or consumer goods on which a great deal of labour had been expended were simply abandoned, often after factories had had to make specialized tools, equipment, and parts for their manufacture and for which they had no further use.[115]

Defective production

The issue of defective production goes far beyond that of spoilt or damaged goods which are so totally unusable that they must be scrapped or remade. This class of products, known as *brak* in Russian, has been notoriously large since the beginnings of Stalinist industrialization, but it constitutes only a small part of the problem of poor quality. More important are the products which fail to conform to the specifications necessary to allow them to be used in either productive or personal consumption. These goods are not scrapped (although some consumer goods remain unsold), but enter circulation where, insofar as means of production are concerned, they deform the nature of the new product, so that it, too, cannot function as intended.

The exact magnitude of defective production in the narrow sense is difficult to assess. In Leningrad it was estimated to equal the annual output of one of the city's major engineering factories.[116] This is a fairly daunting analogy, since it would be equivalent to a large engineering enterprise working an entire year and producing nothing. Yet even this would underestimate the true level, since a large proportion of defective output either went unreported, was passed by quality controllers, or was accepted by customer factories despite the defects, since this was better than receiving no supplies or machinery at all.[117] It also says nothing about factories which fulfilled their plans by increasing their output of second-grade or low-quality products, while leaving plans for high-grade lines underfulfilled.[118]

The poor quality of Soviet consumer goods has long been notorious in the West. Some of the examples cited in the Soviet press during the Khrushchev period were indeed extraordinary. The Vasil'kov factory in Kiev produced refrigerators which carried a two-year guarantee, yet in 1961 one out of four broke down within a month of purchase (to make matters worse, the factory would not repair them). According to *Trud*, defective output 'wanders about from shop to shop ... Fridges with defects, like a veritable boomerang, are sent back to the beginning of the conveyor. Here, in a special section, they remake them all over again'.[119] Similarly, shoes made at the Skorokhod footwear factory in Leningrad, one of the country's oldest and largest, were of such poor quality (25 to 30 per cent were defective; styles were outdated) that retail outlets throughout the USSR were refusing to stock them or to pay for shipments already received.[120] In general, it was alleged that warehouses were bulging with unwanted consumer goods such as watches, coats, and shoes, whose quality was so poor or styles so unattractive that people would not buy them, despite existing shortages.[121]

As important as the low quality of consumer goods was – and I shall have cause to return to this issue in discussing domestic labour in chapter 7 – it was really only the ultimate manifestation of the way in which defective output affected production proper. No industry escaped its impact. Coal – especially that from the Moscow coal-fields – was adulterated with ash and slag. At some tractor factories, the ash and slag carted away from factories weighed as much as the shipments of their own finished output, placing added and totally unnecessary burdens on rail transport.[122] In construction, new projects were in need of repair even before they were opened because defective building materials had been used. A section of a housing block in Orel collapsed, while other units needed rebuilding because the local brick factory had falsified a consignment of defective bricks.[123] Moreover, builders' tools were made of defective metal, thus further reducing the already poor quality of construction work.[124] The tractors produced at the Lipetsk and Altai tractor factories during the early years of Khrushchev's reign were of appalling quality. Tractors from Altai came off the assembly line without cabins, bonnets, or even radiators. At Lipetsk, tractors were shipped out with loose bolts, their motors overheated, and valves and other parts wore out prematurely. Whole consignments were returned by customers, 50 to 100 at a time. Even without these added difficulties, state and collective farms faced the problem that, as late as 1958, Soviet tractors could barely go faster than a horse.[125]

No industry better encapsulates the problems caused by defective production than engineering. With the probable exception of iron and steel, where poor-quality metal was the perpetual bane of production, the quality of machines had the greatest ramifications for an enterprise's ability to function. Everything – the organization of labour, the use of work time, the quality of output – hinged on the efficiency and quality of equipment. Thus the performance of the engineering industry was crucial to all sectors of the economy.

The engineering industry was both victim and cause of defective production. In terms of its own output, the most serious problem it faced was the poor quality of castings. In automobiles, tractors, and other branches of engineering with large foundry shops, losses from outright defective production came to between 3 and 8 per cent of total factory production costs.[126] For engineering as a whole, nearly three-quarters of defective output occurred in foundries.[127] Castings, however, were not the only difficulty. The quality of electric components could also cause a bottleneck. The Kolomensk engineering works (Kolomna, Moscow *oblast'*) had a special section which did nothing but repair faulty components received from just one Georgian supplier, but those from elsewhere in the USSR were equally bad.[128]

No doubt partly because of the problems they had with their own supplies, the quality of equipment made in engineering enterprises was often poor.[129] The causes behind these defects lay in the interrelation of various factors, all indigenous to Soviet production: carelessness, poor-quality supplies from outside, faulty equipment, and general disorganization. Some sense of how these different factors reinforced each other can be obtained by looking at the Lepse engineering works in Leningrad, which made hydraulic, steam, and gas armature for different sectors of Soviet industry. This type of production involved precision work, and parts had to be kept clean. Yet work areas were filthy, and the proportion of defective output was high. Some articles were manufactured satisfactorily, but were *ruined during testing*. Electromagnetic valves, for example, were tested using water that ran through rusty pipes. The valves then had to be remade. One automatic line was so dirty and produced so much unusable output (between 60 and 90 per cent) that five of the 24 workers who staffed it did nothing but rectify its defects. In effect, the products were made first time around on a conveyor, *but then remade by hand*. Even then, a large share had to be redone a third time. To make matters worse, quality control was terrible, because controllers were paid on piece-rates, and so rushed to check as many articles as they could.[130]

Still another side of the problem is revealed in a portrait of Moscow's Frezer instrument factory published in 1964.[131] Frezer was one of the most important cutting-tool and instrument factories in the country, yet its products were so bad that factories had come to find it easier to make their own tools, even though it was more expensive and they had to take workers off production jobs in order to do it.[132] The root causes were several. To begin with, the factory had no proper testing stations to carry out quality control. If a tool worked on a lathe for 30 seconds it passed inspection. More importantly, the factory's own equipment was old and outdated. There were almost no automatic machine tools for carrying out finishing jobs, such as sharpening or grinding, *which made these processes dependent on the diligence of the individual worker.*[133]

It is significant that the Soviet press associated manual labour not simply with a lack of uniformity (which mechanization would certainly have improved), but almost automatically with poor quality – a clear reflection on the lack of diligence and commitment with which workers related to their work. Despite limited attempts to make workers more accountable for defective output through the imposition of penalties, or through experiments to make workers responsible for their own quality control,[134] the poor quality of Soviet products remained at the heart of the country's long-term economic crisis.

The repair and maintenance sector

Soviet industry employed a huge army of repair and maintenance workers. In industry as a whole, they accounted for 1 out of every 10 workers, but the figure was much higher in key sectors. In engineering, nearly 1 out of every 5 workers was in maintenance; in iron and steel over 1 in 4.[135] Repair of equipment was costly and inefficient, and for many machines it nearly matched their original cost. To some extent this is inherent in the nature of repair work, which relies heavily on manual labour. It was, however, primarily due to the specific conditions of Soviet production, which meant that repairs were unnecessarily expensive, long and drawn out, and poorly executed. The costs were exacerbated by the relatively poor construction of much, if not most, Soviet equipment, which shortened its lifespan and necessitated more frequent repairs.

According to the veteran labour economist S. Kheinman,[136] outlays on repair and servicing of machinery in the engineering industry in 1955 came to between 10 and 25 per cent of the total value of equipment. These figures rose steeply as equipment became older. On one particular type of machine tool, the cost of repair rose from 17 per cent of its value in the fifth year of life to 260 per cent in the tenth. For other machines the number of person-hours needed to repair it could be 1.5, 2, or even 4 times the number expended on their initial manufacture. This phenomenon was not confined to machine tools. The cost of repairing an old tractor was between 60 and 100 per cent that of manufacturing a new one.

Kheinman identified four major reasons behind the sorry state of the repair and maintenance sector.

1 As discussed in chapter 1, the engineering industry produced only a small proportion of the spare parts needed to fix and maintain machinery; as a result, enterprises had to make parts themselves, in small quantities, and using inefficient and costly methods. Parts were, therefore, expensive and o poor quality. The few centralized repair factories which existed were hampered in their work by the poor quality of metal.

2 To guarantee that parts would be on hand when needed, repairs were scattered over a multitude of small, decentralized repair stations, each with its own nucleus of equipment, which was under-utilized and produced parts badly and expensively.[137] This proliferation of miniature repair sections impeded the adoption of more efficient methods of restoring worn-out parts, which required high-grade metal, testing laboratories, a sufficient number of accurate measuring devices, and trained maintenance personnel. It was virtually impossible to accumulate adequate supplies, equipment, and expertise over such a large number of small-scale units. Moreover, the quality of parts suffered from the shortage of measuring tools and skilled repair workers. Parts often failed to meet required specifications, thus undermining the integrity of repairs from the very beginning.

3 Within enterprise repair shops there was almost a complete absence of specialization. Shops were badly equipped, yet were prepared to work on almost any type or model of equipment the factory possessed. This prevented economies of scale that could have been achieved had repairs of each kind of machine been centralized in shops or enterprises specializing in their maintenance.

4 Engineering factories dispatched machinery without enclosing detailed drawings. Whenever a part broke or wore out, customer factories had to make their own sketches based on the worn-out part. Inaccuracies were therefore built into the repair process. At the same time, the absence of proper drawings meant that factories had to keep on hand their own team of designers and technologists, thus duplicating those working at the original engineering enterprises.

Although this portrait dates from early in the Khrushchev period, conditions changed little over time. Capital maintenance of machine tools by customer factories continued to consume two or more times as much labour as their original manufacture, while the total cost of capital maintenance ranged from 60 to 80 per cent of the cost of a new machine. The cost of making spare parts in repair shops was 5 to 10 times their cost at specialized factories in 1959, and 4 to 5 times in 1962. In 1962 some 60 per cent of repair workers continued to be concentrated in small maintenance workshops, whose efficiency was further eroded by the fact that they were saddled with additional jobs that had nothing to do with repairs. Finally, capital maintenance was a lengthy process, subject to inordinate delays. On average it took equipment out of service for 30 to 60 days, against a planned period of 10 days. Stoppages for this reason alone came to 8 per cent of potential machine time, which added up to substantial amounts of lost production.[138]

The regime made various attempts to overcome these shortcomings by centralizing repair services, including the production of spare parts, at specialized enterprises. Indeed, some improvement in this direction was reported in the oil industry of Bashkiriya, Volgograd *sovnarkhoz*, and individual engineering works in Moscow and Gor'kii.[139] The reform was not, however, an overwhelming success. In Leningrad, a special maintenance shop was set up at the Sverdlov factory to carry out repairs on precision machine-tools and machinery for other Leningrad enterprises. The first problem was that the factory had no suitable premises. Although they finally found a spare building, the shop's equipment would not fit into it, and so it had to be dispersed among several other shops, whose workers then began to use it themselves. This 'centralization' of repair thus led to the ludicrous situation where maintenance workers, whenever they had a job to do, had to go to another shop, only to find that the workers there would not let them on to their own equipment. In addition, because the maintenance shop's machinery was scattered over so many other parts of the factory, its workers had to shuttle back and forth from one shop to another with each stage of machining, often coming back to the same place several times. The end result of this 'reform' was long delays in meeting repair orders.[140] A similar attempt to centralize machine-tool repairs in Moscow also met with near disaster, this time because the factory was unable – or unwilling – to exercise strict control over the work of the fitters it sent out to different factories. The latter effectively set their own hours. The work of the parent factory – Mosremstanok – was equally bad. It was located in ramshackle premises, without even a foundry or a forge shop. Instead of casting parts, it had to cut them out of ingots, which was time-consuming and wasted metal (80 per cent of ingots ended up as shavings).[141] The irony of the Leningrad and Moscow experiences was that these specialist shops and enterprises had been established specifically to provide centralized, efficient capital repair of equipment, more cheaply and at a higher level of technique and quality than ordinary enterprises could do themselves. The result was exactly the opposite. On balance, efforts to centralize repair and maintenance made little impact on reducing the bloated size of this sector of the auxiliary workforce.

It was the poor quality and slowness of repairs, however, that did the greatest damage to production. Machinery, as we have noted, as a rule stayed out of action far longer than planned. Because repairs were so badly carried out, equipment often left service soon after going back into operation. At Leningrad's Elektropul't factory it was apparently routine for machines to break down within hours of being fixed. Each capstan lathe at the factory averaged three months a year under repair, and factory folklore had it that machinists and repair persons virtually took it in turns to work on a machine.[142] The poor work of maintenance workers was compounded by managers' unwillingness to carry out regular preventive maintenance, because they did not want to take equipment out of production. This of necessity led to more serious and longer breakdowns.[143] Managers at many enterprises were equally unwilling to invest necessary resources in repair and maintenance shops, preferring to concentrate them directly in production. This was a problem with the auxiliary sector as a whole, but it had devastating effects when applied to repairs, since the ability to keep essential machinery working depended to a large degree on the efficiency and productivity of repair shops.[144]

Many of the difficulties with the repair sector were legitimately attributed to the wages and incentives system. Prior to the wage reform, it was common for repair and maintenance workers to be paid on piece-rates, according to the volume of work carried out. Earnings were almost totally divorced from qualitative criteria – for example, how long repaired equipment remained in service, or overall plan fulfilment of the shop or section to which repair persons were attached.[145] The wage reform was designed to address precisely these shortcomings, by tying the earnings of maintenance workers to the quality of repairs, as measured by shop or equipment performance. As with other aspects of the wage reform, however, it failed to achieve the desired results. At many iron and steel plants, for example, plans for machine shops – which worked overwhelmingly on making parts for the servicing of furnaces and mills – continued to be set in tons and machine-hours spent on parts manufacture, rather than specifying required quantities of each type of part. As elsewhere in Soviet industry, workers and shop management quite naturally concentrated on producing the heaviest parts or those which required the most machine time, irrespective of need or product-mix.[146] In the reinforced-concrete products industry, the earnings of repair workers continued to be based on the number of breakdowns repaired. Thus workers had a direct incentive in carrying out faulty repairs and increasing their frequency. At one building-materials factory in Lyubertsy, for example, fitters could maintain their customary earnings only if concrete mixers and other equipment were repaired on average between 18 and 37 times a month! Despite such incongruities, management in the building-materials industry was generally reluctant to put repair workers on time-rates, where bonuses depended on how long equipment stayed in service. Many breakdowns were due to the careless handling of machinery by equipment operators, and repair workers would lose bonuses for stoppages which had not been their fault.[147]

Time-bonus rates, where actually applied, had other shortcomings. According to one engineer at a factory using this system, both workers and shop management came to view bonuses as 'an inalienable part of the wages of repair workers', and thus paid them automatically, without any account of equipment performance. In fact, this particular enterprise – the Por'shen factory in Kharkov – shifted maintenance workers back on to piece-bonus rates, organizing them into integrated brigades, each of which was made responsible for the comprehensive care of all the equipment in the section to which they were assigned (preventive maintenance, capital repairs, and between-service upkeep). If equipment broke down earlier than stipulated by the brigade's plan, the brigade had to rectify the problem without pay. Despite the alleged successes of this system in the first half-year of its use, it failed to overcome one major structural obstacle, namely, the shortages of spare parts, materials, and tools, which caused delays in repairs and compromised their quality.[148] Thus what must have seemed a completely rational reorganization of repair work was undermined by factors outside the control of local workers or managers.

Conclusion

In analysing the phenomenon of waste, two distinct aspects to its reproduction can be identified. The first and most obvious is that of its circulation through the economy. Defective products, be they metal, machines, or raw materials, pass from one stage of production to the next, deforming the utility of all products into which they enter as means of production. The second and more essential aspect of waste is its actual production, the nature of which is determined by the way in which waste circulates: namely, by the fact that what are being circulated are strictly use values, and not commodities embodying exchange value. To understand the connection between these two aspects, we must look at the relationship between waste and the nature of labour power in the Soviet system.

One of the primary consequences of Stalinist industrialization was that it eliminated the market and its attendant value relations from the Soviet economy. Until late 1990, when the Soviet leadership accelerated moves towards the market, Soviet producers had not created goods for exchange on an anonymous market; rather, in distinction from early commodity production or capitalism, production and circulation were organized through a bureaucratic system of imperfect commands and directives, which attempted to control production immediately, rather than through the mediation of a market.[149] Prices existed, but they were mere accounting devices, which had no relation to the actual amount of labour power embodied in the production of an article or service.

Without a market there has been no exchange value in the USSR either. For the existence of exchange value and a market are inseparable. Exchange value arose as a necessary social abstraction, because when anonymous producers confront each other on the market there is no way to determine equivalence (how many hats are worth one coat, etc.) strictly from the concrete properties of the commodities in question. Some abstract property has to be found which is common to all commodities, irrespective of their concrete form, a property to which all commodities can be reduced in order to determine equivalence and ratios of exchange. This abstract property is value, based in its most simple form on the amount of labour power – both living and past – embodied in a commodity's production. The other side of exchange value is abstract labour – labour stripped of its concrete content as the labour which produces specific use values, and reduced to simple, universal labour, whose only defining characteristic is its ability to create value.

Given the absence of the market in the USSR, producers have not confronted each other seeking an exchange of goods; thus no abstract property on which equivalence could be determined has until now been necessary. Instead, producers confronted each other directly, as the creators or possessors of concrete objects which other parties needed, in short, as the creators of use values. This applied equally to labour power, which was not bought and sold as a commodity, and whose price (wages) still bears little relation to the value of its reproduction. There was a 'labour market', in the sense of labour mobility strongly influenced by supply and demand, but this market has been distorted by the fact that workers could always find work and once hired could not be dismissed (barring exceptional circumstances). The other side of this relation is that the worker was compelled to work, both by law and by necessity.[150] The worker, therefore, has confronted the employer – in this case, enterprise management – not as an embodiment of abstract labour (labour whose sole useful characteristic is its ability to create value), but as concrete labour, labour applied to the production of specific goods or services, that is, use values. There was exploitation in the Soviet Union, in that a ruling group appropriated a surplus product created by the working population, but this surplus product also existed only in its concrete form. It received no value expression and could not be bought and sold or otherwise circulated *as value* – although this will change as the market is established. Exploitation has existed in every society. What is unique about capitalism is not exploitation *per se*, but its specific form, namely the transformation of labour power into a commodity which produces a surplus product, whose subsequent appropriation by the capitalist only has economic or social significance if that product can first be realized as surplus value. In the Soviet Union, the surplus product was appropriated directly, as a collection of concrete objects of use intended for specific application. That they could not function in that fashion stems from the antagonistic social relations prevailing in the society.

Under capitalism there is a contradiction between the social form of the product (exchange value) and its concrete existence as use value. Under socialism this contradiction should be overcome, as the useful form of the product becomes its social form. In the Soviet Union this contradiction is re-established, but within the social form itself. The contradictions that have existed in the Soviet Union between workers and management and between workers and the Soviet elite are congealed in the product these workers produce. The worker has been atomized and alienated, because this has been an essential condition of the elite's ability to maintain political control over the society. The price of this control has been that the worker is able to place distinct limits on the creation and expropriation of the surplus product. Workers do this in part by limiting their work effort, reducing the intensity of labour, and thereby attenuating the rate of exploitation. The mechanisms through which they have accomplished this were outlined in the above discussion of the use of work time. But workers also limit the size and disposal of the surplus through the product itself, by creating a deformed product which does not meet the demands of its intended use. Following Ticktin's analogy, if under capitalism the essential contradiction is that between use value and exchange value – the fact that commodities must be realized on the market before their useful properties can be appropriated – in the Soviet Union the contradiction exists within use value itself, that is, in the creation of a use value which cannot fully function as a use value because of its defective nature.[151] If this product enters into circulation, as most products do, it will pass its inherent defects to other products. But the losses to the economy do not stop there. Some products are lost, others squandered. Still others require the expenditure of a great deal of extra labour power and means of production to rectify or adapt them so that they can be used at all. The net result is a hypertrophied productive apparatus which absorbs large quantities of labour power and means of production which are inefficiently used. Hence they do not create the output which they could under a different form of social and political organization.

It would be wrong to reduce the entire phenomenon of waste, with all its varied manifestations, to the behaviour of workers at the point of production. It is clear from our account that it is the nature of the Stalinist-bureaucratic system as a whole which gives rise to waste, although the relationship between workforce and management at shop-floor level is central to this process. Managers must also protect their position, which means violating and circumventing plans and instructions in order to achieve production results which will assure their continued receipt of privileges and further their careers. The planning system, too, was directly responsible for many of the losses and irrationalities affecting industry and agriculture. Workers, managers, planners, and bureaucrats do not exist as separate entities, however, each influencing the course of the economy through their own discreet spheres of activity. They exist only through their relationship to each other. These relationships are reproduced through the reproduction of the social product no less than is the relationship between wage labour and capital under capitalism. The actions of each engender a complex array of reactions and counter-actions which in their surface manifestation give the Soviet economy its appearance of chaotic disorganization. Their common root, however, is the political atomization of society, which causes each individual to pursue and defend her or his perceived individual interests in a system which has no effective mechanism for imposing conformity with central instructions. On the contrary, the uncontrollability of the system by bureaucratic methods makes individual action a necessity. It undermines economic efficiency and at the same time, as will be discussed in more detail in chapter 8, forces individuals to reintroduce a degree of rationality which would not exist if people carried out plans strictly *pro forma*. But this rationality comes only at a price. If managers circumvent the plan in order to meet their targets, this causes distortions felt elsewhere in the chain of production. If workers agree to intercede to make good the shortage of tools, improper designs, or defective materials, it is only at the cost of extracting concessions from management, granting them greater control over work organization, work speeds, and earnings.

This system is not a historical accident. It is a specific system of economic organization through which the elite has attempted to maintain its control over society, and with it, its class position and its privileges. It exists because, historically, the emerging Soviet elite of the early 1930s was unable to root itself in capitalist production relations (which would have passed power on to other social groups, primarily international capital) or in socialism, which would have required the surrender of political power to the working class. Whether the working class of the late NEP period and early 1930s was politically capable of taking power is probably doubtful, given the enervation which resulted from the Civil War, the market conditions of NEP, and the Revolution's continued international isolation.[152] This is not the point. What is important is that the elite could consolidate its rule only through what has now become known as the 'administrative-command' system, that is, through Stalinist 'planning'. It is a system where the elite perceived the need to attempt to control everything from the centre. Even in the 1930s this was politically and administratively impossible, and it became all the more so during de-Stalinization. In both periods what appeared to be the rigidities or even the foibles of the system were in reality the inevitable result of the limited options imposed by such a contradictory social formation. When plans were set in tonnage or ruble value – which had the absurd effect of forcing factories to produce heavy and /or unneeded objects – this was not because the planners were incompetent, but because, with access to neither the market nor genuine democratic planning, they had no other mechanism for trying to administer the economy. These were not mistakes or accidents. The elite's historically contradictory position – embodying a system that was neither capitalist nor socialist – left it no other choice.

Prior to Gorbachev, the elite was able to sustain political power through a secret police, but only at the price of creating an economy that was increasingly flying out of control. Gorbachev's political mission was to try to overcome this contradiction by reorganizing the system, in the hope that decentralization and greater political relaxation would allow improved economic efficiency and still permit the elite to remain in power. Experience has shown that this merely creates a new historical dilemma. If the command system becomes discredited, what will the elite put in its place as a regulator of the economy? The existing class structure excludes the creation of genuine socialism, although heightened social conflict could, under the right historical conditions, lead to a re-formation of the Soviet working class and its challenge for power. The alternative is the one pursued by Gorbachev and his successors, namely the reintroduction of the market. Even this solution holds little hope of overcoming the essential contradictions within the society and economy, so long as the existing class structure remains intact. The consistent application of the market, however, must of necessity lead to a gradual restoration of capitalism, in which case the old contradictions may be superseded, but only by creating new ones, equally as severe.

7   The position of women workers

As under capitalism, patriarchy has played an important role in consolidating the class relations of Soviet society. Where women workers
were concerned, Stalinism did two things. It brought masses of women
into the non-peasant workforce and at the same time attempted to
reinforce the family as a centre of authority and patriarchal attitudes.
At the height of the campaign in 1936 to overturn Bolshevik family
legislation and outlaw abortion, commentators openly identified the
strengthening of family relations with the consolidation of the Stalinist
order. This same hierarchy was replicated within the workplace. Millions of women entered social production, but were marginalized into
the most unskilled and lowest-paid jobs.[1] The two processes reinforced
each other. Women became proletarianized, while their domestic
burdens remained unabated or grew heavier. They retained almost
total responsibility for looking after the home while doing a full day's
labour. Their plight was made worse by the poverty of the country,
itself exacerbated by the Stalinist elite's deliberate policy of underin-
vesting in consumer-goods industries, housing, education, and essential communal services like laundries and child care. It is generally
assumed that the regime starved these areas of resources because of its
near-pathological emphasis on the development of heavy industry.
This may have been the conscious motivation behind the planners'
decisions, but this policy served one other important function. It
would have been extremely difficult to build up the nuclear family as
an authoritarian structure if society had provided the resources to free
women from much, if not most, of their domestic burden. In addition,
the general hardships of the period acted to promote political passivity
among men and women workers alike, as the struggle for survival
helped to atomize the working class and undermine its potential for
collective action. This possibly affected women even more than men,
since they were the ones who had to stand in endless queues, scour the

177

markets for scarce foods or consumer goods, prepare the meals, mend the clothes and the furniture, and look after the children.

In all aspects, women were relegated to a subordinate position within Soviet society, a position simultaneously reproduced within the home and at work. It is common to refer to this as women's double burden, but this terminology is misleading because it implies that these are discreet phenomena, the one merely an accretion to the other. They are not. Rather, women's positions at work and in the home mutually determine one another. Their subordinate status in the home profoundly affects the attitudes of male workers and managers, so that discrimination against women in jobs and pay seems completely natural.[2] Conversely, the perpetuation of women in low-paid, unskilled, and heavy manual labour reinforces male prejudice (and women's own aspirations) about women's ability to do skilled work or to assume positions of authority, be it in society, the workplace, or the household. In more practical terms, the burdens of domestic labour and the drudgery of most female industrial jobs combine to make it difficult for women to find the time or energy to upgrade their skills and earn promotions, over and above the inbuilt discrimination which relegates them to the lowest skill grades in the first place.

In the middle and late 1960s, the new discipline of Soviet sociology began to examine a whole range of issues dealing with social inequality, very often producing work of surprising insight and candour. As part of this wave, a small group of sociologists and labour economists, most of them women, began to investigate the position of women workers, supporting their studies with their own surveys of women in particular industries and localities. In addition to supplementing already existing time-budget studies of men and women, they took a detailed look at the marginalization of women into particular trades and industries, wage discrimination, and the specific content and conditions of female labour. These studies were far more detailed than any of male workers carried out at this time. Other than in short articles, much of this work was presented only in dissertations and not officially published. The rigour and theoretical sophistication of these investigations was extremely uneven, but some were truly noteworthy and showed a high degree of political awareness. Long before Western feminists had discovered the importance of class, they understood the need to examine the position of women in production, and to develop from this a damaging critique – sometimes overt, sometimes only implicit – of the position of women within Soviet society. Even where the main contribution of certain authors was simply to present unpublished statistics on job discrimination and wages, the choice of these data – as opposed to others – presupposed a definite political outlook radically at variance with the prevailing official line on women's role in Soviet society. This is not to overlook the real political limitations imposed by their 'Sovietized' marxism. They saw the phenomena they uncovered as inadequacies that could be overcome within the bounds of the system, rather than as expressions of its immanent nature whose solution demanded its radical overthrow.

Whatever the strengths of these studies of women workers, they did not – and indeed, given the political constraints of the time, could not – address the real issue, namely the political economy of female labour, and its specific role in regulating the Soviet economy. This goes far beyond the issue of the reproduction of labour power. For what we shall find is that women workers were subjected to relations within production which in important ways deviated from those generally prevailing within industry, particularly among male workers. Women constituted a reserve army of workers marginalized for the most part into two types of jobs. First were those where the technology allowed management to exercise relatively tight control over the labour process. The intensity of labour was high and wages poor. The most important of these were in the textile industry, but women on conveyor work in engineering (especially light engineering) and women in other areas of light industry found themselves in similar conditions. Secondly, women formed the overwhelming majority of auxiliary workers doing heavy, manual, and usually unskilled or semi-skilled labour. Their working conditions were harsh and their pay often quite low, although as manual workers they had greater control over the pace of work. The existence of each of these two sectors was predicated on the other. It was possible to induce women to enter the textile mills – be they urban women or rural migrants – only because the alternative was potentially more unattractive, namely manual labour in auxiliary shops.[3] Together these two spheres of employment gave the elite an important lever for recouping part of the control over production which it was forced to cede to male workers in heavy industry. First, these women were taking jobs that male workers could not be persuaded to do. In this sense they were fulfilling the function of female, black, and migrant labour in developed capitalist countries and of the internal migrants (the so-called *limitchiki*) in the USSR today.[4] Secondly, as a low-wage workforce subject generally to a high intensity of labour, the surplus product they produced afforded the elite a certain buffer, allowing it to tolerate the concessions over earnings and the intensity of labour which managers were forced to grant other, usually male, workers in less easy-to-control sectors.

Unlike the other topics dealt with so far, the discussion of women workers is not confined precisely to the Khrushchev period. Many of the available sources cover not simply the Khrushchev years, but those immediately following his downfall. This is of little consequence, since the position of women in the home or in industry altered little over the course of the 1950s and 1960s. Indeed, the problems of low pay, marginalization into manual and low-skilled jobs, harsh working conditions, and the unequal sexual division of labour within the home appear as pressing today as they did 30 years ago.[5]

The structure of female employment

Tables 1.2 and 1.3 showed the size of the total industrial workforce and the proportion of women workers in major industries. Women industrial workers made up approximately one-third of total female employment outside collective farms. Nationally, women were 44 per cent of industrial workers in 1960 and 46 per cent in 1967. Of the roughly 10.2 million women workers in Soviet industry in 1965 (just after Khrushchev's fall), virtually two-thirds were employed in just four main industries: engineering, food, textiles, and the garment industry. In addition, there were 1.4 million women working in construction, an increase of over 60 per cent since 1958. These results are summarized in table 7.1.

It is noteworthy that there were nearly as many women employed in engineering as there were in the three main branches of light industry combined (food, textiles, and garments). It is also significant that in the non-Slavic republics (that is, excluding the Russian Federation, Belorussiya, and the Ukraine) the share of native women among native workers was almost uniformly smaller than the overall percentage of women workers in these republics, a fact which reflects the agrarian, and in many cases also the Muslim, character of their populations, both of which created serious obstacles to the entry of native women into industrial work.[6]

As in the West, women also made up the largest proportion – about three-quarters – of the so-called 'non-productive' sector, that is services, trade, health, education and science, and administration. By 1965, this sphere employed around 17.6 million women workers and clerical employees, or about half of all women outside the collective

Table 7.1. *Women workers by major industries, 1965 (thousands)*

Industry	10,159
Including:	
Engineering	2,998
Food[a]	1,243
Textiles	1,239
Garment	1,206
Building materials[b]	707
Footwear	270
Construction	1,419

[a] 1962 estimate.
[b] 1960 data.
Sources: Calculated from tables 1.2 and 1.3, taking 1965 data for the number of workers in each industry and interpolating the percentage of women from the 1960 and 1967 figures in table 1.3.

farms.[7] According to the 1959 census, there were also more than 16 million non-working women of working age, accounting for 90 per cent of the non-working able-bodied population.[8]

The distribution of female employment varied considerably from region to region. In the RSFSR at the start of 1960, women were a slightly larger proportion of industrial workers than in the country as a whole, a pattern reflected in engineering, iron and steel, wood-working, printing and publishing, and the food and garment indus-tries. Conversely, their share of workers in building materials, chemi-cals, and oil-extraction was slightly lower.[9] A quite different picture emerged in the Urals, where, because of the almost total absence of light industry, women were a far higher proportion of workers in heavy industry and construction than they were in the USSR as a whole. In Sverdlovsk *oblast'* in 1965, for example, they were roughly a third of workers in coal- and ore-mining and in iron and steel, and 36 per cent of workers in non-ferrous metallurgy.[10] In Chelyabinsk *oblast'*, they were approximately a third of workers in iron and steel and non-ferrous metallurgy, 44.4 per cent of engineering workers, and 61 per cent of chemical workers.[11] In the construction industries of Sverd-lovsk and Chelyabinsk *oblasti*, women were 35 and 36 per cent respectively, as against only 29 per cent nationally.[12]

If we look at how women workers as a whole divided up over different industries, we find that a full 24 per cent in Sverdlovsk *oblast'* worked in iron and steel and non-ferrous metals, 32 per cent in engineering, and only 3 per cent in textiles.[13] While the numbers in engineering were only slightly higher than the national average, those for metallurgy and textiles were quite striking. Nationally, only about 3 per cent of women workers were in iron and steel (as against 14 per cent in Sverdlovsk *oblast'*); conversely, 12 per cent of women industrial workers in the USSR were employed in textiles.[14] As we shall see, this concentration of women workers in Urals heavy industry did not give them better access to skilled trades or easier working conditions.

The marginalization of women into manual labour

One of the distinguishing features of Soviet industrialization was the attraction of women into branches of heavy industry from which they are normally excluded under capitalism. Once there, however, they found themselves pushed primarily into low-paid, manual work. This pattern was partially broken during World War II, when, as in Britain and the United States, large numbers of women entered industry to take over jobs – many of them skilled – left vacant by male workers now at the front. With the end of the war, these women – like their Western counterparts – were pushed out of these jobs, a process that probably reached its completion during the Khrushchev years.[15] In 1965, over a third of women workers were in low-paying branches of light industry (food, textiles, garments, and footwear). Access to other industries, such as engineering, had not, however, provided them with more skilled or better-paying jobs. Within production they tended to perform routine, often monotonous jobs as machine operators. As auxiliary workers, where women predominated, they found themselves concentrated in low-skilled, and often heavy manual jobs such as quality controllers, weighers, sorters and packers, warehousing and store-room attendants, and ancillary jobs in lifting and transport. At the other extreme, women were almost universally excluded from highly skilled jobs such as tool-setters and electricians, even within industries such as textiles, where they predominated numerically.

According to the population census of 1959, 15 per cent of turners were women, 48 per cent of other machine-tool operators (primarily capstan-lathe operators), and 64 per cent of press and stamp operators. At the same time, a mere 10 per cent of welders were women, 10 per cent of tool- and pattern-makers, 6 per cent of fitters, mechanics, and assemblers, and 6 per cent of tool-setters and tuners.[16] By the late 1960s this situation remained virtually unchanged: women were 80 per cent of ancillary workers in industry, 86 per cent of sorters, 98 per cent of packagers, and 80 per cent of packers (balers, etc.). By the same token, they continued to be an almost insignificant percentage of skilled tool-setters, even in industries where women workers predominated.[17]

More comprehensive All-Union data are not available, because the 1959 census gave only a partial list of the percentage of women in different industrial trades; similarly, the Occupational Censuses of 1959, 1962, and 1965 were never published, except for their most general sections. Fortunately, considerable material from the Occupational Censuses carried out in different regions and industries was presented in dissertations, from which we can piece together a more detailed picture of women's employment.

In the Ukraine, for instance, where women were 35.6 per cent of industrial workers, they were 40 per cent of machine-tool operators (15 per cent of metal turners, however), but 74 per cent of quality controllers, 76 per cent of store-room attendants, 64 per cent of ancillary workers, 20 per cent of milling-machine operators (a more skilled trade than capstan lathes, on which women traditionally predominated), 10 per cent of electricians, and such a small number of electrical fitters that they did not register in the statistics.[18]

In the Urals there was a very clear pattern, by which women were marginalized into certain trades: control and measuring; sorting and packing; warehousing; and manual ancillary jobs. In addition, they were over 80 per cent of sand-mixers, and over 90 per cent of core-makers in foundries; 97 per cent of signalworkers on factory railway networks; and 80 per cent of manual workers in the meat industry (much of which is extremely heavy work).[19]

The same pattern was true of the engineering industry, as table 7.2 shows. The pattern here is unmistakable. Women are shunted either into routine, mostly manual auxiliary jobs, or the less skilled production trades. The more skilled, better-paid, and rewarding the work, the fewer women there are doing it.[20]

Perhaps even more striking was the situation in the textile industry, where women made up three-quarters of the workforce and nearly 100 per cent of basic production trades, such as spinners, weavers, winders, twisters, and knitters. As in engineering, however, they were an infinitesimal percentage of skilled tool-setters, deputy foremen (whose main job was also tool-setting), and tuners. This had not always been the case, however, as the figures in table 7.3 make clear.

Table 7.2. *Women as a percentage of selected trades in engineering,*
2 August 1965

All workers	39.0
Storeroom attendants	90.0
Manual ancillary workers	73.0
Capstan-lathe operators	66.0
Painters	57.5
Milling-machine operators	21.0
Turners – metal-cutting machine tools	19.5
Fitters on machining–assembly jobs	16.0
Tool-setters, machine-tool tuners, instrument adjusters	7.8
Tool-setters of automatic machine tools	4.7
Maintenance electricians	3.8
Fitter–tool-makers, fitter–pattern makers	1.6
Fitter–assemblers	1.3
Maintenance fitters	0.7

Source: Starodub, dissertation, pp. 57, 84, citing unpublished Occupational
Census of August 1965.

Table 7.3. *Women as a percentage of tool-setters and related trades: Textiles,*
1959–1965

	1 August 1959	1 August 1962	1 August 1965
Tool-setters of automatic machines	48.1	20.0	3.0
Tool-setters, machine-tool tuners and instrument adjusters	25.3	9.7	9.2
Deputy foremen	17.0	—	11.0
Deputy foremen on mechanical ribbon looms	4.0	1.2	1.0
Foremen on automatic weaving machines	1.6	0.5	0.4

Sources: Starodub, dissertation, pp. 57–8; Maloletova, pp. 210–11.

Thus, as late as 1959 women had made up a quarter to a half of
skilled manual trades, *from which they were systematically displaced.* A
very similar, though less drastic, pattern was repeated in the engineering industry of Sverdlovsk *oblast'*, where the proportion of
women model-makers declined from 6.5 per cent in 1959 to 0.5 per cent

in 1965; tool-setters from 13.1 to 11.5 per cent (which was still twice the national average); and fitters–tool-makers from 2.8 to 1.2 per cent. The trend was much more pronounced in woodworking, where the percentage of women machine tuners fell from 11.7 per cent in 1959 to 1.7 per cent in 1965. According to Korobitsyna, the proportion of women was falling in other skilled manual trades: instrument adjusters, fitters, electrical fitters, and electricians.[21]

It is likely that three processes were taking place here. First, some skilled women manual workers were being pushed out of these jobs, partially through the enforcement of protective legislation. Secondly, as women who had entered these trades during the war reached retirement, their jobs were given not to a new generation of skilled women workers, but to men. Thirdly, and probably more significant, was the fact that, as the absolute number of tool-setters and similar occupations expanded with automation and increased mechanization, these jobs, too, were going almost exclusively to men, so that the proportion of women fell.[22] The cumulative result of these three trends was a *relative de-skilling of female labour*.[23]

The process of actually excluding women from skilled trades which they once held appears to have been most pronounced in ferrous and non-ferrous metallurgy, where a ban on women from a number of heavy and hazardous jobs which they had moved into during the war was clearly used as a pretext to remove them from work they could easily have carried on performing. In Sverdlovsk *oblast'*, the number of women manual metal-cutters fell from 79.2 per cent of the trade to 18.3 per cent; the number of teamsters in mines from 67 per cent to 6.5 per cent; hot-metal stampers from 36.6 per cent to 19.5 per cent; and workers with refractory materials in iron and steel from 40.6 per cent to 0. These were indeed dangerous and heavy jobs. At the same time, however, the share of women control-panel operators on furnaces and rolling presses also fell, from well over half to less than a quarter, a change that could in no way be justified on the grounds of labour safety.[24] A similar process occurred in ore-mining, where, in 1957, women were removed from underground work, with many being shifted to lower-paying and less-skilled jobs.[25]

Especially pronounced was the tendency for skilled jobs created as a by-product of automation (tool-setters and machine tuners; repair and maintenance) to go almost exclusively to men. This is illustrated by the case of Sverdlovsk *oblast'*, the data for which are presented in table 7.4. These show a fall in the proportion of men doing unskilled manual labour and a corresponding rise in those doing skilled manual

Table 7.4. *Male and female workers by degree of mechanization, Sverdlovsk 'oblast'', 1959–1965 (percentage of workers in each group)*

	Year	Group I	II	III	IV	V
Male Workers	1959	0.3	36.8	9.2	37.7	16.0
	1962	0.5	40.4	8.7	32.6	17.8
	1965	0.4	39.2	9.6	30.2	20.6
Women Workers	1959	0.5	37.5	9.2	52.0	0.8
	1962	0.8	38.5	9.4	50.4	0.9
	1965	0.8	39.5	9.2	49.1	1.4

Source: Brova, dissertation, p. 106, using data from the 1959, 1962, and 1965 Occupational Censuses of Sverdlovsk *oblast'*.

jobs. Brova, who presented these data, used the following categories, at that time standard in Soviet sociology.[26]
Group I   Automated jobs, involving numerous control functions.[27]
Group II Mechanized jobs using machinery and mechanical devices.
Group III Manual labour carried out on machinery and mechanical devices. This group included workers on specialized machinery, individual machines, or conveyors.
Group IV Manual labour without the aid of machinery or mechanical devices. Workers in this group carried out heavy physical labour.
Group V   Workers carrying out repair and maintenance on machinery and mechanical devices. This work combined manual and mental labour.
Whereas the percentages of women and men in the first three groups were roughly equal, women were far more likely than men to do heavy unmechanized labour, while men had virtually exclusive access to skilled manual trades.

This picture was repeated in virtually every industry in the *oblast'*. In iron and steel, women were one-third of all workers in 1965, but 42.5 per cent of those on heavy manual labour – this was over half of all women workers in the industry. Conversely, they were less than 5 per cent of skilled maintenance workers. In chemicals, where they were half the workforce, women were two-thirds of those doing heavy manual work (again over half of all women) and 2 per cent of skilled manual workers. In textiles, women had been 100 per cent of workers in Group I (fully automated labour) in 1959, but were only a third of such workers in 1965. Meanwhile, the percentage of women on heavy manual work climbed from 60 per cent to 70 per cent in the same period. Here, as elsewhere, they were a mere 5 per cent of skilled maintenance trades. In practically all industries except textiles women were a far higher percentage of those performing heavy manual work than they were of the workforce as a whole. Outside light industry, textiles, and food (where women predominated among production workers), at least half – and usually well over half – of all women workers were confined to these types of jobs.[28]

There is also anecdotal evidence to suggest that when heavy manual jobs were mechanized, women were removed from them and these jobs were given to men.[29] If true, this would explain why the trend in the USSR was quite different from that usually observed under capitalism, where mechanization is often accompanied by a simplification of tasks and the displacement of skilled male workers by lower-paid women. Such a tendency was excluded in the USSR by the absence of a labour market and the political impossibility of creating large-scale male unemployment. What was politically excluded for the regime became a determinant of economic necessity for industrial managers, who depended on their ability to carry out informal bargaining with workers on the shop floor in order to keep the enterprise functioning relatively smoothly. Here male workers were able to protect themselves from displacement or de-skilling in a way that women could not, since managers required their cooperation in other areas of factory life.

The issue was not simply that women were pushed out of skilled production trades into auxiliary jobs, but that these jobs remained unmechanized.[30] This was perpetuated by the managerial practice of concentrating investments and efforts at mechanization in production shops, neglecting auxiliary sections of the enterprise. While the main pressure for this undoubtedly came from the planning system, which placed a premium on gross production results, the fact that women were virtually a captive workforce in the auxiliary sector undoubtedly left managers free to feel that they could continue to ignore the problem. This profoundly influenced the job motivations of women workers: a Leningrad study published in 1965, found that, with the exception of women tool-setters and control-panel operators (who were insignificant in number), the most prevalent factor affecting women's choice of occupation was the absence of any alternative. Their selection of a job was a mere means to an end: earning their subsistence; minimizing distances between home and work (an essential consideration for women with pre-school or school-age children); the opportunity to work only one shift; the availability of dormitory space for single women; or just taking a job wherever they found one. Moreover, as will be discussed in the next section, most women felt that the combination of their jobs and their domestic situation offered them no prospects for upgrading their skills. This contrasted sharply with male workers, who were much more likely to take up a particular trade because it interested them (although a large minority of men also had entered their current job because they felt there was little choice).[31] The other side of this was that many women agreed to take jobs with hazardous and heavy working conditions (for example, in chemicals or iron and steel) because these offered better pay and were the only way out of the trap of low wages.[32]

Wage discrimination

Women workers earned on average less than 70 per cent of what men did.[33] Wage discrimination against women took three forms. First, a large proportion of women – well over a third – were concentrated in low-paying industries, primarily light industry and food, which together ranked at the bottom of industrial wages. As was noted in chapter 4, the average wage of industrial personnel (workers, clerical employees, and technical personnel) in light industry was less than half that in the fuel industry, where wages were highest.[34] Secondly, in heavy industry, women were marginalized into lower-paid manual jobs, usually in the auxiliary sector. Thirdly, even where women worked alongside men in the same trades and shops, they tended to be confined to the lowest wage and skill grades with poor prospects for promotion or skill enhancement. This applied not just to heavy industry, but to those branches where women workers predominated.

The low wages of women were a reflection of the fact that they were marginalized not just into low-paying trades, but into the lowest skill and wage grades, which were the determinant of earnings. In Leningrad industry, fewer than 20 per cent of men were in the first two skill grades, against 30 per cent of women. More interesting was the fact that for men there was a clear correlation between age, experience, and skill grades which simply did not exist for women. As men became older they also moved up the earnings ladder. Women did not.[35]

The situation in Leningrad was duplicated in other regions and industries. In the Urals, various surveys found that women were consistently in lower skill grades than their male counterparts, even where they had the same level of education.[36] Labzin's studies of women engineering workers in the Volgograd region and Moscow showed the same trend: the average skill grade of women was 20, 35 or even 50 per cent below that of men, depending on the trade and factory.[37] The latter data strongly suggest that the low grading of engineering workers brought about by the wage reform, which caused the industry such difficulties in holding on to its workers, was especially severe for – and was, indeed, to some extent at the expense of – women.

The trapping of women into lower skill grades was blamed in large part on the lower educational level of women workers, especially older women from the generation who had entered production in World War II. This to some extent reflected the artificial demographic bulge left by the war, with a large core of unskilled women workers in the upper age groups, alongside a younger – and hence better-educated – cohort of men. The actual picture, however, was clearly more complicated. For one thing, the textile industry, which had a relatively low age composition, still showed a lower average level of schooling than did heavy engineering.[38] This suggests that girls were still receiving less schooling than boys. At the same time, however, a trend was emerging where young women workers had better schooling than men but, despite this, ended up in the bottom skill grades.[39] One must also challenge the underlying assumption that women who were older or who had less than a complete secondary education were intrinsically unable to master machinery and equipment. Women workers in the Soviet Union at this time were certainly better educated than Soviet men during the 1930s or workers in capitalist countries during their big industrialization drives in the middle and late nineteenth century.[40] Perhaps more significant is the fact that educational levels of skilled manual workers in Britain in the 1950s were not especially high, but this did not impede them from acquiring a mastery of their jobs.[41]

Perhaps more relevant was the fact that very few women had the time or opportunity to enhance their training and thereby compensate for poorer initial schooling. One cause was simply housework, practically all of which fell on women. Labzin found, for example, that four-fifths of the women he surveyed gave up attempts to raise their qualifications as soon as they got married.[42] Brova reported an almost identical situation at the Chelyabinsk tractor factory. Among unmarried workers, about half of both sexes were enrolled in various courses.

Among married workers, however, the difference was striking: about half of married men still pursued further training, but only 15 per cent of married women.[43] This result went hand in hand with the huge increase in housework for women that came with marriage.[44] Of young people enrolling in vocational training colleges (PTU), a very small proportion were women – a mere 20 per cent for the country as a whole in 1965, and only 30 per cent in urban areas.[45] Access was somewhat better to factory-run training courses in heavy industry, where young women formed 30–40 per cent of the intake, but this still left them at a relative disadvantage, especially as women continued to be trained in 'female' trades.[46] In fact, up to 1967 women were actually barred from PTU training in a range of skilled trades: pattern-makers; foundry-core makers and mould-makers on machine moulds; tool-setters on automatic and semi-automatic turning lathes and on gear-cutting and gear-milling machines; fitters on machine-assembly work; electrical fitters; fitter–tool-makers; electricians on radio installations; and operators on various types of hazardous equipment. With the exception of the last category, none of these prohibitions could have been justified on safety grounds. And although the restrictions were eased in 1967, they continued to operate informally, since the PTU based their intake on the demands of factory directors, who often specified that they wanted male trainees, even in trades which women could easily do.[47]

Compounding these factors was the simple lack of incentive that low-skilled and badly paid work provided to participate in training courses or other efforts to upgrade skills. Yet these tendencies were all reinforced by the deep-rooted prejudices against women taking skilled jobs in heavy industry or challenging men as the chief bread-winners in the family. Here, too, women were caught in a self-perpetuating spiral: their low skills were used as a pretext for keeping them in this type of work, yet the pressures of this work, combined with their domestic situation, conspired to hinder them from acquiring the qualifications needed to advance to better jobs. Even as their general level of education improved, women continued to be marginalized into less qualified trades and lower wage and skill grades. The obstacles were more deeply rooted than just educational achievement. They were located in the structure of the economy and the specific role that women played in its reproduction. Better insight into this is provided by an examination of the working conditions of women workers, especially in so-called female industries and occu-pations.

Working conditions

Despite the reduction in the numbers of women on heavy or hazardous jobs, women still made up a substantial proportion of such workers. In non-ferrous metallurgy in Kazakhstan, for instance, they were nearly half of ore-crushers and almost all of transport workers on ore enrichment. In recognition of the difficulties of this work, the women who did it were accorded the right to an early pension: ore-crushers and some underground workers could retire at 45 with just seven and a half years' service; transporters in ore enrichment could take their pension at 50 after 15 years' service.[48] In the Urals, women were a substantial minority of workers carrying out various difficult manual foundry operations (including about one-third of stokers and nearly half of loaders working by hand). Here, too, women were willing to take these jobs because of material compensations, in this case the higher pay attached to heavy and hazardous jobs.[49]

There were a number of jobs which technically complied with existing health and safety standards, but where the work was none-theless extremely heavy. This was especially true of lifting jobs, since regulations limited the maximum weight of any one load that women could lift and transport, but placed no limit on the cumulative weight that could be carried over the course of a shift. Brick-making was a particularly graphic example. Women brick-moulders would lift up to 5,000 raw bricks in a shift, each weighing from 4 to 6 kilograms. Although this conformed to the law, the women were lifting 25 tons in a shift. When it came to unloading finished bricks, conditions were even worse, since in addition to the excessive weight (on some operations, shifting 10,000 bricks weighing 3 to 5 kilograms each) the women had to cope with the intense heat of bricks that had not yet cooled down after coming out of the ovens.[50] Women packers and loaders in the soap industry faced similar conditions, lifting and carting from 5 to 7 tons in a shift. In the paint and varnish industry the poor design of conveyors forced women in some factories to lift 40-kilogram drums on to the conveyor a hundred or more times over the course of a day.[51] This is not to say that managers did not also violate regulations. A 1964 survey of over 200 Leningrad factories allegedly uncovered a vast number of violations, with women having to cart 400-kilogram loads in wheelbarrows or haul 25 kilograms up a flight of stairs.[52]

The persistence of such heavy labour was directly connected, of course, with the undermechanization of primarily female auxiliary jobs. To some extent this was a by-product of managers' general unwillingness to apply innovations or new technology. Yet this trend – while encouraged by the planning system – was further reinforced by the fact that managers saw no reason to mechanize jobs done by cheap female labour.

The physical toll of heavy and/or intense work made itself felt in high turnover, often associated with women leaving their particular industry altogether. At a time when the regime was still finding it difficult to recruit non-working women into the workforce, the fact that women were not staying in such traditional industries as textiles or light engineering until retirement age must have seemed particularly alarming. A survey of spinners found almost two-thirds under the age of 30, and a mere 4 per cent working past the age of 45. Among weavers, over 80 per cent were younger than 40, and only 4 per cent over 50.[53] The same pattern emerged at the Svetlana electrical-appliance factory in Leningrad, where half of women were under 30, and nearly 80 per cent younger than 40.[54] These figures can in no way be attributed to women's family circumstances. On the contrary, women tend to drop out of the workforce when they are younger and their children are of pre-school age. It is precisely after the age of 40 that they have the time and independence to resume work. This exodus of women who, in terms of experience and ability, should have been at the prime of their working life, could be due only to working conditions.[55]

For many women a major problem was monotony. Whether they carried out heavy manual labour or worked on a conveyor, a large proportion of women's jobs involved highly repetitive operations that allowed little variation in the work routine. The work was further impoverished by the fact that it was often broken down into minute sub-operations. In the Sverdlovsk garment industry, for example, the women were so highly specialized in what they did that when a worker was absent it was difficult to find someone to replace her.[56] Conveyor work was especially bad in this regard, because the repetitiveness was compounded by the workers' lack of control over the speed and rhythm of the job, which remained more or less constant throughout the day and were the same for all workers, irrespective of abilities. The same applied to press operators, nearly two-thirds of whom were women. Their work involved just three basic operations: inserting the piece, stamping, and removing it. Given the technology prevailing in the 1960s, in the course of a shift a worker would carry out between 13,000 and 15,000 identical, monotonous movements. In addition, the work demanded speed, accuracy, quick reaction, and intense concentration.[57] As one would expect in these conditions, it was also very dangerous.[58]

Yet women were able to find definite compensations in monotonous jobs. Some allegedly felt that, although their work was tedious and boring, it was nonetheless socially useful, which gave them an indirect satisfaction.[59] More common was the feeling that the work was undemanding and left women time and space to think about themselves and their problems and to interact with their friends.[60]

Conditions in the textile industry

Perhaps the most detailed studies of working conditions for women workers were in the textile industry, where they revealed a portrait of high intensity and stress in what were frequently unsafe or unhealthy working conditions. In 1965 there were over 1.2 million women working in textiles. This was more than 1 in 20 of all industrial workers, and nearly 1 out of 8 women. The textile and garment industries, taken together, accounted for nearly a quarter of all women industrial workers.

Work in textiles was, and remains, noisy, dusty, hot, and humid. About one-third of a worker's time was spent repairing broken threads, an operation demanding speed, dexterity, and high concentration. It was estimated that the average weaver covered 15–20 kilometres walking between machines in one shift. The average spinner did less walking – a 'mere' 6 to 9 kilometres. In addition, the design and construction of spinning machines was poor, so that spinners had to work in uncomfortable positions. Mending broken threads, for example, had to be done in a stooping position. As spinners performed this operation some 1,500–2,000 times a shift, or between 35 and 38 per cent of their work time, this meant about three hours a day constantly bending over and straightening up. The work rate was also intense. Women were on the job more than 95 per cent of the time, with only one short break of 8 to 10 minutes. Compared with the accounts of the use of work time given in chapter 5, this was far higher than in any other industry. Work in textiles was also unhygienic, and associated with numerous health problems, including cardiovascular disease, deafness (due to excessive noise), back trouble, varicose veins, and rheumatic ailments.[61] A comparative study of textile and iron and steel workers found, for example, that the incidence of cardiovascular and rheumatic disease was higher in textiles.[62]

The stress and intensity of the work was, in Kalinina's words, 'right at the physiological limit of human capabilities'.[63] Equipment utilization in textiles, as measured by the so-called shift index (see chapter 3), was nearly 100 per cent, as against barely 50 per cent in engineering. Yet for all this, workers in light industry received less annual leave than workers in any other industry.[64] In addition to the strains of carrying out basic operations, there was also that caused by the threat of injury and the need to avoid it (shuttles flying off, burning one's fingers on high-speed spindles). Moreover, women had the additional burdens of child care and housework which, as we shall see, took up nearly as much time as their work in production.[65]

It was the technology of production itself, however, which placed women in textiles under the greatest strain, a problem which appears to have grown worse with mechanization. Quality controllers, for example, performed movements of only 0.5 to 3 seconds' duration, repeated some 70–79 times a minute, or 27,000 times a shift. This demanded considerable concentration and placed great strain on the eyes. In addition, they spent 11 per cent of their time doing heavy lifting. Most controllers did their entire job standing, with just a 20-minute rest over the course of a seven-hour day. Spinners and winders took 5 to 6 seconds to repair a thread-break, 1.5 seconds to remove a cop of spun thread and 7 to 9 seconds for a cop of wound thread. For weavers it took from 16 to 60 seconds to repair a broken thread. Like the work of controllers, all of these operations were repeated hundreds if not thousands of times in the course of a shift, involving the constant repetition of brief movements and terrible monotony. Thus a winder doing thread-rewinding, who had less than 14 minutes' rest over an entire shift, performed in that time over 2,000 monotonous operations, involving over 200 repetitive physical movements a minute – all while standing up in a semi-bent position.[66]

Some, if not most, of this stress could have been alleviated had equipment been better designed and manufactured. New automatic weaving looms introduced into the woollen industry in 1958 were so badly designed that in order to carry out quality control, a controller had to lie on the floor in the space between the looms, and carry out the inspection under ambient light.[67] Kalinina estimated that much of the bending done by spinners and weavers could be eliminated if the main work area of machines was raised a further 15 centimetres from the floor. Under then current construction, spindle bars were too low, requiring women to bend at a 60° angle when mending broken threads.[68] Similarly, the poor quality of raw cotton or wool increased thread-breaks, and thus imposed even greater strain on spinners and weavers.[69]

Fatigue was made worse by prevailing shift schedules, which compelled many women to work night shifts, usually in combination with a six-day week. The problems with night work were legion. Productivity and quality were notoriously worse than on day shifts. The physical toll on the women was also severe: they had less sleep, did more housework, and had a higher accident rate while on the job.[70] Night shifts were understandably unpopular, so much so that in Moscow women were prepared to move from factories on a three-shift system to one with just two shifts even if this meant a cut in pay.[71]

Conditions in the mills were poor. Temperatures in the summer months routinely reached 30°C to 42°C, causing even greater fatigue, which in turn increased the danger of accidents. The machinery generated a lot of vibration and noise. In addition to deafness, it also affected neurological functions and slowed down motor reactions. The result was both reduced productivity and increased risk of accidents, not least because women were unable to hear the warnings of other workers when dangerous situations developed.[72] Lighting and ventilation were also bad. A number of production and quality-control jobs already caused eye strain, which was made worse by the fact that lighting conditions in a number of mills were below even officially set standards, sometimes providing as little as one-third, or even one-fifth the permitted minimum.[73] Dust levels created a number of hazards. The main contaminants were natural-fibre particles, together with admixtures of earth and sand, and their concentrations at times exceeded statutory maxima by as much as fiftyfold. In addition, sizing and dyeing operations involved the use of other toxic substances – sulphuric, hydrochloric, and acetic acids, as well as caustic soda – which gave off harmful vapours. The problem was compounded by the poor state of Soviet ventilation systems. Soviet industry produced very little air-conditioning equipment, and what it did produce was often ineffective. Many ventilation systems only blew air into the workplace and did not extract it. They therefore did nothing to alleviate high temperatures in the summer months or high dust levels.[74]

The nature of the textile industry imposed a very different type of work regime than that which existed in most areas of heavy industry. If the characteristic feature of Soviet production is the worker's ability to appropriate a large degree of control over the labour process, such opportunities were much fewer – if not almost non-existent – in textile production. The intensity of labour, and the attendant degree of concentration and stress, were higher even than in those areas of light engineering and automobiles where the pace of work was largely dictated by the conveyor belt, but where workers still could 'conceal' certain 'reserves' (to use modern-day Soviet parlance) and expect important breaks in their routine due to problems with supplies and equipment breakdowns. The importance of a sphere of production where the regime could exercise greater control will be discussed in more detail at the end of this chapter. Conditions in the textile industry have changed little over the past two decades. The intensity of labour remains high and the women continue to work in hot, poorly ventilated, and unhealthy surroundings. One of the long-term consequences has been to make it increasingly hard to recruit women to the industry. The tradition of daughters following their mothers and grandmothers into the Ivanovo mills has virtually disappeared, and the industry has become dependent on migrant labour from smaller towns and the countryside. In the words of the manager of one Ivanovo weaving factory, 'What mother who has experienced all the "delights" of a weaving or spinning shop, is going to send her own daughter there?'[75] In the 1960s the mills undoubtedly seemed a more attractive alternative to unskilled manual work in heavy industry. With the expansion of the service sector, young women today have more of a choice of occupation, even though the alternatives are almost universally low-paid. Thanks to the continued migration from the countryside, however, the reserve army of cheap female industrial labour is still far from exhausted.

Domestic labour

The unequal division of labour within the home has long been documented in the Soviet Union, beginning with Strumilin's time-budget studies in the 1920s.[76] The Khrushchev period, too, saw the publication of numerous surveys of domestic labour on both an All-Union and a regional basis. At the same time it has been part of both official ideology and popular attitudes that women, despite participating fully in social production, should also bear the major responsibility for running the home. With few exceptions, those who have discussed the problem have seen the solution in the provision of better public services and labour-saving domestic appliances. Few have been so bold as to suggest that the problem lies not with technology, but with the organization of society and the attitudes of men which it engenders.[77]

The cost to women of their domestic burden was high. Together with the inequalities and discrimination women faced at work, it blunted their advancement within society and their all-sided development as human beings. The combination of a full day's work and half again as many hours afterwards doing housework left women little time for study, rest and leisure, or physical recreation. At the same time, for a certain section of women the poor prospects offered by employment acted to perpetuate domestic labour, by making it economically advantageous for women to stay at home – a factor which in turn reinforced existing prejudices about women's domestic role and helped reproduce the traditional division of labour.[78] The latter undoubtedly placed women under considerable emotional as well as physical strain, especially given that the man's refusal to help with housework was in many cases accompanied by heavy drinking. The two together were a major cause of divorce.[79]

Time-budget studies from the Khrushchev period universally showed that women spent more than twice as many hours a day on domestic labour (housework, shopping, and child care) as men, although the absolute amount varied from region to region. A 1959 survey of women workers (not necessarily in industry) in Moscow, Leningrad, Tbilisi, and Pavlovskii Posad (a small town in Moscow

Table 7.5. *Time budgets of women workers, 1959*

	Moscow		Leningrad		Tbilisi		Pavlovskii Posad	
	I	II	I	II	I	II	I	II
Work time	8:00	(33.3%)	8:00	(33.3%)	8:00	(33.3%)	8:00	(33.3%)
Other time spent at work[a]	1:30	(6.2%)	1:20	(5.6%)	1:40	(6.9%)	1:30	(6.2%)
Housework and child care	3:20	(14.0%)	4:40	(19.4%)	3:20	(14.0%)	5:30	(22.9%)
Rest	1:40	(6.9%)	1:10	(4.9%)	2:00	(8.3%)	0:25	(1.8%)
Sleep	6:40	(27.8%)	6:50	(28.5%)	7:40	(31.9%)	7:10	(29.9%)
Other	2:50	(11.8%)	2:00	(8.3%)	1:20	(5.6%)	1:25	(5.9%)

[a] Dinner break, travel to work, social work, etc.
Column I = hours and minutes.
Column II = time as a percentage of each 24-hour period.
Source: *Trudovye resursy SSSR*, p. 150 (M. Ya. Sonin). The survey covered 47 women in Moscow, 77 in Leningrad, 53 in Tbilisi, and 58 in Pavlovskii Posad.

Table 7.6. *Time budgets of men and women Ivanovo, Rostov, Gor'kii, and Sverdlovsk oblasti 1963 (hours and minutes)*

	Men			Women		
	Work days	Half day	Day off	Work days	Half day	Day off
Housework	2:03	2:17	2:58	5:27	5:53	6:13
Satisfaction of physiological needs	9:15	9:40	11:25	9:05	9:17	10:43
Free time	4:30	5:09	8:43	2:54	2:52	6:29

Source: Statistika byudzhetov vremeni, p. 57.

oblast') showed that women spent nearly half as many hours on domestic labour as they did at work (table 7.5).

Despite the small size of the survey, and its skewing in favour of the small town of Pavlovskii Posad,[80] its results were reproduced in other local studies. Sakharova's survey of workers' families in Krivoi Rog and Odessa and workers and clerical employees in Kiev found that urban women averaged 4 hours a day on housework, as against 1.5 hours for men. This extra time that women spent on housework was equivalent to 112 *extra working days a year*. Other surveys showed that women devoted even more time to domestic labour on weekends, when they were nominally off work a half day on Saturdays and all day Sunday. A 1963 survey of Ivanovo, Rostov, Gor'kii, and Sverdlovsk *oblasti*, carried out by the USSR's Central Statistical Administration, showed the pattern in table 7.6.

A separate study of Sverdlovsk *oblast'* in 1960 showed the same pattern. Men did 2 hours 36 minutes' housework on work days, and 4 hours 11 minutes' on their day off; women, by contrast, did 4 hours 23 minutes and 6 hours 27 minutes respectively.[81] The difference between men and women is even more stark when we realize that a sizeable share of the 'housework' done by men was on the private plot: about one-third of all male 'domestic labour' in Gor'kii and Ivanovo, and over 40 per cent in Sverdlovsk and Rostov (women's input into the private plot represented less than 10 per cent of their total housework).[82]

What this meant in concrete terms was illustrated by a survey of 100 workers in one shop of Leningrad's Kirov engineering works. There the average worker spent 11 hours a week on some form of study (an important means of upgrading skills and earning promotion in Soviet industry), and another 7 hours reading books and journals, but the distribution was highly unequal between men and women. Describing a typical day for one woman worker, she arrived home after spending 1.5 hours shopping, and then had immediately to get down to her other household chores: feeding the family, cleaning and tidying the flat, and doing the washing. She, like her husband, would have liked to study, but had not a single free minute. The only assistance she received from her husband was that he picked up their daughter from kindergarten on his way home from the factory. On Sundays she was up making breakfast while her husband slept. In the afternoon he took the child out for a walk for a few hours while his wife studied, but she was then back in the kitchen preparing dinner. The survey as a whole found that women averaged 22 hours a week on housework and men only 9. As this included men and women without families, the gap for married couples was even larger. Interestingly, the article reporting these findings saw the root of the problem not solely in the poor provision of services, but in the reactionary attitudes of men, who justified their non-involvement by reference to 'the right and title of the husband'.[83]

Women on night shifts proved to be at an even greater disadvantage. According to a survey of five textile mills in Kostroma, Leningrad, and Novosibirsk, women on the day shift averaged 3.5 hours' housework as against almost 6 hours for those on night shift. Most of the difference came at the expense of sleep: women working nights averaged a mere 5.5 hours, 1 to 1.5 hours less than women on days and evenings.[84]

Closer examination of time-budget studies reveals that the structure of domestic labour was determined by two main factors: the traditional sexual division of labour, and the shortages of food, household appliances, and communal services endemic to the Soviet economy. Table 7.7 shows how different household tasks divided up between men and women members of workers' families in Moscow and Novosibirsk in 1959.[85] With the exception of looking after children,[86] which in Moscow (but not Novosibirsk) was quite evenly distributed, women shouldered the burden of almost every household task. They spent an hour a day standing in queues and shopping, plus 90 minutes to 2 hours preparing food once they got home. In fact, shopping and preparing food together accounted for half of their housework in both cities. But it was also the women who cleaned the flat, did the household repairs, and washed and mended the clothes.[87]

Table 7.7. *Contributions to domestic labour by men and women in workers'*
families, Moscow and Novosibirsk, 1959 (hours and minutes per day)

| | Men | | Women | |
	Moscow	Novosibirsk	Moscow	Novosibirsk
Total on domestic labour and personal needs	1:53	2:30	5:16	7:14
Shopping (consumer goods and foodstuffs)	0:22	0:23	0:57	1:00
Preparing food	0:13	0:10	1:38	2:04
Looking after premises	0:07	0:27	0:30	0:51
Looking after clothing	0:03	0:03	0:42	0:47
Looking after children	0:29	0:22	0:36	1:11
Looking after oneself	0:35	0:32	0:34	0:37
Other expenditures of time	0:04	0:33	0:19	0:44

Source: Statistika byudzhetov vremeni, p. 52.

Given the length of time required to carry out given domestic tasks, women's burden was, therefore, increased first of all because most of the work fell on them. The other determinant, however, was the time needed to do these chores, irrespective of who executed them. Almost all washing was done by hand. In the late 1950s there were only 300,000 domestic washing machines among the entire urban population of the RSFSR, all of which were primitive, semi-automatic machines which were themselves time-consuming to use. Nevertheless, they still cut washing time to one-third of what it took to do it by hand.[88] By the mid-1960s, ownership of washing machines had expanded considerably, so that one out of 10 workers' families in the RSFSR had one, but this still left 90 per cent of working women without one. Other appliances were in equally short supply. Just over 2 per cent of workers' families had a vacuum cleaner; only 3 per cent had refrigerators.[89] Commercial laundries and similar services offered little by way of saving labour, due to their inefficiency and poor quality. In the mid-1960s, only 13 per cent of women used laundries, and even these women gave them only a small portion of their total washing.[90] Attempts to set up self-service launderettes came to very little. They were too few in number, underequipped, and the machines had inadequate capacity.[91] In all, for the average woman in an urban family in early 1964, the use of public services – including eating in cafeterias and canteens instead of shopping for food and cooking at home – made up a mere 5 per cent of the time spent on household chores.[92]

The time wasted standing in queues, although due mostly to chronic shortages, was needlessly extended by the primitive organization of retail trade. I am referring not so much to the somewhat baffling Soviet system of double queuing (where a shopper first waits to order goods and have them weighed and priced, and then has to stand in a separate line to pay for them), as to the shortage of prepackaged goods and food-stuffs. In Leningrad, the country's second most important city and rela-tively privileged by way of supplies, the percentage of prepackaged foods actually declined over the course of the early 1960s. In 1961, 47 per cent of milk sold in Leningrad was prepacked, but this fell to 41 per cent in 1964, and 38 per cent in 1965. A vast proportion of such items as butter, porridge, sour cream, macaroni, and even sugar was sold loose; like milk, the proportion worsened over the years 1959–65. It took con-siderably longer (three to six times, in Starodub's estimate) to buy loose produce than items that were prepackaged, entailing an otherwise needless expenditure of time and effort by shop assistants and shop-pers alike.[93] Moreover, the shortage of prepackaged foodstuffs would have made it impossible to introduce self-service grocery stores, even if the trading network had been inclined to go in that direction.[94]

The chronic shortage of child-care places – which could accommo-date only one-fifth of all children in the appropriate age group and probably only about half the demand for places[95] – affected domestic labour in ways not always recorded by the statistics. For one thing, it influenced how families organized shift schedules. At the Kirov Elek-trosila electrical-engineering plant in Leningrad, for instance, it was common (as it is in the West) for parents to work different shifts, so that someone would always be home to look after the children.[96] Families could thus spend an entire working week without being together except when they were asleep. Overcrowding in creches and kindergartens increased the frequency with which children took sick. When the children were ill, it was almost always the mother – never the husband – who stayed off work to look after them, often taking unpaid leave to do so. At the turbo-generator factory in Novosibirsk, women averaged 6 days' unpaid leave a year, compared to just 0.6 days for men.[97] Even where mothers had places for their children this did not solve the problem, since often the children were looked after only while the mother was working. After her shift, the mother would have to drag them around while she did the shopping or have them underfoot while trying to do the housework.[98]

Table 7.8. *Amount of housework per week by different age groups, Sverdlovsk oblast' (hours and minutes per week)*

	18 and under	19–24	25–9	30–4	35–9	40 and over
Total housework	17:10	19:23	30:16	39:49	44:42	37:17
Total free time	34:00	22:51	11:01	7:43	6:04	7:44

Source: Korobitsyna, dissertation, appendix, table 4.

The other important feature of domestic labour was the way in which its structure and character altered by age and family status. Korobitsyna's survey of women in Sverdlovsk *oblast'*, for example, found an incredible jump in the number of hours devoted to domestic labour as women entered their mid- to late twenties, with a corresponding fall in their free time (table 7.8).

These results are in no way surprising, and merely indicate that as women married and had children their domestic burden mushroomed, so that women in their thirties – the prime of their working lives – were putting in as many, if not more, hours in the home as they were at work. The increase in housework was extremely sharp, and indicates that the husband played almost no role in helping the women cope with increasing family responsibilities. Only when women reached 40, and their children were in their teens or older, did the amount of housework begin to fall.

These results were confirmed by other studies measuring changes in housework with family status. Korobitsyna found, for example, that an unmarried mother with one child did almost the same amount of housework (approximately 36 hours per week) as a married woman with one child.[99] In other words, the addition of a husband did absolutely nothing to ease the woman's domestic burden. What help he may have given was negated by the extra demands he placed on his wife to service *his* needs. A study of women workers in Krasnoyarsk *krai* (1963 data) showed a similar pattern. Single women averaged just over 2 hours of housework a day (including work on a private plot), as opposed to 5.5 hours a day for an unmarried mother and just over 6 hours a day for a married woman with young children. The main increase came with children, and only grew worse after marriage.[100] A smaller-scale study at Leningrad's Kirov engineering works showed the same result: whereas marriage meant a huge increase in housework for women, it brought no new commitment from the man.[101]

Instead of being serviced by his mother, he could now be tended by his wife.

As families grew in size and the amount of domestic labour increased, the entire burden fell on the woman. The Gor'kii study of the mid-1960s found that the amount of housework done by women workers went up by over 50 per cent with the first child and by two-thirds with the first two. Conversely, the amount of leisure or free time left to women more than halved, as did the time devoted to study.[102] Indeed, a study of three large enterprises in Kemerovo *oblast'*, including the Kuznetsk iron and steel combine, showed that men began to help with the housework in large families only when there were three or more children, although even then the added work of extra children fell disproportionately on the wife, who still put in 5 hours of housework on work days and nearly 10 hours on days off.[103]

Perhaps equally important was the fact that men and women became conditioned to these inequalities in domestic labour at a very early age. A 1963 RSFSR survey found that among teenagers aged 16 to 19, boys put in on average 24 minutes a day helping with the housework, as against 1 hour and 40 minutes for girls. Young men aged 20–4 gave 43 minutes a day, while women in this age group gave nearly 3 hours.[104] Danilova, commenting on these findings, noted that the idea of housework as 'women's work' was thus inculcated very early on, with young girls learning to do it and young boys being excused. These attitudes were in turn reinforced in school, where – as in the West until very recently – 'home economics' was taught only to girls.[105]

The domestic position of women workers – and women in general – was economically, culturally, and politically determined. Women provided countless hours of unpaid domestic labour, receiving little help from their husbands or sons. Men, and very probably most women, accepted this situation as a more or less 'natural' state of affairs. Men saw it as their right and women as their natural role. This situation was not going to change through better consumer goods or improved communal services. It would change only when women decided that the situation had to change, and to confront men over the unequal division of labour. As in the West, women were unlikely to do this as individuals. Only through an organized feminist movement would they acquire the awareness and the confidence to articulate and press these demands. Unfortunately, even now, when there has been a huge growth in political activism in the Soviet Union as a consequence of liberalization, no feminist movement has emerged.

The perpetuation of traditional attitudes towards women and domestic labour reinforced their marginalization into low-paying and low-skilled jobs at work. It made it much harder for them to acquire the skills needed to move into more skilled trades or to win promotion. At the same time, it helped reinforce prejudices about 'women's work', which then became a pretext for excluding them from better jobs. It was a vicious circle, for their marginalization at work in turn gave support to men's conviction that housework was unskilled labour and women, and women alone, should do it.

Conclusion: the contradictions of female labour

With the exception of wartime, one of the major functions of women industrial workers under capitalism has been as so-called 'dilutees', where mechanization has allowed management to replace skilled male workers with non-skilled and lower-paid women. This has either occurred as direct displacement (for example, textiles in the nineteenth century), or by creating new industries or industrial processes which were staffed by women, and which supplanted older industries or processes that employed men.[106] This pattern has been only partially repeated in the USSR. Prior to the Revolution, for example, men made up almost half of all textile workers, but by the end of the First Five-Year Plan this industry was almost exclusively female.[107] Women also have made up the bulk of the workforce in new conveyor- and assembly-based industries, especially light engineering. But there have also been important differences with capitalism. With Stalinist industrialization, women entered many 'male' trades, especially as machinists in engineering, but also in the building trades (as crane operators, for example), where they faced a different kind of discrimination. They were kept in lower wage and skill grades, so that they received less money and found it difficult to win promotion. Parallel with this trend, women became – and have remained – the bulk of workers in manual, unmechanized, and largely (although not exclusively) low-paid auxiliary jobs on internal transport, loading, packing, sorting, and quality control, some of which (packing and sorting) are also female occupations in the West, but others of which (primarily heavy manual work) are usually done by men.

The role of the family in determining the structure of female employment has also differed under capitalism and in the USSR. Under capitalism, women have been the flexible element in the workforce, a pool of labour able to be drawn into production at times of a labour shortage (during the World Wars, for example), and readily expelled when their labour power was no longer needed. As Beechey has noted, women, unlike men, can be made redundant at little cost to the state, for when they lose their jobs, they are reabsorbed back into the domestic economy.[108] At the same time, women have been readily recruitable into low-wage areas, because earnings were still higher than unpaid domestic labour. Women workers in the Soviet Union are in a quite different position. The problem – at least until the end of the 1970s – was not how to use women as an easily unemployable work-force, but, on the contrary, how to attract them back into the labour market. In fact, during the Khrushchev period, the problem, as we have noted, was how to overcome the economic incentives that many women had to remain within the domestic economy, where their labour was more advantageous to the family budget than work in industry or services.[109] Moreover, once recruited, there was no question of women being made redundant, although they could be displaced from certain mechanized jobs if management felt compelled to offer this work to men.

Thus the decision by Soviet women to enter social production has brought with it a multi-dimensional exploitation, based on the fact that they will hold down a full-time job and shoulder almost the entire burden of domestic labour. In fact, this has been both official policy and the dominant ideology of women and men. Most married women decide to stay in employment because the family needs the extra wage, even though it is significantly lower than that of their husbands. Women also value work in its own right and, as we have seen, find various social compensations even in the most monotonous and tedious jobs. The role of the family is crucial here, because it establishes structural limits to women's acquisition of skills (little free time, exhaustion) and concurrently reproduces a patriarchal ideology which also circumscribes their occupational opportunities.

In general, we can identify a duality in female industrial employment in the USSR. In industries such as textiles, the garment industry, and light engineering and other processes based on conveyors and assembly lines, women hold jobs which are relatively tightly regulated in terms of the intensity of labour and the use of work time, and they subsequently find it far harder than their male counterparts in heavy industry to extract concessions from management over work organization or earnings. On the contrary, the percentage of utilized work time is high – far higher than for industry as a whole – while wages are low. This, then, is a sector where the elite is relatively successful in controlling the extraction and disposal of the surplus product, a fact which is indirectly reflected in the high profits generated by light industry, which are skimmed off into the state coffers.[110] There, instead of providing resources for new investment in light industry and an expansion of consumer goods, they allow the elite a certain leeway in tolerating its relative lack of control over the labour process in other sectors of industry, including the granting of concessions to male workers over the use of work time and adherence to formal wage regulations. This does not mean that heavy industry is being 'subsidized' by 'super-profits' extracted from light industry. It does mean, however, that the limits on the surplus due to waste and the elite's relative lack of control over the labour process are partially compensated and kept within bounds which, until recently, allowed the economy to continue to carry out expanded reproduction, albeit in crisis-ridden form.[111]

The other main area of female employment is in non-skilled, manual auxiliary jobs. These jobs are generally heavy and unpleasant, and usually low-paid. Productivity in this sphere is low, partly because these jobs are unmechanized, and partly because the prevalence of manual labour gives these workers greater control over the intensity and pace of their labour.

If we look at this latter area of employment first, we see that it engenders its own contradictions, rooted in the conflict between the needs of the economy as a whole and those of the individual enterprise. This was partly recognized by Starodub, who described it in the following terms:

> At the current state of development of our society a clear contradiction is taking place. On the one hand, our country possesses highly mechanized enterprises, where the process of production places growing demands to raise the level of general education and skills among workers. On the other hand, about half of industrial workers – the majority of them women – are still employed on manual labour, which at times does not permit them to raise their cultural–technical level. The existence of low-skilled jobs lowers the average level of labour productivity. Since it is mainly women who work at low-skilled jobs, it is precisely owing to them that the general level of labour productivity is falling.[112]

Starodub's observations bring together two basic problems: the impact of undermechanization on the performance of the economy as a whole, and its particular effect on women workers. The duality of female employment means that, thanks to the existence of jobs where the labour process is tightly controlled and wages are low, the elite can tolerate concessions to more strategically important sections of the workforce, primarily men.[113] At the same time, women constitute a pool of unskilled, low-productivity workers whose labour is harder to control, which thus undermines the performance of the entire economy and of the enterprise itself. The undermechanization of auxiliary jobs, as we have seen, is a major source of bottlenecks and disruptions to production, lowering overall productivity and in many cases negating the results of the more mechanized labour of workers in direct production.

On the surface, the retention of this sector, therefore, appears wholly irrational, due solely to the structural rigidities of the planning system. This, however, overlooks two important economic functions which it serves. First, from the enterprise's point of view, it is possible, indeed probable, that individual managers have found it economically more expedient to maintain an inefficient, but low-wage auxiliary sector – despite its impact on overall production results – than to invest in the equipment needed to mechanize these operations. Here the expectations and assumptions about low female wages have surely played a key role.

Secondly, there is another, deeper level at which the maintenance of this army of unskilled women workers is crucial to the regulation of the Soviet economy, even while it acts to undermine its efficiency and erodes the production of the surplus. For at a society-wide level, the existence of this 'reserve army' of low-skilled manual workers has been essential for two reasons. First, these workers (who, since the late 1960s have been made up not just of women, but of migrant workers of both sexes from rural areas) have done jobs that men have refused to do, at least under prevailing working conditions and wages. Secondly, and equally as important, this reserve army has been vital in getting women to take jobs in tightly controlled areas of production, where the rate of exploitation and extraction of the surplus is higher (textiles, light industry, conveyors, stamp-press operators, etc.). If women had a real choice, if they were not effectively barred from skilled and highly skilled production jobs, if auxiliary jobs in industry were better-paid with acceptable working conditions, it would be extremely difficult to recruit and hold women in high-intensity industries. This has already become the case today in textiles, which now relies overwhelmingly on rural migrants, since urban women are no longer willing to put up with the strains and stresses of this type of employment.[114] Women prefer to enter the service sector, where the pay is also bad, but conditions are far less strenuous. Insofar as the existence of this high-intensity sector has played an important role in helping the elite to regulate the economy, maintaining a steady flow of low-paid women workers has been a central task. Yet this supply of labour has in large part been conditioned upon the existence of the reserve army of low-paid manual workers, who in effect act as a disciplining factor, limiting alternatives.

In this sense, the concessions granted to workers in heavy industry (most, but not all, of whose beneficiaries are men), while being largely reproduced by the actions of the workers themselves, are to a significant extent also made possible by the subordinate position of women workers in high-intensity areas of production and the unskilled auxiliary sector. Thus the privileges men enjoy in the home are mirrored in those they are granted at work. The position of women workers is, therefore, even more contradictory than the above discussion may have indicated. Their specific role in production involves an enormous waste of human resources and potential, and acts to perpetuate the relatively backward structure of the Soviet economy. Yet at the same time it provides the elite with the means partially to compensate for the loss of control which is both reflected in and perpetuated by this same backwardness. Politically, the relative privileges that men derive in the home and at work at the expense of women act further to atomize the workforce and undermine its eventual re-emergence as a class for itself, able to act as a self-conscious collective historical agent and challenge the elite for power. The position of women thus impinges upon the most basic contradiction of all in Soviet society: the need for the elite to maintain the atomization of the working class as a means of ensuring its own domination, and the inherent instability of the system that arises from that atomization. It is only now, with the potential re-emergence of politics and class struggle in the Soviet Union that events may allow the working class to transcend this contradiction. But it will do so only as a universal class, fighting to satisfy the radical needs of all workers. This means not just overcoming racial and national conflict, but gender divisions as well. As the experience of the West has shown, this process is unlikely to begin until the women themselves organize to initiate it.

8   Skill, de-skilling, and control over the labour process

The Braverman debate

One of the essential arguments of this book has been that the labour process within Soviet industry plays a fundamental (although in no way exclusive) role in defining the society's overall system of production. Implicit in this argument is the idea that, if this system of production is historically unique and different from capitalism, then so, too, are its labour process and the underlying relations between workers, managers, and the ruling elite (ruling class) within production. This does not mean that the labour processes (for the labour process, as we have seen, is by no means identical from one branch of production to another) within Soviet industry do not share many common features with the labour processes observed under capitalism. I have argued that, on the contrary, the survival and eventual promotion of capitalist technology and forms of industrial organization and management in the 1920s were a major factor which weakened the post-revolutionary Soviet working class and paved the way for Stalinism. Many of the forms of work organization and defensive practices developed by Soviet workers on the shop floor are also found in capitalist factories, although not as universally and systematically as they occur in the USSR. More to the point, because the overall economic and political context in which they take place is fundamentally different between the two systems, the meaning of these practices also differs. While capitalist management has learned either to adapt to these practices or to break them down, and indeed, as Burawoy has argued,[1] even to transform them into one of the ideological pillars of capitalism's continuing stability, in the Soviet Union they constantly lead the system to the point of crisis.

The nature of the labour process under capitalism has itself been the subject of intensive debate and study, most notably following the publication in 1974 of Harry Braverman's outstanding book, *Labor and Monopoly Capital*. This was a detailed investigation, informed by Braverman's own experiences as an industrial worker, as well as by his painstaking research and critical marxist theory, of the way in which capitalism in the twentieth century has gradually denuded work in both industry and services of its skill content, leaving the worker as a simple executor of functions defined and determined by management. The advance of contemporary monopoly capitalism has, according to Braverman, in fact been predicated upon the capitalist gaining increasing control over the labour process and removing all decision-making, as well as control over work speeds and organization, from the worker. Braverman views this process primarily from the perspective of the skilled manual craft worker of the late nineteenth century, who had used his (rarely her) skills and knowledge of production to regulate the intensity of labour and to enrich the content of his work through control over job design. For such workers (who were by no means typical of all workers even in the period Braverman takes as his model), their skills and knowledge of craft processes gave them considerable control over the labour process precisely because they possessed them and management did not. Management was dependent on the workers' assessment of how much could be produced and in what fashion.

To Braverman, management's aim was to raise the intensity of labour by breaking down this control. This it achieved by separating the worker from conception, job design, and other areas of decision-making within the work process, and transferring these functions to itself. Among the vehicles for accomplishing this were automation, the assembly line, the creation of a new managerial stratum of rate-fixers, and later on the introduction of machine tools with programmed controls. Central to this process for Braverman was the adoption of so-called scientific management techniques, as pioneered by F. W. Taylor. Braverman devotes a great deal of his discussion to Taylorism, which he sees as the model that capitalist management was to follow. Taylor, by his own admission, was attempting to find a system of management which would deprive workers of both the incentive and the means of restricting output. He believed that by careful study of any particular job a single, optimal way could be found to do it, and that, through the 'correct' system of incentives and work organization, the worker could be made to carry it out along these lines. Naturally, the adoption of more efficient work methods would lead to greater output, not to mention greater effort on the part of workers, but a precondition to this was that essential decisions regarding job organization and design must now rest with management. Braverman interpreted the implications of Taylor's system as follows:

> Workers who are controlled only by general orders and discipline are not adequately controlled, because they retain their grip on the actual process of labor. So long as they control the labor process itself, they will thwart efforts to realize to the full the potential inherent in their labor power. To change this situation, control over the labor process must pass into the hands of management, not only in a formal sense but by the control and dictation of each step of the process, including its mode of performance. In pursuit of this end, no pains are too great, no efforts excessive, because the results will repay all efforts and expenses lavished on this demanding and costly endeavor.[2]

As scientific management techniques became more widespread, the worker was reduced increasingly to a mere extension of the machinery he or she operated or, as in the case of strictly manual labour, to a simple executor of management instructions. The result in practice was the de-skilling of work and the workforce, and the impoverishment of the content of labour.

Braverman's argument has come in for considerable criticism from a number of quarters. There have been three principal objections to his analysis. First, he has relied almost exclusively on the experience of industry in the United States, and has generalized these observations to apply to capitalism as a whole, when in fact the US experience has not necessarily been typical of other countries.[3] Secondly, Braverman has tended to romanticize the skilled manual craft worker, holding him or her up as an ideal type who was able to combine intellectual and manual labour. He cites, for example, the training of skilled machinists in the late nineteenth century, who in order to do their jobs required a knowledge not just of how to operate equipment, but of mathematics and metallurgy.[4] But even if he has not idealized the actual work experience of these workers, the fact remains that they were typical only of certain branches of American industry, and were hardly representative of the working class as a whole. Thirdly, and most importantly, Braverman has tended to identify managerial *policy* with its actual implementation on the shop floor. In fact, reality was and remains far more complex, as any student of the Soviet economy will know. Workers did not accept management attempts to introduce scientific management passively, but reacted to it and developed various defensive mechanisms through which they could retain control over vital areas of the work process.[5] In fairness to Braverman, however, while it is true that he tends to treat the working class as passive and overlooks the defensive responses of workers and lower-level managers alike, it is probable that their actions have not nullified the long-term tendency towards de-skilling and the divorce of workers from job-related decision-making.

The debate over Braverman's book is too complex for me to do it justice here. What is important here is that several aspects of this debate are directly relevant to the themes taken up in this book. Primary among these are the similarities between patterns of worker–manager behaviour in Soviet industry and apparently similar forms of behaviour in the West. The control over output by workers under capitalism dates back to well before Taylor's day, so that it was already long established by the time he developed his system. 'We who were the workmen of that shop', noted Taylor about his early days as a machinist, 'had the quantity of output carefully agreed upon for everything that was turned out in the shop. We limited the output to about, I should think, one-third of what we could very well have done. We felt justified in doing this, owing to the piecework system – that is, owing to the necessity for soldiering under the piecework system.'[6] By 'soldiering' Taylor meant the regulation of effort 'with the deliberate object of keeping their employers ignorant of how fast work can be done'.

> So universal is soldiering for this purpose, that hardly a competent workman can be found in a large establishment, whether he works by the day or on piece work, contract work or under any of the ordinary systems of compensating labor, who does not devote a considerable part of his time to studying just how slowly he can work and still convince his employer that he is going at a good pace.[7]

It was Taylor's view, however, that output restriction had a rational basis. Workers had discovered through hard experience that if they worked harder and raised output, they would simply have their piece-rates cut, since employers already had a fixed idea of the maximum daily wage they were prepared to pay. If workers exerted themselves and produced more, employers would simply lower job prices in order to keep overall earnings constant.

> After a workman has had the price per piece of the work he is doing lowered two or three times as a result of his having worked harder and increased his output, he is likely to entirely lose sight of the employer's side of the case and to become imbued with a grim determination to have no more cuts if soldiering can prevent it.[8]

Taylor's account shows clearly that attempts by workers to control the labour process, and thereby to regulate the amount of effort they must expend in order to achieve a 'reasonable' level of earnings, are neither specifically Soviet nor an especially modern-day phenomenon. Roy, too, observed an almost identical rationality when he worked as a radial-drill operator in an American machine shop in 1944–5. Workers were careful not to turn in too much work, since experience showed that high output levels would provoke almost immediate rate cuts by management. This led to enormous losses of work time, since more experienced workers could fulfil their self-imposed quotas in barely more than half a shift, leaving them idle for the rest of the time. Roy himself reached a point where he averaged two free hours a day. By the same token, if jobs were poorly paid, workers might still be able to make money on them by running them – against factory regulations – during the 'free' time they built up on easier jobs. If this failed, they might deliberately cut their work effort as an expression of their discontent, even if this cost them money in the short run.[9]

Although the idea of an accepted level of earnings which workers must be allowed to reach clearly prevailed in Soviet factories, I have found little evidence from either the Stalin or Khrushchev periods to suggest that workers restricted output specifically as a means of avoiding rate cuts.[10] The emphasis, rather, was on controlling the amount of effort they had to expend to achieve what they deemed to be an acceptable level of earnings. This meant keeping norms low so that targets might be reached without excessive strain within the context of highly uncertain conditions of production. Where norms were held low enough, this merely led to high levels of overfulfilment.[11] The significance of the Taylor and Roy accounts, however, is not the specific form of control which they highlight, but the fact that the possibilities to exercise this control exist in both systems. There are other areas within the labour process where the parallels between capitalism and the USSR are more direct, some of which were noted in earlier chapters.[12] These similarities are not superficial, but in many cases are structurally rooted in the conditions of production prevailing in both capitalist and Soviet factories. Tom Lupton, for example, describes how workers in an engineering plant in which he worked as a young man during the 1930s routinely left work 15 minutes before the end of a shift, and took unofficial tea breaks or time off for informal discussions.[13] Roy relates how, whenever management attempted to block workers from manipulating the incentives system, the workers would immediately counter with even more 'ingenious' methods of manipulation, involving quite complex forms of collusion between production and service workers.[14] For both Lupton and Roy, these were not capricious acts by workers, but attempts to protect themselves from the uncertainties of production (which might cost them earnings) or from managerial pressures.

Another similarity with the Soviet Union is the apparent willingness on the part of many lower-level shop managers – at least outside the United States – to collude with workers in various fiddles, primarily in order to win a quiet life. Littler notes how foremen and even some managers opposed job analysis and time-and-motion studies in British industry between the World Wars, because they resented the potential erosion of their authority. At one Birmingham factory, lower management subverted time-study schemes by having a separate time-study man in each shop under the jurisdiction of the foreman. Littler quotes one observer in an account that could easily have appeared in the Soviet press:

> Chargehands are in effect running the shop as a collection of almost independent small factories ... each man making what he thinks is required, or what happens to be an easy job for any machine.[15]

Shop managers often preferred to by-pass rate fixers and deal directly with their workers, since this allowed them to maintain flexible working relations and at the same time preserve their authority. Littler cites another passage from Lupton on precisely this point:

> There is little wonder that there is much common ground between shop stewards and front-line supervision in many industries on the point that work-study men are a 'pain in the neck.' It is much easier for them to reach agreement, say about piece-work prices, where there is plenty of vagueness and room for manoeuvre than it is when there is someone around with sheets full of synthetic times to 'blind you with science.'[16]

The other side of this, as Lupton noted in his book, was that even rate fixers had to agree to keep rates within reasonable limits if they wanted a comfortable existence.[17]

At an even deeper level, Lupton noted that the engineering enterprise where he worked was able to tolerate wages manipulations and limits on effort precisely because it had a secure market and was under no pressure to reduce wage costs.[18] This is important, for it indicates that those areas of capitalism where 'Soviet-type' phenomena can be observed are precisely those where the market – either the sales market or the labour market – has been eroded and enterprises have acquired a certain freedom from budgetary constraints, similar in type (although not·in scale) to those enjoyed by Soviet managers. Equally significant was Lupton's observation of the reproducibility of workers' control over the labour process, at least within British engineering in the 1950s. Essentially, the piece-work system encouraged workers to falsify their records of how much time they spent on each job. Management, however, used this false data when making the calculations needed to co-ordinate production. The result in many cases was severe disruptions to the flow of components and supplies, which then compelled workers *to carry on* manipulating the system in order to protect their earnings from these same dislocations.[19] Thus the workers, by pursuing perfectly rational actions in defence of their own interests, became in turn a partial cause of the very conditions that necessitated these actions. This was a system which then reproduced itself from one production period to the next. The difference with the USSR is that in Britain and other capitalist societies this system was confined to particular enterprises or sections of industry, whereas in the Soviet Union it has become characteristic of the economy as a whole. It does, however, neatly point up the problems of acquiring the knowledge needed for planning in a society based on class antagonisms. It was these antagonisms that were ultimately responsible for the workers' need to distort the system, thus depriving the planners of the information they needed to draw up a workable plan.

It is important, however, to recognize just how *contingent* many of these institutions and practices in the West are upon the particularities of given industries, the specificities of their local labour markets, or transient historical factors. Roger Penn, for example, points to the example of Rochdale and Peterborough engineering workers, who, through their strong trade union organizations, were able to take advantage of tight local labour markets and forestall de-skilling by securing for skilled workers a monopoly over jobs that could have been done by workers with lower skills.[20] Perhaps equally important here is David Lee's argument that trade union attempts to prevent skill dilution have in the long run proved unable to resist structural changes in capitalism, which have undermined workers' ability to defend their control on the shop floor. On the one hand, new industries or processes have by-passed, or grown up alongside older enterprises where craft skills were not eroded. On the other hand, recessions have successfully driven craft workers out of their trades or industries.[21]

We must emphasize that the protection of skills is not necessarily the same as control over the labour process, although under capitalism the erosion of craft has been an important mechanism for diluting this control, while defence of skills has been an equally important vehicle for retaining it. As the experience of the Soviet Union has shown, there are large areas of unskilled manual labour where workers preserve a great deal of control, at least over how they dispose of their work time. What we see, however, is that in capitalist industry both the protection of skills and retention of control over the labour process do not assume the generalized and systematic character that they do in the USSR. We shall deal with this argument in greater detail later on. For the moment, it is important to note that, whatever the limits of Braverman's argument as applied to capitalism, it has a great deal of applicability to the USSR, although here, too, the process of removing workers from decision-making within the labour process provoked strong counteracting tendencies.

De-skilling in Soviet industry

Braverman's argument about the separation of conception and execution finds clear evidence among machine-tool operators in Soviet industry, particularly in engineering. As was noted in chapter 6, one of the strategies for gaining control over the workforce in the 1930s was the breaking up of job assignments into minute repetitive tasks. This was in sharp contrast to the generalist–machinists of the pre-Stalinist period, who carried out his or her own auxiliary tasks and determined the organization and speed of work. One of the long-term legacies of Stalinist policy was considerable amounts of lost work time, as machinists had to wait for tool-setters and adjusters to come and tune their machines every time they began a new job.[22]

This divorce from decision-making was in fact a generalized phenomenon, and not confined to machine-tool operators or to engineering. We have already seen how a large proportion of women workers are in jobs where they have virtually no control over job design or work organization, at the same time as they find fewer opportunities within the labour process to ease the intensity of labour. The huge pool of semi- and unskilled manual labour within Soviet industry is also indicative of a large reserve of workers carrying out menial tasks with little room for 'conceptualization', although they often have considerable control over how they make use of their work time.

In the 1960s, Soviet sociologists carried out a number of surveys of workers in particular localities and industries which highlighted the process of de-skilling and the economic problems that derived from it. Perhaps the largest and most ambitious was a study carried out in Gor'kii in the early 1960s. The authors divided workers into six skill classifications, similar but not identical to the more standard divisions cited by Brova in her study of the skills of women workers in the Urals.[23]

1. Workers employed on automatic machine tools, automatic lines and assemblies, and on control panels of electric power stations and chemical plants. This group, although rapidly growing, was still a very small percentage of all workers. It was, in fact divided into two subgroups. The first were workers who combined tool-setting and the tending of automatic lines or machine tools with programmed controls, or with the supervision of complex assemblies in the chemical, oil, or similar industries. This work was complex and demanded considerable engineering knowledge. Workers in these jobs tended to be highly educated (sometimes possessing even some higher education) and, because of the considerable amount of mental labour involved, generally found their work interesting. They were, however, a small portion of Group I. Far larger were operators of various automatic machine tools, who did only a limited amount of their own tool-setting or skilled auxiliary operations. These were by far the largest component of Group I, and their work was broken up and monotonous. Thus a large portion of this group of skilled manual workers was in fact working under conditions which differed little from those of less skilled workers.

2. Workers employed on mechanized labour on metal-cutting machine tools, hammers, presses, forge-press machinery, open-hearth and thermic furnaces, etc. They were the largest group of industrial workers, making up some 35 per cent of all production workers (that is, excluding auxiliary workers) in the USSR. At some Gor'kii factories, their percentage was even higher. With automation, this group was contracting and some of its workers were moving into jobs in Group I – although without necessarily enriching the content of their labour. As the authors of the Gor'kii study later point out, these workers were engaged primarily on mechanical, physical labour with little scope for conceptualization or exercising direct control over the labour process. We shall see at the end of the chapter, however, that this assessment must be qualified, for the almost constant hitches and bottlenecks in production frequently impelled these workers to assume more control over work organization and design than the formal structure should have allowed.

3. Workers carrying out manual labour on machines and mechanical devices, for example loaders and transporters on conveyors, sorters sorting parts and raw materials, and so on. Although this group was small within Gor'kii enterprises, it was *growing* due to the poor integration of the mechanization of different processes.

4. Workers using manual tools (shovels, hammers, chisels, etc.). This was a heterogeneous group which included both highly skilled workers, such as fitters and tool-makers, and unskilled workers, such as carriers, store-room attendants, and manual sorters. At most of the enterprises surveyed, this group was quite large, accounting for up to one-quarter of factory establishments. The exception was the Gor'kii Automobile Factory, which underwent comprehensive mechanization in the early 1960s, and managed to reduce the size of its manual workforce to 7 per cent of its total establishment.[24]

5. Tool-setters and repair and maintenance workers. These were highly skilled manual workers, whose work was labour-intensive, but relatively rewarding and interesting. The size of this group varied from factory to factory, ranging from a low of 7 per cent of the establishment at the Gor'kii milling-machine factory, to a quarter of the workers at the city's Motor factory. On the whole, we know from the Occupational Census that this group, if we include electricians and electrical fitters engaged on repair, formed a sizeable minority of industrial workers – to the order of 10 per cent in 1965.[25]

6. Workers on conveyors. These represented a surprisingly small share of workers in Gor'kii, including a mere 10 per cent of workers at the Gor'kii Automobile Factory.

When the authors of the Gor'kii study set about analysing the job content of each of these groups, the separation of conception and execution was obvious. Unlike tool-setters, whose work involved a wide variety of operations, most of which combined physical and manual labour (analysing jobs, making necessary calculations), the labour of workers on conveyors, machine tools, and semi-automatic and automatic machines was dismembered and repetitive. It entailed a continuous cycle of identical movements, and was monotonous and tiring.[26] These observations, in fact, conformed to those of an earlier, more general study, which found that the typical machine-tool operator spent less than 10 per cent of her or his time on tasks requiring conceptual input from the worker (job analysis, adjusting and setting equipment, etc.). This contrasted sharply with tool-setters, over 80 per cent of whose time was spent on job analysis, instructing other workers, drawing up job sheets, setting and adjusting, and technical maintenance.[27] The impoverishment of work was even more pronounced for workers on conveyors. Commenting on the mechanization of foundry shops (where manual labour was especially heavy and unpleasant), the Gor'kii study noted:

> The process of conveyorization is contradictory. Mechanization, which makes labour easier and raises its productivity, the regulation of labour functions, the reduction in the time needed to transfer an object of labour from one operation to another, [and] rhythmical work, are obtained at the price of impoverishing the content of labour and making it more monotonous. The conveyor introduces harmony into the general organization of the labour collective, but limits the possibility of an all-round application of each worker's mental and physical energies. The expenditures of physical energy on the conveyor in many cases are quite significant, but always one-sided.[28]

Earlier studies of assembly-line work in light engineering had come to the same conclusion. At the First Moscow Clock Factory the assembly of wrist-watches involved a number of operations requiring only 1 to 1.5 minutes to carry out. Assembly-line work at factories manufacturing electric meters was even more strenuous, with some operations being carried out in 27, 12, or even 6 seconds. The economists reporting these findings noted that, taking into account the fact that during this time the worker had to carry out a complex range of assembly functions, 'it becomes clear that such a division of labour, while it simplifies the labour of the assemblers, [also] makes it monotonous, which worsens the workers' conditions of labour'.[29] This trend was not confined, however, to light engineering (where the majority of workers would have been women). At major automobile plants, assembly work was broken down into a hypertrophied number of trades, each carrying out a relatively minute part of the assembly process.[30]

It is not surprising that monotony and the general lack of creative stimulus in work profoundly affected workers' attitudes. The Gor'kii study found that workers doing purely physical labour (that is, without the aid of any equipment) were generally dissatisfied with their jobs. They considered their work uninteresting and wanted to move into jobs requiring more skill. This was especially a problem among young workers, who were better educated and, therefore, more discontented with the discrepancy between their training and the content of the jobs they were actually doing.[31] In a well-known study of young Leningrad workers, those doing heavy manual work (men and women alike) cited pay as their only motivation for staying in their particular job.[32] This contrasted sharply with the motivations of skilled manual workers, who cited the need to 'use their wits' as the most attractive feature of their work. This prompted two of the survey's authors to challenge the traditional Soviet view that 'manual labour is virtually always a basic obstacle to the transformation of labour into a primary, vital need', and to point out that the issue was not manual labour *per se*, but *its content*.[33] It is interesting that young machine-tool operators in this study did not consider their work to be dull, although it was taxing; for them the main problem was the limited opportunities to raise their skills. By contrast, as in the Gor'kii study, workers on automatic machines who also did their own tool-setting, found monotony a problem, because once the equipment was running properly there was nothing for them to do.[34] Among assembly-line workers, monotony – together with their relatively low pay – was a major cause of labour turnover, and in some industries (electrical or automobile components, for example) the assembly worker who had been at her or his factory for more than 10 years was an exception.[35]

The sociological studies of the 1960s can give us only an approximate idea of the skill structure of Soviet workers. Precise estimates of the percentage of Soviet workers in each skill category are almost impossible to come by. We can partially overcome this problem by referring to the Occupational Census of 1965.[36] Nearly 1 in 15 Soviet industrial workers was a machine-tool operator, most of whose jobs, though the workers did not necessarily find them dissatisfying, had only a limited creative content. In terms of the formal structure of these jobs (informally, as we shall see in the next section, the situation was quite different), there was little room for the worker to make an independent contribution to job design or to vary the routine by setting and repairing her or his own equipment. The Census also shows that 1 in 30 workers was a fitter–assembler. Unfortunately, the Census does not disaggregate this category to show how many were manual fitters, in engineering for example, whose work was independent, skilled, and for the most part varied and interesting, and how many worked on assembly lines, where the conditions were precisely the reverse. Other trades stand out for their similarly meagre demands for skills. Foundry work was heavy and difficult, and auxiliary operations (such as knocking out foundings) were tedious. Predominantly female occupations such as press operators and virtually all trades in the textile and garment industries were repetitive and physically taxing, and offered the women few opportunities to control their work methods or even to vary their routine. Finally, there was the myriad of auxiliary operations, the vast majority of which involved manual labour which, although it gave the worker in many cases greater control over the speed and intensity of the job, was extremely routine in its content. The one exception among this group was the vast army of fitters and electricians on repair and maintenance, who made up a full 10 per cent of Soviet industrial workers, and whose work gave them considerable scope to control most aspects of the labour process and to exercise independent skill. The fact that this work was often, if not usually, badly carried out is another issue, reflecting the inadequacies of the wages system and, more generally, the politics prevailing on the shop floor and within Soviet society at large. Thus, although there was a sizeable minority of Soviet workers who could be said to have retained a considerable degree of control over the skill content of their jobs, for the overwhelming majority such control was excluded.

This does not mean that Soviet workers have not resisted the process of de-skilling or found compensations to offset its effects. Women assembly-line workers, while not being in a position to reverse the monotony of their jobs, have been able to counter the boredom through their network of on-the-job social relationships.[37] As to resistance, attempts in the 1960s to introduce machine tools with programmed controls – which would have further reduced the skills required of machine-tool operators and at the same time eliminated a great deal of the free time they were able to appropriate during the normal course of work – met with almost no success. It is impossible to tell from the press accounts just how much of this failure was due to workers' refusal to work with the machines, and how much to their poor construction or the inability of factories to maintain the essential steady flow of components and supplies necessary to their efficient utilization. Certainly, both sets of reasons are cited.[38] What is true is that their introduction in the 1960s was extremely slow and sparing, a situation that has continued to the present day.[39]

Far more important, however, has been the fact that the nature of Soviet production itself has provided workers with countless opportunities, indeed the necessity, to reappropriate various decision-making functions within the work process. Workers, and machine-tool operators in particular, may have to make their own tools or components when they are in short supply, or redesign a job when the drawings are faulty or the required materials are not on hand. I shall discuss the implications of this in greater detail at the close of the chapter. What we should note is that these interventions allow, or even require, workers to develop and utilize skills which, according to the formal requirements of their jobs, they should not in fact possess. Moreover, this reacquisition of skills, together with the need to exercise other, more simple decision-making functions (for example, where to find missing parts, or how to speed up the delivery of awaited materials), gives workers a great deal of control over the labour process, which has become an important source of power for workers in their shop-floor dealings with lower management.

This is not to say that the process of de-skilling has not had serious negative effects on the workforce. The authors of the Gor'kii study themselves associated the relatively low skill level of most industrial jobs with the effective appearance of a substratum of poorly paid and poorly qualified workers whose conditions of work discouraged them from improving their skills or education.[40] What they were in effect describing was the appearance of an inherited working class (or at least here, of a subgroup within that class), which first became visible in the 1960s, as the social mobility of the Stalin years began to subside.[41] The growing disparity between the educational levels of new workers and the relatively low level of skills demanded of them at the workplace has proved to be a continuing source of tension and dissatisfaction among young people, and a major cause of labour turnover.[42] From a political point of view, de-skilling was an important component of the process of atomizing the working class, as it facilitated the process of isolating workers from one another through the breaking down of the labour process. At the same time, it discouraged (but did not prevent) workers from developing an interest in the overall problems of job design and organization, which, if realized, would have exacerbated dissatisfaction with the hierarchical structure of management imposed by the Stalinist system. The results of this policy have, of course, been contradictory, since the removal of workers from decision-making within the labour process and the consequent over-fractionated division of labour have themselves become a source of crisis in the economy.

The labour process and shop-floor bargaining

It is clear from various Western studies that when de-skilling does take place, workers are often able to develop compensating mechanisms of control over their work. As the Western studies suggest, these often affect the relationship between effort and pay, the so-called 'effort bargain'.[43] As a perfectly rational vehicle for protecting earnings, the control of output obviously involves workers in considerable decision-making, as well as a quite sophisticated calculus, but the control that workers consequently exert is essentially *negative*, a set of decisions and actions which limit the extent of their exploitation, but do not necessarily overcome the separation of conception and execution. It is clear that these forms of controlling the labour process, especially as they affect the use of work time and manipulation of earnings, bear a great deal of similarity to the practices employed by Soviet workers. However, there are important differences, associated both with the specificities of industrial production in the USSR and more generally with the nature of economic regulation and, in the conditional sense of the term, the Soviet 'mode of production'.

Virtually all Western studies indicate that workers' ability to regulate output and earnings is contingent upon strong local trade union organization and a well-organized workforce. Lupton's study of the women at the 'Wye Garment Factory' is a case in point, for there the women were weakly organized and the trade union had no strength. Virtually the only sanctions open to the women when they had a grievance were *individual actions*, mainly absenteeism or quitting.[44] These practices are also common in the USSR for precisely the same reason: the inability of workers to press their grievances collectively, leaving individual action as the only recourse. This situation has obviously started to change, as strikes have become both common and legal, but it was certainly the case until 1988.

In the USSR, at least until now, virtually all the restrictions imposed by workers (and not just truancy or labour turnover) have arisen not out of their organized strength, but specifically out of their atomization, and represent the attempt by individuals, or groups of individuals, to defend their position on the shop floor in the absence of other, more organized tactics. We must, however, be careful of what we mean by atomization. One of the most important sources of the strong shop-floor organization in the 'Jays' engineering works where Lupton worked was the social cohesion that developed as a natural consequence of the way work was organized there. Soviet-style delays in waiting for parts or components, or the need for workers to travel from one shop to another in order to expedite deliveries, contributed to workforce solidarity.[45] Although we have little direct evidence of it, other than the occasional anecdotal press report, this type of solidarity must have grown up in Soviet factories subject to similar working conditions. The work day in most Soviet industrial enterprises is simply too full of disruptions, throwing workers into constant contact with each other, for this not to be the case. Of course this situation also gave rise to conflicts, such as those already indicated between older and younger machinists in engineering. Even in this situation, however, individuals and small groups of workers had to build some forms of cooperation in order to exercise the controls that they did, or to overcome various shop-floor difficulties when they chose to do so. At this level, the atomization of Soviet workers had definite limits. No regime, no matter how brutal, can impose total isolation and individualization in a modern society based on cooperative, socialized (in Marx's sense of the term) forms of production. Even here, however, the process is differentiated. Just as under capitalism, there is a clear pattern in the Soviet Union where stronger workers, namely those in the more vital production and auxiliary trades in large-scale industry, are better placed to extract concessions from managers than weaker sections of the workforce (women, migrant workers, those in peripheral industries, and so on).

The issue of atomization must also be seen at a deeper, political level, however, and here the difference between capitalism and the Soviet Union is striking. For despite the social cohesion that must certainly exist in Soviet factories, there have been very definite limits on how workers have been able to make use of it. Here we must ultimately return to the fundamentally different *political* relationship in the USSR between the elite and the workforce on the one hand, and between the capitalist class and the proletariat on the other. The Soviet elite controls the means of production in the Soviet Union not by virtue of ownership or legal titles to these means of production and to the products produced by them, but only through its political control over the society, which means in the first instance the working class. Historically, it has been able to consolidate and maintain its political power only through the atomization of the population. Politically, workers in the Soviet Union have been atomized to an extreme degree. Until Gorbachev they had virtually no means of influencing or affecting political events, either individually or through political parties or trade unions. Political opposition was impossible, both for the individual and for organized groups: workers could not form or join political parties or organizations (other than the Communist Party) or form independent trade unions. This was enforced by a ubiquitous and brutal secret police, so that even the smallest conspiracy, to lead a strike, for instance, was likely to be broken up and its leaders arrested; if strikes did occur, the organizers were invariably arrested and imprisoned as soon as the trouble had been defused. Workers might exercise some degree of solidarity with each other on the shop floor over work-related issues (such as covering up for absent comrades or promoting various wages fiddles), but open political contact or discussion was dangerous and therefore rare. The methods of management and work organization adopted during the Stalin years all tended to reinforce this atomization. The work process was broken up both organizationally and by the absurd emphasis on individual piece-rates and individual record-breaking. This had the 'positive' effect from the regime's point of view of further impeding collective action within the factories, especially in a situation where generalized scarcity and the struggle for survival further reinforced the disintegration of workers' solidarity and the growth of individualism. Workers were encouraged to react as individuals, and the regime exerted every effort to make it clear that this was the only avenue open to them.

This process was, as I have argued in *Soviet Workers and Stalinist Industrialization*, highly contradictory. The emergent Soviet elite gained politically from the individuation of the workforce, which it correctly saw as indispensable to its ability to consolidate its rule and to remain in power. But this came at great cost, for it led directly to the breakdown of coordination within factories, and contributed greatly to the loss of coordination between different industrial units, already fostered by the bureaucratic system. It also created a situation where workers, if they were to affect their working conditions at all, could do so only through individualistic actions: absenteeism, insubordination, job-changing, and – what eventually became the most important of all – by controlling the speed and quality of their work. The result was the imposition by workers of very definite limits on the production and disposition of the surplus product, not just through 'effort bargaining' in the Western sense, but through the phenomenon of waste, which negated a large proportion of the surplus and deformed the utility of what was actually circulated for use.

This control over quality is one of the most prominent differences between control over the labour process under capitalism and in the USSR, for under capitalism the pressures of the market (and, according to some accounts, also a certain residual pride in the quality of one's work[46]) act to block the circulation and reproduction of defective products, so that their impact on the overall reproduction of the system is contained. Here we come to another fundamental divergence between the two systems: the nature of the market and the impact of workers' limited control over the labour process on the ruling class's (or ruling elite's) ability to dispose of the surplus.

Under capitalism there are quite definite limits to the extent to which capitalists can tolerate such control, since ultimately it will impinge on the rate of profit and the valorization of the surplus product, that is, its transformation into surplus value. At some point, a capitalist firm can go bankrupt and lay off its workers. Politically, the capitalist class can attempt a wholesale assault on shop-floor relations in order to change the conditions under which the surplus is produced. This was the political function of fascism, but it has also been the policy of less radical and authoritarian capitalist regimes, as in Great Britain under Margaret Thatcher, where the main weapon in the attack on traditional shop-floor practices was the deliberate introduction of mass unemployment.

Until now, these types of limits to workers' control over the labour process have simply not operated in the Soviet Union. Production does not require realization as value, since market exchange does not exist. Goods are circulated either through administrative direction or via black- or grey-market arrangements between factory managers. In both cases what are being circulated or 'exchanged' are values in use (use values), not commodities seeking realization as exchange value. As far as the official state supply system goes, this should be self-evident, but even where managers enter into direct exchange to swap scarce supplies, materials, or even equipment, what they are interested in is not the 'value' of these products in abstract, money terms, but their functional utility in allowing managers to meet their plan. Moreover, a Soviet enterprise (at least until the implementation of Gorbachev's market reforms) could not go bankrupt and its workforce could not be laid off. Firms have therefore been under little pressure to challenge traditional work practices and the limits these have placed on surplus extraction. When at times, as under Stalin, managers did face this kind of pressure, the instability this introduced into shop-floor relations threatened to jeopardize their ability to fulfil other economic objectives, in the first instance their plans. Managers were, therefore, more than willing to collude with workers to try to ease the legal and penal restrictions on workers' freedom, at least until they themselves were faced with imprisonment.[47]

All this has given shop-floor relations in the Soviet Union their unique character. Because workers have been politically atomized and unable to exercise collective power within the enterprise, they have had to establish this power individually, via control over the work process. They have been encouraged in this by the process of atomization itself, which depended on the hyper-individualization of the labour process and incentives. This has meant that concessions which managers have granted to workers have essentially been concessions to the individual, or at best to groups of individuals, rather than concessions won collectively and applying to an entire shop, an enterprise, or even a whole industry.[48] This conforms to the general pattern of power relationships within Soviet society, where, in the absence of the market and the meritocratic system of advancement on which the market depends, individuals must rely for promotion on the arbitrary decisions of their immediate superiors. More generally, 'exchange' in the Soviet Union has been based on personal connections and exchange of favours, rather than on the cash nexus of the outright bribe. This is clearly changing, as money, and with it the monetarization of corruption, have become more important in the Soviet economy, despite persistent shortages, and promise to become more important still with the introduction of the market.

Insofar as relations between workers and management on the shop floor are concerned, managers grant concessions over work speeds or earnings precisely because they require reciprocal 'favours' from the workforce. In my study of the 1930s I argued that the main drive behind managerial willingness to cede workers their substantial, though still partial, control over the labour process was the need to achieve a certain degree of stability in an otherwise highly unstable factory environment. In a situation where managers could never be certain about the availability of supplies, the presence of the necessary tools, the reliability of equipment, or even the constancy of their plan assignments, it was important to win at least the passive cooperation of the labour force in an effort to dissuade workers from aggravating real and potential disruptions. This alone would have given workers considerable bargaining power, but the severe labour shortage which has plagued Soviet industry since the First Five-Year Plan has made the individual workers' position stronger still. Managers were willing to tolerate poor discipline, time-wasting, and bad quality because if they did not, workers, through negligence or even more concerted lack of effort, were quite capable of making this state of affairs even worse. Had managers possessed effective sanctions against workers, they might have been able to weaken this essentially negative control over the work regime, but the labour shortage deprived them of such weapons. A worker who worked badly was still preferable to no worker at all, which explains why managers, from the 1930s to the present, have been generally unwilling to fire workers for poor discipline (and in the 1930s refused to enforce legislation calling for mandatory dismissal for truancy and related offences) and have made considerable concessions over wages and norms in order to keep them from quitting. What can happen when the state constrains managers from making such concessions was amply illustrated by the experience of the engineering industry during the Khrushchev wage reform.

The weakness of this interpretation is that it locates the power of the individual worker in an essentially passive relationship between managers and workers. It is accurate as far as it goes, but it illuminates only part of the dynamic behind shop-floor relations. This study of the Khrushchev period has shown the need to emphasize an additional aspect of the problem, namely the need for workers who are structurally divorced from decision-making to reappropriate considerable decision-making power in the normal course of work in order to deal with the myriad of disruptions and potential disruptions which occur throughout the Soviet working day. In certain areas of production in capitalist factories, workers also are forced to assert this kind of initiative,[49] but in the Soviet Union this has become a systematic feature of the labour process which has determined the entire shape of shop-floor bargaining and concessions.

The forms of such intervention are literally as varied as the difficulties with which workers have to cope. It may involve something as seemingly trivial as taking time to hunt down a missing tool in the store-room or scouring the factory to try to borrow it from another worker. Yet management is absolutely dependent on the workers' willingness regularly to undertake such excursions in order to keep production going. 'A lot of talk goes on about the prompt provision of workers in machine shops with semi-finished components, materials, tools, and technical documentation,' noted *Moskovskaya pravda* in late 1963. 'But, in fact, machine-tool operators frequently have to provide themselves with all that they need for uninterrupted work. Sometimes as much as 10 per cent of work time goes on all this "self-service".'[50]

Other interventions, however, require the worker to possess a considerable degree of knowledge about production techniques, materials, and designs. If metal components or forgings are too large and workers have to shave them down, to do this accurately presupposes a knowledge of the process for which the metal will be used. When materials are late or of the wrong specifications workers require not just the administrative know-how of where to dig them out from, but a knowledge of what alternative materials they might use. Technically, these decisions, which might also involve changes to the plan or product-mix, are the prerogative of management, but in reality it is the workers who often make them and carry them through. In this sense, every worker – at least in production – becomes potentially both a *tolkach* (a 'pusher' or expediter), and an engineer.

Just how extensive such intervention could be is illustrated from various press accounts. At Leningrad's Lenmashzavod, fitters routinely received parts that needed further work. They had to decide their own sequence of operations and modify the parts to make them suitable for assembly.[51] At the Ekonomaizer plant in Leningrad, workers received incorrect job plans and drawings. One skilled turner was given a job card where the designers had changed the technical specifications but specified the wrong tools. The turner had to manufacture his own measuring device, for example, since the one called for on the card was not precise enough for the job.[52] The outcome of this enforced independence was not always a success. The need to make their own tools or to manufacture or modify parts without adequate technical designs, as was commonplace at Leningrad's Reduktor works, caused even experienced workers to get poor results.[53] This is less important, from the point of view of our discussion, than the fact that these workers had to make parts and tools 'by eye', which presupposed a considerable knowledge of the machine process and job design.

Interventions such as these, which took place countless times in the course of the Soviet work day, affected the nature of shop-floor disputes and bargaining. Disputes over wages, for example, must certainly have revolved around more than just the protection of established earnings levels, important as this was. There was also the question of how much workers were to be paid for using their 'creative powers' to help overcome problems. The clearest example of this is the payment of *namazki*, or palm-greasing, to workers in exchange for agreeing to engage in storming.[54] Other disputes need not have involved pay at all, but issues such as staffing levels or job allocation. The issue, however, goes deeper than shop-floor disputes *per se*. Soviet workers had built up a distinct pattern and tradition of control over various aspects of the labour process to which managers had accommodated themselves, in part because they had no choice, and in part because the planning system as a whole evolved in such a way that this control did not jeopardize managers' plan fulfilment and they could therefore tolerate it. There was thus a constant process of bargaining over the extent to which workers were to be allowed to set their own pace of work, to deviate from prescribed norms of work organization, or turn out work of poor quality. And one of the issues over which such bargaining must necessarily have taken place was the extent to which workers were willing to help compensate for the poor work of other workers, whether from their own or from another factory.

The need for workers to exercise independence within the labour process did not generally mean a reappropriation of craft skills in the sense used by Braverman. They still did not have positive control over job design, choice of tools and materials, or even fully over the intensity of work, much less *political control* over how plans were drawn up and implemented at either a society-wide or enterprise level. Insofar as they were able, or required, to exercise these skills, this naturally gave them a degree of control over their immediate working conditions. But the importance of their active reinsertion back into the work regime was more general: it was another bargaining chip in the ongoing give and take of the shop floor. Workers had something – the ability to exert themselves to help alleviate the day-to-day disruptions to production – which management needed, and this allowed them to extract concessions in other areas of the labour process. The evidence presented in chapter 6 certainly indicates that workers' ability, if not willingness to cope with these difficulties, was distinctly limited. This did not make the issue any less important for management, who had to contemplate how taut the situation might become if workers were not prepared to lend what cooperation they did.

The concessions which workers could in this way extract acted further to reinforce the reproduction of their partial control over the labour process. By being able to moderate the intensity and speed of their labour, by ignoring quality requirements, or by defending the retention of 'irrational' forms of work organization, workers were constantly recreating the conditions which required them to go beyond their formal responsibilities and adopt varying degrees of independence within the production process. Like the reproduction of the labour shortage, they were in effect permanently reproducing the conditions which made management dependent on their cooperation, since the scale and nature of the dislocations within Soviet factories is such that managers cannot possibly cope with them on their own. From the point of view of the individual enterprise, this system became functional. It generally allowed managers to meet their plans and to further their own careers. From the point of view of the society as a whole, however, it helped precipitate the economy into a deep crisis which the elite only began to address under Gorbachev.

Conclusion

De-Stalinization, civil society, and socialism

The main argument of this book has been that de-Stalinization was faced with one overriding task to which all others – no matter how great their historical ramifications – were subordinate, namely the need to increase the efficiency of surplus extraction. In part this was attempted through various roundabout methods which did not involve tampering with the essential structure of the system: in industry the reorganization of administration into *sovnarkhozy*; in agriculture, the opening up of virgin lands and the constant tampering with regulations governing private plots, state purchase prices for grain and other farm products, and ownership of agricultural machinery. None of these measures could obviate the need to address the more fundamental issue of how the surplus was produced within industry. This meant inevitably raising the rate of exploitation. Given the failure of Stalinist policies, when the elite had attempted to rule through sheer coercion, it was evident that the working class would have to accede to this process or it would be doomed to failure. Significant improvements in economic performance would, therefore, require sweeping political changes, for only then could the regime hope to re-establish some form of legitimacy in the eyes of the population. The terror would be removed, and other methods of motivating the workforce would have to be found. Insofar as the scope for political reform was limited by their destabilizing effect on the elite's hold on power, they would have to be supplemented by coercion – only now, economic coercion rather than the coercion of the labour camps.

Labour policy under Khrushchev reflected this abortive character of de-Stalinization. It was a mixture of political gestures – efforts to create the appearance of democratization, coupled with the relaxation or

231

repeal of the repressive Stalinist labour laws – and efforts to exert more direct influence over worker behaviour, in particular over the issues of labour mobility and job performance. To this end, labour policy followed three main directions, each of which failed because they were unrealizable within the bounds of the existing system.

'Democratization' of the workplace. The Draconian Stalinist labour laws of 1940 – which had criminalized job-changing and absenteeism – were repealed, thus removing a major source of worker resentment. New discipline regulations made it more difficult for managers to dismiss workers, as they now had to gain trade union sanction before a worker could be fired. This was in line with a general reform of the trade unions, designed to make the unions appear more accountable to their members. The unions were also given a formal veto over norm rises within the factories. At the same time, the press took up campaigns against managerial abuses of labour legislation, unfair dismissals, and failure to provide safe working conditions, again to foster the appearance that the regime was once again acting in the workers' 'interests'.

Efforts to control labour mobility. The main task here was to solve the labour shortage, both in the established industrial centres of the western and central USSR, and in the newly developing regions of Siberia and the Far East. There was a concerted campaign to persuade the large reserve of non-working women to enter industrial employment; hundreds of thousands of recruits were enlisted to build and staff new factories in Siberia; and the vocational training system was overhauled in an effort to make it more responsive to industry's demands for particular occupations and skills.

The reform of the wages and incentives system. Piece-rates and norm-overfulfilment bonuses were made less important in determining workers' overall earnings. Norm-setting was decentralized, in the hope that managers would be more willing to raise norms in line with local improvements in equipment and productivity. Simultaneously, workers were more tightly graded into wage and skill categories, and an attempt was made to impose more rigorous 'scientifically based' norms. Greater emphasis was placed on bonuses for plan fulfilment, economizing on materials and fuel, and improving quality.

The effectiveness of these reforms was stunted by their inbuilt limitations. In the case of the 'democratization' campaign, insofar as it actually did broaden workers' rights, this was confined to the *individual* worker, and not the workforce as a collective entity. The trade unions did become slightly more aggressive in defending individuals against unfair dismissal, but not overly so. Nor did they intervene very often to block norm rises. This was the logical outcome of a system in which the masses were granted no real political power, and the trade unions continued to function as an arm of the state. There was no question of workers building genuinely independent, collective organizations capable of articulating and defending the interests of workers as a class. As such these reforms were incapable of solving the problem of morale. The various legal changes did, however, have the contradictory effect of increasing labour turnover and legalizing workers' *de facto* guarantee of employment. They thus made discipline more difficult to enforce and, at least indirectly, reinforced long-standing patterns of shop-floor bargaining between workers and managers.

By facilitating labour turnover, the liberalization of labour law also undermined efforts to ease the labour shortage. Far more important in this regard, however, were the structural backwardness of the economy and its lack of infrastructure, both a legacy of Stalinist industrialization and the low priority it afforded to popular consumption. It was simply impossible to keep recruits in Siberia when housing, transport, working conditions, and food supplies were so poor, not just in absolute terms, but in relation to the rest of the USSR. It was equally hard to attract women into industrial employment when the jobs available to them were arduous, often dangerous, and almost uniformly low-paid.

Finally, the wage reform failed because it made workers' earnings more directly dependent on overall enterprise performance in a system where the latter depended on an array of outside variables over which workers had no control. Managers could not guarantee performance bonuses or impose tighter norms when irregularities in supplies and frequent equipment breakdowns might jeopardize earnings. In the one industry where the reform was more rigidly applied – engineering – it led to a severe crisis, as machine-tool operators left the factories in response to lower wages, tighter regrading, and their reduced control over job execution. The reform, intended to coerce (albeit indirectly) workers into surrendering their traditional control over the work process, was simply inadequate to such a task: the behaviour it was intended to curb played a major role in creating the very uncertainties which made the application of the reform unworkable.

All three components of Khrushchev's labour policy were in different ways distorted, if not negated, by the system. In this they mirrored the general experience of de-Stalinization, where reform after reform came undone because it could not address the real problems at the heart of the system's crisis: the property and power relations which sustained the elite's domination. In the field of labour policy this meant that the regime addressed only the externalities of the problem and not its essence. The real need was to force a restructuring of the labour process, for only this would have directly confronted the factors determining surplus extraction. It was precisely on this issue that the regime had no coherent policy.

With the failure of the terror, the only means by which the elite could have imposed such a restructuring was mass unemployment. But this would have undercut workers' *de facto* security of employment without any of the compensating social and ideological structures through which capitalism controls popular unrest at times of crisis. In the Soviet Union of the 1950s and 1960s, mass unemployment would have provoked possibly uncontrollable protest and disorder. The rising in Novocherkassk, sparked off not by the threat of massive job losses, but by a threat to workers far less severe, namely an increase in food prices, would have disabused any in the elite who might have entertained illusions in this regard. Thus even economic coercion was unlikely on its own to allow the elite to achieve its goals. Something more was required, namely the passive cooperation of the workforce through its political integration into the system. For, without some political identification with the system (no matter how illusory it might have been), workers would not have surrendered their individual control over the labour process. It demanded, in short, the creation of a Soviet equivalent of capitalist civil society.

Capitalism gave rise to a civil society of 'free' individuals because this and only this type of society corresponded to the demands of its reproduction. Capitalism had liberated society from the fetters of feudal privilege, which had constrained trade and industry and prevented the new mode of production from achieving the unrestrained expansion it required. The political freedom of bourgeois society was an expression of capitalism's need for a society of 'free' individuals as the agents of the free movement of capital and labour power. It was a freedom based on market competition and exploitation, a freedom which was therefore illusory in that it subjugated the mass of the population to a state of dependence, want, and distorted personal development, and, through the bourgeois state, deprived this majority of access to real political power.

What held – and still holds – this civil society together is not simply the coercive power of the state, but a consensual ideology, which Gramsci, in his concept of hegemony, defined as the '"spontaneous" consent given by the great masses of the population to the general direction imposed on social life by the dominant fundamental group', that is, the ruling class.[1] This ideology is not something ephemeral or illusory. It is a functional system of popular beliefs derived from everyday experience, through which subordinate classes – and the working class in particular – accept capitalism as the natural order of things, as a system which can perhaps be altered or adjusted, but not transcended. Such an ideology is as much a part of capitalist reality as its economy, and the reproduction of this ideology is a fundamental and indispensable part of the reproduction of capitalist social relations as a whole.

Under capitalism, the 'free' politics of civil society and a hegemonic bourgeois ideology are inseparably linked. The difficulty confronting Stalin's successors was this: how was the elite to create a Soviet equivalent of civil society, which would generate an organic, hegemonic ideology binding the workforce to the existing system of class domination? The civil society of the capitalist market was excluded, for it would have meant subverting the very property relations through which the elite maintained its domination and extracted its privileges. So, too, was the creation of working-class power and socialism which would have resolved the antinomies of both capitalism and Stalinism, but equally at the cost of displacing the elite from power. This meant that the task would have to be resolved within the Stalinist system itself. Yet this system had shown itself incapable of generating such an ideology from within. Despite the survival of certain residual beliefs from the early years of Bolshevik power, in particular workers' attachment to egalitarianism and a basic sense of social fairness, the overriding result of the Stalin years was depoliticization, apathy, and a sullen attitude towards both the regime and the workplace that manifested itself in workers' general indifference to appeals and sanctions designed to prompt them to work harder or more efficiently.

In theory, the elite might have attempted to create a 'free' politics within the existing social relations, but this would have come into conflict with the elite's tenuous hold on power. For the elite's domination, unlike that of the bourgeoisie, is not automatically reproduced through ownership of the means of production and the reproduction of a capital–wage labour relationship (for the elite has no direct ownership of the means of production, and capital, given the absence of production for profit, does not exist). Rather, it is sustained through the elite's control over the state apparatus, a control secured and maintained only through the political atomization – the antithesis of a 'free' politics – of the population. Without this atomization, the elite cannot reproduce its hold on power and the elite–workforce relationship, which, for all its instability, is the only means through which the elite can produce and appropriate the surplus from which it derives its privileges. This appreciation of the dangers of even limited democratic reforms explains the timidity with which de-Stalinization was actually carried out. It received practical confirmation in Eastern Europe, where the risings in East Berlin in 1953, and in Hungary and Poland in 1956, brought home with full force to the elite the true nature of its position and the inherent dangers of political relaxation.

This being the case, de-Stalinization could not resolve the contradiction between the elite and the workforce decisively – or even fundamentally – in the elite's favour. The elite could not incorporate the workforce into society, yet it could not enslave it. Stalin's attempt at the latter had led, in fact, not to a 'totalitarian' society, in which the population passively carried out the leaders' bidding (such a society is a mythical construct of anti-communism and has never existed in history), but to a society that was almost totally unorganizable and whose dysfunctionality was recognized by Stalin's successors as the source of the country's crisis. Under Khrushchev, the elite was left with no choice but to try to achieve its economic objectives while leaving intact the prevailing relationship between the worker and the labour process, for only this would guarantee the survival of the social relations on which the society had been founded and from which the elite derived its power. This, however, meant that the seeds of the society's long-term decline and ultimate crisis were allowed to germinate. In the contradiction between the elite and the workforce nothing was resolved. The labour process characteristic of the Stalinist system consolidated itself as a fundamental feature of production, and remained unchallenged until Gorbachev came to power.

The historical impasse of *perestroika*

Gorbachev's original labour policy conformed closely to his understanding of the nature of the economic crisis he and his entourage had inherited. Like Khrushchev, he recognized that the main task facing the elite was to rationalize the economy and with it the elite's appropriation of the surplus, but without jeopardizing the class relations which kept the elite in power. Fundamental to this task was the need to restructure the labour process so as to eliminate the worker's partial control. Here Gorbachev showed a greater appreciation than Khrushchev of the need to combine significant political liberalization (although the eventual extent of democratization was surely not part of his original conception) with economic levers. In the political realm this meant not just a relaxation of political life, but attempts to incorporate the workforce directly at the workplace through the latter's 'democratization'. At the same time, economic pressure was to be put on the traditional structures of shop-floor bargaining through the introduction of mass unemployment, a reform of the wages system (remarkably similar to Khrushchev's wage reform), and the transfer of enterprise finances to profit-and-loss accounting (*khozraschet*), which would, in theory, compel them to reduce production costs – and labour costs in particular – in order to maximize revenues. The decision, announced in September 1990, for a wholesale shift to the market was a *de facto* admission that these policies had failed to produce the type of restructuring that would have been necessary to allow the Stalinist class relations to survive intact, and that the elite was now prepared to accept the eventual restoration of capitalism – despite the uncertainties this would pose for the fate of its individual members, who might or might not survive as members of the new capitalist class that will be created.

The failure of the economic aspects of Gorbachev's labour policy is perhaps easiest to assess.[2] Unemployment, despite an initial rise among industrial workers, did not have the disciplining effect on work relations that was intended. Nor did the wage reform, whose provisions were almost identical to those of the Khrushchev reform of 1956–62, except that they were backed up by the introduction of enterprise self-financing. Although detailed data on losses of work time are not available, global losses in industry are still high – some 38 per cent of calendar time (which includes time lost by not utilizing second or third shifts).[3] Workers' deliberate use of output restriction has also been receiving more open discussion in the press and journals, and is acknowledged as widespread, especially as a device for fending off norm rises or rate cuts.[4] Perhaps more important, the traditional difficulties besetting production, and which have provided the fertile soil for workers' partial control over the labour process, have actually worsened under *khozraschet*, as ministries have ceased guaranteeing supplies and materials, and suppliers increasingly fail to honour contracts. As pressure on earnings has mounted and more and more skilled workers have quit state enterprises for jobs in cooperatives, managers have responded by pushing up prices on their products – without necessarily increasing output – and using the additional revenues to finance wage rises. Norm-setting, the central element of any coercive incentives system, has lost almost all significance in this regard, as managers in many industries have virtually ceased revising norms in order to push up earnings. The result was the abandonment of the 1986 wage reform, and its replacement in 1991 by a decentralized system, which devolved all decisions over wage rates and norms on to individual enterprises.[5] This move, while clearly threatening to make many of the adverse trends even worse, was essential for the full-scale move to the market. Finally, the economic reforms failed to overcome another major structural weakness of Soviet industry, namely its continued high share of manual labour, a large stock of worn-out, obsolete equipment, and managerial and worker resistance to the introduction of more modern technology, such as machine tools with programmed controls, which would loosen machinists' control over work execution.

As for the political dimension of the reforms, Gorbachev clearly saw the need to create the Soviet 'civil society' which had been absent from the reforms of the 1950s and 1960s. For only then could the society generate a truly hegemonic ideology through which the workforce would accept the need to make sacrifices for the sake of preserving a class structure which left it still disenfranchised. On such a scenario, workers could be expected to struggle around specific issues, but such struggles would not lead to a perception of the need to transcend the system, to overthrow it and build a society in which workers exercise genuine collective power. Had the elite been able to lay the groundwork for such a society, they could in theory have transformed the Soviet economy to make it efficient and no longer dependent on the arbitrariness of the bureaucratic structure, while still ensuring their class position as expropriators of the surplus product.

The idea that the elite (or at least its reform wing) could accomplish this short of the actual restoration of capitalism was a complete illusion. The market reformers themselves recognized that once the political relation between the elite and the working class changes, the economic relationship could not also remain intact. On the contrary, it was their recognition of the dire crisis into which this economic relationship had led the society that prompted them to demand and begin to implement the dismantling of the political relationship and its attendant bureaucratic control. That the latter had also become a fetter on the intelligentsia's own ability to appropriate and exercise its privileges only strengthened their vision and motivation to carry the reforms through. But the fact is that the elite could survive as managers of the economy only through a command-type structure. How else could they exercise their function as planners, organizers, and administrators of the economy and the state? The logic of the market, however, is that once the command economy begins to give ground it must be totally dismantled, as the rapid disintegration of the economy has shown. This has now been tacitly recognized, but there is as yet no clear strategy of how the elite can shift to capitalism and ensure that its members become the new class of capitalists. Those strategically placed, such as bureaucrats in the old industrial ministries and enterprise directors, have been trying to secure their position by converting the enterprises under their command into joint-stock companies, with the ministries or management retaining the majority of shares. But for others in the upper echelons of the bureaucracy, including many ex-Communist Party functionaries, the future is less secure. An alternative out of the impasse would, of course, be genuine democratic planning, but that would mean the working class coming to power, an alternative that the elite is unlikely to accept peacefully, and which the working class is not itself yet in a position to demand and fight for.

The political relaxation that has taken place, together with the accelerated disintegration of both the economy and central authority have led to workers increasingly replacing individual controls and defensive measures with collective ones, including the development of independent workers' organizations and the traditional weapons of collective mass struggles. Strikes and mass demonstrations are commonplace, and increased in frequency throughout 1990 and 1991. To date, most strikes have been over very immediate shop-floor issues, although the 1991 miners' strike and the brief but no less significant strikes in Belorussiya and elsewhere against the April 1991 price rises were overtly political. The other side of this process is that the market will lead to a greater assault on the workers' position within the enterprise, including the threat of mass unemployment and attempts to intensify the rate of exploitation. These will almost certainly lead to sharper social conflicts, which workers will increasingly wage on a collective rather than an individual basis. This will be all the more so now that the regime has abandoned its cynical experiments with enterprise 'democratization' and enshrined enterprise ownership as the sole source of managerial authority.[6]

There is no guarantee that the re-emergence of class struggle will necessarily create the possibility of a revolutionary transformation of the system and the development of a genuine socialism. The Soviet workforce, which is once again becoming a working class, is deeply divided, most obviously along national and ethnic lines, but also, as has been indicated in this study, by gender and hierarchical privileges as well. It is already clear that the elite intends to try to ameliorate the discontent of male workers in privileged sectors at the expense of women and migrants, who have been among the first to feel the whip of unemployment and whose earnings will remain low. Only time will tell whether the Soviet working class will be able to overcome these intrinsic weaknesses better than their counterparts under capitalism. Workers' confusion and ambiguity over the market, wanting 'independence' for their enterprises but not the unemployment and falling living standards that the market must bring, is part of this process of historical maturation, but it is at present a servere limitation on the working class's combative ability. What is true is that the historical blockage created by Stalinism has finally begun to loosen. It is now possible, to paraphrase Marx, for the Soviet working class once again to make its own history. Whether or not the original, libertarian promise of the October Revolution will be fulfilled we can only wait and see.

Notes

Introduction: the contradictions of de-Stalinization

1 Nove, conomic History, p. 325; Narodnoe khozyaistvo SSSR za 60 let, p. 7.
2 Hosking, pp. 327–32.
3 A slightly different version of this argument appears in Brus, pp. 112–21.
4 Service, 'The Road to the Twentieth Party Congress', p. 236; 'De-Stalinisation in the USSR', pp. 290–5.
5 Nove, conomic History, pp. 323–4.
6 For the events surrounding the Beria Affair, see Roy Medvedev, Khrushchev, pp. 56–64.
7 The July Plenum and other events in the early phases of 'de-Stalinization' are discussed in detail by Service in the two articles listed in note 4.
8 This was summed up quite well at the time by Edward Crankshaw, the Observer Soviet affairs correspondent: 'What is important, however, is that the post-Stalin reforms, or some of them, were inevitable. The problem facing the new leadership, collective or individual, was how to massage life back into the numbed limbs of society, how to encourage the new vitality to express itself and fructify, and how, at the same time, keep it within bounds, so that the whole elaborate edifice of administration was not swept away' (Crankshaw, pp. 60–1).
9 Roy and Zhores Medvedev, Khrushchev: The Years in Power, pp. 151–6.
10 McCauley, pp. 127–8; G. A. E. Smith, 'Agriculture', pp. 107, 113–14.
11 Roy and Zhores Medvedev, Khrushchev: The Years in Power, pp. 73–4; Roy Medvedev, Khrushchev, pp. 89–92; Deutscher, pp. 11ff.; Khrushchev, pp. 347–51.
12 This is one of the least explored aspects of de-Stalinization, yet one of the most central because it is directly bound up with the production and reproduction of the social product. It is thus curious that while Khrushchev's other major reform programmes have received relatively extensive treatment by historians or contemporary commentators, there have been few specialist studies of labour in this period, and none on the position of workers within the production process proper.
13 Filtzer, Soviet Workers and Stalinist Industrialization.

14 In 1931 and 1932, the average industrial worker was absent without permission six days a year; in coal-mining the average was 13 days (1931) (*ibid.*, pp. 52–3).
15 *Ibid.*, p. 52.
16 *Ibid.*, pp. 112–15.
17 These are described in detail in *ibid.*, chapters 6 and 8.
18 It is important that this process be understood in its proper political context. These actions by individual workers were not resistance, but the highly individualized responses of a depoliticized, atomized workforce.
19 This argument is developed in more detail in chapter 5. See also Filtzer, *Soviet Workers and Stalinist Industrialization*, pp. 16–22.

1 The worker and the work environment

1 This argument is developed more fully in chapter 5.
2 A further incentive to storming was the fact that managers' bonuses depended on plans being fulfilled on time.
3 *Sotsiologicheskie issledovaniya*, no. 1 (1988), pp. 35–6 (I. S. Gudzovskaya, A. G. Kosaev).
4 Nove, conomic History, pp. 327–39; Roy and Zhores Medvedev, *Khrushchev: The Years in Power*, pp. 24–37; G. A. E. Smith, 'Agriculture', pp. 95–117.
5 Service, 'The Road to the Twentieth Party Congress', p. 237.
6 Nove, conomic History, p. 353.
7 P G, 27 July 1956 (Chimtensk automatic-press factory), 30 September 1956 (Dnepropetrovsk metallurgical-equipment factory).
8 P G, 12 September 1956.
9 P G, 1 July 1956.
10 The Rostov agricultural-machinery factory (Rostsel'mash) acquired wire from Lyubertsy, an industrial suburb of Moscow, at a cost of 1,000 rubles per ton for the wire and 7,000–8,000 rubles for its transport (*Izvestiya*, 30 June 1956). See also the case of the AMO car factory in Moscow (P G, 13 July 1956).
11 *Izvestiya*, 30 June 1956.
12 P G, 14 September 1956.
13 P G, 18 July 1956. According to the *Izvestiya* article about Rostsel'mash (note 10), the planning and allocation of non-existent metal from non-existent factories was a deliberate policy, aimed to pressurize construction firms to complete these factories on schedule. The policy was, of course, a failure. In 1955, of the 800,000 tons of metal planned and allocated for production by enterprises nearing completion, only 200,000 tons were ever received. It is interesting that this practice even survived into the 1960s. See the example of the Orsk synthetic-alcohol factory (Orenburg *oblast'*) in *Trud*, 19 April 1963.
14 Decree of TsK KPSS following the speech of N. S. Khrushchev, 'O dal'neishem sovershenstvovanii organizatsii upravleniya promyshlennost'yu i stroitel'stvom' (On the Further Improvement in the Organization of the Administration of Industry and Construction) (*Izvestiya*, 16 February

1957); and the law of the Seventh Session of the Supreme Soviet of the USSR, 10 May 1957, 'Zakon o dal'neishem sovershenstvovanii organizatsii upravleniya promyshlennost'yu i stroitel'stvom' (*P G*, 11 May 1957).

15 For two very good accounts of the general failures of the *sovnarkhoz* reform, see Nove, *conomic History*, pp. 342–4, 354–9, and Roy and Zhores Medvedev, *Khrushchev: The Years in Power*, pp. 103–7.

16 *ST*, no. 9 (1960), p. 26 (B. Machekhin); *Trud*, 23 May 1963 (Severnyi iron and steel works, Sverdlvosk *sovnarkhoz*), 14 July 1963 (Gur'ev chemical factory, Kazakhstan).

17 *P G*, 2 February 1958 (Podol'sk machine factory, Moscow); *LP*, 18 April 1962 (Lentrublit).

18 *Trud*, 3 October 1963.

19 *SG*, 13 January, 24 February, 21 March, and 27 June 1956.

20 *MP*, 23 March 1956.

21 *SG*, 11 January 1961; *LP*, 1 August 1964; Utkin, p. 36.

22 Granick, *Management*, p. 281; Berliner, pp. 39–40, 138, 235.

23 *Trud*, 11 September 1962.

24 *P G*, 12 September 1958.

25 *LP*, 3 August 1963. See also the accounts of the steam-turbine shop at the 22nd Congress of the CPSU Metal Factory in Leningrad (*LP*, 14 September 1962), the Saratov machine-tool factory (*Trud*, 19 July 1969); and the Kolyushchenko road-building machinery factory (Chelyabinsk *oblast'*) (*ChR*, 10 December 1957).

26 *RK*, 11 June 1964 (Ivanovo carding-machinery factory).

27 *LP*, 5 January 1962. See also the similar account from a turner in the first machine shop of the Leningrad excavator factory in *LP*, 26 August 1962.

28 *LP*, 29 July 1964 (Pnevmatika factory, Leningrad). At the Dmitrov milling-machine factory, it was estimated that during storming 15 per cent of workers in the factory's maintenance-machine shop were diverted to production shops to help fulfil the monthly plan. Storming, however, was only one culprit among many. A survey of 400 engineering factories carried out in 1959 found that maintenance-machine shops in general spent a full 60 per cent of their time carrying out jobs that had nothing to do with repair and maintenance (*ST*, no. 9 (1962), p. 65 (K. Kuznetsova, A. Rybkina)).

29 'Sometimes at Tambovkhimmash it's the workers who give in. They talk about it, they make a lot of noise, but they do their job on time. Sometimes management gives in' (*Trud*, 21 February 1963).

30 *Trud*, 16 August and 27 September 1963. The practice of offering miners drink as an incentive to boost output (and not just as compensation for storming) apparently had a long tradition in the Donbass. See the lengthy article on this subject in *Izvestiya*, 4 June 1958.

31 See chapter 2.

32 *Izvestiya*, 18 May 1956 (coal-mining equipment); *P G*, 28 March 1958 (Magnitogorsk).

33 *Izvestiya*, 11 July 1958.

34 *LP*, 17 May 1958, 5 January 1962. The situation in Moscow appears to have been little better. See *MP*, 21 January and 29 November 1962, and 7

February 1963 (which cites alleged improvements in the organization of metal supplies).

35 *MP*, 23 March 1956; *SG*, 22 January 1961; *Trud*, 22 May 1964.

36 *LP*, 5 January 1962, 10 April 1964.

37 For this reason there was a concerted campaign in the early 1960s to prompt factories to adopt the so-called 'group manufacture' of parts, that is, the mass production of parts and components used in single-item and small-batch production which could be used in the manufacture of several different types of equipment. The system was extremely slow to get off the ground, and by 1964 appears to have achieved only modest results (*LP*, 23 June and 22 July 1960, 15 September and 18 November 1964; *MP*, 4 April 1961).

38 The problem of internal coordination was by no means exclusive to the Soviet Union. Lupton gives a detailed account of the difficulties engineering factories engaged in batch production faced when trying to calculate and coordinate the flow of parts and materials for final assembly (Lupton, pp. 100–3, 109).

39 *TZP*, no. 9 (1960), p. 43 (S. Pinskii); *ST*, no. 9 (1960), p. 47 (I. Rossochinskii).

40 *TZP*, no. 3 (1958), pp. 9–10 (N. Gavrilenko); *ST*, no. 6 (1959), pp. 66, 69 (I. Priimak).

41 Labour hoarding was, of course, facilitated by the fact that enterprises were, at least until Gorbachev's market reforms, guaranteed their wage funds, so that maintaining swollen establishments did not impinge on an enterprise's financial well-being (so-called 'soft-budget constraints').

42 Davies, pp. 322–3. For some interesting examples, see *Pravda*, 24 May 1955 and *LP*, 7 April 1956.

43 'The existing system of bonuses does not create any material interest among the [administrative] personnel of enterprises to introduce new technology; more than that, to a certain degree it creates an obstacle to technical progress. The introduction of new technology demands from these personnel a certain risk and the expenditure of a great deal of time; it makes it difficult for an enterprise to fulfil its production plan and in many cases leads to a temporary rise in production costs and a fall in wages. All this stands in contradiction to the striving to fulfil the plan using habitual methods and resources, and to receive the bonuses that are coming. [Existing] planning practice also slows down the introduction of new technology, for under this system soon after the introduction of highly productive equipment tighter plans are set, which again leads to reduced opportunities for their overfulfilment and the receipt of bonuses' (Manevich, pp. 142–3).

44 *RK*, 3 October 1962; *UR*, 10 January 1963; *DP*, 21 March 1963.

45 Throughout 1956 there was a concerted press campaign attacking ministries for their neglect of new technology. See, for example, *Izvestiya*, 10 January and 26 May 1956, and *P G*, 25 April, 27 April, 8 July, and 18 July 1956.

46 Two labour economists noted that the poor mechanization of assembly-line production meant that, as each individual worker became accustomed to

her or his work and improved the methods by which she or he performed their job, this *disrupted synchronization* and led to losses of work
time (*ST*, no. 6 (1960), p. 61 (V. Vorotnikova, V. D'yachenko)). In other
words, the lack of mechanization allowed workers to impose their own
idiosyncrasies on the production process, making it difficult to coordinate
different stages in what should have been a uniform, virtually automatic
process.

47 *ChR*, 27 January 1957 (productivity brigades, coal-mining); *LP*, 6 January
1961, 15 May 1962 (Baltiiskii factory), 22 May 1962 (Kotlyakov engineering
factory); *Trud*, 21 May 1963; *MP*, 23 May 1964.

48 *RK*, 3 October 1962, 19 February 1963; *LP*, 23 July and 26 July 1964.

49 See chapter 8.

50 See chapter 4. On the 1930s, see Filtzer, *Soviet Workers and Stalinist
Industrialization*, pp. 148–9, 177, 191–2.

51 Vaisman, p. 122; *Trudovye resursy SSSR*, p. 60; *VS*, no. 2 (1964), p. 34 (O. Shafranova).

52 *VS*, no. 2 (1964), p. 34 (O. Shafranova); *Promyshlennost' SSSR*, p. 85. The 1962
Occupational Census covered only 86 per cent of all workers in Soviet
industry. It is unclear if Shafranova's figures are taken directly from the
Census or extrapolated to arrive at a global total.

53 *Trud v SSSR* (1968), p. 83. As well as a myriad of minor auxiliary trades,
these figures exclude those trades most directly involved in production
(trimmers of castings in foundry shops, crane operators, bulldozer drivers,
compressor operators, etc.), which came to a further 1.8 million workers
(*VS*, no. 6 (1966), pp. 88–91). Shafranova's figure of 2 million repair and
maintenance workers in 1962 is almost surely an underestimate. Of the 3.2
million workers on maintenance, tool-setting, and tool-making in 1954,
approximately 2.8 million were on repair and maintenance (*Trud v SSSR*
(1968), pp. 177, 204–5). According to a later study by Shafranova, by 1969
this group had grown to 3 million (Shafranova, p. 56). This would represent
an increase of 40 per cent between 1962 and 1965, and 50 per cent between
1962 and 1969, which is hard to credit. As the Occupational Censuses all
covered only about 90 per cent of industrial workers, this cannot account
for the discrepancy.

54 *Trud v SSSR* (1968), pp. 208, 227, lists 158,000 cleaners in engineering and
food, but gives no figures for other industries. Maloletova (p. 240) gives
25,000 cleaners in light industry. This figure seems incredibly low,
especially considering the nature of work in textile mills. Thus the number I
have cited should be taken as a bare minimum.

55 Granick, *Job Rights*, pp. 183, 185.

56 *VS*, no. 2 (1964), pp. 30–4 (O. Shafranova). Only 25 per cent of loaders and
transport workers worked 'with the aid of' any kind of machinery (only a
small proportion of these jobs would have been fully mechanized). Of the
industry's 283,000 quality controllers, a full 92 per cent carried out their
work completely by hand.

57 *Trud v SSSR* (1968), p. 83. When we consider that in 1965 there were 3.5
million production workers in engineering compared to just under 3

million workers on repair and maintenance within Soviet industry as a whole, we have the incredible situation where there were nearly as many people in the economy employed on the repair of machines as on their construction.

58 *P G*, 5 April 1959; *ST*, no. 5 (1958), p. 52 (E. Voronin); no. 12 (1960), p. 57 (E. Voronin); no. 4 (1962), pp. 48–9, 50–3. In one machine shop of the carding-machinery factory in Ivanovo, workers were forced to put up with castings and shavings being piled up on the floor because the factory had no equipment for carting them away (*RK*, 11 June 1964).

59 This covers workers in iron and steel plants only.

60 *VS*, no. 2 (1964), pp. 24–30 (O. Shafranova). In Ukrainian iron and steel plants – which tended to be older and less efficient – there were some 180 auxiliary workers for every 100 production workers (*ST*, no. 6 (1963), p. 69 (M. Luk'yanov, N. Tereshchenko)). The 1965 Occupational Census showed virtually no change in these figures (*Trud v SSSR* (1968), pp. 187–97).

61 *TZP*, no. 5 (1960), pp. 19–21 (I. Kryzhko, N. Prokopenko).

62 *TZP*, no. 2 (1962), pp. 20–1 (A. Bakelov).

63 *ST*, no. 3 (1962), pp. 71–3 (G. Tataryan); Krevnevich, pp. 21, 23. Krevnevich divided manual workers into two groups: workers of average or above-average skill, and semi- or unskilled. The first group predominated among those in direct production, and the second among those servicing the production process. Among manual workers engaged in general factory servicing, the two groups were fairly evenly split (*ibid.*, pp. 25, 28, 34).

64 *P G*, 29 April 1956 (S. Kheinman).

65 *LP*, 10 December 1959.

66 *ST*, no. 9 (1962), p. 63 (K. Kuznetsova, A. Rybkina).

67 *Trud*, 13 July 1963.

68 Ore-mining: *ST*, no. 6 (1957), p. 46 (S. Zhuravlev, I. Zabolotnyi); *DP*, 20 September 1962. Paper and cellulose: *LP*, 7 July 1964. Textiles: *RK*, 11 June 1964. Iron and steel: *TZP*, no. 3 (1958), p. 10 (N. Gavrilenko). Footwear: *Trud*, 8 June 1963. Construction: *SG*, 27 March 1957. Ore mines in the Marganets basin had to rely for parts on a small local repair factory because the original equipment manufacturers would not provide them. The local parts would last only a matter of days, whereas the originals had a lifespan of several months (*DP*, 20 September 1962). Ivanovo textile mills found it almost impossible to obtain simple fastenings like nuts and bolts. Most were made at two local foundries which had not changed their assortment for 30 years, and were thus incompatible with new, high-speed textile equipment then being introduced (*RK*, 16 May and 13 September 1962). The No. Four Footwear Factory in Kiev had neither parts nor cutting tools. Workers were forced to sneak out to the local bazaar to buy tools that had been pilfered from other factories (*Trud*, 8 June 1963). One construction trust in Dnepropetrovsk had to make its own hinges (*SG*, 27 March 1957).

69 *ST*, no. 9 (1957), pp. 82–3 (Ya. Ulasenko, Ch. Naidov-Zhelezov); *UR*, 21 May 1963. The shortage of spares impeded the introduction of new coal-cutting equipment. The new machines were soon out of action, allegedly because

sovnarkhoz bureaucracies had issued risibly low plans for the manufacture of spares (*Trud*, 18 September 1964).

70 *MP*, 13 December 1961.

71 *ST*, no. 1 (1958), p. 51 (I. Polyakov); *LP*, 16 May and 23 October 1963.

72 *ST*, no. 1 (1958), p. 51 (I. Polyakov).

73 *ST*, no. 9 (1960), pp. 25–6 (B. Machekhin).

74 *Trud*, 22 November 1962 (Grishin, speech to Plenum of TsK KPSS).

75 Maloletova, pp. 193–5.

76 In 1963 there were 4,578,000 industrial workers in the Ukraine, including 431,000 in iron and steel (45 per cent of all iron and steel workers in the USSR), 1,500,000 in engineering, and a mere 555,000 in light industry (excluding food) (*Promyshlennost' i rabochii klass Ukrainskoi SSR*, p. 433).

77 *Rabochii klass SSSR*, pp. 144, 147.

78 Sonin, pp. 121–2. For a more detailed discussion of industrial recruitment, see chapter 3.

79 Khlusov, p. 108. There were still pockets of industry where a significant share of young workers were from peasant backgrounds. In the open hearth shop of the Kuznetsk iron and steel combine in 1965, 37.5 per cent of workers aged 18 to 25 were of 'non-working class' origin (*Problemy istorii sovetskogo obshchestva Sibiri*, p. 125 (A. A. Khaliulina)). Most of these would have been young people from the countryside. Nevertheless, the share of rural migrants among new industrial recruits in Siberia – which relied on the countryside to a far greater extent than the older industrial conurbations of the western USSR – fell from 59 per cent in 1956 to 38 per cent in 1965 (*Chislennost' i sostav rabochikh Sibiri*, p. 114 (A. A. Khaliulina)).

80 *Itogi vsesoyuznoi perepisi*, pp. 99, 159, 161. Of the 99.1 million people in active employment, only 92.7 million were of actual 'working age'. The rest were presumably pensioners or juveniles. The implications of this pool of non-working adults for the labour shortage of the early 1960s is discussed in chapter 3.

81 Alastair McAuley, 'Social Policy', pp. 144–5.

82 See chapter 4.

83 Based on a survey of workers' families in Moscow, Gor'kii, and Ivanovo carried out in 1951, with follow-up surveys in 1956 and 1959 (*TZP*, no. 12 (1960), p. 25 (F. Aleshina, Ya. Kabachnik)). We do not know the average wage of industrial workers in these years. The average wage of workers and clerical employees in the economy as a whole was officially reported as 63.9 rubles a month in 1950, and 71.5 rubles a month in 1955 (*Narodnoe khozyaistvo SSSR v 1965 g.*, p. 567). Judging from later years for which statistics are available, the average wage of industrial workers *per se* would have been approximately 10–12 per cent higher.

84 Alastair McAuley, 'Social Policy', pp. 146–7; Nove, 'Wages', p. 219. The minimum wage was raised by a decree of the Council of Ministers of the USSR, Central Committee of the CPSU, and the All-Union Central Council of Trade Unions (VTsSPS), 8 September 1956, 'O povyshenii zarabotnoi platy nizkooplachivaemym rabochim i sluzhashchim' (On Raising the Wages of Low-Paid Workers and Clerical Employees). Workers and white-

collar employees employed directly in industrial enterprises, construction projects, and transport and communications enterprises were to earn no less than 300 to 350 rubles (30 to 35 new rubles) a month, excluding payments for norm overfulfilment, bonuses, and other special payments. The decree was to come into force on 1 January 1957 (*P G*, 9 September 1956). In 1959 the minimum wage was raised again, this time to 40–5 rubles (Alastair McAuley, 'Social Policy', p. 146).

85 *TZP*, no. 12 (1960), p. 25 (F. Aleshina, Ya. Kabachnik).
86 During the late 1950s the Institute of Labour and the Scientific Research Institute of Trade and Public Catering projected a total need in 1965 for 9 billion linear metres of cotton cloth, 855 million linear metres of wool cloth, and 742 million pairs of leather footwear. Planned production in 1965 for these items was set respectively at only 8 billion linear metres and 500 linear metres of cotton and wool cloth, and 515 million pairs of leather footwear. Actual production in 1965 fell short of the planned levels by 11 per cent in the case of cotton cloth, 27 per cent in woollen, and 5.5 per cent in footwear (*TZP*, no. 8 (1960), p. 48 (F. Aleshina, N. Kuznetsova); *Narodnoe khozyaistvo SSSR za 60 let*, pp. 244–5.
87 *TZP*, no. 12 (1960), p. 28. (F. Aleshina, Ya. Kabachnik). A study of Leningrad textile workers in 1958 found that they spent 45.5 per cent of their income on food (*TZP*, no. 1 (1959), p. 35 (N. Kuznetsova, I. Nemchinova)). The amount going on food and housing in 1959 was actually greater in the Moscow–Gor'kii–Ivanovo survey than that recorded in a 1956 study of Leningrad engineering workers, Baku oil workers, and Ivanovo textile workers, who on average spent between 47 and 49 per cent of family income on these items (*Rabochii klass SSSR*, p. 232 (V. N. Kazantsev)).
88 *TZP*, no. 12 (1960), p. 35 (N. Kuznetsova).
89 G. A. E. Smith, 'Agriculture', pp. 108, 112; Roy and Zhores Medvedev, *Khrushchev*, pp. 159–70; *Rabochii klass SSSR*, p. 229 (V. N. Kazantsev). For the events in Novocherkassk, see chapter 2, note 26.
90 *ST*, no. 2 (1960), p. 77 (V. Kryazhev, M. Markovich).
91 *TZP*, no. 6 (1959), p. 52 (V. Kryazhev, M. Markovich).
92 *Trud*, 13 August 1964.
93 Zemtsov, pp. 66–7. The settlement attached to a mine-construction site in Voroshilovgrad *oblast'* housed 4,000 workers, yet during six years of building work no one had provided either a movie theatre or a club. The foyer of the club had been under construction for four years, but no one knew when the rest would be completed (*SG*, 10 May 1957).
94 *TZP*, no. 10 (1958), p. 39 (V. Kryazhev, M. Markovich); no. 1 (1959), p. 33 (F. Aleshina); no. 9 (1959), p. 32 (P. Eidel'man).
95 *LP*, 13 September 1962.
96 *Trud*, 16 March 1963.

2 The reform of labour legislation and the re-emergence of the labour market

1 Livshits and Nikitinskii, p. 77.

2 Filtzer, *Soviet Workers and Stalinist Industrialization*, pp. 107–115, 146–7, and chapter 9.
3 Gliksman, p. 22.
4 Calculated from Smirnov, p. 79. Smirnov notes that in heavy engineering the proportion of those leaving without permission actually fell during the post-war period, from a surprising 22.5 per cent of all leavers in 1946, to a low of 1.6 per cent in 1956. Those leaving with the sanction of enterprise management correspondingly rose from 32.8 per cent in 1946 to 54.5 per cent in 1956. 'Consequently', comments Smirnov, 'turnover acquired unique legal forms – dismissal at one's own desire with the permission of the administration' (*ibid.*, pp. 83–4). His 1956 figure for those quitting without managerial permission seems impossibly low, but his basic point is still valid.
5 According to Bulganin, in 1954 some 2.8 million industrial workers – or nearly 25 per cent of the total – and 1.5 million building workers (about 50 per cent) left their jobs (Davies, p. 324). Senyavskii claims that in 1955 some 60 per cent of industrial leavers and 50 per cent of those in construction left at their own desire, from which we can deduce the turnover rate in 1954 at about 12 per cent in industry and 25 per cent in construction (Senyavskii, *Rost rabochego klassa* p. 180). As the case of heavy engineering suggests, however, a large number of those leaving with the permission of enterprise management were probably going at their own desire with managerial protection, so that real turnover must have been higher.
6 *Trud*, 19 January 1952.
7 *Trud*, 2 February 1956.
8 During the first nine months of 1955, the factory took on 759 workers but lost 547, and in October it lost more workers than it had hired – all primarily because of poor housing and working conditions (*Izvestiya*, 5 February 1956).
9 *Sbornik postanovlenii i opredelenii Verkhovnogo Suda RSFSR*, pp. 10–11, 75–6.
10 Edict of the Presidium of the Supreme Soviet of the USSR, 'Ob otmene sudebnoi otvetstvennosti rabochikh i sluzhashchikh za samovol'nyi ukhod s predpriyatii i iz uchrezhdenii i za progul bez uvazhitel'noi prichiny' [On the Repeal of Legal Accountability of Workers and Clerical Employees for Wilfully Leaving Enterprises or Institutions and for being Absent without Just Cause], 25 April 1956, *Vedomosti Verkhovnogo Soveta SSSR*, 1956, no. 10, art. 203. An editorial in *Izvestiya* of 14 April 1956 had signalled the impending change by calling for a revision of obsolete labour legislation and the protection of the 'labour rights' of Soviet citizens, in line with the drive for socialist legality following the 20th Congress of the Communist Party.
11 *Trud*, 6 February 1957.
12 Edict of the Supreme Soviet of the USSR, 25 January 1960, 'O posobiyakh po vremennoi netrudosposobnosti rabochim i sluzhashchim, ushedshim s predydushchei raboty po sobstvennomu zhelaniyu' [On Temporary Disability Benefits for Workers and Clerical Employees who have Left Their Previous Employment at Their Own Desire], *Vedomosti Verkhovnogo Soveta SSSR*, 1960, no. 4, art. 36. The extension of full benefits to job-leavers was

made retroactive by a further edict of the Presidium of the Supreme Soviet of 8 August 1960 (*Vedemosti Verkhovnogo Soveta SSSR*, 1960, no. 31, art. 288). A condition of receiving full benefits was that the worker had to enter new employment within 30 days.

13 *Direktivy KPSS*, vol. iv, pp. 620–6 (p. 622). The letter was dated 16 May 1956.

14 See chapter 4.

15 For a discussion of this issue, see Filtzer, *Soviet Workers and Stalinist Industrialization*, pp. 107–15.

16 *Sbornik zakonodatel'nykh aktov o trude*, p. 546. The Draconian law of December 1938 had defined absenteeism as lateness of more than 20 minutes (later reduced to 15 minutes by the law of June 1940). The new Internal Labour Regulations defined truancy as the worker's unauthorized non-appearance for a whole day. A worker showing up for work drunk was also considered to be truant and subject to the appropriate penalties (*ibid.*, p. 546; *Sbornik postanovlenii i opredelenii Verkhovnogo Suda RSFSR*, pp. 72–3).

17 *Ibid.*, pp. 63–4.

18 *Ibid.*, pp. 59–60.

19 Filtzer, *Soviet Workers and Stalinist Industrialization*, pp. 23, 108.

20 *Trud*, 14 February 1957.

21 Edict of the Presidium of the Supreme Soviet of the USSR, 15 July 1958 (*Izvestiya*, 16 July 1958).

22 *Sbornik postanovlenii i opredelenii Verkhovnogo Suda RSFRS*, pp. 9, 10–11. In fact, this right, which had existed up to the introduction of compulsory labour in 1940 (Filtzer, *Soviet Workers and Stalinist Industrialization*, p. 147), was reaffirmed by the Supreme Court of the RSFSR as early as 1953, which gives further indication of how far the old restrictions were being disregarded, even before 1956.

23 This ruling, too, dated from 1953 (*Sbornik postanovlenii i opredelenii Verkhovnogo Suda RSFSR*, pp. 97–8). The use of temporary hiring had been widespread in the 1920s, and played a not unimportant role in undermining the confidence and cohesion of the working class. With the end of unemployment and the emergence of a severe labour shortage during the First Five-Year Plan, the practice virtually died out (Filtzer, *Soviet Workers and Stalinist Industrialization*, pp. 26–7). It is not clear just what the practical significance of the court ruling was in the post-war period, other than in individual cases. The regulations must have continued to be abused on at least some scale, since discussion of them cropped up again in 1961 (*ST*, no. 1 (1961), p. 148).

24 *ST*, no. 10 (1961), p. 143; no. 10 (1963), p. 115.

25 Edict of the Presidium of the Supreme Soviet of the RSFSR, 4 May 1961, *Vedemosti Verkhovnogo Soveta RSFSR*, 1961, no. 18, art. 273. The law stated that able-bodied adults who refused to do socially useful labour, lived off unearned income, or committed 'anti-social acts' could be exiled with confiscation of their property and forced to do corrective labour.

26 For brief accounts of the events in Novocherkassk and other evidence of workers' protests in the Khrushchev years, see Holubenko, pp. 10–14 and

Belotserkovsky, pp. 44–6. After long being a taboo subject in the Soviet press until as late as 1989, the incident is now beginning to receive public discussion. Petr Siuda, a participant in the Novocherkassk events, has written a detailed samizdat account of the rising; this, together with an interview he gave in 1988 to David Mandel from the University of Quebec at Montreal, offer the most detailed portrait of the protests. Hopefully they will soon appear in English. Siuda was killed under mysterious circumstances early in 1990.

27 *Rabochii klass SSSR*, p. 360 (L. S. Rogachevskaya); McAuley and Helgeson, 'Soviet Labour Supply', p. 28a.

28 *ST*, no. 5 (1957), p. 33 (G. Podorov); no. 9 (1958), p. 53 (L. Meshchaninov); no. 10 (1959), p. 75 (V. Selivanov); *Trud*, 15 May 1962 (Kuibyshevkabel'); *LP*, 12 June 1963 (Ekonomaizer), 28 March 1964 (Leningrad excavator factory).

29 In 1930 the average Soviet industrial worker was truant 6 days, ranging from a high of 13.8 days for coal-miners to a low of 1.6 days for textile workers (Filtzer, *Soviet Workers and Stalinist Industrialization*, pp. 52–3).

30 *SG*, 7 July 1961; *Trud*, 4 February 1964.

31 McAuley and Helgeson, 'Soviet Labour Supply', p. 28a. Senyavskii cites similar figures for excused absence in the RSFSR in 1961–3. (*Rost rabochego klassa*, p. 199).

32 See, for example, *LP*, 6 September 1963 and *Trud*, 3 April 1964. The use of work time is discussed in chapter 6.

33 *Rabochii klass SSSR*, pp. 360–2 (L. S. Rogachevskaya); *ST*, no. 7 (1959), pp. 99–100 (I. Andrianov); no. 11 (1963), p. 68 (A. Mukhina, A. Frolov); *LP*, 17 March 1964.

34 *Trud*, 25 December 1962 (speech by V. Grishin to 11th Plenum of VTsSPs); *ST*, no. 2 (1963), p. 10 (A. Sergeev).

35 *Rabochii klass SSSR*, p. 368 (L. S. Rogachevskaya). See also *LP*, 23 March 1960, 18 April 1961; *ST*, no. 2 (1963), p. 9 (A. Sergeev).

36 *Rabochii klass SSSR*, pp. 366–7 (L. S. Rogachevskaya); *ST*, no. 2 (1963), pp. 9–10 (A. Sergeev).

37 *Trud*, 25 August 1963; *LP*, 9 April 1960, 3 June 1961. According to the latter, a brigade of Communist Labour made up of women workers in the machine shop of the Lengazapparat factory in Leningrad ran afoul of their shop superintendent when one brigade member criticized him for not cutting stoppages. He retaliated by taking away the woman's bonus. The response of her brigade was interesting: the other seven women then *pooled their earnings and paid her bonus themselves*. This egalitarianism – which ran counter to the whole spirit of the wages system under Khrushchev and, indeed, since the end of the 1920s – indicates the seriousness, if not idealism, with which some workers treated Khrushchev's promises to build communism in 20 years.

38 *Rabochii klass SSSR*, p. 368 (L. S. Rogachevskaya).

39 Headlines such as 'How We Participate in the Administration of Production' (*LP*, 12 January 1957) were commonplace. Typical, too, was this comment from *Moskovskaya pravda* in late 1964: 'Soviet man is simultaneously the creator and the corrector of the production plan. Our plans are

born at the base, where their fate is decided – in the factories, on the construction sites. And this is understandable. Who better than the producers of material values can know the possibilities of their own enterprise?' (*MP*, 3 September 1964).

40 *Trud*, 7 December 1962.

41 See, for example, *Trud*, 15 June 1956; *Izvestiya*, 8 July 1956; *LP*, 26 January 1962; *MP*, 31 March 1964.

42 *Trud*, 15 March 1959; *UR*, 22 February 1962.

43 *ST*, no. 1 (1958), pp. 136–7 (M. Yakovlev); *Trud*, 22 December 1962, 7 March 1963, 29 January 1964; Mary McAuley, *Labour Disputes*, pp. 100–1, 123–8, 205.

44 *SZ*, no. 12 (1959), pp. 20–2 (Ya. Yanovskii); *Trud*, 13 September 1962, 12 January 1964.

45 *ST*, no. 1 (1958), p. 134 (M. Yakovlev).

46 Mary McAuley, *Labour Disputes*, pp. 206, 213. In 1963, Union-wide 53 per cent of appeals for reinstatement were granted by the lower courts, while in Leningrad (1962 data) the figure was only 35 per cent (*ibid.*, p. 213). Between 1960 and 1980 the rate of reinstatement by the courts remained fairly stable, at 50–60 per cent for the USSR as a whole (Lampert, p. 266). It should be borne in mind that many of these cases involved not workers, but clerical employees or specialists.

47 According to Lampert (p. 265), in the 1970s only about 2 per cent of those fired went to court. It is, of course, impossible to know whether this reluctance to appeal was because people anticipated an unsympathetic hearing or because most dismissals were uncontentious. Lampert points out that in handling dismissal cases both the courts and trade unions were sensitive to the political realities of the environment they were operating in. Courts tended not to challenge powerful managers from large enterprises; trade unions were loath to defend workers fired due to personal conflicts with management, but were more prone to back workers when the issues involved were less overtly 'political' (*ibid.*, pp. 264, 270–1, 276 note 28).

48 These usually involved cases of managers keeping unsafe equipment in operation. See *LP*, 10 February 1962; *SG* 11 January 1963; *Trud*, 1 June and 13 June 1963.

49 *Trud*, 9 March 1963 (chemical industry, Bashkiriya), 20 April 1963, 13 June 1963 (Khimmash, Pavlograd). In the latter case, a health inspector colluded with the head of a Dnepropetrovsk construction firm to eliminate a vital skylight from the factory's building plans, and even claimed a 412–ruble bonus for it as a rationalization measure! The inspector was later fired.

50 *Trud*, 12 August 1964; *RK*, 10 January 1962.

51 *Trud*, 16 January 1964.

52 According to the law, overtime was permitted in only four circumstances: (1) The need to cope with problems of national defence or social or natural disasters; (2) the need to finish off work already begun which, if left unfinished, might cause damage to machinery or materials; (3) the need to carry out temporary repair and maintenance of equipment if its being out of action would cause stoppages to large numbers of workers; and (4) the

need to complete loading or unloading jobs in order to free warehouses essential to rail and water transport or to prevent goods piling up at points of dispatch or receipt (*ST*, no. 5 (1961), pp. 137–9 (Yu. Orlovskii)).

53 A worker at one Moscow car factory recently told me that what the workers at his plant most resented was forced overtime, especially on weekends.

54 *Trud*, 31 May 1963 (Middle Volga machine-tool factory); 8 September 1963 (Staraya Russa garment factory, Novgorod *oblast'*); *LP*, 19 June 1962 (Il'ich machine-tool factory, Leningrad). In the very worst cases, managers could be disciplined or even gaoled for imposing illegal overtime (*Trud*, 9 January 1963 (Donbass building-materials factory), 13 April 1963 (Kemerovo construction)). These were extreme cases, however, in which managers were punished for offences duplicated by other managers all over the USSR.

55 *LP*, 5 October 1963 (Lentrublit), 29 July 1964 (Soyuz factory); *Trud*, 26 August 1964 (Vpered).

56 See also the account of the factory committee meeting at Leningrad's Skorokhod footwear factory, where shop superintendents blamed overtime on unrealistically high plan targets, which the planning authorities compelled them to meet with (in managers' eyes) inadequate establishments (Mary McAuley, *Labour Disputes*, pp. 118–20).

57 The labour economist I. Kaplan argued that even this definition was too broad, and claimed that survey data showed that nearly a quarter of those listed as leaving a job at their own desire in reality took their pension, re-entered education, stayed home to raise children, or needed prolonged medical treatment. Others who quit their jobs voluntarily went to take up work in Siberia or the Far East, and their mobility was, therefore, consistent with government policy. In all, Kaplan estimated that around one-third of those officially listed as turnover in the narrow sense (*tekuchest'*) actually did not belong in this category (*V* , no. 10 (1963), pp. 45–6 (I. Kaplan)). Unfortunately, we have no way to verify Kaplan's assertion. The major sociological surveys of turnover conducted in the mid-1960s (some of which were extremely thorough) continued to apply the conventional definition.

58 Filtzer, *Soviet Workers and Stalinist Industrialization*, pp. 134–44.

59 *V* , no. 10 (1963), p. 47.

60 *V* , no. 10 (1963), p. 48 (I. Kaplan). In 1965 turnover among workers stood at 20.5 per cent in industry and 34.2 per cent in construction (*Trud v SSSR* (1988), p. 258). In early 1963 there was a momentary spurt in job-changing, at least in the RSFSR, where turnover shot up to 35.6 per cent on an annual rate, allegedly as a response to the increasingly severe labour shortage (Senyavskii, *Rost rabochego klassa*, p. 177). This appears to have been no more than a temporary aberration, however. Although international comparisons are difficult to make, Granick has estimated that total separations in the USSR in the late 1960s and early 1970s (that is, just after the period we are dealing with here) were on a similar order of magnitude to those in Western economies, and were even slightly below those in the United States and Australia. He emphasizes, however, the difficulties of finding comparable data, since Soviet statistics exclude temporary and part-time

employment, which make up a large component of separations in the West (Granick, *Job Rights*, pp. 15–16).

61 Sochilin, p. 5 (Leningrad); Smirnova, pp. 86–7 (Ivanovo); T. P. Malakhova, p. 136. As will be noted in chapter 3, the labour shortage in engineering made this industry an important exception in both Leningrad and the Urals.

62 *Rabochii klass SSSR*, p. 130 (S. L. Senyavskii).

63 Krevnevich, p. 95.

64 T. P. Malakhova, pp. 141–2. A similar problem affected machine-tool operators in Moscow chemical enterprises. The Kauchuk rubber plant in 1962 lost 704 machine-tool operators and took on only 469. This reflected the general shortage of (and high turnover among) machinists in Moscow at the time.

65 *TZP*, no. 6 (1959), pp. 28–30 (I. Kaplan).

66 *SG*, 22 February 1961.

67 Blyakhman *et al.*, pp. 73, 75, 76.

68 *V* , no. 10 (1963), p. 48 (I. Kaplan). A 1962 Urals survey of 10,500 leavers claimed to find that 79 per cent were manual labourers. It is difficult to assess whether the Urals – with its predominance of heavy industry and a large share of unmechanized, heavy auxiliary jobs – was an exception, or whether the definition of 'manual labour' was looser here than that applied in other studies (Pysin, p. 21).

69 Fakiolas, p. 28; Sochilin, p. 8; *LP*, 21 November 1964 (A. Slepukhin); Pysin, p. 13; *ST*, no. 2 (1961), p. 26 (N. Kokosov).

70 Sochilin, p. 8; Blyakhman *et al.*, pp. 61–2; Ovchinnikova and Brova, p. 42; Pysin, pp. 13–14.

71 The proportion of workers who changed trades in Leningrad ranged from a low of 27 per cent among fitters to a high of 65 per cent for textile workers (Blyakhman *et al.*, p. 72). A survey of job-changers in Moscow claimed that nearly three-quarters of workers who moved from one enterprise to another also changed their occupation (*Puti likvidatsii*, p. 18). While this figure seems incredibly high in light of the Leningrad study, the two surveys together suggest that a large share of leavers also changed profession.

72 *ST*, no. 12 (1963), p. 45 (V. Ivanovskii, N. Tikhonov).

73 *Ibid.*, p. 45; *Puti likvidatsii*, p. 17.

74 *TZP*, no. 6 (1959), p. 27 (I. Kaplan); *UR*, 27 October 1962 (Sverdlovsk garment factory).

75 The 27 days lost to legal absences (excluding annual leave and public holidays) made up roughly 10 per cent of potential shift time. If we assume that there were very roughly 1 million workers in Leningrad in this period, this was equivalent to over 100,000 person-years in lost production – more than 10 times the figure for time lost to turnover (*LP*, 21 November 1964 (A. Slepukhin)). For a more detailed breakdown of lost work days see chapter 6.

76 The figures were higher in Moscow and Leningrad, where large-scale surveys found that respectively 23 per cent and 28 per cent of leavers quit for this reason (*Puti likvidatsii*, pp. 76–7; Blyakhman *et al.*, pp. 53–4).

77 *V* , no. 10 (1963), pp. 50–1 (I. Kaplan).

78 One mine in the Shchekinougul' trust (Tula *oblast'*) was put into operation in 1954 without providing housing for a full 25 per cent of its miners (*Izvestiya*, 1 May 1956). Housing was still a major cause of turnover in coal-mining at the end of the 1950s (*TZP*, no. 6 (1959), p. 30 (I. Kaplan)). For similar problems in construction, see *SG*, 3 June and 19 October 1956.

79 *ChR*, 6 February 1957; *SG*, 17 February 1957; *Izvestiya*, 5 February 1956 (Penza chemical-equipment factory).

80 *Narodnoe khozyaistvo SSSR za 60 let*, pp. 492–6. Of the 22.7 million new flats erected between 1956 and 1965, nearly 5 million were built by workers and clerical employees either at their own expense or with the aid of state credits.

81 T. P. Malakhova, p. 147.

82 Korobitsyna, dissertation, pp. 116–17.

83 *TZP*, no. 12 (1960), p. 37 (V. Vasil'eva). In Moscow, over half the surveyed families had these amenities. In Gor'kii and Ivanovo, the figures were lower, although the actual share of families was not given.

84 *LP*, 5 July 1960.

85 *Trud*, 14 March 1963.

86 *Trud*, 19 May 1963.

87 *Trud*, 6 March 1963. In general, the quality of construction during the Khrushchev period was so poor that the population termed the new housing units *khrushchoby*, or 'Khrushchev slums', a play on the Russian word *trushchoba* (slum) and Khrushchev's name.

88 *V*, no. 10 (1963), p. 48 (I. Kaplan).

89 *ST*, no. 4 (1963), pp. 34–5.

90 *UR*, 4 October 1963.

91 The No. 1 motor-assembly shop at Kharkov's Serp i molot lost half its workforce during 1958. At Moscow's Likhachev auto factory (ZIL) in the same year, the assembly and automobile-testing shop had half its workers either discharged or transferred to other sections of the factory (*ST*, no. 6 (1960), p. 61 (V. Vorotnikova, V. D'yachenko)).

92 Blyakhman *et al.*, pp. 61–2.

93 Starodub, dissertation, pp. 123–4. Starodub's caveat, if valid, would have applied only to textiles. According to the Leningrad survey, the shortage of child-care places was overall a major cause of turnover among women workers.

94 Blyakhman *et al.*, pp. 105–7; Sochilin, p. 40. For those on 60 to 80 rubles a month at their old job, only a third had bettered their position by changing jobs. Towards the top of the scale, large numbers of workers actually moved to jobs with lower wages in order to win better working or living conditions.

95 See above, note 64.

96 T. P. Malakhova, p. 142. In general, turners and fitters in auxiliary shops in Kuzbass chemicals could earn 13 to 20 per cent more by becoming production workers. This was due partly to the low earnings potential of these trades, and partly to the fact that production workers earned bonuses for working in hazardous conditions. By the same token, workers under 18

were barred from working in dangerous conditions, and so tended to be put on ancillary jobs where they could not acquire an interesting trade (*ibid.*, pp. 142, 148). It was a general trend for young workers, irrespective of their skills, to be put on menial, unskilled tasks, sometimes (as in Leningrad construction) without proper payment for stoppages. Turnover among these workers was high, because of their low wages and the boredom of their jobs (*Trud*, 7 October 1962; Blyakhman *et al.*, p. 95). The Kuzbass had the additional problem that its wages were some 8 per cent lower than those offered by comparable chemical enterprises in the Urals, while prices averaged 15 per cent higher. This led naturally to a migration of skilled chemical workers from the Kuzbass to the central and European parts of the USSR (T. P. Malakhova, pp. 144, 146, 149).

97 Ore-mining: *Trud*, 26 September 1962 (Shamlugskaya ore mine), 26 November 1963 (Krivoi Rog). Engineering: *Trud*, 17 November 1962 (Yuzh-uralmash, Orsk), 7 December 1962 (Kuibyshev engineering). Although the wage reform led to high turnover among, and eventually to a severe shortage of, machine-tool operators in engineering, one of the devices used by managers to try to ease these problems was precisely to make norms easier to fulfil. See chapters 3 and 4.

98 Blyakhman *et al.*, pp. 56–8. See also p. 52 and note 93 for Starodub's objection that working conditions, and not a shortage of child-care places, was the main cause of turnover among Leningrad textile workers.

99 L. K. Malakhova, p. 16.

100 *SG*, 10 May 1963.

101 Forstman, p. 224.

102 *Trud*, 7 December 1962.

103 The factory was the turbine-motor factory, Sverdlovsk (*UR*, 7 January 1964). By the same token, the director of the Association responsible for manufacturing equipment for light industry criticized a similar scheme as inadequate and in need of supplementation through a tightening up of the labour laws (*LP*, 19 September 1963).

104 *LP*, 2 August, 3 August, and 30 August 1963. Although the press campaign did not get properly under way until 1963, an interesting precursor of what was to come – in the form of a letter from an older woman worker at Leningrad's Kotlyakov factory – appeared in *LP*, 11 October 1962.

105 *LP*, 1 November 1963; *Trud*, 23 November 1963; *MP*, 8 July 1964.

106 Cited in *ST*, no. 12 (1963), pp. 49–50 (V. Ivanovskii, N. Tikhonov).

107 *LP*, 18 January and 24 January 1963.

108 *Trud*, 23 August 1963; *LP*, 7 February 1963. The latter also contained letters from workers at the Baltiiskii, Krasnoe znamya, and Bol'shevik factories complaining that many workers – including skilled workers with con-siderable experience – were leaving 'unwillingly', in response to bad conditions.

109 *Trud*, 14 August 1963.

110 *SG*, 10 May 1963. To his credit, the author of this letter did state that the major problem was the lack of finance for new house-building.

111 *Trud*, 30 August 1963.

112 *Izvestiya*, 23 September 1962. The opponent was V. Acharkan (*ST*, no. 8 (1964), p. 129). The letter in *Izvestiya*, from four workers at Leningrad's Kirov works, proposed that 'labour veterans' should receive extra holidays and preferential housing allocation, while 'flitters' should have their pensions cut.

113 *ST*, no. 12 (1963), p. 50 (V. Ivanovskii, N. Tikhonov).

114 *Izvestiya*, 26 February 1964.

115 See *Izvestiya*, 29 February 1964; *Trud*, 1 March, 3 March, and 2 April 1964; *MP*, 27 February 1964; *LP*, 28 February, 29 February, 1 March, and 13 March 1964; and *UR*, 23 May 1964.

116 One Leningrad worker claimed that workers had to be protected from malicious entries by making the factory collective the arbiter of which penalties should be recorded. (*LP*, 13 March 1964). Other opponents had their views printed in *SG*, 27 May 1964.

3 The labour shortage

1 For a discussion of the emergence of the labour shortage during the early years of industrialization, see Filtzer, *Soviet Workers and Stalinist Industrialization*, chapter 2.

2 Hanson, pp. 88–9.

3 Senyavskii, *Rost rabochego klassa*, pp. 168–70; Khlusov, pp. 103–4. The absolute size of the labour surplus in industry was insignificant, amounting to a mere 108,000 workers in February 1951 (*ibid.*, p. 104). This masked the unevenness of the process as it affected different industries and regions.

4 Senyavskii, *Rost rabochego klassa*, p. 171. In the first quarter of 1963, Moscow *oblast'* recorded a surplus of 15,900 workers while Moscow city was seriously short of labour power. The First State Ball-Bearing Factory, for example, was 1,000 workers below the level needed to allow the plant to work more or less normally.

5 Sonin, pp. 108, 113.

6 There were various causes for the shortages. *Sovnarkhozy*, for example, issued wages funds to new chemical shops only several months after they had started up, making recruitment of full establishments difficult. New plants were also built without training schools, which made it hard to train the numbers of skilled workers they required. In fact, as late as mid-1964, the USSR did not possess a single school to train workers to install chemical equipment (*UR*, 22 March 1964; Krevnevich, p. 95; *Trud*, 19 April 1963; *SG*, 27 May 1964).

7 Starodub, dissertation, p. 195. Mills made up the shortage by taking on pensioners and students and by having existing production workers tend more equipment (that is, by increasing the intensity of labour).

8 Manevich, p. 132.

9 *Itogi vsesoyuznoi perepisi*, pp. 98–9.

10 Sonin, pp. 195–6. Here, as elsewhere in his discussion, Sonin has been careless with his handling of the census data. He claims that many of those working private plots were pensioners who could not enter production.

However, the 5 million listed as looking after private plots were adults of working age; thus pensioners were excluded from this figure.

11 *Rabochii klass SSSR*, pp. 98–9 (S. L. Senyavskii).

12 Sonin claimed that, although no figures were available, the number of non-working adults of working age fell after 1959. This is undoubtedly true, but it is worth bearing in mind that between 1960 and 1970 the number of women workers (not necessarily industrial workers) and clerical employees grew by 16.3 million – exactly equal to the size of non-working female population aged 16–54 in 1959 (*Narodnoe khozyaistvo SSSR za 60 let*, pp. 463, 469). At the same time, collective-farm employment was declining. Thus a group equivalent to the entire natural growth of this age group (new entrants minus those dying or retiring) would have remained outside of social employment even in 1970.

13 *ST*, no. 2 (1961), p. 25 (N. Kokosov).

14 *ST*, no. 7 (1962), p. 19 (V. Pizikov). Kazakhstan was atypical insofar as religious and cultural factors, including a high birth rate and a large number of dependants per household, meant that women were a far smaller share of the workforce than in the USSR as a whole. This disparity showed up mainly in rural areas, however, and not in industry, where women were 43 per cent of the workforce, as against 46 per cent nationally (Sagimbaeva, pp. 6–8). This in turn reflects the predominance of the Muslim population in the countryside, versus the largely Russified cities.

15 *Rabochii klass SSSR*, p. 98 (S. L. Senyavskii); Starodub, dissertation, pp. 179, 182.

16 *Trudovye resursy SSSR*, p. 154 (M. Ya. Sonin). The chemical industry in the Kuzbass was able to provide only 65 per cent of its planned number of places (and probably even a smaller share of actual demand) (T. P. Malakhova, p. 148). At the other end of the spectrum, the Kuznetsk needle-platinum factory was able to ease its labour shortage by building three new kindergartens, which allowed out-of-work women machine-tool operators to return to their jobs (*MP*, 26 June 1964).

17 Danilova, p. 46.

18 *Rabochii klass SSSR*, pp. 97–8 (S. L. Senyavskii). In 1962, women were 32 per cent of building workers in Kemerovo *oblast'*, as against a national figure in 1960 of 18 per cent (Senyavskii, *Rost rabochego klassa*, p. 75).

19 *ST*, no. 7 (1962), p. 20 (V. Pizikov). Planning of industrial location in this region was appalling. Industries were planned and developed without taking account of the local availability of workers, and there was little attention paid to the problems of how to re-employ people when construction projects were completed or ore mines exhausted. Rather than planning new enterprises in these localities, the population was expected to migrate to other towns and districts, leading not just to wasteful population movements, but to a total squandering of whatever infrastructure (housing, productive plant, and roads) had been laid down (*ibid.*, p. 21).

20 Sagimbaeva, pp. 12–13.

21 Brova, abstract, p. 9, dissertation, pp. 117–18; Korobitsyna, dissertation, pp. 101–2.

22 Sonin, pp. 203–4.
23 Sakharova, abstract, p. 11, dissertation, pp. 151–2, 154–61, and appendix 14. She argues that families would actually be worse off if a woman took up employment and earned less than 50 rubles a month, since additional use of public services would absorb whatever she earned. The argument, while correct in principle, had little actual relevance. Public services like canteens and laundries were generally shunned because of their relatively high cost and poor quality. If women went out to work, this merely added to their domestic burden, since they still did the shopping, cooking, and washing when they got home. The disincentive for the wives of skilled workers was not, therefore, so much financial as one of *time*. Skilled male workers in Ukrainian heavy industry could earn enough to support the family without the woman working. The woman, on the other hand, found no point in taking a job if this was not going to improve the family's standard of living appreciably, but was merely going to double her work-load. For a detailed discussion of women's domestic burden, including time budgets of women workers, see chapter 7.
24 The *perestroika* campaign was also motivated, at least in part, by the recognition that a strong family reinforces political conservatism and strengthens the authoritarian state. This was bluntly stated in a *Pravda* editorial: 'Yes, recently we have been talking ever more frequently about a woman's problems, about her spiritual, physical, and moral conditions, about the fact that it is necessary for her to return to the family. True, *the stronger the family the stronger the state*. We talk about it, we understand it, but alas, in practice we do little about it' (*Pravda*, 11 June 1988; my emphasis).
25 *Voprosy trudovykh resursov*, pp. 12–13 (V. I. Zanin).
26 *ST*, no. 7 (1962), pp. 26–7 (V. Starikov); Sonin, pp. 203–7.
27 *V* , no. 5 (1962), p. 49 (V. Perevedentsev).
28 *Rabochii klass Sibiri*, pp. 90, 99.
29 *V* , no. 5 (1962), p. 50 (V. Perevedentsev).
30 *Voprosy trudovykh resursov*, p. 20 (V. I. Perevedentsev).
31 *ST*, no. 6 (1961), p. 21 (I. Korzinkin, I. Matrozova, N. Shishkin). This claim has to be treated with care. The authorities regularly put a ceiling on new building projects to try to clear the huge backlog of unfinished construction.
32 *ST*, no. 6 (1961), p. 24 (I. Korzinkin, I. Matrozova, N. Shishkin).
33 Pysin, p. 9.
34 *V* , no. 5 (1962), p. 53 (V. Perevedentsev).
35 Komogortsev, pp. 240–2.
36 Senyavskii, *Rost rabochego klassa*, pp. 176–8.
37 *Rabochii klass Sibiri*, p. 100.
38 *V* , no. 5 (1962), p. 53 (V. Perevedentsev).
39 *ST*, no. 6 (1961), p. 24 (I. Korzinkin, I. Matrozova, N. Shishkin).
40 *Rabochii klass Sibiri*, p. 89; Komogortsev, pp. 241, 243.
41 *TZP*, no. 4 (1960), p. 43 (I. Matrozova); *ST*, no. 6 (1961), p. 25 (I. Korzinkin, I. Matrozova, N. Shishkin).

42 *Ibid.*, p. 25.
43 *TZP*, no. 4 (1960), p. 40 (I. Matrozova).
44 *Ibid.*, p. 41.
45 *ST*, no. 2 (1961), p. 25 (N. Kokosov). Kokosov's point received interesting confirmation in a lively discussion in the construction newspaper in late 1964, devoted precisely to the issue of women workers in Siberia. One woman argued that the real problem was women's double burden: once they had children they were expected to give up work to look after them. Another woman pointed out that many women were forced to leave construction due to the lack of child care and other facilities. A third, however, countered that many women used the dearth of services as a pretext for giving up work so that they could live off their husbands. Unfortunately, the paper gave no indication of how representative each of these views was of the total number of letters they had received (*SG*, 20 November 1964).
46 Komogortsev, p. 245.
47 Khlusov, p. 108; *Rabochii klass SSSR*, pp. 104–5.
48 This was particularly notable in the engineering industry, which is discussed in the second part of this chapter. But the economy as a whole was heavily reliant on ex-soldiers. In the Ukraine, for example, during the fourth quarter of 1965 they accounted for 36.6 per cent of new workers (Shelest, p. 181).
49 *Rabochii klass SSSR*, p. 105 (S. L. Senyavskii).
50 On *orgnabor* in the 1930s, see Barber, 'Organised Recruitment' and Filtzer, *Soviet Workers and Stalinist Industrialization*, pp. 60–1, 141–2.
51 *Rabochii klass SSSR*, p. 105 (S. L. Senyavskii); *ST*, no. 4 (1960), p. 73 (V. Moskalenko). Despite these failings, *orgnabor* still provided Siberia and the Far East with two-thirds of new hirings in 1955–8 and 58 per cent in 1959–60 (*ibid.*, p. 73 (V. Moskalenko)); *ST*, no. 6 (1961), p. 22 (I. Korzinkin, I. Matrozova, N. Shishkin)).
52 *ST*, no. 4 (1960), pp. 75–7 (V. Moskalenko).
53 *Ibid.*, pp. 74–5.
54 *Rabochii klass SSSR*, pp. 106–7 (S. L. Senyavskii).
55 *Ibid.*, p. 106.
56 *Ibid.*, p. 107.
57 *Izvestiya*, 19 May 1956.
58 *Rabochii klass SSSR*, pp. 108–9, 112 (S. L. Senyavskii).
59 *SG*, 17 March 1957; *Rabochii klass SSSR*, pp. 110–12 (S. L. Senyavskii).
60 For a fuller discussion, see Filtzer, *Soviet Workers and Stalinist Industrialization*, pp. 146–7.
61 Edict of the Presidium of the Supreme Soviet of the USSR, 18 March 1955, 'Ob otmene prizyva (moblizatsii) molodezhi v remeslennye i zheleznodorozhnye uchilishcha' (On the Repeal of the Call-Up (Mobilization) of Young People to Industrial and Railway Trade Schools), *Direktivy KPSS*, vol. iv, p. 371.
62 *ST*, no. 2 (1957), pp. 20–2 (I. Kiparenko); no. 11 (1960), p. 70 (V. Raguzov).
63 *P G*, 7 April 1957. The mine training schemes themselves left much to be

desired. A December 1956 survey of the 127 instructional long-walls allegedly operating in the Donbass found that many of them were bogus. Some had only one new worker, some even none on them: they had been given over to skilled workers who were allowed to work with the lower production targets these long-walls were assigned, thus achieving high overfulfilment figures (*ST*, no. 2 (1957), pp. 18–19 (I. Rossochinskii, A. Dovba)).

64 *ST*, no. 4 (1957), pp. 66–8 (I. Slepov); *SG*, 18 January 1956, 12 April and 14 June 1957. To try to meet some of these drawbacks, the Council of Ministers in 1957 extended construction courses to two years (*ibid.*).

65 *ST*, no. 4 (1957), p. 69 (I. Slepov); *SG*, 10 May 1957. Construction was not the only industry where trainees were neglected. At the Ordzhonikidze heavy-engineering factory in Podol'sk (Moscow *oblast'*), young turners coming out of labour-reserve schools were put to work on machine tools without any prior training or assistance. When they ran into trouble, management allegedly made little effort to help them out. Its only solution was to transfer one young woman turner to an office job (*MP*, 3 August 1956).

66 See, for example, two articles in *P G*, 17 April 1957.

67 Decree of Council of Ministers, 2 August 1954, 'Ob organizatsii proizvodstvenno-tekhnicheskoi podgotovki molodezhi, okonchivshei srednie shkoly, dlya raboty na proizvodstve' (On the Organization of Production and Technical Training for Youth Completing Secondary School for Work in Production), *Direktivy KPSS*, vol. iv, pp. 247–50. The decree provided for the establishment of technical colleges open to those finishing a general secondary education.

68 Kostin, p. 196; Krevnevich, p. 88.

69 Kostin, pp. 193–4.

70 *LP*, 21 December 1962.

71 *ST*, no. 10 (1960), p. 64 (M. Liberman); no. 11 (1960), pp. 71–3 (V. Raguzov).

72 *LP*, 1 February and 5 March 1963. For similar problems at Moscow's Frezer cutting-tool factory, see *MP*, 15 March 1963.

73 Krevnevich, pp. 89–90, 95 ff.; *UR*, 22 March 1964.

74 Roy and Zhores Medvedev, *Khrushchev: The Years in Power*, pp. 143–4; Matthews, pp. 268–70. For an account of polytechnical education during the 1920s and the ensuing impoverishment of the school curriculum under Stalin, see Helmert, 'The Reflection of Working Life', and *Schuler*, pp. 144–57. For a more general account of Khrushchev's educational reform, see Matthews, pp. 267–74, 288–96. The problems of the present-day vocational training schools are discussed in two recent articles: *Sobesednik*, no. 29 (1988), pp. 12–13 and E. Ya. Butko and N. A. Denisov, 'Inogorodnyaya molodezh' v proftekhuchilishchakh Moskvy i Leningrada' (Youth from Other Towns in the Industrial Trade Schools of Moscow and Leningrad), *Sotsiologicheskie issledovaniya*, no. 4 (1988), pp. 73–4.

75 *LP*, 1 April 1961, 14 April 1962, 14 July and 26 September 1963, 12 March 1964.

76 See, for example, the front-page article praising the attitude of older workers at Leningrad's Kirov works in *LP*, 5 August 1964.

77 See, for example, the problems faced by the Kauchuk rubber factory (*MP*, 14 March 1964) and the construction of Leningrad's Neva chemical plant

(*LP*, 3 March 1964). At the latter, jobs requiring 50 to 100 workers had only 15 or 20 people on them; other jobs begun the year before had been abandoned because of the labour shortage.

78 Utkin, pp. 29–30. Considering that for the whole of the USSR there were in 1962, 6,600,000 engineering workers, of whom 1,500,000 were in the Ukraine (not to mention the engineering industries in the Baltic states, Belorussiya, and the Trans-Caucasus), the shortage in the RSFSR was equivalent to well over 12 per cent of the actual number of employed workers. See table 1.2.

79 One Soviet historian, with whom I recently discussed this problem, told me that labour turnover in Moscow exceeded 20 per cent throughout the early 1960s, but that we would not find a single word about it published in the local press. This was a slight hyperbole, in that *Moskovskaya pravda*, like other local newspapers, did make occasional references to the labour shortage, but these were relatively few and far between.

80 *DP*, 18 September 1962, 21 March 1963. Another *Dneprovskaya pravda* article (20 September 1962) refers to a shortage of spare parts in the Marganets ore mines, because mining-equipment factories in the Krivoi Rog and Dnepropetrovsk were not manufacturing them. This may have been partially due to the shortage of turners in machine shops.

81 Pysin, pp. 19–20. According to Pysin (p. 10), turnover was worst in the timber, food, fuel, building-materials, and construction industries, not in engineering.

82 *Ibid.*, p. 21. By 1963, however, the factory was also losing experienced foundry hands, allegedly because of the heaviness of the work and absence of mechanization (*UR*, 22 February 1963).

83 *UR*, 21 May 1963 (Uralmash), 21 November 1963 (Uralkhimmash). The report on Uralmash mentions that one of its assembly shops was beset by the common problem of receiving castings that were too large. As the factory's iron and steel plant refused to change the profile of its castings, shop management decided to earmark a milling machine that would do nothing but trim castings down to a usable size. Yet the machine went for six months without anyone to operate it – we can only assume because management had no one to spare.

84 *MP*, 23 November 1962. The first oblique reference to a labour shortage had been published six weeks earlier, in an article about the Ordzhonikidze machine-tool factory, in *MP*, 5 October 1962.

85 *MP*, 10 September and 13 September 1963.

86 *MP*, 26 September 1963.

87 Great play was made in particular of the experiences of the Stankoliniya and Stankoagregat factories, which had managed to stem the loss of machinists by helping workers to move into higher-skill grades and by substantially expanding their housing stock (*MP*, 24 January and 20 April 1963, 26 June 1964).

88 Nor were machine-tool operators the only trade to be affected. A labour shortage at the ZIL car plant in 1963 was blamed for the relatively high number of workers unable to meet their norms, since the factory had been

forced to replace experienced workers with people unfamiliar with its production (*ST*, no. 2 (1964), p. 113 (Yu. Dostovalov)). Perhaps more illuminating was the case of one shop at Moscow's Dinamo factory, which could not find a single electrician or specialist to repair an automatic line, because the only electrician trained to service it had quit to take up a higher-paying job at an institute, and the factory had been unable to replace him (*MP*, 31 January 1963).

89 *LP*, 3 March 1961.

90 *LP*, 29 March 1961. The five enterprises were the Izhora works, Russkii dizel', the State optical-equipment factory, the Karl Marx factory, and the printing and publishing machinery factory. This was tied to a national campaign to improve equipment utilization. Unlike the Leningrad press, *Moskovskaya pravda* at no time hinted that this was linked to a labour shortage. See *MP*, 28 April, 10 May, and 30 November 1961.

91 *LP*, 24 August 1963.

92 *LP*, 14 May 1961. The Elektrik factory later managed to recruit 150 new workers and at the same time have its production plan reduced. This, combined with the difficulties machine shops had acquiring metal, led to a situation where turners then did not have *enough* work to keep them fully occupied. Earnings were threatened and many young workers quit the factory (*LP*, 27 July 1963).

93 *LP*, 21 April 1961.

94 *LP*, 20 May 1961.

95 *LP*, 17 May 1962.

96 *LP*, 13 November 1963.

97 *LP*, 3 July 1962.

98 *LP*, 31 July 1962.

99 *LP*, 11 October 1962. Machinists, for example, consistently received pig-iron that was too hard, causing cutting tools to break, and this factor had previously been taken into account when setting norms. For some reason, management changed the norm-setting procedures, eliminating this allowance for poor-quality metal, which must have put considerable pressure on earnings. Wages were also hit by lost work time, as workers had to wait around for parts to be planed because the factory's planing shop had insufficient capacity.

100 Blyakhman *et al.*, p. 71; Sochilin, p. 6.

101 The study did not include workers who transferred from one job to another within the same enterprise, and therefore failed to catch a considerable number of machinists.

102 Blyakhman *et al.*, pp. 72–4. The Kirov works, which was generally portrayed by *Leningradskaya pravda* as a near-model factory in terms of creating attractive conditions for young workers, was able to fill only half its training places for machine-tool operators between 1960 and 1964 (*ibid.*, p. 74). On the Kirov's alleged successes with young workers, see *LP*, 5 March 1963 (where it is contrasted with the dismal record at the Kotlyakov factory) and 5 August 1964.

103 Again, we must emphasize that these conclusions are based only on data

for workers who left their enterprise when quitting a job. We do not know how many machine-tool operators stayed within the same factory (although press reports suggest it was not small) or what proportion of these became fitters as opposed to auxiliary workers.

104 Blyakhman *et al.*, pp. 72–3, 76. By the same token, nearly 10 per cent of construction workers who left their jobs became machine-tool operators. This did not necessarily mean that they were accepting lower pay in exchange for better conditions, since these may have been unskilled labourers for whom a job as a machinist offered both more money and easier work. We simply do not know.

105 One commentator pointed out the dangers of viewing the shift of auxiliary workers to production jobs as an end in itself. If transferring a maintenance worker to a machine tool leads to more breakdowns, or if switching an ancillary worker means that machinists have to lose time wandering around looking for tools and components, then the exercise becomes self-defeating because it does not lead to any increase in actual production (*LP*, 7 June 1964 (N. Chirskov)).

106 The Volgograd (formerly Stalingrad) tractor factory was held up as the model in this regard. Over three years it was able to cut its establishment of maintenance workers by 32 per cent, quality controllers by 30 per cent, tool-setters by 26 per cent, and transport workers by 22 per cent (Utkin, pp. 30–1). In Leningrad, the Kinap factory allegedly managed to cover a shortage of 400 workers by improving internal organization and to fulfil its plan without them (*LP*, 11 September 1962). Of course, the original plan may have been very slack.

107 *UR*, 7 December 1962.

108 *MP*, 14 August 1963.

109 *MP*, 13 September 1963. The Kompressor campaign was built around the 'initiative' of a woman office worker – Z. V. Nilova – who gave up her job to become a machine-tool operator. In an attempt to prompt more women to become machine-tool operators, *Moskovskaya pravda* published an account of a group of women at the Kommunal'nik factory who learned to be capstan-lathe operators and formed their own brigade of Communist Labour – despite widespread prejudices that this was 'man's work'. However impressive the efforts of these women might have been, they were really a drop in the ocean compared to the additional 100,000 machinists the city needed.

110 *LP*, 8 June 1961 (Sverdlov engineering works); *LP*, 17 May 1962 (machine-tool and automatic machine factory).

111 *LP*, 24 August 1963.

112 *LP*, 29 January 1963. One of the few reported successes in Leningrad was the Izhora works, which claimed to have covered a shortage of 600 workers via a combination of outside recruitment, expanding its training programmes, and redeploying an unspecified number of auxiliary workers (*LP*, 13 June 1963).

113 *LP*, 13 November 1963.

114 *LP*, 26 April 1964. This is all the more interesting in that the factory tried

desperately to hold on to these workers by assigning them looser norms and making it easier for them to earn bonuses (*LP*, 1 June 1963).

115 *LP*, 26 April 1964.

116 *LP*, 1 June 1963.

117 *MP*, 16 October 1963, for example, noted that for all the efforts to raise the prestige of machine-tool operators, unless the 'scissors' between their wages and those of fitters could be closed, the problem was insoluble.

118 See chapter 4.

119 *VS*, no. 3 (1966), pp. 92–4. The only industry that even remotely duplicated such a tight grading structure was coal-mining, where, in 1965, 63 per cent of pit workers were in the bottom four skill grades in a seven- and eight-grade scale. In practically all other industries, just over half of workers were in the bottom half of their scale. The exception was iron and steel, where, because of its hazardous conditions, over 60 per cent of workers were in the top grades.

120 Blyakhman *et al.*, pp. 72, 109–10, 122; *Trud v SSSR* (Moscow 1968), pp. 141–5.

121 This may have been the case at the Neva works when it lost a turner of 18 years' experience (*LP*, 18 December 1962). The man had spent the entire time in the second skill grade, but was always given work at a higher rating. *Leningradskaya pravda* claimed that he left as a matter of pride over his lack of promotion, but the fact is that he would have always been dependent on the goodwill of his shop management to protect his earnings.

122 *LP*, 12 February 1963.

123 The bureaucratic hurdles in the way of workers seeking upward regrading were at times nothing short of a nightmare. A group of fitters at Leningrad's Krasnogvardets factory had for years been carrying out skilled work, and had even acquired a second trade as machine-tool operators – despite which they remained in the lowest grades (one was still classed as a trainee after six years). They could not move into higher grades, because regulations stated that they had first to complete a course to upgrade their skills. The factory, however, did not run such courses. After three years of empty promises, the factory finally put on the appropriate course, at the end of which the workers had to pass an exam, consisting of manufacturing two parts. But because they were all skilled workers, their foreman gave them a full production programme of 20 parts, which they duly made. The factory official responsible for certifying their exam refused to do so, however, because they had made 20 items, instead of the required two. After a prolonged dispute, they repeated the exam, machining just two parts, and only then did they receive their new grades (*LP*, 16 February 1963).

124 *V* , no. 10 (1963), p. 50 (I. Kaplan). It is important to note that one factor pulling down the average skill grade in engineering was the marginalization of women at the bottom of the scale, an issue discussed in more detail in chapter 7. Nevertheless, it is clear from the press and monograph discussions of the labour shortage in engineering that the discontent and labour turnover fostered by the industry's rigid grading was extensive among male machine-tool operators, despite their relatively 'privileged'

position. Unfortunately, we do not know whether women machinists were as prone to quit their jobs over this issue as their male counterparts.

125 *Sbornik zakonodatel'nykh aktov o trude*, p. 282.

126 *ST*, no. 4 (1964), p. 57 (Yu. Nazar'yants, I. Galitskii). Earnings in engineering were further limited by the fact that bonuses for overfulfilling technically based norms were paid only on those items passed as defect-free. Moscow engineering factories made the rules even more stringent by refusing to pay bonuses on articles which failed initial inspection. Even if workers subsequently rectified any defects, they were paid at the normal rate (*ST*, no. 10 (1964), p. 82 (M. Glyantsev)).

127 See chapter 4, pp. 105, 111–12.

128 *UR*, 9 May 1964; *ST*, no. 4 (1964), pp. 56–7 (Yu. Nazar'yants, I. Galitskii), no. 7 (1964), pp. 35–6 (D. Vladimirov), no. 10 (1964), p. 83 (M. Glyantsev). The decree establishing the new bonus regulations was apparently never published. Glyantsev dates its issue as 12 March 1964, but it never appeared in the *BGK* [State Labour and Wages Committee's Bulletin], which listed all that Committee's laws and regulations.

129 *ST*, no. 7 (1964), p. 35 (D. Vladimirov). The new changes had their opponents. The authors of the Moscow study of labour turnover claimed that such bonuses failed to take into account the greater intensity of the labour of machine-tool operators, as opposed to fitters (for whom accepting tighter norms would involve far less physical effort). Instead, they advocated higher basic wages for work which was more intensive, although they admitted that they had no way accurately to measure different degrees of intensity (*Puti likvidatsii*, pp. 83–5).

130 *MP*, 29 January 1963.

131 *UR*, 16 November 1962.

132 *RK*, 19 September 1964.

133 See *MP*, 28 April, 10 May and 30 November 1961.

134 *LP*, 26 May 1963.

135 *LP*, 4 September 1963 (Machine factory), 1 November 1963 (Vibrator factory), and 28 November 1963 (Lepse and Znamya truda factories). In the Kuzbass, the Kuznetsk needle-platinum factory raised its shift index to 1.76 – far higher than the vast majority of engineering enterprises – through a combination of extending mechanization and improving the work environment (*MP*, 26 June 1964).

136 *LP*, 10 May 1964 (Kotlyakov), 13 November 1963 (Admiralty ship-building factory). In one section of Leningrad's Machine factory, a piece of equipment was recorded as in use during the dinner break, but only because its operator had forgotten to switch it off (*LP*, 4 June 1963).

137 *LP*, 7 May 1964 (I. Lebedinskii). At the Sverdlov machine-tool factory, some metal-reamers spent over half their time rectifying defects in castings or finished output. One reamer needed an entire shift to put 10 windows into equipment casings that been left out in their original manufacture.

138 Utkin, pp. 33–6. 'In practice it often happens that the liquidation of one "bottleneck" leads to another portion of the equipment – which pre-

viously had not been limiting production – becoming a "bottleneck" in its turn" (*ibid.*, pp. 33–4).

139 *LP*, 29 January 1964.

140 *LP*, 6 May 1964 (I. Kozlov); Utkin, p. 38. Out of 235,000 machine tools in Ukrainian industry in 1962, a full 100,000 were in repair and maintenance sections (*KU*, no. 2 (1966), p. 34 (S. Kul'chitskii)).

141 *MP*, 6 October 1963, 7 April 1964. In one case, a factory was ordered to buy a piece of equipment in 1957, for which it spent *six years* looking for the drawings. When they finally looked inside the crates, the equipment had deteriorated so badly that it was useless (*ibid.*).

142 *LP*, 6 May 1964 (I. Kozlov).

143 *RK*, 7 May 1963. The Sverdlov metal-construction factory in the Urals had, out of its stock of 650 machine tools and other pieces of equipment, 200 in storage, 100 in the process of installation, 30 out of action, and 27 which simply were not needed for the factory's production – in sum, over half its stock was immobilized in one way or another (*UR*, 17 March 1964).

144 *LP*, 26 April 1964.

145 *LP*, 10 May 1964. This was just the equipment in production shops used to calculate the factory's shift index. It does not include machinery in auxiliary shops, which would have been much older.

146 *LP*, 28 November 1964.

147 Utkin, p. 41. Engineering was not the only industry to experience this problem. In 1962, over 20 per cent of equipment in the Ukrainian iron and steel industry was more than 20 years old (*KU*, no. 2 (1966), p. 32 (S. Kul'-chitskii)).

148 *MP*, 6 October 1963 (A. Kogan).

149 *LP*, 1 August 1964.

150 *KU*, no. 2 (1966), pp. 27–8 (S.Kul'chitskii). Referring to the vast growth of capital investment, Kul'chitskii noted: 'While all this has been going on, the rates of technical re-equipment of existing enterprises have barely risen. The fact is that the growth of production capacities has often been achieved not by replacing obsolete equipment with the latest, high-productivity technology, nor even by building new shops which make use of existing auxiliary services, but rather by creating a large complex of shops (both production and auxiliary) which have no technological connections with order production units. In other words, new construction has been taking place under the guise of reconstruction' (*ibid.*, p. 28).

151 *Ibid.*, pp. 31–4.

152 For an account of these pressures in the contemporary Soviet economy and their interrelationship with the labour shortage, see Hanson, pp. 101–2.

153 *LP*, 26 April 1964 (V. Kazakov).

154 *VS*, no. 11 (1966), p. 87; Utkin, p. 5.

155 *ST*, no. 8 (1988), pp. 41–2.

156 See chapter 8.

4 The wage reform

1 On the redistributive aspects of Khrushchev's wages policies, see Alastair McAuley, 'Social Policy', pp. 144–7.
2 See chapter 3, pp. 68–9.
3 Leonard Joel Kirsch, *Soviet Wages*.
4 *Trudovye resursy SSSR*, pp. 74, 75 (R. A. Eidel'man).
5 Filtzer, *Soviet Workers and Stalinist Industrialization*, chapter 8.
6 At the Kalibr instrument factory in Moscow, which employed a large number of highly skilled workers, the basic hourly rate for piece workers on so-called 'hot' and dangerous jobs (the highest paid category) was a mere 1.44 rubles, which would have earned them a paltry 300 rubles a month without payments for norm overfulfilment. In fact, norms were kept low enough for fulfilment to average 240 per cent, more than doubling workers' earnings (*TZP*, no. 7 (1958), p. 14 (S. Karshenbaum)).
7 Batkaev and Markov, pp. 201–3; Davies, pp. 325–6. In coal-mining, where many women and factory training-school graduates took up work during the war, norms were cut far below their pre-war levels. Although norms were raised in 1950, 1953, and 1955, the rises were very small. In addition, many norms on mechanized jobs were still pegged at the levels set when these jobs had been done by hand (*ST*, no. 4 (1960), pp. 66–7 (B. Labkovskii)). At the Neva Lenin engineering works in Leningrad, the basic wage for some piece workers came to only 35 to 40 per cent of their total earnings (*PEG*, 28 November 1956).
8 *ST*, no. 10 (1958), p. 74 (R. Batkaev); *SG*, 8 August 1956.
9 *ST*, no. 10 (1958), pp. 74–5; *SG*, 20 April 1956.
10 *ST*, no. 2 (1960), p. 48 (M. Zagorchik).
11 *TZP*, no. 10 (1959), pp. 6–7 (S. Shkurko); no. 6 (1959), p. 9 (F. Libina). A certain degree of care has to be taken when assessing claims of different payment for identical work under allegedly equal conditions. The fact is that conditions which the centre might have deemed 'identical', even where the equipment used was nominally the same, need not have been so, due to differences in the age of equipment, non-standardization of parts and components, problems with supplies, storming, etc.
12 *PEG*, 28 November 1956 (Lenin engineering works, Leningrad); 27 February 1957 (K. Petkevich).
13 In November 1956, the coal-machinery factory in Gorlovka fulfilled its plan for gross output by 85 per cent against an average norm fulfilment of 214 per cent; at the mining-equipment factory in Stalino, the corresponding figures were 97 per cent and 187 per cent; and at the Laptevo coal-machinery factory, the plan that month was fulfilled by 99.8 per cent while norm fulfilment averaged 221 per cent (*PEG*, 27 February 1957 (K. Petkevich)).
14 *PEG*, 24 July 1957 (E. Kasimovskii). On the fragmentation of norm-setting in the 1930s, see Filtzer, *Soviet Workers and Stalinist Industrialization*, p. 210.
15 *ST*, no. 1 (1958), p. 69 (T. Ignat'eva, N. Senchenkova).
16 *ST*, no. 2 (1957), p. 10 (I. Rossochinskii, A. Dovba); no. 6 (1958), pp. 39–40.
17 *TZP*, no. 5 (1959), p. 21 (P. Rasines).

18 *Izvestiya*, 4 November 1958; *ST*, no. 5 (1959), p. 8.
19 *TZP*, no. 10 (1959), p. 7 (S. Shkurko); *ST*, no. 7 (1958), p. 90 (S. Aptekar'). The original decree called for the reform in iron and steel to be completed by the end of 1957 (*Direktivy KPSS*, vol. iv, pp. 703–10). The fact that a further degree was issued in 1958 stipulating completion of the reform in iron and steel and other industries during that year (*Izvestiya*, 22 April 1958) indicates that the introduction of the reform had met with substantial delays.
20 *ST*, no. 2 (1958), p. 141; no. 5 (1958), p. 11.
21 *ST*, no. 2 (1960), p. 49 (M. Zagorchik).
22 *ST*, no. 5 (1959), p. 8; *TZP*, no. 10 (1959), p. 7 (S. Shkurko).
23 *ST*, no. 2 (1958), p. 142.
24 *TZP*, no. 8 (1960), p. 37 (G. Veselova, V. Dol'nik).
25 Engineering: *ST*, no. 5 (1959), p. 11. Chemicals: *ibid.*, p. 13; *ST*, no. 7 (1958), p. 36 (N. Aleksandrov, B. Latov, S. Pogostin, I. Pushkov). Coal-mining: *ST*, no. 9 (1958), p. 52 (L. Meshchaninov); *TZP*, no. 6 (1958), p. 13 (L. Semenov); *ST*, no. 5 (1958), p. 78 (L. Nikolskii).
26 For example, fitters at one lead and zinc combine in the non-ferrous metals industry had their norms raised 85 per cent (*TZP*, no. 7 (1960), p. 44 (V. Rugin)). Norms in the tool shop of the Karacharovsk plastics factory went up by 88 per cent (*TZP*, no. 8 (1959), p. 36 (Yu. Vinogradov, G. Tataryan)).
27 *ST*, no. 5 (1958), p. 11 (chemicals); no. 2 (1960), p. 49 (M. Zagorchik) (building materials); *VS*, no. 6 (1963), p. 90 (engineering). By 1962, some 72 per cent of industrial workers were on a six-grade scale (*ibid.*).
28 Iron and steel, for example, was to have just three basic wage rates in the first skill grade: (1) for time workers in so-called 'cold' shops (the lowest rate); (2) for time workers in so-called 'hot' shops and piece workers in 'cold' shops; and (3) for piece workers in 'hot' shops (*TZP*, no. 10 (1959), p. 7 (S. Shkurko)). Arrangements were similar in other major industries (*ST*, no. 2 (1960), p. 49 (M. Zagorchik); no. 10 (1963), pp. 66–7 (R. Batkaev)).
29 *ST*, no. 9 (1958), pp. 53–4 (L. Meshchaninov); no. 9 (1960), p. 45 (I. Rossochinskii).
30 *Ibid.*, p. 46 (I. Rossochinskii).
31 *ST*, no. 5 (1959), p. 9; no. 11 (1963), p. 15 (S. Shkurko).
32 *ST*, no. 5 (1958), p. 12; no. 2 (1961), pp. 54–8 (N. Aleksandrov).
33 *TZP*, no. 4 (1959), p. 14 (Yu. Vinogradov, G. Tataryan); *ST*, no. 12 (1960), p. 49 (S. Shkurko).
34 *Trud*, 28 August 1957 (L. Semenov); *ST*, no. 2 (1958), pp. 21–7 (V. Pyss, N. Kabanov).
35 *VS*, no. 6 (1963), p. 94. The only industry where progressive piece-rates continued to be applied on any significant scale was iron and steel, where despite its low global figure (3.2 per cent of piece workers) (*ibid.*), progressive rates were widely used in some shops – it was alleged, often improperly (*ST*, no. 9 (1960), pp. 52–3 (Ya. Gomberg)). The share of piece workers in industries applying the wage reform actually fell to 53.4 per cent in 1959, before rising back to its 1962 figure (Manevich, p. 137).
36 Calculated from Batkaev and Markov, pp. 221–2.

37 *Ibid.*, p. 208; *Trud*, 22 November 1962 (speech by Grishin to the Plenum of the TsK KPSS). Grishin gives a higher figure for underfulfillers in coal-mining (35 per cent) than do Batkaev and Markov.

38 Nove, 'Wages', pp. 213, 219; Adam, p. 47; *Narodnoe khozyaistvo v 1965 g.*, p. 567.

39 Nove, 'Wages', pp. 213, 219; *Narodnoe khozyaistvo v 1965 g.*, p. 567.

40 *Ibid.* This contrasts with construction workers, whose monthly money wages in 1965 averaged 106.4 rubles (versus 101.3 rubles for industrial workers), an increase of 28 per cent over 1958.

41 Manevich, p. 147. These are, of course, Soviet calculations, but they nevertheless indicate the trend in which wages and productivity were moving. According to Adam, who cautioned that his calculations were very rough, average productivity within the economy as a whole (again, not just industry) grew at an annual rate of 7.2 per cent between 1956 and 1960, compared to an average rise in money wages of 2.1 per cent. The gap narrowed considerably in the period 1961–5 (when the Khrushchev wage reform was supplanted by the Kosygin reforms), with an average annual rise in productivity of between 4.8 and 5.2 per cent (depending on the source of the estimate), against an average increase in money wages of 3.4 per cent (Adam, pp. 36–7).

42 This issue is discussed at length in chapter 7, pp. 179–80, 205–8.

43 Manevich, pp. 131–3. Manevich also lists wages in electric energy above those in engineering, but this is not supported by the data in table 4.2.

44 The basic wage of a worker in the first skill grade (*razryad*) in coal-mining was 1.33 times that of a comparable worker in the food industry (Manevich, p. 131). The comparison here understates the discrepancy, since in 1962 there were no workers in the first skill grade in coal-mining, and only 7.3 per cent of workers in the first two grades, while in the food industry over a third of workers fell into this category (*VS*, no. 6 (1963), pp. 90–3). More telling is the fact that the basic wage of the highest paid worker in coal-mining was almost three times that of the highest paid worker in the food industry and five times that of a worker at the bottom (Manevich, p. 131). Given that bonuses and norm-overfulfilment payments would have been higher in coal-mining than in food, the gap in earnings would have been even greater. Where zonal or regional coefficients were paid, as in Siberia, the difference in nominal earnings would have been wider still.

45 *ST*, no. 8 (1959), pp. 85–6 (N. Gapeev); no. 8 (1960), pp. 86–7 (M. Belkin).

46 *ST*, no. 2 (1957), p. 17 (I. Rossochinskii, A. Dovba); no. 4 (1960), p. 67 (B. Labkovskii); no. 9 (1960), p. 45 (I. Rossochinskii).

47 *ST*, no. 4 (1960), pp. 68–9 (B. Labkovskii).

48 *ST*, no. 2 (1957), p. 18 (I. Rossochinskii, A. Dovba).

49 See chapter 3, pp. 76–7, 80–2.

50 *LP*, 11 October 1962.

51 Blyakhman *et al.*, p. 122.

52 *UR*, 19 June 1962, 15 May 1963; *ST*, no. 10 (1964), p. 118 (O. Kuznetsov).

53 *LP*, 12 February 1963.

54 Kirsch, p. 30.

55 Manevich, p. 133.
56 Building materials: *TZP*, no. 10 (1959), p. 21 (A. Arkhipov, A. Bakelov), pp. 38–9 (I. Baltrushevich, T. Shatova); *ST*, no. 7 (1962), pp. 68–9 (P. Boroshnev, N. Nevolin). Chemicals: *ST*, no. 10 (1959), p. 68 (S. Pogostin); no. 7 (1963), p. 128 (N. Naumenko, N. Delektorskii). Iron and steel and non-ferrous metallurgy: *TZP*, no. 3 (1958), p. 9 (N. Gavrilenko); *ST*, no. 9 (1959), p. 54 (S. Levin *et al.*); no. 2 (1960), pp. 66–7 (E. Smirnov, M. Rudnitskii); no. 11 (1960), p. 58 (M. Rudnitskii); no. 5 (1962), p. 72 (M. Sudrab). As a result of these practices, a number of iron and steel factories then found it difficult to recruit workers to work in sections with heavy or dangerous working conditions, since the differential between these and ordinary shops had been eroded (*ibid.*).
57 Mary McAuley, *Labour Disputes*, p. 92.
58 At Leningrad's Mikoyan confectionery factory, for example, the factory trade union committee resisted *sovnarkhoz* pressure to lower the skill grades of cleaners because it was becoming impossible to recruit them. Similarly, the committee, with the support of the factory's Labour and Wages Department, wanted to raise the grade of pipe-liners to stem turnover among them (*ibid.*, pp. 97–8).
59 *ST*, no. 4 (1962), p. 80 (P. Parfenov, M. Shor); no. 5 (1962), p. 72 (V. Sudrab).
60 Blyakhman *et al.*, p. 120.
61 *MP*, 1 December 1963.
62 *ST*, no. 3 (1961), pp. 48–9, 52 (L. Kunel'skii); no. 4 (1962), p. 82 (P. Parfenov, M. Shor).
63 Blyakhman *et al.*, p. 129. An article from the director of the Krasnopresnensk building-materials combine in Moscow (*MP*, 4 January 1963) illustrates the problems faced by small factories. The *Gosbank* [State Bank] allocated the combine's foundry a wages bill based on the assumption of fairly modest plan overfulfilment. Results even slightly in excess of these limits led to the wage fund being overspent, and the loss of bonuses by technical staff, who then had little incentive to see that plans were overfulfilled.
64 *TZP*, no. 6 (1959), p. 8 (A. Arkhipov).
65 *TZP*, no. 5 (1960), p. 38 (K. Petkevich).
66 *ST*, no. 9 (1960), p. 61 (B. Chernyshev); *TZP*, no. 10 (1959), pp. 42–3 (I. Akimova). In a slightly different case at the Elektrostal' iron and steel works, new penalties for defective output led to a large share of workers in all sections of the plant receiving lower bonuses, which almost certainly meant a cut in their earnings (*ST*, no. 9 (1963), pp. 91–4 (A. Teverovskii)).
67 *ST*, no. 11 (1963), p. 100 (G. Shtefan).
68 *ST*, no. 7 (1963), pp. 129–30 (M. Naumenko, N. Delektorskii).
69 *ST*, no. 5 (1962), p. 73 (V. Sudrab), p. 55 (I. Kulagin).
70 *Trud*, 9 January 1963.
71 *ST*, no. 12 (1957), pp. 13–15 (V. Shuruev); no. 3 (1958), p. 74 (V. Retivoi); no. 1 (1961), p. 77 (N. Krivtsov); no. 4 (1957), p. 46 (V. Korneev).
72 Petr Siuda describes how rates were cut in his factory in Novocherkassk just before the strikes and demonstrations there in June 1962 precisely

because the factory could not otherwise meet its productivity plan (interview with David Mandel, unpublished transcript, pp. 15–16).

73 This is well illustrated by the case of a foreman at the printing and publishing machinery factory in Leningrad who routinely assigned the best equipment and most lucrative jobs to older workers in order to protect their earnings, and left younger workers to make do with worn-out machinery and the worst jobs. The position of young workers was aggravated by the fact that the older workers would not take them into their brigades of Communist Labour, which they reserved only for the top workers with the highest earnings potential (*LP*, 14 April 1962).

74 This was especially true in construction. See the examples in *SG*, 19 February, 13 September, and 29 November 1964.

75 Managers in certain sections of capitalist industry confront similar problems. Lupton describes how shop managers in the engineering firm where he worked wanted to keep rates loose to avoid constant bickering with the workers. In like manner, foremen allowed workers to inflate performance figures in exchange for their assistance in clearing backlogs (Lupton, pp. 151, 154). Burawoy observed the same type of bargaining process in his American engineering plant. See chapter 8, note 48.

76 At the Leningrad carburettor factory, over 32 per cent of workers in the third skill grade were doing jobs rated in skill grade four; at the city's electric-meter factory, well over half the assembly workers in grade three were carrying out work rated at grades four and five. Since payment was based on the rating of the job, and not the skill grade of the worker, they could thus neutralize the effects of the reform's regrading (*ST*, no. 6 (1960), p. 63 (V. Vorotnikova, V. D'yachenko)).

77 See *ST*, no. 2 (1957), pp. 15–16 (I. Rossochinskii, A. Dovba); *TZP*, no. 2 (1958), pp. 6–7 (A. Dovba, K. Karetina, S. Punskii); no. 6 (1958), p. 16 (L. Semenov); *ST*, no. 8 (1959), pp. 87–8 (N. Gapeev); no. 4 (1960), p. 68 (B. Labkovskii), p. 70 (L. Zudina).

78 *ST*, no. 2 (1961), p. 54–8 (N. Aleksandrov); no. 1 (1963), pp. 103–4 (M. Medvedev); no. 8 (1963), pp. 108–9 (O. Kravchenko). For similar accounts in construction, iron and steel, and non-ferrous metallurgy, see *ST*, no. 11 (1963), p. 100 (G. Shtefan); *TZP*, no. 4 (1959), p. 13 (Yu. Vinogradov, G. Tataryan); *ST*, no. 2 (1960), pp. 66–7 (E. Smirnov, M. Rudnitskii); no. 11 (1960), p. 58 (M. Rudnitskii); no. 5 (1962), pp. 72–3 (V. Sudrab).

79 *ST*, no. 3 (1958), pp. 61–2 (A. Balaban, I. Dzhioev); no. 2 (1959), pp. 63–4 (S. Andreev); no. 11 (1963), p. 101 (G. Shtefan).

80 *Izvestiya*, 4 June 1958; *Trud*, 16 August 1963. See chapter 1.

81 *ST*, no. 2 (1957), p. 14 (I. Rossochinskii, A. Dovba); no. 1 (1960), p. 52 (A. Dovba); no. 10 (1962), p. 77 (A. Dovba, M. Tyurin).

82 *TZP*, no. 6 (1959), pp. 25–31 (I. Kaplan).

83 *MP*, 23 May 1964.

84 *ST*, no. 3 (1957), pp. 112–13 (S. Shkurko); no. 8 (1959), p. 87 (N. Gapeev); no. 1 (1960), p. 50 (A. Dovba). See also note 7 above.

85 *TZP*, no. 10 (1959), p. 9 (S. Shkurko); *ST*, no. 10 (1963), p. 67 (R. Batkaev); *TZP*, no. 10 (1959), p. 22 (A. Arkhipov, A. Bakelov).

86 *TZP*, no. 10 (1959), pp. 34–5 (I. Baltrushevich, T. Shatova). For similar practices in iron and steel, see *ST*, no. 2 (1961), pp. 30–1 (L. Meshchaninov).
87 *MP*, 1 December 1963.
88 *Trud*, 19 November 1963.
89 In Leningrad *sovnarkhoz*, for example, revisions were rare: only 10 per cent of all norms in the *sovnarkhoz* were revised in 1960, and 9 per cent in 1962. Of those that were, some were pushed up by only a few per cent (Mary McAuley, *Labour Disputes*, p. 91).
90 *ST*, no. 3 (1961), p. 5.
91 *ST*, no. 4 (1962), p. 80 (P. Parfenov, M. Shor); no. 3 (1963), p. 82 (A. Kosichkin).
92 *V* , no. 5 (1962), p. 41 (S. Shkurko); *ST*, no. 1 (1958), p. 93 (M. Amel'-chenko).
93 *ST*, no. 1 (1960), pp. 73–4; *Trud*, 22 September 1962; *ST*, no. 5 (1964), pp. 122–5 (V. Mikhailov). Mikhailov's article was followed by further discussions in *ST*, nos. 10 and 11 (1964).
94 Kirsch (p. 46) maintained that there was little resistance to norm rises, but the number of references to cases where factory trade unions blocked revisions makes this claim questionable. One even finds occasional references to workers objecting to the new norms. Although the evidence does not suggest that this was widespread, it nonetheless indicates that resistance was far from insignificant. See *LP*, 29 April 1962; *Trud*, 9 March 1963; *ST*, no. 12 (1957), p. 14 (V. Shuruev), p. 82 (Z. Lukashin); no. 1 (1958), pp. 91, 93 (M. Amel'chenko); no. 3 (1958), p. 76 (V. Retivoi); no. 3 (1961), pp. 5–7; no. 3 (1963), pp. 114–16 (L. Ganichev); and Senyavskii, *Rost rabochego klassa*, p. 191.
95 In the oil industry in Azerbaidzhan norm-setting handbooks introduced in 1960 had taken six years to prepare, so that the norms were already well outdated by the time they were introduced. New handbooks started to be drawn up in late 1959, but they would not be ready for use until 1963 (*ST*, no. 6 (1962), pp. 82–6 (A. Martkovich)). Similarly, one Leningrad furniture factory had one rate-setter to revise some 600 norms in just one shop. With no other work to do, it would have taken her or him two full years to complete the job. In reality, given the rate-setter's other duties, the revisions would take twice that long (*LP*, 16 June 1962).
96 *ST*, no. 1 (1960), pp. 71–3.
97 *ST*, no. 7 (1963), pp. 85–6 (M. Zelikson).
98 *ST*, no. 10 (1961), pp. 55–6 (M. Glyantsev).
99 *ST*, no. 12 (1962), pp. 73–4 (V. Udovichenko) (iron and steel); no. 7 (1962), p. 68 (P. Boroshnev, N. Nevolin) (building materials).
100 For the early stages of this campaign see *LP*, 29 April and 25 November 1962, and 6 February 1963.
101 *ST*, no. 2 (1963), pp. 68–86; no. 5 (1963), pp. 30–6. For accounts of the Bureaux at individual factories, see *Trud*, 20 March and 24 April 1963; *UR*, 7 February, 15 May, and 3 September 1963, and 1 February 1964; *RK*, 2 November and 14 November 1963, 14 January 1964.
102 *RK*, 29 October 1964.

103 *UR*, 1 September 1963.
104 *RK*, 14 January 1964 (Ivanovo melange-yarn combine).
105 *MP*, 11 April 1964 (Elektrozavod). It is interesting that this same article praised the Bureaux at Elektrozavod for successfully parcelling out profitable and unprofitable jobs and overcoming the situation where experienced workers had simply refused to carry out jobs offering lower earnings.
106 Kirsch, p. 69.
107 *SG*, 9 December 1964.
108 *SG*, 29 November 1964. In one construction trust in Ufa, *annual* bonuses to top management came to 760 rubles, as against 55 rubles for technical specialists, and a mere 11 rubles for the workers.
109 Calculated from figures given in Batkaev and Markov, p. 221. The veteran labour economist A. Kromskii cites a similar figure for piece workers in Kuibyshev *sovnarkhoz* in 1962 (*Trud*, 8 June 1962).
110 *ST*, no. 7 (1963), p. 88 (M. Zelikson); no. 11 (1963), p. 15 (S. Shkurko). See also chapter 3.
111 *Trud*, 4 October 1962 (E. Manevich); *ST*, no. 7 (1963), p. 130 (M. Naumenko, N. Delektorskii). According to the latter, in 1962 total bonuses made up a mere 8 per cent of the wage fund in chemicals, against a prescribed range of 30 per cent for production workers and 20 to 25 per cent for auxiliary workers.
112 *TZP*, no. 10 (1959), p. 19 (Yu. Vinogradov, G. Tataryan); *ST*, no. 10 (1959), p. 68 (S. Pogostin); *TZP*, no. 8 (1960), pp. 40–1 (G. Veselova, V. Dol'nik); *ST*, no. 7 (1963), p. 129 (M. Naumenko, N. Delektorskii). For similar examples in the footwear and tractor parts industries, see *Trud*, 19 August and 15 December 1964.
113 *ST*, no. 12 (1960), pp. 48–9 (S. Shkurko). The Petrovskii iron and steel works in Dnepropetrovsk established a bonus to be paid out of a so-called foremen's fund, formed out of economies on wages. Wages, however, were 'economized' only when plans were underfulfilled or brigades were short-handed due to illnesses or absenteeism, that is, when a shift or a brigade was working poorly or below its full potential. When the plan was met there were no wage economies and no bonus was paid! (*TZP*, no. 4 (1959), p. 14 (Yu. Vinogradov, G. Tataryan)).
114 *ST*, no. 9 (1960), p. 56 (Ya. Gomberg) (Sebryakovskii cement factory); no. 12 (1960), p. 49 (S. Shkurko) (Serp i molot and Gigant); no. 3 (1962), pp. 102–3, 106–8 (S. Chursanov) (Kalinin *sovnarkhoz*); no. 4 (1962), p. 65 (A. Arkhipov) (Urals engineering); no. 6 (1963), pp. 47–9 (V. Veretennikov) (Tambov); no. 8 (1963), pp. 93–4 (A. Teverovskii) (Elektrostal'). A similar system applied at the First State Ball-Bearing Factory in Moscow, which claimed to have cut defective production considerably, nevertheless ran into problems. Because of the poor mechanization of quality control, assessments of controllers were not accurate. Moreover, the system was used in only two shops. In the rest of the factory, workers continued to be able to claim full payment for defective parts (*MP*, 7 July 1964).

115 *ST*, no. 11 (1963), pp. 99–101 (G. Shtefan). During the Khrushchev years there were numerous experiments with collective payments in construction. Workers were organized into so-called 'finished-output' brigades, where they were paid for completing an entire unit of construction, including finishing jobs. Workers in most construction trusts found it difficult to keep to contracted completion dates, which cut bonuses and made the system increasingly unpopular. For more detailed descriptions see *ST*, no. 5 (1961), pp. 54–5 (I. Chernenzon); no. 10 (1962), pp. 68–72 (N. Bystrova, V. Zolotorev); and *SG*, 7 July and 26 November 1961, 30 September and 7 December 1962.

116 *Trud*, 21 February 1963 (Tambov chemical-equipment factory).

117 *LP*, 12 July 1962.

118 At Leningrad's Russkii dizel' works, a great deal of work time was lost at the end of each shift because machinists would not start work on jobs they could not finish. It was proposed that workers operating the same equipment on successive shifts share a common job sheet, so that each would be paid according to the output of all shifts taken together. In that way, jobs left unfinished would be completed by the worker taking over the equipment on the succeeding shift. Workers opposed the plan because they feared their earnings might suffer if they shared their equipment with a worker who was less productive. Management, however, also rejected the system because they wanted to retain the flexibility to assign workers to new jobs if production plans were suddenly changed (*LP*, 5 January 1962). The system was not uniformly a failure, however. For accounts of its successful application in various Gor'kii factories, see *Rabochii klass i tekhnicheskii progress*, pp. 133, 135–6. An interesting attack on the use of collective job sheets – which claimed that they prompted an unhealthy move away from individual piece-rates – appeared in *UR*, 18 May 1962.

5 The historical genesis of the Soviet labour process

1 Granted, the Soviet Union had many of the features of a distinct mode of production, the most important of which was the fact that the society carried out production in a uniquely definable way which was predicated upon, and in turn reproduced definite social relations of production. On the other hand, the system was too unstable and historically transient to be categorized as a mode of production in the sense that either feudalism or capitalism warrant this designation. The elite, having eliminated capitalism without introducing genuine social regulation of the economy, was able to maintain control only through its political control of the state. This did not prevent the economy and society from falling into profound crisis, characterized by prolonged stagnation and rising popular discontent. The tendency was for the society to unravel, as administrative regulation of the economy failed and the elite groped for some other form of regulator to put in its place, one that would still allow it to remain in power. It is difficult to see what such a regulator could have been, for if the elite surrendered its political tutelage over society, then its role as organizer of the economy

would become unsustainable. That the elite could not maintain itself in this role was demonstrated even before the *putsch* of August 1991 by the market reforms and the reformers' attacks on the 'bureaucratic system', which, if truly eliminated, would leave both the elite and the huge bureaucratic stratum that supports it without any political or economic function. What is left, other than a gradual evolution of capitalism or the involuntary ceding of power to the working class? Current events in the USSR have justified this argument. Hypothetically, had Gorbachev succeeded in creating the conditions whereby the elite were able to stabilize its position as controller of the economy and at the same time create a Soviet equivalent of civil society, then we may, indeed, have seen the emergence of the Soviet Union as a unique mode of production different from both capitalism and an imputed genuine socialism. The reality, however, is that the Stalinist system has disintegrated and begun evolving towards some form of capitalism. The argument for its historical transience has, in my view, thus been validated. The general argument is developed further in the conclusion. On the issue of mode of production, see Ticktin, 'Contradictions', pp. 27–31 and 'Class Structure', p. 61.

2 Although I touch on this point at various times in the course of the book I do not view attempts to categorize the Soviet Union as a form of capitalism or 'state capitalism' as either valid or analytically useful. Internally, at least until the current economic reforms, it was impossible to identify commodity exchange except in the peripheral area of certain private sales of foodstuffs. This is for good reason. There was no market in the Soviet Union, at least not in the capitalist sense. Goods were produced not for sale to anonymous buyers, but on order from the state. Supplies were acquired in the same fashion. Unlike capitalism, there was no market where anonymous producers confront other producers with goods, seeking exchange. Under capitalism it is this situation which gives rise to the social abstraction of exchange value, since so long as goods embody merely the concrete properties of use values, there is no means of establishing an equivalence between them, which must form the basis of exchange. Exchange value, or value, arises precisely out of the need for such an abstract measure. By effacing the concrete properties of the products of labour and reducing them to their one common abstract property – the amount of labour bestowed on their production – value becomes the social basis on which exchange can take place. Even the black and grey markets in the Soviet Union did not (and still do not) conform to this principle, since here what are being exchanged are use values, sought precisely for their concrete utility (for example, metal, machinery, or even consumer goods in short supply), rather than because they embody value. Nor can we say that labour power was bought and sold as a commodity. There was a market for labour power in the Soviet Union, but it bore little resemblance to a capitalist labour market, where the purchase and sale of labour power are subject to the law of value. Wages were determined by the state, bearing only an indirect relationship to the 'value' of labour power's reproduction. Insofar as a labour market existed, it was badly distorted by the fact that, on

the one hand, the worker was legally compelled to work, while on the other hand, the worker could not be dismissed except under exceptional circumstances. Thus the free movement of labour essential to the capitalist market did not exist. The fact that there was exploitation of labour, and that the worker created a surplus product, does not mean that labour power had a commodity form. At most one can say that labour power had a partial or distorted commodity form (insofar as some type of exchange takes place between worker and employer), reflecting the hybrid nature of the Soviet system in general, but one cannot deduce from this that the law of value therefore operated, even imperfectly. Even today, as the market emerges and state control over wages has disappeared, the severe labour shortage, itself provoked by the transition to the market, continues to reproduce these distortions. As for those variants of state capitalism that attempt to adduce the existence of the law of value in the Soviet Union from the pressures of external competition from the West, we can only say that we find such an analysis – which deliberately refrains from looking at the concrete essence and inner workings of a social formation and posits the drive of the system in external factors – methodologically suspect, to say the least.

3 Filtzer, *Soviet Workers and Stalinist Industrialization*, pp. 34–44, 117–18, 268–9. Ticktin has noted that while planning in the terms defined here does not exist in the USSR, the elite nevertheless attempts to exercise control through 'administration' and 'organization' (Ticktin, 'Class Structure' pp. 44–55).

4 I take up this argument in more detail in chapter 8.

5 For an illustration, see the discussion of the *sovnarkhoz* reform, pp. 16, 18, 26.

6 This process is described in detail in Filtzer, *Soviet Workers and Stalinist Industrialization*, chapter 3.

6 Limits on the extraction of the surplus

1 By absolute surplus I mean the expansion of the surplus through increasing the amounts of means of production and labour power applied to production; by relative surplus I refer to the expansion of the surplus through the increased efficiency of means of production or greater intensity of labour, whereby a given quantity of labour power produces a greater quantity of output. Historically, the elite has relied on extension of the absolute surplus as the main vehicle of economic growth, because production relations within the enterprise have made increases in the relative surplus difficult to obtain. This is not to say that the relative surplus has not also expanded. Clearly it has, as workers have gone on to work with more modern equipment or more streamlined methods of work organization. But this process has been so haphazard and so impeded by resistance from both factory managers and workers, that it has been far easier for the elite to build more production units than to rely on managers to introduce new technology or workers to accept a greater intensity of labour.

2 This argument is developed in detail in Filtzer, *Soviet Workers and Stalinist Industrialization*, chapters 6 and 7.

3 *Ibid.*, pp. 262–3.

4 McAuley and Helgeson, p. 28a. There was a wide discrepancy between the estimates of work-time losses made by Soviet labour economists (based primarily on time and motion studies) and official factory reports, which grotesquely underestimated the actual size of the problem. In Novosibirsk, for example, engineering works in 1959 reported losses of less than 1 per cent of shift time, versus the 22–7 per cent recorded by workers in question-naires (*ST*, no. 1 (1961), p. 103 (V. Zanin)). For other examples, see *ST*, no. 3 (1960), pp. 120–1 (I. Bryukov, Ya. Chernyavskii); no. 8 (1961), pp. 77–8 (R. Eidel'man); no. 9 (1961), pp. 141–2.

5 Losses could range anywhere from 7 per cent to 21 per cent even between factories engaged in similar production or between shops inside the same enterprise (*ST*, no. 8 (1961), p. 77 (R. Eidel'man); no. 11 (1961), pp. 38–9 (G. Prudenskii); *TZP*, no. 12 (1962), p. 21 (A. Dovba, A. Golov, D. Gorokhova)).

6 *ST*, no. 10 (1961), p. 57 (M. Glyantsev).

7 *ST*, no. 8 (1961), pp. 78–9 (R. Eidel'man).

8 *ST*, no. 6 (1959), pp. 57–8 (E. Voronin).

9 *PEG*, 24 June 1959. Although the article does not say so directly, these figures must have excluded idle or stoppage time, which we know from other studies to have been substantial. In Kharkov, for example, the average worker faced equipment stoppages of 40 minutes a shift at the city's Tractor Factory, 60 minutes at Serp i motol, and 26 minutes at the Turbine Factory (*ST*, no. 10 (1959), pp. 76–7 (V. Selivanov)).

10 *ST*, no. 9 (1958), p. 53 (L. Meshchaninov); no. 1 (1960), p. 54 (A. Minevich), pp. 64–5 (Yu. Cherednichenko).

11 *ST*, no. 6 (1961), pp. 70–7 (S. Mekkel').

12 *Ibid.*, pp. 71–3.

13 *ST*, no. 1 (1960), pp. 55–6 (A. Minevich). In addition to interruptions suf-fered within production proper, miners also lost a great deal of time waiting for job sheets, receiving maps, washing and dressing, and going to and from their assigned workplace. All of these were done outside official working hours and were, in effect, a *de facto* extension of the working day – although they contributed nothing to output.

14 For a detailed analysis of the use of work time in the 1930s, see Filtzer, *Soviet Workers and Stalinist Industrialization*, chapter 6. A critique of this analysis appears in Lewis Siegelbaum's review of the book in *Slavic Review*, vol. 46, no. 2 (summer 1987), pp. 308–9.

15 *LP*, 14 April 1962.

16 *Trud*, 25 March 1964.

17 *MP*, 2 July 1964.

18 *MP*, 17 March 1964.

19 *ST*, no. 10 (1959), p. 83 (V. Patrushev); *Trud*, 25 March 1964.

20 *LP*, 22 May 1962. It is interesting that, despite such a casual attitude to work schedules, virtually all workers in the factory substantially overfulfilled their norms. Norms were deliberately kept low so that the losses of work time would not affect worker's earnings.

21 *LP*, 9 August 1963.

22 *ST*, no. 9 (1963), pp. 76–7 (P. Kozlov); *LP*, 7 May 1964.

23 *LP* 5 October 1963. See also chapter 2, p. 45.

24 *ST*, no. 9 (1963), pp. 76–7 (P. Kozlov) (Egor'evsk melange-yarn combine, Moscow *oblast'*); *LP*, 7 March 1963 (Sovetskaya zvezda combine, Leningrad); *MP*, 31 March 1964 (Dzerzhinskii Trekhgornaya Manufaktura, Moscow).

25 *TZP*, no. 2 (1958), p. 37 (E. Kasimovskii); no. 3 (1960), p. 31 (A. Denisov, E. Makarov).

26 *ST*, no. 6 (1957), pp. 113–14 (N. Udovenko); *TZP*, no. 2 (1958), p. 37 (E. Kasimovskii).

27 *ST*, no. 6 (1957); pp. 113–14 (N. Udovenko); no. 7 (1961), pp. 121–5 (A. Denisov); *TZP*, no. 2 (1958), p. 37 (E. Kasimovskii); no. 3 (1960), pp. 31–3 (A. Denisov, E. Makarov).

28 That enterprise managers must have recognized this implicitly is suggested by the experience of Chelyabinsk, where workers at the Ordzhonikidze factory allegedly proposed to do away with timekeepers and police themselves as part of socialist competition. The factory's 100 timekeepers were subsequently retrained. However, when the same system was proposed to other factories in the city, their directors refused to adopt it, claiming their enterprises were too large (indeed, the experiment was tried out only at small factories) (*Trud*, 23 September 1962). Management clearly had a better appreciation of the level of commitment of their workers than the people who dreamed up this proposal. The idea of making workers responsible for overseeing the one area of discipline they were most likely to violate must have seemed quite preposterous.

29 *SG*, 21 November 1956.

30 *Trud*, 13 August 1964. Perhaps the supreme irony was the canteen at a large building site in Moscow, which could nowhere nearly accommodate the 3,000 workers who ate there and where the wait for a meal was substantial, yet over whose exit hung the slogan, 'All 420 Minutes to Construction Work' (*MP*, 29 November 1961).

31 *ST*, no. 10 (1959), p. 80 (N. Klimov).

32 *Trud*, 15 December 1963.

33 *LP*, 24 June 1962. The milling-machine operator who wrote about this was, of course, citing it as an example of the poor organization reigning in his shop, but this does not change the fact that some, if not most, workers would have greatly appreciated this pause in the work routine.

34 This was well documented by time and motion studies carried out in the Kuzbass coal-fields in late 1959 and early 1960. Although some stoppages acted to increase workers' rest time, this was cancelled out by the extra work caused by others. The result was that workers on coal combines more or less kept to their regulation rest time (45 minutes per shift), while workers involved in blasting were well below it (*ST*, no. 6 (1961), p. 74 (S. Mekkel')).

35 *ST*, no. 3 (1958), p. 138 (A. Bochkov). A drill operator at Leningrad's Russkii dizel factory described a similar situation at his factory, and concluded:

'Having stumbled along in this way with equipment breakdowns and shortages of tools, we've come to the end of the shift. Strictly speaking there are still an hour and a half to go, but the worker is already beginning to think about whether it's worth it to start on a new batch of parts. He won't be able to finish it. And he still has to clear up and get the machine tool ready to hand over to the next shift' (*LP*, 5 January 1962).

36 *Trud*, 12 July 1959. At the machine-tool and automatic-machine factory in Leningrad, turners in one, allegedly well-equipped shop still had to make their own mandrels before they could machine parts, an operation more complicated and time-consuming than machining the parts itself (*LP*, 3 January 1964). Problems also arose due to the absence of supervisory personnel on evening shifts. At Leningrad's Second Five-Year Plan engineering works the lack of such staff meant that machinists finishing a job early had no one to assign them new work, while young workers had no one from whom to seek assistance or instruction when they ran into difficulties. The factory also had no repair and maintenance personnel on the second shift, so that if equipment broke down it had to stay out of action until the morning (*LP*, 23 July 1963).

37 *LP*, 27 July 1963. The problems were partly caused by poor supplies, and partly due to the factory's ability to have its plan reduced in response to an earlier labour shortage. See chapter 3, note 92.

38 *Trud*, 10 May 1957.

39 *TZP*, No. 5 (1960), p. 42 (I. Kryzhko, N. Prokopenko).

40 *LP*, 30 March 1961.

41 *LP*, 17 May 1962.

42 *LP*, 5 January 1962 (B. Rokin), 19 June 1962 (Il'ich machine-tool factory), 11 August 1962 (Elektropul't factory), 30 August 1962 (Vibrator factory).

43 *LP*, 26 August 1962.

44 *ST*, no. 10 (1959), pp. 78–9 (N. Klimov).

45 *LP*, 13 November 1962.

46 Sonin, p. 107.

47 *ST*, no. 11 (1960), pp. 60–1, 63 (Yu. Cherednichenko). These problems were not unique to the older Donbass coal-fields, but were reproduced in the Kuzbass and Karaganda (*Izvestiya*, 27 June 1957 (Karaganda); *ST*, no. 6 (1961), p. 71 (S. Mekkel') (Kuzbass)).

48 *ST*, no. 5 (1958), p. 52 (E. Voronin); *TZP*, no. 9 (1959), p. 9 (E. Voronin).

49 *ST*, no. 12 (1960), p. 57 (E. Voronin).

50 *Ibid.*, p. 61. The Russian word *mekhanizm* (literally, mechanism) could refer to something as simple as a vacuum cleaner, which even today would be seen in many places as a revolutionary piece of labour-saving technology.

51 *ST*, no. 6 (1960), p. 61 (V. Vorotnikova, V. D'yachenko).

52 *LP*, 23 July and 26 July 1964; *MP*, 10 April 1962.

53 *LP*, 14 May 1964 (Leningrad shale-mining combine).

54 *PEG*, 7 August 1959.

55 *Trud*, 6 March 1963 (Uralmash), 6 April 1963 (Zaporozhstal'). The regime's penchant for 'campaigns' also negated the benefits of many inventions. Innovators were given so much publicity and spent so much time at

conferences or giving demonstrations of their improvements that they ceased to be 'innovators' (*Rabochii klass SSSR*, p. 368 (L. S. Rogachevskaya)).

56 *LP*, 1 October 1964.

57 *ChR*, 21 March 1957 (No. 4 Metal-Construction Factory, Chelyabinsk); *PEG*, 15 March 1959 (coal-mining).

58 See chapter 8, p. 221.

59 See chapter 1, pp. 23–6. In 1960, 60 per cent of loading and unloading jobs were mechanized, but most of this was accounted for by the high degree of mechanization in loading ore. When this was excluded, the degree of mechanization fell to 30 per cent (*ST*, no. 12 (1960), p. 71 (N. Izvol'skaya, N. Trusikhin)).

60 *Ibid.*, pp. 72, 77.

61 *ST*, no. 4 (1962), pp. 48, 50–1.

62 *ST*, no. 12 (1960), pp. 72–3 (N. Izvol'skaya, N. Trusikhin); *LP*, 5 March 1964.

63 *ST*, no. 10 (1960), p. 58 (L. Karpov).

64 *TZP*, no. 2 (1958), p. 16 (L. Karpov).

65 *LP*, 4 June 1963. for similar reports in other enterprises, see *MP*, 23 May 1964 (Second State Ball-Bearing Factory, Moscow), and *RK*, 8 September 1962. In general, the conveyors installed on transport operations in Ivanovo textile mills were so badly designed and constructed that they actually required *more* workers than when these jobs had been done manually (*RK*, 19 February 1963).

66 *ST*, no. 10 (1960), p. 58 (L. Karpov).

67 *UR*, 10 January 1962.

68 In one machine shop at Leningrad's Il'ich works, there were not enough cranes to move parts around as fast as workers required. One machine-tool operator spent nearly four and a half hours out of a seven-hour shift waiting for a crane to mount or transport parts. It is interesting that management's solution was to take machinists – who were idle anyway – off machining jobs and have them relieve the shop's overworked crane operators (*LP*, 19 June 1962).

69 *ST*, no. 6 (1959), pp. 56–7 (E. Voronin).

70 Filtzer, *Soviet Workers and Stalinist Industrialization*, chapter 3 and p. 159.

71 *TZP*, no. 9 (1959), p. 10 (E. Voronin).

72 *TZP*, no. 12 (1962), p. 22 (A. Dovba, A. Golov, D. Gorokhova).

73 *ST*, no. 6 (1962), p. 65 (M. Korbov, N. Silant'eva).

74 *ST*, no. 6 (1959), p. 59 (E. Voronin); *TZP* no. 9 (1959), p. 11 (E. Voronin).

75 *ST*, no. 6 (1959), p. 61 (E. Voronin).

76 *TZP*, no. 9 (1959), p. 11 (E. Voronin).

77 *ST*, no. 5 (1959), p. 73 (M. Glyantsev); no. 1 (1963), pp. 62–3 (V. Gorodetskii).

78 *ST*, no. 6 (1959), pp. 59–60 (E. Voronin).

79 *ChR*, 12 June 1957.

80 The factories most prominently mentioned were automobile plants in Moscow, Gor'kii, and Ul'yanovsk, and the Stalingrad tractor factory (*ST*, no. 5 (1959), p. 74 (M. Glyantsev)). Some non-automobile engineering works attempted to restructure the organization of labour of tool-setters by having them work in integrated brigades. But there was no question here

of actually doing away with tool-setters and letting machine-tool operators carry out their jobs (*ST*, no. 1 (1963), p. 65 (V. Gorodetskii)).

81 *ST*, no. 5 (1959), pp. 116–17 (N. Maiorskaya, F. Chaikin); *Rabochii klass i tekhnicheskii progress*, p. 139.

82 *Ibid.*, p. 140.

83 *ST* no. 1 (1958), p. 53 (I. Polyakov); no. 5 (1958), p. 54 (E. Voronin).

84 A less controversial but equally pressing problem was the work of foremen. Foremen were in theory the shop-floor link between workers and shop management, but the nature of Soviet production often reduced them to little more than trouble-shooters. At Moscow's First State Ball-Bearing Factory, foremen were routinely tied up with such extraneous tasks as tracking down components, tools, and materials, helping out with repairs, and filling out forms. The latter took up nearly a fifth of their work time (*MP*, 5 April 1956). This posed considerable hardship for young workers, who had no one from whom to seek assistance because the foremen were always off on other jobs (*MP*, 10 October 1956). Nor does the problem appear to have attenuated over the course of the Khrushchev period. In the Donbass, the vast areas over which sections ranged, coupled with their constant distractions, meant that each foreman could average a mere 10 minutes a day with each worker (*ST*, 23 December 1962). In Sverdlovsk light industry, they spent little time on actual instruction, since most of their time was taken up with paperwork, replacing absent workers at their machines, or repairing equipment (*UR*, 23 December 1962).

85 *LP*, 3 March 1961.

86 *TZP*, no. 9 (1959), p. 39 (A. Arkhipov); *ST*, no. 6 (1959), p. 59 (E. Voronin).

87 *TZP*, no. 9 (1959), p. 11 (E. Voronin).

88 *SG*, 26 January 1962.

89 In addition to the references cited in notes 44 and 45, see also *ST*, no. 5 (1963), p. 76 (G. Podorov).

90 See, for example, the reviews of *Soviet Workers and Stalinist Industrialization* by Lewis Siegelbaum, *Slavic Review*, vol. 46, no. 2 (summer 1987), pp. 308–9, and John Barber, *Soviet Studies*, January 1988, pp. 149–50.

91 The major comparison drawn in *Soviet Workers and Stalinist Industrialization* is with workers in Nazi Germany just prior to the outbreak of World War II, and in the United States during the war. For references, see *ibid.*, chapter 6, notes 4 and 5.

92 The Report went on to comment: 'bad time-keeping can become a practice in the sense that late starts, early finishes and prolonged tea-breaks can become so regular and so frequently condoned that attempts at enforcing punctuality would be resented perhaps to the point of unofficial action' (Eldridge, p. 49, citing Ministry of Labour, Final Report of the Committee of Inquiry under the Rt. Hon. Lord Devlin into certain matters concerning the Port Transport Industry, HMSO, 1965, p. 19).

93 'He [the Assistant Deputy Manager] was unable convincingly to stress that wasting of time was a bad thing when the workers were encouraged by the situation created by the planners to believe that management did not care about wasted time. How else were they to interpret management's failure

to create a smooth flow of work which would keep them busy?' (Lupton, p. 158). In another passage with a close parallel to Soviet working conditions, Lupton describes the time workers lost due to shortages of tools (*ibid.*, pp. 122–3).

94 See chapter 8.

95 *ST*, no. 6 (1960), p. 60 (V. Vorotnikova, V. D'yachenko).

96 *ST*, no. 4 (1962), p. 51.

97 *MP*, 21 January 1962; *Trud*, 2 April 1962; *LP*, 23 June 1960 (Second Five-Year Plan engineering works); 15 May 1961 (A. Demoshko); 9 June 1962; 14 September 1962 (22nd Congress of the CPSU Metal Factory); 15 May 1963; *P G*, 23 February 1958; *UR*, 14 January 1964 (Uralkhimmash), 28 February 1964.

98 *P G*, 28 February 1958.

99 *P G*, 13 January 1957. The newspaper estimated that the weight of the tractor – the model DT-54 – could be reduced by 150 to 180 kilograms, simply on the basis of standardizing metal consumption for all three factories.

100 *LP*, 30 November 1962.

101 *Ibid. Leningradskaya pravda* ran a small campaign on this issue during October and November 1962.

102 *Ibid. Leningradskaya pravda* disputed this claim, arguing that increasing the weight of components led to more defects, because it encouraged workers to take a slack attitude towards production methods. The two sides in the dispute were clearly talking past each other here. *Leningradskaya pravda* was undoubtedly correct, but the fact was that, given poor-quality metal, component shops had no choice but to compensate for this by making metal articles heavier.

103 *LP*, 3 January 1964.

104 Filtzer, *Soviet Workers and Stalinist Industrialization*, pp. 119, 120–1, 264, 266.

105 *LP*, 14 June 1962.

106 *MP*, 23 March 1956; *SG*, 22 January 1961 (No. 1 Reinforced Concrete Products Factory, Omsk). An equally, if not more important, cause of shortages was the fact that construction firms would put in preliminary estimates of their required supplies, which the planning authorities would use to draw up production plans for the building-materials industry. Firms would then make supplemental requests which the building materials factories could not meet (*ibid.*).

107 *ST*, no. 5 (1961), p. 120 (I. Akimova, T. Shatova).

108 *P G*, 23 August 1959. The factory also sent out equipment that was incomplete, thus passing the problem on to its customers.

109 *P G*, 19 August 1959.

110 *P G*, 9 March 1956 (Petrov factory, Stalingrad); *Trud*, 8 February 1957 (Likhachev automobile factory, Moscow).

111 *LP*, 11 March 1964.

112 *UR*, 22 February 1963.

113 *LP*, 5 January 1962.

114 *UR*, 10 February 1962.

115 *ST*, no. 9 (1960), p. 26 (B. Machekhin); *UR*, 27 October 1962 (Sverdlovsk garment factory).
116 *LP*, 21 November 1964.
117 The Vilnius drill factory, for example, reclassified defective drills as 'specially made for agriculture' and included them in its plan fulfilment figures (*Trud*, 28 March 1964). Factories were so desperate to obtain metal that 'pushers' (*tolkachi* – agents sent out to suppliers to expedite deliveries) would accept anything that iron and steel plants had on hand, irrespective of its quality or how closely it matched their original order. This invariably meant that customers ended up taking metal that was thicker and heavier than they required. At the same time, it allowed iron and steel factories to dispose of second-grade or even defective metal (*Izvestiya*, 3 December 1957).
118 *Pravda*, 23 July 1960 (cement industry). See also the case of the Vilnius drill factory cited in the preceding note.
119 *Trud*, 10 January 1962.
120 One trade organization in Voronezh wrote to the Russian Footwear Trading Organization (Rosobuv'torg), refusing to pay its account: 'Despite this, you continue to ship this type of shoe, obviously reckoning that it is possible to send any kind of shoe to Voronezh for which there is no demand in Leningrad. We have already informed you that boots made by Skorokhod lie as dead freight in the warehouses of the depot. Instead of glutting the trade network with these shoes, you would do better to stop accepting them from the factory'. In fact, the quality of shoes was just as bad in Leningrad (*LP*, 13 May 1960).
121 *Trud*, 11 January 1962.
122 *ST*, no. 10 (1960), pp. 58–9 (L. Karpov).
123 *Trud*, 16 July 1963. The potential malice here was incidental. The building-materials trust in Dnepropetrovsk was poorly equipped and had inadequate storage facilities, so that materials spoiled sitting out in the open. Because it had nowhere to dry its timber, building firms used green, unpainted wood, and so floors and window frames warped. (*Trud*, 2 April 1964).
124 *SG*, 29 January 1956.
125 *P G*, 1 April, 6 June, and 27 June 1956; *Izvestiya*, 5 December 1958.
126 *ST*, no. 4 (1964), p. 58 (Yu. Nazar'yants, I. Galitskii).
127 *ST*, no. 5 (1961), p. 43 (F. Kasatkin); *LP*, 17 March 1961. At the machine-tool and automatic-machine factory, also in Leningrad, on some parts 4 out of 10 had to be discarded. Often the defects showed up only during the final stages of machining, so that the time spent working on them was also wasted (*LP*, 3 January 1964). At Leningrad's Lepse factory, defective castings of non-ferrous metals routinely came to 80 per cent, and on some parts was 100 per cent – that is, the entire output had to be scrapped. Yet management refused to switch to cheaper and more efficient methods of stamping or welding parts (*LP*, 30 September 1964).
128 A switch from a Moscow components manufacturer when installed on a turret lathe actually started up the wrong part of the equipment. The

quality of other components from Kharkov and Odessa was so bad that they lasted only a quarter of their required lifetime (*Trud*, 23 May 1963).

129 *P G*, 17 October 1956, 19 August 1959; *LP*, 29 July 1964. Many of the defects were due to poor design. Of 40 models of polishing machinery manufactured at Leningrad's Il'ich works, only four worked satisfactorily. Twenty-eight were refused by customers for design faults or needed further finishing work, seven were never put into production, and one was discarded as totally defective in its experimental phase (*LP*, 14 May 1963).

130 *LP*, 3 March 1960.

131 *MP*, 28 July 1964.

132 As *Moskovskaya pravda* commented, 'It is safe to say that a tool manufactured after the 20th of the month will almost completely fail to meet standards and technical specifications' (28 July 1964).

133 The article claimed that the factory's wages system did nothing to encourage workers to work more carefully. Instead of putting these workers on time-and-bonus rates, they were kept on piece work, where quality inevitably suffered.

134 On penalties for defective work see chapter 4, p. 115. Experiments to encourage workers to control their own quality were reported, with allegedly modest – but not total – success at the First State Ball-Bearing Factory in Moscow (*MP*, 7 July 1964) and the Slantsy shale-mine combine, Leningrad (*LP*, 30 November 1963). Such experiments must have been more widespread, but their long-term impact was clearly negligible.

135 See chapter 1, pp. 24–5.

136 *P G*, 29 April 1956.

137 In the iron and steel industry, for example, some 70 per cent of all metal-cutting machine tools used for repairs were scattered in small groups over a plethora of shops, where they were used only sporadically.

138 *ST*, no. 9 (1962), pp. 23–4 (F. Aunapu), pp. 62–3 (K. Kuznetsova, A. Rybkina – 1959 data); *TZP*, no. 12 (1962), pp. 15–16 (A. Dovba, A. Golov, D. Gorokhova); *LP*, 4 June 1963.

139 *ST*, no. 10 (1959), p. 79 (N. Klimov) (engineering); no. 9 (1962), p. 18 (V. Sopin) (Bashkiriya), p. 66 (K. Kuznetsova, A. Rybkina) (Volgograd *sovnarkhoz*).

140 *LP*, 13 April 1963. An almost identical article describing the situation at the Sverdlov factory appeared in *LP*, 5 October 1963.

141 *MP*, 17 March 1964.

142 *LP*, 11 August 1962.

143 *P G*, 17 March 1957; *ST*, no. 10 (1959), p. 79 (N. Klimov); *LP*, 11 August 1962.

144 A good example was the Dzerzhinskii iron and steel works in Dnepropetrovsk, where chronic underinvestment in repair and maintenance led to stoppages of blast-furnaces for twice as long as those at Magnitogorsk. The factory's repair shops were simply unable simultaneously to carry out preventive maintenance and manufacture the necessary stock of spare parts needed for preventive and running repairs (*P G*, 27 March 1959).

145 For examples in the oil and geyser-drilling industries, see *TZP*, no. 5 (1958), pp. 42–5 (E. Shimchishin) and no. 7 (1958), pp. 41–5 (K. Volodchenko, T. Mostinskii). For a brilliant account of how piece-rates affected equipment maintenance in the 1930s, see Andrew Smith, *I was a Soviet Worker*, pp. 41–2.

146 *ST*, no. 7 (1960), p. 82 (I. Medvedev, I. Moshkevich, Kh. Zaitsev).

147 *SG*, 26 August 1959. The reinforced-concrete products industry revealed an interesting cycle. Repairs were badly carried out, increasing the amount of equipment needing full-scale capital maintenance. Managers, on the other hand, were unwilling to have machinery taken out of service for such long periods, and so kept inflated establishments of duty fitters who did nothing but tend breakdowns.

148 *ST*, no. 12 (1963), pp. 86–9 (M. Mokrin).

149 Even during the first phase of market reforms prior to August 1991, production was still based mainly on the plan. Indeed, one of the problems enterprises increasingly faced was the imposition of market-style financial arrangements (the need to finance wages and investment out of revenues, declining subsidies from ministries, and the end of ministerial guarantees of supplies) without a true market. As a result they faced the worst of both systems, as supplies and investment resources both became increasingly hard to obtain.

150 This, too, will be changing under the provisions of the new draft employment law, which will no longer make employment compulsory. This is, of course, essential if the regime is going to introduce large-scale unemployment, an inevitable result of any shift to the market.

151 Ticktin, 'Class Structure' pp. 48–53.

152 On this, see Filtzer, *Soviet Workers and Stalinist Industrialization*, chapters 1 and 3.

7 The position of women workers

1 On women in the 1930s, see Lapidus, *Women in Soviet Society*, chapter 3; Filtzer, *Soviet Workers and Stalinist Industrialization*, pp. 63–7, 131–3; and Trotsky, pp. 144–59.

2 At a woodworking factory in Okhta (Leningrad *oblast'*), the workers had adopted the egalitarian (and illegal) practice of assigning wage and skill grades according to seniority rather than actual skill. At the same time, however, they institutionalized discrimination against women, who were put in lower grades than male workers doing the same work (*LP*, 2 August 1964). See also the example of the woman trainee machine-tool operator at the Ordzhonikidze heavy-engineering factory, cited in chapter 3, note 65.

3 For women with established residency in the large towns, there was increasingly the alternative of work in the growing service sector, which by the end of the Khrushchev period accounted for nearly half of all female employment (see note 7 below). Although the pay was low, for the most part the work was easier and often more prestigious; on some jobs, such as shop assistants in food stores, women could supplement their income

through bribes or by pilfering food supplies. This still left a third of employed women with no choice but to work in industry, which in turn could not survive without its millions of female workers.

4 There are many jobs in the older industrial conurbations (Moscow, Leningrad, Ivanovo, etc.) which local workers simply will not take up. They are filled by internal migrants (known formally as workers from other towns – *inogorodnie*) on temporary residence permits (hence the term *limitchiki*). For a fuller discussion, see *Sotsiologicheskie issledovaniya*, no. 3 (1987), pp. 80–5 (V. S. Dunin, E. A. Zenkevich) and no. 4 (1988), pp. 73–4 (E. Ya. Butko, N. A. Denisov).

5 The most detailed discussion of women workers in the Brezhnev period is Alastair McAuley's *Women's Work and Wages in the Soviet Union*. See also Lapidus, *Women in Soviet Society*, chapter 5 and her collection, *Women, Work, and Family*, which provides translated extracts from Soviet sources published in the Brezhnev years.

6 Senyavskii, *Rost rabochego klassa*, p. 223. The one exception to this pattern was Kirgiziya, where in 1959, 38.5 per cent of native workers were women, whereas women were only 36.4 per cent of workers in the Republic as a whole.

7 In 1965, trade (which Soviet statistics usually include in the productive sector), services, health, education, and other non-productive areas employed 23.8 million people. According to Starodub (dissertation, p. 65), in 1964, 74 per cent of workers and clerical employees in these branches were women. This comes to 17.6 million, or 47 per cent of all women workers and clerical employees (excluding collective farms) (*Narodnoe khozyaistvo SSSR za 60 let*, pp. 463, 469). Both the size of the non-productive sector and the importance of women within it grew rapidly over the course of the Khrushchev period. Excluding trade and public catering, it accounted for 15.9 per cent of total employment (including *kolkhozy*) in 1958, and 20 per cent in 1965. If we include trade and public catering, the 1965 figure rises to 25 per cent. In 1961, only 70 per cent of workers and clerical employees in this sphere were women, as against 74 per cent in 1964 (Starodub, dissertation, p. 65; *Narodnoe khozyaistvo SSSR za 60 let*, pp. 459–60).

8 See chapter 3, pp. 62–3.

9 Kotlyar and Turchaninova, p. 40.

10 Korobitsyna, dissertation, p. 39.

11 Brova, dissertation, p. 111.

12 *Ibid.*, p. 103. Women were also a higher proportion of workers in transport (30–2 per cent, compared to 24 per cent nationally), communications (76–9 per cent, compared to 65 per cent nationally), and health (90–2 per cent, compared to 86 per cent nationally). The higher share of women in what were already 'female' sectors reflected the limited prospects for employment in light industry.

13 Korobitsyna, dissertation, p. 41.

14 Calculated from tables 1.2, 1.3, and 7.1.

15 We do not have figures for the proportion of women in different trades

before 1959. Overall, the proportion of women workers and clerical employees in industry rose from 38 per cent in 1940, to 52 per cent in 1945, and fell back to 46 per cent by 1950. In construction the proportion of women rose from 23 per cent in 1940, to 32 per cent in 1945, and 33 per cent in 1950. Only in the 1960s did it begin to fall, which is perhaps a reflection of the rapid expansion of construction (especially housing) in the 1950s, combined with the relative unattractiveness of these jobs (*Trud v SSSR* (1968), p. 76). Although these data show only global trends, the following discussion makes it abundantly clear that women were pushed out of skilled trades they had entered during the war.

16 *Itogi vsesoyuznoi perepisi*, p. 167.

17 Mikhailyuk, pp. 67–8. Women made up less than 7 per cent of tool-setters in chemicals, and just over 7 per cent in light industry. In the food and printing and publishing industries, less than 3 per cent were women, and in the porcelain and pottery industry there were practically no female tool-setters at all.

18 Sakharova, dissertation, pp. 98–101. The year for these data is not given, but they are probably from the 1959 population census. Elsewhere she gives figures from the Occupational Census of August 1959, showing women to command a slightly higher share of some trades: 47 per cent of machine-tool operators (including 17 per cent of metal turners), 28 per cent of milling-machine operators, and 11 per cent of electricians (*ibid.*, p. 92). The pattern in the Ukraine was confirmed by the Occupational Census carried out in Odessa industry in August 1965, where women were 81.4 per cent of ancillary manual workers, 100 per cent of sorters and packers, 83.1 per cent of store-room attendants, yet only 17 per cent of metal-cutting machine-tool operators and 4.4 per cent of electricians. Starodub, dissertation, pp. 61–2, citing data of the Statistical Administration of Odessa *oblast'*.

19 Korobitsyna, dissertation, pp. 42, 44.

20 Korobitsyna's figures for machine-tool operators in Sverdlovsk *oblast'* show a similar pattern, and also include trades not listed by Starodub. In 1965, women were 60.8 per cent of drill operators, and 52.6 per cent of polishers/grinders. In addition, they were 74.5 per cent of capstan-lathe operators and 31.8 per cent of milling-machine operators (Korobitsyna, dissertation, p. 53).

21 Korobitsyna, dissertation, pp. 50–1. In light industry, the fate of women tool-setters followed a peculiar pattern. In the food industry, where women were a majority of workers, women were 3.9 per cent of tool-setters and tuners in 1959; this rose to 7.0 per cent in 1962, and yet by 1965 there were no women in the trade at all. It was the same in light industry, where the share of women tool-setters rose from 16.6 per cent in 1959 to a surprising 26.5 per cent in 1962, then fell to 11.7 per cent in 1965 (*ibid.*, p. 50).

22 This was certainly the trend in engineering, where between 1948 and 1959 the number of tool-setters increased 2.3 times, while the share of women in the trade remained extremely small (Mikhailyuk, p. 67).

23 This was recognized by Starodub, who, noting the low proportion of women among skilled manual occupations in various All-Union and Lenin-

grad industries, commented: 'These data permit us to conclude that the share of women employed in leading trades of automated production remains extremely insignificant. This must necessarily arouse concern, since the solution to the problem of how to attract women into social production and how to keep them there lies not only, and not so much, in the mass employment of female labour, as in the character of the jobs and trades on which female labour is employed, and on the level of skills of women workers' (Starodub, dissertation, p. 60).

24 Korobitsyna, dissertation, p. 48. The share of women on fully automated jobs in iron and steel actually rose in this period, so that by 1965 they formed more than half the workers in this category. But this accounted for so few jobs in the industry that these women still made up less than 1 per cent of all female steel workers. This same process occurred in non-ferrous metals (Brova, dissertation, pp. 108, 110–11). At the same time, women were excluded from virtually all skilled trades in Ukrainian iron and steel (where in 1959 they made up 31 per cent of all workers) which did not involve especially heavy or dangerous work: welders, tool-setters, moulders, lathe operators, and metal turners (Sakharova, dissertation, p. 103). It is also worth noting that there was little if any attempt to transform working conditions in hazardous jobs, to make them safe for men and women alike. They remained perilous, and the confines of men, who at least had the compensation of the higher pay that went with them.

25 Sagimbaeva, p. 20. Given the small size of the industrial workforce in Kazakhstan, this trend, although important, would have affected a relatively small number of women. We do not know if it was reproduced elsewhere in metallurgy. According to Mikhailyuk, for the whole of the USSR, 150,000 women were displaced from ore-mining, but many (she does not specify the exact percentage) were re-employed on heavy physical labour, for example, loaders or excavators (Mikhailyuk, p. 83).

26 With regard to Groups II and III, it should be kept in mind that the Soviet definition of working 'with the aid' of machinery or mechanical devices included anyone using the simplest type of mechanical tool, for instance drills, air hammers, electric carts, conveyors, or, where factory cleaners were involved, something as basic as a vacuum cleaner. Such tools did not necessarily make work easier or even appreciably less labour-intensive.

27 Other sociological studies divided this group into two subgroups. The largest carried out routine control functions, not requiring special skills, and the work was often monotonous. A minority in this group were highly skilled and derived considerable satisfaction from their work (see chapter 8). Group I as a whole was extremely small: in 1965 in Sverdlovsk it employed only 0.4 per cent of male workers and 0.8 per cent of women workers (Brova, dissertation, p. 106).

28 Brova, dissertation, pp. 108, 110–11. Although the data for Sverdlovsk *oblast'* are the most complete, this trend for women to be marginalized into heavy manual jobs was practically universal. In the engineering industry in 1965, for example, women were 39 per cent of workers, yet they were 55 per cent of manual carters and transport workers and 73 per cent of manual ancilla-

ries. In Leningrad industry in 1962, women made up three-quarters of manual workers on loading and hauling, and 86 per cent of manual ancillary workers (Starodub, dissertation, pp. 60–1).

29 Brova, dissertation, p. 115; Starodub, dissertation, pp. 63–4, citing *Rabotnitsa*, no. 7 (1966), p. 10.

30 A survey of auxiliary jobs in light industry carried out by the Central Statistical Administration of the USSR and cited by Maloletova, gives the following proportions of auxiliary workers whose jobs were totally unmechanized: loaders – 6 out of 7; controllers – 4 out of 5; factory cleaners – 15 out of 16; transporters – 7 out of 10; packers – 3 out of 4 (Maloletova, p. 240). The survey covered roughly 15 per cent of auxiliary workers in light industry and lists only the most important occupations. Without knowing the basis of the sample, it is impossible to assess how indicative these figures are of the entire industry. The general picture it portrays of a badly undermechanized auxiliary sector is certainly accurate.

31 *Trud i razvitie lichnosti*, pp. 82–4, 86, 94–5 (V. V. Vodzinskaya). The survey covered 2,665 people – all under 30 – from a wide spectrum of trades at 25 Leningrad enterprises. Kharchev and Golod obtained similar results from their survey of women workers in Leningrad and Kostroma, carried out between 1966 and 1968 (Kharchev and Golod, pp. 47–53).

32 Brova, abstract p. 10. One of the additional attractions of construction was that it had no night shifts and offered many of its workers housing space in dormitories (Shishkan, p. 116). The issue of financial inducements to take dangerous jobs is still being raised in contemporary discussions of women workers. Boldyreva, for example, claims that there is a disproportionate share of widows, divorcees, and women with large families doing heavy and hazardous jobs precisely for the extra pay. Managers, on the other hand, rather than investing in safety improvements, find it easier to pay extra wages to workers in unsafe jobs, since such supplements come out of the state budget rather than enterprise investment funds. At present, some 80 per cent of funds going to 'improve' working conditions are actually paid out as danger money (Boldyreva, pp. 141–2, 150–1). I am grateful to Alastair McAuley for bringing the Shishkan reference to my attention.

33 Calculated from figures provided in Ovchinnikova and Brova, pp. 37, 40; Starodub, dissertation, p. 78, citing Labzin, dissertation, pp. 111–12. The data are from 1963. I was unable to obtain access to Labzin's dissertation while in the USSR, although a summary of its results is available in his author's abstract and a major published article.

34 See table 4.2. According to the 1959 population census, there were also about 7 million women employed in low- and semi-skilled jobs in the service sector: cleaners, laundry workers, nurses and nurses' aides, nannies, kindergarten teachers, librarians, cashiers and bookkeepers, waitresses, cooks, etc. (Labzin, *Filosofskie nauki*, p. 100, fn). All of these, of course, were low-paid occupations. Danilova (p. 28) associated the low wages in light industry with that industry's very high profits. This issue has recently been raised again by those concerned that the high turnover tax on consumer-goods production is depriving these enterprises of the resources

needed to create adequate incentive funds or otherwise go over to self-financing. See *Sotsialisticheskaya industriya*, 22 January 1988 (Lyudmila Telen').

35 For men aged 26–30, only 13 per cent were in the two lowest skill grades, compared to 28 per cent of women (Blyakhman *et al.*, pp. 65–6).

36 Brova, abstract p. 13; Forstman [Brova], p. 217; Brova, dissertation, pp. 155–7.

37 Labzin, *Filosofskie nauki*, p. 99 and abstract, pp. 4–5; Starodub, dissertation, p. 77, citing Labzin, dissertation, pp. 102–3. Labzin's study deliberately selected shops where women and men were employed in identical trades.

38 Starodub, dissertation, p. 80, citing *Rezervy rosta proizvoditel'nosti truda v narodnom khozyaistve* (Leningrad, 1962), p. 143. Nearly twice as many textile workers as heavy-engineering workers had fewer than four years of school; 80 per cent had fewer than eight years, as opposed to 68.5 per cent in heavy engineering.

39 According to Brova, a survey of nine large enterprises in Chelyabinsk and Sverdlovsk *oblasti* in heavy industry, light industry, and chemicals, showed a higher percentage of women with at least nine grades of school (Brova, dissertation, pp. 136–8). These may have been concentrated among women technical specialists or clerical employees. However, later studies have confirmed this as a general tendency. Brova maintained (without presenting any data) that even in the middle and late 1960s women with the same educational level as men were being put into lower skill grades. This prompted her to identify the 'contradiction' of improving workers' education and at the same time preserving occupations which did not require a high level of training (Brova, abstract, p. 14).

40 At the Sredneural'sk copper-smelting factory, for example, half of all women were under 35 years old and 44 per cent had more than eight grades of secondary school. Yet they were still marginalized into lower skill grades and few were pursuing further training (Ovchinnikova and Brova, pp. 39–40; Brova, abstract p. 14).

41 In the transformer-assembly shop where Lupton worked, most of the men had only an elementary education. Technically they were classed as semi-skilled, but most were highly skilled at their jobs and certainly would have been classed as skilled workers in the Soviet Union (Lupton, pp. 113–14 and table 4).

42 Labzin, *Filosofskie nauki*, p. 100.

43 Brova, dissertation, p. 169.

44 See pp. 202–3. This in large part also explains the relatively low percentage of workers upgrading their skills in industries with large numbers of women workers (light industry, food, and building materials). An exception was the chemical industry, where nearly a third of workers annually improved their qualifications, but whether or not women and men participated equally in this is impossible to tell from the data (Kostin, p. 196).

45 Brova, dissertation, p. 145; *Narodnoe khozyaistvo SSSR v 1965 g.*, p. 585; Danilova, p. 35.

46 Brova, abstract p. 13. At Kachkanarrudstroi construction trust in the Urals, nearly half of all trainees by 1964 were women, but they were concentrated in such traditional trades as plasterers, painters, laboratory technicians, and crane operators. They made up a far smaller share of trainee bricklayers, boiler-stokers, and electricians (Brova, dissertation, p. 148).

47 Mikhailyuk, pp. 79–80. Mikhailyuk's own survey of training schools in Odessa found that they could roughly be divided into three categories. First were those training skilled fitters, repair and maintenance workers, electric welders, brigade leaders for roadbed repairs on the railways, dock workers, etc. These had no female trainees at all (despite the fact that on the railways, for instance, most of the workers actually carrying out roadbed repairs were women). Second were PTU training tool-setters, maintenance fitters, fitters on machine assembly, etc. Here only 10–15 per cent of the intake were women. Finally, there were PTU training carpenters, moulders–pattern-makers, plasterers, house painters, and seamstresses. In these institutions, responsible for trades where women already predomi- nated, women made up between 80 and 95 per cent of the students (ibid., pp. 80–1).

48 Sagimbaeva, p. 17.

49 Korobitsyna, dissertation, p. 49.

50 Temperatures could range from 50 to 90°C (Korobitsyna, dissertation, pp. 88–9, citing Vrachebnoe delo, no. 6 (1964) (G. E. Zhirnova et al.)).

51 Starodub, dissertation, pp. 55–6, 111.

52 Ibid., pp. 149–50. It goes without saying that women industrial workers were not the only ones having to cope with these kinds of conditions. A great deal of work in services was also hard and boring (cleaners, dish- washers, pot scrubbers, etc.) (ibid., pp. 111–12).

53 Starodub, dissertation, pp. 51–2. It is interesting that Boldyreva recently claimed that the length of continuous service in textiles had halved in the past 20 years, to between seven and nine years, because of the strains of work in that industry. She also noted that 80 per cent of women textile workers had left the industry by the age of 40, but Starodub's reference indicates that this is not as new a phenomenon as Boldyreva may have thought (Boldyreva, pp. 139–40).

54 Starodub, dissertation, p. 51.

55 'Analysis of the age composition of working women in a number of trades shows that a huge number of them over 40 years old are no longer able to carry on working in their own trade and have to transfer to other, lighter, but lower-paid jobs' (Starodub, dissertation, p. 52). In support of her claim, Starodub (pp. 118–19) cites the examples of various enterprises in light industry and engineering where improved conditions – particularly noise levels and lighting – were matched by increases in labour productivity.

56 UR, 27 October 1962.

57 Rabochii klass i tekhnicheskii progress, p. 131; Danilova, p. 24.

58 A Moscow worker with friends working as press operators at the First State Ball-Bearing Factory recently told us that their accident rate is still high. One acquaintance had just lost her hand and forearm.

59 Danilova, p. 25.
60 *Rabochii klass i tekhnicheskii progress*, pp. 131–2; Valentinova, p. 110; Zdravomyslov and Yadov, pp. 188–9.
61 Danilova, pp. 26–7; Kalinina, pp. 12–13; Starodub, dissertation, pp. 114–17. In one shop of Leningrad's Kirov textile combine, carders tending three machines covered four kilometres *per hour* (*ibid.*, p. 115).
62 Cherkasov, p. 204.
63 Kalinina, p. 20.
64 Danilova, pp. 28–9; Starodub, dissertation, pp. 199–201. This prompted Starodub to call for women in textiles and related branches of light industry to receive the same amount of additional leave time as did workers in iron and steel, non-ferrous metallurgy, and other industries with heavy and hazardous conditions.
65 Kalinina, pp. 7, 24.
66 *Ibid.*, pp. 10–11, 22–4.
67 Starodub, *Nauchnye zapiski*, vypusk 27 (1965), p. 225.
68 Kalinina, pp. 13–14. In one experiment, spinning machines were raised 12–15 centimetres off the floor by putting them on a wood and rubber stand. Not only did this do away with the need to work in an uncomfortable position, but it also sharply cut vibration – and with it the number of thread-breaks.
69 *MP*, 10 August 1956; *RK*, 23 January and 3 April 1962.
70 Kalinina, pp. 63–4; *Statistika byudzhetov vremeni*, p. 108. At the Bryansk worsted combine, the accident rate on night shifts was 30 to 50 per cent higher than on day shifts (Kalinina, p. 64).
71 *Puti likvidatsii*, p. 84. In an attempt to cut the amount of night work in textiles, the regime introduced the so-called 'Ivanovo Schedule' in the early 1960s. This was supposed to cut night shifts from seven per month to two. The Ivanovo Schedule is still in operation and has recently come under attack precisely for its failure to affect appreciable reductions in night work. On the contrary, textiles continues to have more night shifts than any other industry (*Trud*, 14 September 1988; Boldyreva, p. 139; *Pravda*, 2 July 1988 (Speech by Z. P. Pukhova to the 19th Party Conference of the CPSU); *Sobesednik*, no. 23 (1988), pp. 4–5; *Sotsialisticheskaya industriya*, 22 January 1988 (Lyudmila Telen')).
72 Kalinina, pp. 39–40.
73 *Ibid.*, pp. 27–8; *RK*, 2 April 1964.
74 Starodub, dissertation, pp. 115, 134.
75 *Trud*, 14 September 1988 (T. Lozhnikova). For other discussions on contemporary conditions in textiles, see sources cited in note 110 below.
76 For a summary of early Soviet time-budget studies, see Barber, 'Notes on the Soviet Working Class Family'.
77 An exception was Danilova, who identified the problem as one of male privilege: 'The existence of the old division of labour in the family between men and women, at a time when women participate equally with men in social production, places the man in a privileged position. Men, and often the women themselves, perceive such a division of labour as a completely

law-governed phenomenon. Men willingly take advantage of the labour of women, and women, by virtue of established custom, take upon themselves essentially all the care of the family.' Moreover, she clearly understood that the inequalities women faced at work 'reinforced the traditional division of labour inside the family', and that the latter played a vital economic function: the provision of *unpaid* labour essential to the reproduction of labour power. 'Domestic labour receives no value expression, and by statistical and planning practice, is not included as part of the total social product. However, this labour is an important condition for satisfying the material and day-to-day needs of workers and provides a definite quantum of vital resources. This labour provides means of subsistence, and is an important condition for the reproduction of labour power' (Danilova, pp. 54–5).

78 On the disincentives to work, see chapter 3.

79 A Novosibirsk study, published in 1966, found that among low- and unskilled workers refusal to help with housework accounted for 10 per cent of all divorces; among skilled and highly skilled workers it was the cause of fully a quarter. A further 22 per cent of break-ups were due to the husband's alcoholism (Danilova, p. 65).

80 It is doubtful, for instance, that Leningrad women had to put in a full 80 minutes' more housework and child care per day than did women in Moscow.

81 Korobitsyna, dissertation, p. 142. The survey was carried out by the Economics Department of the Sverdlovsk Higher Party School. Korobitsyna's own study of women in Sverdlovsk showed them putting in over 7 hours of housework on off-days. This came to 36 hours a week, just 8 hours less than they were putting in at work (Korobitsyna, abstract, p. 14).

82 *Statistika byudzhetov vremeni*, p. 140. These figures apparently include men and women working on *kolkhozy* (Kolpakov and Prudenskii, p. 219). Since the main responsibility for the private plot on collective farms belonged to the women, the plots must have represented an even greater share of men's contribution in the towns.

83 *LP*, 14 April 1963. This is probably the same study cited by Starodub from the doctoral dissertation of M. D. Pliner. See below, note 101.

84 *Statistika byudzhetov vremeni*, p. 108. Detailed data from the Novosibirsk Cotton Textile Combine showed women on night shifts getting less than 5 hours' sleep, more than 2 hours less than other workers. The same pattern was observed among women in engineering (where night shifts were extremely rare, however). It did not apply to women in iron and steel, who, together with men, worked special shift rosters peculiar to that industry (*ibid.*, pp. 144–6).

85 There is a slight discrepancy between the data given here, which cover all family members, and those cited on p. 198, which were for working family members only.

86 The table seriously underestimates the time spent on child care. Often women were looking after children while doing other domestic chores, for example, shopping, cleaning the house, or cooking. Where families lived

with an older parent, the latter, of course, spent much of their time taking care of their grandchildren.

87 The 1963 study of Sverdlovsk *oblast'* showed that women (including those on *kolkhozy*) gave almost twice as much time as men each week to 'maintaining living quarters, furniture, and appliances' (4.6 hours as against 2.5), and 14 times as many hours as men to washing and mending clothes (8.4 hours as against 0.6). As in Novosibirsk, the gap in child care was also wide: 3.4 hours per week for women and 1 hour for men (Kolpakov and Prudenskii, p. 219).

88 *ST*, no. 6 (1959), pp. 34–5 (V. Kryazhev, M. Markovich).

89 Brova, dissertation, p. 205, citing V. G. Baikova, A. A. Zemtsov, and A. S. Duchal, *Svobodnoe vremya i vsestoronnee razvitie lichnosti* (Moscow, 1965), p. 420.

90 Danilova, p. 54.

91 A self-service laundry was opened in Moscow on Leninskii Prospekt in 1962. It had 20 washing machines, each with a capacity of only 4 kilograms – less than the average household machine in Western Europe today, and much smaller than domestic machines in the United States. To do 10 kilograms of washing took 1.5 to 2 hours. Probably more useful was a scheme in Yaroslavl', where in 1962 they opened up 63 self-service laundries in the basements of blocks of flats, and equipped them with 475 machines altogether (Sazonova, p. 69).

92 *Izvestiya*, 15 April 1964 (S. Strumilin, A. Peremyslov).

93 Starodub, dissertation, pp. 165–6.

94 Although foods like milk are now almost totally prepacked, self-service groceries are still a rarity. Shortages make those that exist gloomy affairs. Many items, such as eggs and macaroni, are still mostly sold loose.

95 See chapter 3, pp. 53–4, 63, 69.

96 Trufanov, p. 162.

97 Danilova, p. 47. A major problem with the shortage of child-care places was the high turnover of staff – in turn due to the fact that they did not have the same conditions and privileges as teachers for this same age group (3 to 7), despite the fact that their work was difficult and laborious. Teachers, for example, had 36 days' paid holiday a year and a six-hour day, as opposed to child-care workers who had limited holidays and longer hours (*ibid.*, p. 46). In fact, this division is comparable to that between nursery nurses and primary-school teachers in Britain today. Nursery nurses are extremely low-paid, despite the fact that they work much longer hours than teachers and in many cases carry out comparable responsibilities.

98 L. K. Malakhova, p. 16. By way of an exception, Malakhova cites the Ulan-Ude fine-cloth factory in the remote Buryat-Mongolian ASSR, about 200 kilometres from Irkutsk. The factory had places for 60 per cent of the children open around the clock; the rest were offered extended hours until 8 p.m. The nursery was also open on Saturdays. There is no evidence that this model was widely adopted elsewhere.

99 Korobitsyna, dissertation, appendix, table 5.

100 *Statistika byudzhetov vremeni*, p. 87.
101 The average woman (not just workers) employed at the factory spent 22 hours a week on housework, compared to 9 hours for the average man. For married women, however, this rose to 30.5 hours, as opposed to just 10.5 hours for married men (Starodub, dissertation, p. 158, citing M. D. Pliner, *Problemy vosproizvodstva rabochei sily v promyshlennosti*, doctoral dissertation (Leningrad, 1965), p. 110).
102 *Rabochii klass i tekhnicheskii progress*, p. 240. The data were based on a survey of 1,069 women workers.
103 Men in large families, on the other hand, did 3 hours of domestic labour on work days and just under 5 hours on their days off. This was still a 50 to 100 per cent increase over men in families with only one child (Sazonova, p. 21).
104 *Statistika byudzhetov vremeni*, p. 85. The survey was carried out in 1963. These data are consistent with Korobitsyna's study of Sverdlovsk women, summarized in table 7.8.
105 Danilova, pp. 61–2.
106 Beechey, p. 67.
107 *Zhenshchiny i deti v SSSR* (1969), p. 86.
108 Beechey, p. 70.
109 See chapter 3.
110 This is due, in effect, to light industry's undercapitalization and low wage costs, and consequent 'high return' on investment. Recent discussions of the textile industry have pointed to the problems these factories now face under self-financing: with most of their profits (90 per cent in some cases) being siphoned off to subsidize large-scale industry, they have few resources left with which to carry out necessary modernization (*Sotsialisti-cheskaya industriya*, 22 January 1988 (Lyudmila Telen'); *Sobesednik*, no. 23 (1988), pp. 4–5).
111 As of late 1989, light industry provided 10 per cent of the state's accumulation fund, but received a mere 1 per cent of its total capital investment (*Sotsialisticheskaya industriya*, 18 October 1989 (O. Berezhnaya)).
112 Starodub, dissertation, p. 93.
113 Michael Burawoy has developed a similar interpretation based on his experiences working in a Hungarian engineering works. He identifies two distinct groups within the labour force, whom he calls core and peripheral workers. The former are composed of skilled and experienced workers who manage the exigencies of continually changing production requirements. The latter group is made up of unskilled or semi-skilled workers, who carry out jobs that are more easily routinized. Management is dependent on the core workers, who are thus able to extract concessions, but only at the expense of the peripheral workers (Burawoy, *Politics of Production*, pp. 15–16, 163). I cannot assess how accurately Burawoy's theory fits Hungary, but its applicability to the USSR has two limitations. First, in the Soviet Union this division between core and peripheral workers is primarily (although by no means totally) coterminous with the division of the workforce by gender. Secondly, much hinges on Burawoy's

definition of 'peripheral'. He uses it to refer to auxiliary trades, but within Soviet industry, at least, this is not strictly true: many weaker sections of the workforce, especially where women are concerned, are production workers; conversely, many auxiliary trades retain considerable control over the labour process.

114 See p. 196.

8 Skill, de-skilling, and control over the labour process

1 Burawoy, *Manufacturing Consent*. See in particular, chapters 5–7 and 12. The argument is summarized in his later book, *Politics of Production*, pp. 10–14, 35–40.
2 Braverman, pp. 100–1.
3 Burawoy, *Politics of Production*, pp. 63–8. This criticism also appears repeatedly in the studies published in Stephen Wood, ed., *The Degradation of Work? Skill, Deskilling and the Labour Process* (London, 1982). It would appear that many of Braverman's British critics (Burawoy being an exception) make the same error in the opposite direction, and assume that, because Braverman's analysis has only limited applicability to large sections of British industry, it is therefore not an accurate description of developments elsewhere.
4 Braverman, pp. 133–6.
5 See in particular Burawoy, *Politics of Production*, pp. 40–50.
6 Braverman, p. 93, citing *Taylor's Testimony before the Special House Committee*, in Frederick Winslow Taylor, *Scientific Management* (New York and London, 1947), p. 79.
7 Braverman, p. 98, citing Frederick Winslow Taylor, *Shop Management*, in Taylor, *Scientific Management*, p. 33.
8 *Ibid.*, p. 99, citing Taylor, *Shop Management*, pp. 34–5. It is worth noting in this context that Stakhanovism, far from being an attempt to impose Taylorist methods on Soviet workers, was in fact 'pre-Taylorist'. Taylor blamed 'soldiering' precisely on the piece-rate system, where improvements in output achieved even by a single worker would be used to lower rates for all the others. This, of course, was the entire basis of Stakhanovism, and provoked considerable efforts by Soviet workers to find whatever devices they could to ease the pressures it created on work speeds and earnings. See Filtzer, *Soviet Workers and Stalinist Industrialization*, pp. 212–29. On early attempts to introduce Taylorism into Soviet industry in the 1920s, see Bailes.
9 Roy, 'Quota Restriction', pp. 431–2, 435–8; 'Efficiency and the "Fix"', p. 257.
10 According to one Western firm currently working in the Soviet garment industry, women garment workers do cite the fear of rate cuts as a reason for holding back their performance (interview data).
11 This does not mean that workers had no interest in concealing actual capacities as a protection against rate cuts. It says simply that there was no way that they could finish a day's output in a few hours and take the rest of the day off. Nor did it keep them from reacting with considerable hostility to Stakhanovites or other rate busters, whose records were used to push up

norms for the rank and file. The fact was, however, that under Stalin, workers knew that hefty norm rises and rate cuts were going to come anyway. The struggle, therefore, revolved around compelling local management to keep the new norms attainable. It is significant that when norm-setting was decentralized under Khrushchev, managers were, in the main, less than diligent about revising them. It is also worth noting that Lupton, too, observed how, unlike in Roy's factory, the workers in his plant did not restrict output. Most wasted time was due to stoppages in the flow of work, which were mainly the fault of management. The wage fiddles the workers then engaged in were an attempt to cushion their earnings from the effects of these stoppages (Lupton, p. 182).

12 See chapter 4, p. 272 (n. 75) and chapter 6, p. 159.
13 Lupton, p. 2.
14 Roy, 'Efficiency and the "Fix"'.
15 Littler, p. 142.
16 *Ibid.*, p. 143.
17 Lupton, p. 151.
18 *Ibid.*, p. 185. This was equally true of the engineering plant where Roy, and later Burawoy, worked.
19 *Ibid.*, p. 168. Lupton claimed that recognition of this fact by the engineering employers was one factor behind the shift to measured day work in the 1960s (*ibid.*, pp. 168–9).
20 Penn, p. 100. Penn, on the basis of these observations, argues for the need to differentiate between the skilled trades already present within a factory before automation, which had developed structural supports for preserving skills, and those trades essentially brought into a factory by automation, which had to try to develop means of protecting their skills via strong trade union organization and social exclusion, that is, by keeping other workers away from the machinery over which they wanted to preserve their control.
21 Lee, p. 159.
22 See chapter 6, pp. 152–6.
23 *Rabochii klass i tekhnicheskii progress*, p. 125–9. For Brova's study, see chapter 7, table 7.4.
24 A similar study of workers in the chemical industry found that, as of mid-1962, 40 per cent of workers worked with non-automatic machinery, and 51 per cent carried out manual labour without the aid of any machinery or mechanical devices. This latter group divided up into two subgroups, according to skill: 60 per cent (or 30 per cent of the total) were classed as workers in jobs demanding high or average skills, and 40 per cent (20 per cent of the total) in jobs that were only semi- or unskilled (Krevnevich, p. 23).
25 *VS*, no. 6 (1966), pp. 88–92; *Trud v SSSR* (Moscow, 1968), pp. 180–3.
26 *Rabochii klass i tekhnicheskii progress*, pp. 261–2.
27 *Ibid.*, pp. 259–60, citing *Kommunizm i trud* (Moscow, 1964), p. 94.
28 *Ibid.*, p. 137.
29 *ST*, no. 6 (1960), p. 60 (V. Vorotnikova, V. D'yachenko). As in the textile

industry, the number of movements was unnecessarily multiplied by the poor design of equipment. At the Kharkov machine-tool factory, the controls on polishing machinery were placed so that to use them the worker had to bend over from 450 to 2,300 times a shift. Many controls were placed on the left-hand side of equipment, making them hard for right-handed workers (the obvious majority) to reach. Other machines had controls on both sides, which forced workers to violate safety regulations – which stated that workers had to stand to one side while the equipment was in operation (*P G*, 19 August 1959).

30 *ST*, no. 6 (1960), p. 63 (V. Vorotnikova, V. D'yachenko).

31 *Rabochii klass i tekhnicheskii progress*, p. 130. Discontent among manual workers working at or with machinery was considerably lower, despite the fact that their jobs also involved heavy physical labour. The Gor'kii study attributed this to their greater involvement with the actual operation of equipment and their higher skills (*ibid.*, pp. 130–1). This surely depends on the type of machinery they were servicing. It is hard to believe that workers loading sacks on to a conveyor belt found this particularly stimulating.

32 Zdravomyslov and Yadov, pp. 180–2.

33 *Ibid.*, pp. 183, 186.

34 *Ibid.*, pp. 190–1.

35 *ST*, no. 6 (1960), pp. 61, 63 (V. Vorotnikova, V. D'yachenko). As noted in chapter 4, the low skill grades of many assembly workers in engineering were partially offset by putting them on jobs with a higher skill classification and thus paid at a higher rate (*ibid.*, p. 63).

36 *VS*, no. 6 (1966), pp. 88–92; *Trud v SSSR* (Moscow, 1968), pp. 180–3.

37 See chapter 7, p. 193.

38 See *LP*, 27 January 1961, 31 May and 28 July 1962, and 19 March 1963.

39 *ST*, no. 8 (1988), p. 30 (Yu. Kalmykov); no. 9 (1989), p. 54 (L. Sitnikova); no. 1 (1990), p. 51 (G. Amelina, E. Zhukova); no. 5 (1990), p. 35 (N. Khrulev, L. Salomatina). To put the issue of programmed controls into perspective, in Great Britain in 1976, numerical-control machines represented a mere 1.3 per cent of all metal-cutting machine tools. This slightly underestimated their importance, since each had the capacity of roughly three standard machine tools and were also kept in operation on more shifts. Moreover, they have not in all cases led to de-skilling, since in at least some factories the operators have the freedom to modify the programmes to deal with various operational difficulties (Jones, pp. 186–7, 195–7). The problems with the introduction of these machines in the Soviet Union, however, are quite specific to that country. The machines are expensive and yield improvements in productivity well below their extra costs. Factories therefore refuse to buy them or, if forced to do so, acquire them but leave them unused.

40 *Rabochii klass i tekhnicheskii progress*, pp. 204ff., 208–9, 256–7.

41 The best description of this process is Yanowitch, *Social and conomic Inequality*, chapters 2–4.

42 Yanowitch, *Work in the Soviet Union*, pp. 59–73.

43 Eldridge, pp. 49–64.

44 Commenting on the situation in the Wye workshop where he was working, Lupton noted, 'The threat to leave, made individually, seemed to be the only sanction which the workers were prepared to use to control their conditions of work. In the absence of collective controls and an effective procedure for collective presentation, by a representative from the workshop, it was the only sanction which promised to be effective' (Lupton, pp. 82–3).

45 'Time spent waiting for delivery of components, or for the crane, could, for example, be spent in talk on all sorts of subjects of common interest, and again, some waiting time was almost bound to occur when batch production was, as in this case, planned on flow principles ... All this was conducive to the spontaneous development of friendly groupings on and off the job, and to the spread and exchange of knowledge amongst the whole group of workers in the section. This contributed to the solidarity of the group in its relations with management, but at the same time permitted the development of smaller groups with different interests within the larger group' (Lupton, p. 109).

46 Lupton, pp. 2, 145.

47 Filtzer, *Soviet Workers and Stalinist Industrialization*, pp. 112–15 and chapter 9.

48 To judge from Burawoy's experience, this type of personalized bargaining also takes place in some sections of capitalist industry, in situations similar to storming in the USSR: 'Under such circumstances [a "hot job on the agenda"], operators are expected to drop what they are doing and punch in on the new job, "throwing everything they've got" into it ... On occasions like this, unless the foreman can bring some sanctions to bear, he is at the mercy of the operator who may decide to take it easy. For this reason, foremen may try to establish an exchange relationship *with each individual operator*: "You look after me, I'll look after you." Operators may agree to cooperate with the foreman, but in return they expect him to dispense favors, such as the granting of casual days, permission to attend union meetings during working hours, permission to go home early on a special occasion, etc.' (Burawoy, *Manufacturing Consent*, p. 61; my emphasis). In Burawoy's case, such bargaining relations existed alongside – and were probably enabled by – strong shop-floor organization.

49 Again, Lupton's engineering works is a good example, as workers constantly had to find ways to shortcut the ongoing breakdowns in intra-factory coordination. How generalized this situation was outside the specific context of British engineering, or how applicable it would be today, more than 30 years after Lupton made his observations, it is difficult to say.

50 *MP*, 16 October 1963.

51 *LP*, 17 March 1961.

52 *LP*, 1 April 1961.

53 *LP*, 31 July 1962.

54 See chapter 1, p. 20.

Conclusion

1 Gramsci, p. 12.
2 The following discussion is taken from Filtzer, 'Economic Reform and Production Relations'.
3 *Rabochaya tribuna*, 28 July 1990.
4 *Sotsiologicheskie issledovaniya*, no. 10 (1990) (A. N. Komozin). We know from interview data that this is also the case in the Belorussian garment industry.
5 *Izvestiya*, 8 August and 27 October 1990.
6 Under the 1990 Enterprise Law, the Councils of Labour Collectives (STK in Russian) created under the State Enterprise Law of 1987 have been stripped of most of their powers, including the right of enterprise collectives to elect their own managers. Despite the fact that in most enterprises the STK were never more than shadow organizations, mostly dominated by management, their potential as a focal point of worker protest and attempts to interfere with managerial decisions required their further denaturing (Law of the USSR, 'O predpriyatiyakh v SSSR', 4 June 1990; implemented by the decree of the USSR Supreme Soviet, 'O poryadke vvedeniya v deistvie Zakona SSSR "O predpriyatiyakh v SSSR"', *konomika i zhizn'*, no. 25 (1990), pp. 19–20). Procedures for hiring managers in state enterprises were laid down in a decree of the USSR Council of Ministers, 23 October 1990, no. 1073, 'O poryadke naima i osvobozhdeniya rukovoditelya gosudarstvennogo soyuznogo predpriyatiya', *konomika i zhizn'*, no. 45 (1990), p. 19.

Bibliography

The bibliography lists all newspapers, journals, books, monographs, and dissertations consulted in the course of research. For journal articles, only the titles of non-Soviet articles and those by contemporary Soviet authors are listed. Other articles are referred to only in the notes, where they are listed by journal title, issue number, date, and page number, with the author's name in parentheses. Some Soviet authors whose works might be of special interest to those wishing to do research on the subjects covered in this book are listed in the index. The abbreviations of newspaper and journal titles used in the notes appear next to the full titles below.

Newspapers and journals

KHRUSHCHEV PERIOD

BGK	*Byulleten' Gosudarstvennogo Komiteta Soveta Ministrov SSSR po Voprosam truda i zarabotnoi platy*
ChR	*Chelyabinskii rabochii*, local newspaper, Chelyabinsk
DP	*Dneprovskaya pravda*, local newspaper, Dnepropetrovsk
FN	*Nauchnye doklady vysshei shkoly: Filosofskie nauki*, journal of the Ministry of Higher and Specialized Secondary Education of the USSR
	Izvestiya
KU	*Kommunist Ukrainy*
LP	*Leningradskaya pravda*, local newspaper, Leningrad
MP	*Moskovskaya pravda*, local newspaper, Moscow
	Pravda
P G	*Promyshlenno-ekonomicheskaya gazeta*
RK	*Rabochii krai*, local newspaper, Ivanovo
S	*Sovetskaya etnografiya*
SG	*Stroitel'naya gazeta*
SGP	*Sovetskoe gosudarstvo i pravo*
ST	*Sotsialisticheskii trud*, journal of the State Committee of the Council of Ministers of the USSR on Questions of Labour and Wages
SYu	*Sovetskaya yustitsiya*
SZ	*Sotsialisticheskaya zakonnost'*
	Trud

TZP   *Byulleten' nauchnoi informatsii: Trud i zarabotnaya plata,* journal of the
        State Committee of the Council of Ministers of the USSR on Ques-
        tions of Labour and Wages
UR   *Ural'skii rabochii,* local newspaper, Sverdlovsk
        Vedemosti Verkhovnogo Soveta SSSR
V   *Voprosy ekonomiki*
VF   *Voprosy filosofii*
VS   *Vestnik statistiki*

POST-KHRUSHCHEV PERIOD
        konomika i zhizn'
        Rabochaya tribuna
        Sobesednik
        Sotsialisticheskaya industriya
        Sotsiologicheskie issledovaniya

Articles, books, and dissertations

Adam, Jan, *Wage Control and Inflation in the Soviet Bloc Countries* (London, 1979).

Bailes, Kendell E., 'Alexei Gastev and the Controversy over Taylorism, 1918–
1924', *Soviet Studies,* July 1988, pp. 373–94.

Barber, John, 'The Organised Recruitment of Soviet Labour in the 1930s',
unpublished discussion paper, Centre for Russian and East European
Studies, University of Birmingham, November 1979.

Barber, John, 'Notes on the Soviet Working Class Family, 1928–1941',
unpublished conference paper, Second World Congress for Soviet and
East European Studies, Garmisch-Partenkirchen, October 1980.

Batkaev, R. A., and Markov, V. I., *Differentsiatsiya zarabotnoi platy v promyshlennosti v SSSR* (Moscow, 1964).

Beechey, Veronica, 'The Sexual Division of Labour and the Labour Process: A
Critical Assessment of Braverman', in Stephen Wood, ed., *The Degradation
of Work? Skill, Deskilling and the Labour Process* (London, 1982), pp. 54–73.

Belotserkovsky, Vadim, 'Workers' Struggles in the USSR in the Early Sixties',
Critique, no. 10/11 (1979), pp. 37–50.

Berliner, Joseph S., *Factory and Manager in the USSR* (Cambridge, MA, 1957).

Blyakhman, L. S., Zdravomyslov, A. G., and Shkaratan, O. I., *Dvizhenie rabochei
sily na promyshlennykh predriyatiyakh* (Moscow, 1965).

Boldyreva, Tat'yana, 'Revolyutsionnogo konya na skaku ne ostanovish'',
KO, no. 8 (1988), pp. 138–51.

Braverman, Harry, *Labor and Monopoly Capital* (New York, 1974).

Brova, S. V., *Sotsial'nye problemy zhenskogo truda v promyshlennosti (po materialam
sotsiologicheskikh issledovanii na predpriyatiyakh Sverdlovskoi i Chelyabinskoi
oblastei).* Author's abstract of Candidate dissertation (Sverdlovsk, 1968).

Brova, S. V., *Sotsial'nye problemy zhenskogo truda v promyshlennosti. Po materialam
sotsiologicheskikh issledovanii na predpriyatiyakh Sverdlovskoi i Chelyabinskoi
oblastei.* Candidate dissertation, Ural'skii Gosudarstvennyi Universitet im.
A. M. Gor'kogo (Sverdlovsk, 1968).

Brown, Emily Clark, *Soviet Trade Unions and Labor Relations* (Cambridge, MA, 1966).

Brus, Wlodzimierz, *Socialist Ownership and Political Systems* (London, 1975).

Burawoy, Michael, *Manufacturing Consent: Changes in the Labor Process under Monopoly Capitalism* (Chicago, 1979).

Burawoy, Michael, *The Politics of Production* (London, 1985).

Cherkasov, G. N., *Sotsial'no-ekonomicheskie problemy intensivnosti truda v SSSR* (Moscow, 1966).

Chislennost' i sostav rabochikh Sibiri v usloviyakh razvitogo sotsializma (Novosibirsk, 1977).

Crankshaw, Edward, *Khrushchev's Russia* (Harmondsworth, 1959).

Danilova, E. Z. [Ekaterina Zakharovna], *Sotsial'nye problemy truda zhenshchiny-rabotnitsy* (Moscow, 1968).

Davies, R. W., 'The Reappraisal of Industry', *Soviet Studies*, January 1956, pp. 308–31.

Deutscher, Isaac, 'Khrushchev on Stalin', in *Ironies of History* (Oxford, 1966), pp. 3–17.

Direktivy KPSS i sovetskogo pravitel'stva po khozyaistvennym voprosam, vol. iv (Moscow, 1958).

Dunstan, John, 'Soviet Boarding Education: Its Rise and Progress', in Jenny Brine, Maureen Perrie, and Andrew Sutton, eds., *Home, School and Leisure in the Soviet Union* (London, 1980), pp. 110–41.

Dzhebrailov, N. F., 'Rabochii klass Azerbaidzhana v gody semiletki (1959–1965 g.g.)', in *Iz istorii rabochego klassa SSSR* (Moscow: Mysl', 1968), pp. 62–84.

Eldridge, J. E. T., *Sociology and Industrial Life* (London, 1971).

Fakiolas, R., 'Problems of Labour Mobility in the USSR', *Soviet Studies*, July 1962, pp. 16–41.

Feshbach, Murray, 'Manpower in the USSR: A Survey of Recent Trends and Prospects', in *New Directions in the Soviet Economy*, part 3 (Washington, DC: United States Congress, 1966).

Filtzer, Donald, *Soviet Workers and Stalinist Industrialization: The Formation of Modern Soviet Production Relations, 1928–1941* (London, 1986).

Filtzer, Donald, 'The Soviet Wage Reform of 1956–1962', unpublished seminar paper, Soviet Industrialization Project Seminar, Centre for Russian and East European Studies, University of Birmingham, October 1987.

Filtzer, Donald, 'The Soviet Wage Reform of 1956–1962', *Soviet Studies*, January 1989, pp. 88–110.

Filtzer, Donald, 'Economic Reform and Production Relations in Soviet Industry, 1985–1990', in Chris Smith and Paul Thompson, eds., *Labour in Transition: The Labour Process in Eastern Europe and China* (London: Routledge, forthcoming 1992).

Forstman, S. V. [S. V. Brova], 'Kul'turno-teknicheskii pod"em rabotnits promyshlennykh predpriyatii', in *Novyi rabochii formiruetsya segodnya* (Chelyabinsk, 1966), pp. 209–28.

Fox, Alan, *Beyond Contract: Work, Power and Trust Relations* (London, 1974).

Friedman, Andrew L., *Industry and Labour: Class Struggle at Work and Monopoly Capitalism* (London, 1977).

Gliksman, Jerzy, 'Recent Trends in Soviet Labor Legislation', *Problems of Communism*, July–August 1956, pp. 20–8.

Gramsci, Antonio, *Selections from the Prison Notebooks* (London, 1971).

Granick, David, *Management of the Industrial Firm in the USSR* (New York, 1964).

Granick, David, *Job Rights in the Soviet Union: Their Consequences* (Cambridge, 1987).

Hanson, Philip, 'The Serendipitous Soviet Achievement of Full Employment: Labour Shortage and Labour Hoarding in the Soviet Economy', in David Lane, ed., *Labour and Employment in the USSR* (Brighton, 1986), pp. 83–111.

Helmert, Gundula, 'The Reflection of Working Life in the Teaching Programmes of Soviet Non-Specialist Schools, 1928–1940', unpublished conference paper, Centre for Russian and East European Studies, University of Birmingham, June 1981.

Helmert, Gundula, *Schuler unter Stalin 1928–1940. Über zen Zusammenhang von Massenbildung und Herrschaftsinteressen*, Ph.D. thesis, Gesamthochschule Kassel, 1982.

Holubenko, M., 'The Soviet Working Class: Discontent and Opposition', *Critique*, no. 4 (1975), pp. 5–25.

Hosking, Geoffrey, *A History of the Soviet Union* (London, 1985).

Itogi vsesoyuznoi perepisi naseleniya 1959 goda SSSR (Svodnyi Tom) (Moscow, 1962).

Jones, Bryn, 'Destruction or Redistribution of Engineering Skills? The Case of Numerical Control', in Stephen Wood, ed., *The Degradation of Work? Skill, Deskilling and the Labour Process* (London, 1982), pp. 179–200.

Kalinina, N. P., *Usloviya truda i osnovnye napravleniya ikh uluchsheniya na predpriyatiyakh tekstil'noi promyshlennosti* (Moscow, 1969).

Kalmykov, Yu., 'Intensivnyi rezhim truda v mashinostroenii', *Sotsialisticheskii trud*, no. 8 (1988), pp. 29–33.

Kharchev, A. G., *Brak i sem'ya v SSSR* (Moscow, 1964).

Kharchev, A. G., and Golod, S. I., *Professional'naya rabota zhenshchin i sem'ya* (Leningrad, 1971).

Khlusov, M. I., *Razvitie sovetskoi industrii, 1946–1958 gg* (Moscow, 1977).

Khrushchev, N. S., *Khrushchev Remembers*, with an introduction, commentary, and notes by Edward Crankshaw (London, 1971).

Kirsch, Leonard Joel, *Soviet Wages: Changes in Structure and Administration* (Cambridge, MA, 1972).

Kolpakov, B. T., and Prudenskii, G. A., 'Opyt izucheniya vnerabochego vremeni trudyashchikhsya', in *Sotsiologiya v SSSR*, vol. ii (Moscow, 1965), pp. 209–24.

Komogortsev, I. I., *Promyshlennost' i rabochii klass Sibiri v period stroitel'stva kommunizma (1959–1965 gg)* (Novosibirsk, 1971).

Korobitsyna, M. A., *Zhenskii trud v sisteme obshchestvennogo truda pri sotsializme*. Candidate dissertation, Sverdlovskii Gosudarstvennyi Yuridicheskii Institut (Sverdlovsk, 1966).

Korobitsyna, M. A., *Zhenskii trud v sisteme obshchestvennogo truda pri sotsializme*. Author's abstract of Candidate dissertation (Sverdlovsk, 1967).

Kostin, L. A., *Planirovanie truda v promyshlennosti* (Moscow, 1967).

Kotlyar, A. E., and Turchaninova, S. Ya., *Zanyatost' zhenshchin v proizvodstve* (Moscow, 1975).

Krevnevich, Valentina Vyacheslavovna, *Sovremennye trebovaniya k podgotovke rabochikh khimicheskoi promyshlennosti* (Moscow, 1964).

Labzin, A. L., *Stroitel'stvo kommunizma i ustranenie ostneravnogo polozheniya zhenshchiny v bytu*. Author's abstract of Candidate dissertation (Moscow, 1964).

Labzin, A. L., 'Stroitel'stvo kommunizma i ustranenie ostatkov neravenstva v polozhenii zhenshchiny', *Filosofskie nauki*, no. 1 (1965), pp. 98–106.

Lampert, Nick, 'Job Security and the Law in the USSR', in David Lane, ed., *Labour and mployment in the USSR* (Brighton, 1986), pp. 256–77.

Lapidus, Gail Warshofsky, *Women in Soviet Society* (Berkeley, 1978).

Lapidus, Gail Warshofsky, ed., *Women, Work, and Family in the Soviet Union* (Armonk, NY, 1982).

Lee, David, 'Beyond Deskilling: Skill, Craft and Class', in Stephen Wood, ed., *The Degradation of Work? Deskilling and the Labour Process* (London, 1982), pp. 146–62.

Littler, Craig, 'Deskilling and Changing Structures of Control', in Stephen Wood, ed., *The Degradation of Work? Skill, Deskilling and the Labour Process* (London, 1982), pp. 122–45.

Livshits, R. Z., and Nikitinskii, V. I., 'Reforma trudovogo zakonodatel'stva: voprosy teorii', *Sotsialisticheskii trud*, no. 1 (1989), pp. 76–89.

Lupton, Tom, *On the Shop Floor* (Oxford, 1963).

McAuley, Alastair, *Women's Work and Wages in the Soviet Union* (London, 1981).

McAuley, Alastair, 'Social Policy', in Martin McCauley, ed., *Khrushchev and Khrushchevism* (London, 1987), pp. 138–55.

McAuley, Alastair, and Helgeson, Ann, 'Soviet Labour Supply and Manpower Utilisation, 1960–2000', unpublished discussion paper, 1978.

McAuley, Mary, *Labour Disputes in Soviet Russia, 1957–1965* (Oxford, 1969).

McCauley, Martin, *Khrushchev and the Development of Soviet Agriculture: The Virgin Land Programme, 1953–1964* (London, 1976).

Malakhova, L. K., *Nekotorye voprosy truda i obrazovaniya zhenshchin-rabotnits pri perekhode ot sotsializma k kommunizmu* (Moscow, 1969).

Malakhova, T. P., *Kolichestvennyi i kachestvennyi rost kadrov khimicheskoi promyshlennosti kuzbassa v 1959–1965 gg*. Candidate dissertation (Novosibirsk, 1967).

Maloletova, N. P., *Rabochie legkoi promyshlennosti SSSR v 1945–1965 g.g. (chislennost' i sostav)*. Candidate dissertation (Moscow, 1970).

Manevich, E. L., *Problemy obshchestvennogo truda v SSSR* (Moscow, 1966).

Marx, Karl, and Engels, Friedrich, *The Holy Family* (Moscow, 1975).

Matthews, Mervyn, *Class and Society in Soviet Russia* (London, 1972).

Medvedev, Roy, *Khrushchev* (Oxford, 1983).

Medvedev, Roy A., and Zhores A. Medvedev, *Khrushchev: The Years in Power* (Oxford, 1977).

Medvedeva, T. N., *Problemy dvizheniya i ispol'zovaniya trudovykh resursov Leningrada v sovremennykh usloviyakh*. Candidate dissertation (Leningrad, 1965).

Mikhailyuk, Valentina Borisovna, *Ispol'zovanie zhenskogo truda v narodnom khozyaistve* (Moscow, 1970).

Narodnoe khozyaistvo SSSR v 1965 g. (Moscow, 1966).

Narodnoe khozyaistvo SSSR za 60 let (Moscow, 1977).

Nove, Alec, 'Wages in the Soviet Union: A Comment on Recently Published Statistics', *British Journal of Industrial Relations*, July 1966, pp. 212–21.

Nove, Alec, *An conomic History of the USSR* (Harmondsworth, 1969).

Ovchinnikova, E. P., and Brova, S. V., 'O likvidatsii ostatkov sotsial'nogo neravenstva rabochikh u rabotnits na promyshlennykh predpriyatiyakh', in *Protsessy izmeneniya sotsial'noi struktury v sovetskom obshchestve* (Sverdlovsk, 1967), pp. 36–43.

Penn, Roger, 'Skilled Manual Workers in the Labour Process, 1856–1964,' in Stephen Wood, ed., *The Degradation of Work? Skill, Deskilling and the Labour Process* (London, 1982), pp. 90–108.

Pimenova, A. L., 'Semya i perspektivy razvitiya obshchestvennogo truda zhenshchiny pri sotsialisme', *Filosofskie nauki*, no. 3 (1966), pp. 35–44.

Problemy istorii sovetskogo obshchestva Sibiri (Novosibirsk, 1970).

Promyshlennost' SSSR. Statisticheskii sbornik (Moscow, 1964).

Puti likvidatsii tekuchesti kadrov v promyshlennosti SSSR (Moscow, 1965).

Pysin, L. F., *Tekuchest' rabochikh kadrov v promyshlennosti i puti ee preodeleniya.* Author's abstract of Candidate dissertation, Ural'skii Gosudarstvennyi Universitet im. A. M. Gor'kogo (Sverdlovsk, 1963).

Rabochii klass i tekhnicheskii progress: Issledovanie izmenenii v sotsial'noi strukture rabochego klassa (Moscow, 1965).

Rabochii klass Sibiri, 1961–1980 g.g. (Novosibirsk, 1986).

Rabochii klass SSSR (1951–1965 g.g.) (Moscow, 1969).

Rakovsky, Khristian, 'The Five-Year Plan in Crisis', *Critique*, no. 13 (1981), pp. 13–53.

Romantsov, V. O., *Robotnichii klass Ukrainskoi RSR (1946–1970 rr.)* (Kiev, 1972).

Roy, Donald, 'Quota Restriction and Goldbricking in a Machine Shop', *American Journal of Sociology*, vol. 57 (March 1952), pp. 427–42.

Roy, Donald, 'Work Satisfaction and Social Reward in Quota Achievement: An Analysis of Piecework Incentive', *American Sociological Review*, vol. 18 (October 1953), pp. 507–14.

Roy, Donald, 'Efficiency and the "Fix": Informal Intergroup Relations in a Piecework Machine Shop', *American Journal of Sociology*, vol. 60 (November 1954), pp. 255–66.

Sagimbaeva, R. M., *Problemy ispol'zovaniya resursov zhenskogo truda (na materialakh Kazakhskoi SSR).* Author's abstract of Candidate dissertation (Moscow, 1968).

Sakharova, N. A., *Zhenskie rezervy trudovykh resursov gorodov i rabochikh poselkov Ukrainskoi SSR.* Author's abstract of Candidate dissertation (Kiev, 1962).

Sakharova, N. A., *Zhenskie rezervy trudovykh resursov gorodov i rabochikh poselkov Ukrainskoi SSR.* Candidate dissertation (Kiev, 1962).

Sazonova, O. K., *Perekhod k kommunizma i problema obobshchestvleniya domashnogo khozyaistva* (Moscow, 1963).

Sbornik postanovlenii i opredelenii Verkhovnogo Suda RSFSR po trudovym delam (1953–1958 g.g.) (Moscow, 1959).

Sbornik zakonodatel'nykh aktov o trude (Moscow, 1964).

Senyavskii, S. L., *Rost rabochego klassa SSSR (1951–1965 g.g.)* (Moscow, 1966).

Senyavskii, S. L., and Tel'pukhovskii, V. B., *Rabochii klass SSSR (1938–1965 g.g.)* (Moscow, 1971).

Service, R. J., 'The Road to the Twentieth Party Congress: An Analysis of the Events Surrounding the Central Committee Plenum of July 1953', *Soviet Studies*, April 1981, pp. 232–45.

Service, Robert, 'De-Stalinisation in the USSR before Khrushchev's Secret Speech', in *Il XX Congresso del Pcus* (Milan, 1988), pp. 287–310.

Shafranova, O. I., *Professional'nyi sostav rabochikh promyshlennosti SSSR* (Moscow, 1972).

Shelest, D. S., *Kolichestvennye i kachestvennye izmeneniya v sostave rabochego klassa Ukrainskoi SSR v period kommunisticheskogo stroitel'stva (1959–1970 gg.).* Doctoral dissertation (Dnepropetrovsk, 1972).

Shishkan, Nadezhda Mikhailovna, *Trud zhenshchin v usloviyakh razvitogo sotsialisma* (Kishinev, 1976).

Siegelbaum, Lewis, 'Soviet Norm Determination in Theory and Practice, 1917–1941', *Soviet Studies*, January 1984, pp. 15–68.

Smirnov, A. V., *Rabochie kadry tyazhelogo mashinostroeniya SSSR v 1946–1958 g.g.* Candidate dissertation (Moscow, 1962).

Smirnova, G. M., 'Sostav rabochikh kadrov tekstil'noi promyshlennosti i osnovnye tendentsii ego formirovaniya (1959–1969 g.g.)', in *Iz istorii rabochego klassa SSSR* (Ivanovo, 1972), pp. 78–95.

Smith, Andrew, *I was a Soviet Worker* (London, 1937).

Smith, G. A. E., 'Agriculture', in Martin McCauley, ed., *Khrushchev and Khrushchevism* (London, 1987), pp. 95–117.

Sochilin, B. G., *Kazhdomu predpriyatiyu – stabil'nye kadry* (Leningrad, 1964).

Sonin, M. Ya., *Aktual'nye problemy ispol'zovaniya rabochei sily v SSSR* (Moscow, 1965).

Starodub, V. I. [Valentina Illarionovna], 'Tekhnicheskii progress – uslovie rasshireniya sfery primeneniya truda zhenshchin', in *Nauchnye zapiski* (Leningradskii Finansovo-ekonomicheskii Institut im. N. A. Voznesenskogo), vypusk 27 (1965), pp. 214–31.

Starodub, V. I., 'Tekhnicheskii progress i usloviya truda zhenshchin', *Nauchnye zapiski* (Leningradskii Finansovo-ekonomicheskii Institut im. N. A. Voznesenskogo), vypusk 28 (1966), pp. 52–61.

Starodub, V. I., *Tekhnicheskii progress i trud zhenshchin.* Author's abstract of Candidate dissertation (Leningrad, 1966).

Starodub, V. I., *Tekhnicheskii progress i trud zhenshchin.* Candidate dissertation, Leningradskii Finansovo-ekonomicheskii Institut im. N. A. Voznesenskogo (Leningrad, 1966).

Statistika byudzhetov vremeni trudyashchikhsya (Moscow, 1967).

Ticktin, Hillel, 'Towards a Political Economy of the USSR', *Critique*, no. 1 (1973), pp. 20–41.

Ticktin, Hillel, 'The Contradictions of Soviet Society and Professor Bettelheim', *Critique*, no. 6 (1976), pp. 17–44.

Ticktin, Hillel, 'The Class Structure of the USSR and the Elite', *Critique*, no. 9 (1978), pp. 37–61.

Tol'stykh, N. A., *Zanyatost' i raspredelenie zhenskikh trudovykh resursov v obsh-chestvennom proizvodstve SSSR.* Author's abstract of Candidate dissertation (Moscow, 1967).

Trotsky, Leon, *The Revolution Betrayed* (New York, 1972).

Trud i razvitie lichnosti (Leningrad, 1965).

Trud v SSSR. Statisticheskii sbornik (Moscow, 1968).

Trud v SSSR (Moscow, 1988).

Trudovye resursy SSSR (Problemy raspredeleniya i ispol'zovaniya) (Moscow, 1961).

Trudy II S"ezda Akusherov-ginekologov RSFSR, 29 June–3 July 1965, Rostov-on-Don (Moscow, 1967).

Trufanov, I. P., 'Opyt etnograficheskogo izucheniya rabochikh leningradskogo zavoda "elektrosila" im. S. M. Kirova', *Sovetskaya etnografiya*, no. 4 (1963), pp. 157–65.

Utkin, E. A., *Rabotu mashin – na polnuyu moshchnost'* (Moscow, 1964).

Vaisman, I. A., 'O sootnoshenii chislennosti osnovnykh i vspomogatel'nykh rabochikh v promyshlennosti', *Voprosy truda*, vypusk 1 (Moscow, 1958), pp. 118–41 [journal of the Scientific Research Institute of Labour, State Committee of the Council of Ministers of the USSR on Questions of Labour and Wages].

Valentinova, N. G., 'O psikhicheskikh osobennostyakh lichnosti rabochego, svyazannykh s soderzhaniem truda', in *Sotsiologiya v SSSR*, vol. ii (Moscow, 1965), pp. 99–115.

Vodzinskaya, V. V., 'Otnoshenie molodogo rabochego k svoei profesii', in *Trud i razvitie lichnosti* (Moscow, 1965), pp. 77–109.

Voprosy trudovykh resursov i urovnya zhizni naseleniya vostochnykh raionov (Novo-sibirsk, 1966).

Wood, Stephen, and Kelly, John, 'Taylorism, Responsible Autonomy and Management Strategy', in Stephen Wood, ed., *The Degradation of Work? Skill, Deskilling and the Labour Process* (London, 1982), pp. 74–89.

Yanowitch, Murray, *Social and conomic Inequality in the Soviet Union* (White Plains, NY, 1977).

Yanowitch, Murray, *Work in the Soviet Union: Attitudes and Issues* (Armonk, NY, 1985).

Zdravomyslov, A. G., and Yadov, V. A., 'Vliyanie razlichii v soderzhanii i kharaktere truda na otnoshenie k trudu', in *Opyt i metodika konkretnykh sotsiologicheskikh issledovanii* (Moscow, 1965), pp. 144–96.

Zdravomyslov, A. G., Yadov, V. A., and Rozhin, V. P., *Chelovek i ego rabota* (Moscow, 1967).

Zemtsov, A. A., 'Svobodnoe vremya i razvitie lichnosti', *Voprosy filosofii*, no. 4 (1965), pp. 61–9.

Zhenshchiny i deti v SSSR (Moscow, 1969).

Index of industrial, mining, and construction enterprises

General index

absenteeism, 41, 232, 251, n29
abstract labour, 172–3
All-Union Central Council of Trade
    Unions, 38, 52
atomization, *see* workers
auxiliary workers, 22–6, 151, 245, n53
    and control over labour process, 24
    and labour shortage in Leningrad
        engineering, 27–8, 81–2
    and use of work time, 150
    and wage reform, 104, 109, 110

baking industry, norm fulfilment in, 100
barter, between industrial managers, 21
Beechey, Veronica, 205
Beria, Lavrenti, 2
Bolshevik Party, 123–4
bonus regulations
    abuse of to cut wages, 108
    and labour shortage in engineering, 84
    as cause of low norm fulfilment, 100
    failure of as incentives, 114–15
    under wage reform, 98, 109–10
Braverman, Harry, xii, 210–13, 216, 230
brigades of Communist Labour, 75
Brova, S. V., 186, 189, 217
building-materials industry
    and incomplete production, 162–3
    average wages in, 104
    labour turnover in, 67, 80
    norm fulfilment in, 100
    wage reform in, 96, 97; and
        manipulation of wages system, 105,
        111, 112
    wages system prior to wage reform, 94
Burawoy, Michael, 209, 272, n75, 296–7,
    n113
bureaucracy, *see* elite

chemical industry
    average wages in, 104
    inadequacy of bonus systems in, 114

labour shortage in, 61, 257, n6
labour turnover in, 48, 53, 255–6, n96
manual labour in, 25–6, 298, n24
norm fulfilment in, 100
poor training provision in, 74
wage reform in, 96, 97, 98, 99; and
    manipulation of wages system, 105,
    109–10
child care
    poor provision of, 201, 295, nn97, 98; as
        cause of labour turnover, 53–4, 69;
        preventing women from joining
        labour force, 63, 258, n16
civil society, 234–6, 238, 276, n1
coal-mining
    average wages in, 104
    Labour Reserve Schools in, 73
    labour shortage in, 61, 62
    labour turnover in, 49
    manual labour in, 25, 149
    norm fulfilment in, 100, 268, n7
    undermechanization of, 149
    use of work time in, 138–9, 146–7, 278,
        n13, 279, n34
    wage concessions in, 20
    wage reform in, 96, 97, 98, 100; and
        manipulation of wages system,
        103–4, 109, 110–11, 112
collectivization, 59, 128
construction
    and organized recruitment, 70–1
    average wages in, 104
    Labour Reserve Schools in, 73
    labour turnover in, 49, 67, 71; caused
        by wage reform, 106–7
    manipulation of wage reform in, 110,
        117
    see also unfinished construction

Danilova, Ekaterina Zakharovna, 203,
    293–4, n77
de-skilling, 122, 216–22

313

de-Stalinization
 as strategy to improve labour
  discipline, 46
 economic necessity of, 2
 failure of to change
  workforce–management relations, 8,
  159–60, 231–6
 limits of, 9
defective production, 86, 164–7, 284,
  nn120, 127, 285, n129
 reproduction of, 134–5
 see also quality, waste
division of labour, 128
 and losses of work time, 152–6

education reform, 73–4, 91
elite
 and Gorbachev reforms, 176
 historical origins of, 122–5, 175
 relationship with working class, 4,
  127–8, 231–6
engineering industry
 average wages in, 104
 defective production in, 165–7
 hostility towards younger workers in,
  75
 inadequacy of bonus systems in, 114
 labour shortage in, 60, 62, 76–89
 labour turnover in, 53, 54
 manual labour in, 25, 149–50
 norm fulfilment in, 100, 112
 poor training provision in, 74
 use of work time in, 138, 146, 147, 150
 wage anomalies in, 105, 106
 wage reform in, 76, 80, 82–3, 92, 96, 97,
  98, 99, 100; and manipulation of
  wages system, 105, 106, 111, 112
 wages system in prior to wage reform,
  95
equipment modernization, resistance to,
 see managers, workers
equipment utilization, campaign to
  improve, 85–9
exchange value, 172–4, 226, 276, n2

food industry
 average wages in, 104
 labour turnover in, 80
footwear industry
 average wages in, 104
 low wages in, 83
foremen, 282, n84

garment industry
 average wages in, 104
 low wages in, 83
 norm fulfilment in, 100

Gorbachev, M. S., xi, xii, 176, 236–8
 see also perestroika

housing conditions, as cause of labour
  turnover, 50–2, 68–9, 71, 72, 255, n78

incomplete production, 162–3
industry
 disproportions in, 16
 location policy, as cause of labour
  shortage and labour turnover, 63–4,
  258, n19
 output, 1950–65, 15
 see also sovnarkhoz reform
integrated brigades, 97
internal passport, 59
iron and steel industry
 average wages in, 104
 inadequacy of bonus systems in, 114
 labour turnover in, 5
 manual labour in, 25
 norm fulfilment in, 100
 wage anomalies in, 105
 wage reform in, 96, 98, 100; and
  manipulation of wages system,
  105–6, 111, 112
 wage system in prior to wage reform,
  94–5

Kaganovich, Lazar, 2
Kalinina, N. P., 194
Kaplan, I., 253, n57
Kazakhstan, non-working population in,
  63–4
Kheinman, S., 167–8
Khrushchev, N. S., xi, xii, 2, 3, 236,
  237
Kirsch, Leonard, 93, 105, 113
Komsomol, 71, 72
Korobitsyna, M. A., 185, 202
Kuzbass
 housing conditions in, 51
 labour shortage in, 61
 labour turnover in, 48–9, 255–6, n96

labour camps, rebellions in, 1
labour discipline
 in 1930s, 5, 46
 campaign to improve through moral
  appeals, 42–3
 see also absenteeism, labour turnover,
  work time
labour hoarding, 22, 60
labour legislation
 Model Internal Labour Regulations
  (1957), 38–9, 250, n16
 protection against dismissal, 39–40

Soviet and East European Studies

Soviet and East European Studies

Soviet and East European Studies

DATE DUE